100 Most Popular Contemporary Mystery Authors

100 Most Popular Contemporary Mystery Authors

Biographical Sketches and Bibliographies

Bernard A. Drew

Popular Author Series

AN IMPRINT OF ABC-CLIO, LLC
Santa Barbara, California • Denver, Colorado • Oxford, England

Library of Congress Cataloging-in-Publication Data

Drew, Bernard A. (Bernard Alger), 1950–
100 most popular contemporary mystery authors : biographical sketches and bibliographies / Bernard A. Drew.
    p. cm. — (Popular author series)
  Includes index.
  ISBN 978-1-59884-445-0 (acid-free paper) — ISBN 978-1-59884-446-7 (ebook)
1. Detective and mystery stories, American—Bio-bibliography—Dictionaries.   2. Novelists, American—21st century—Biography—Dictionaries.   I. Title.   II. Title: One hundred most popular contemporary mystery authors.   III. Title: Contemporary mystery authors.
  PS374.D4D74   2011
  813'.087209—dc22
  [B]   2011008551

ISBN: 978-1-59884-445-0
EISBN: 978-1-59884-446-7

15 14 13 12 11   1 2 3 4 5

This book is also available on the World Wide Web as an eBook.
Visit www.abc-clio.com for details.

Libraries Unlimited
An Imprint of ABC-CLIO, LLC

ABC-CLIO, LLC
130 Cremona Drive, P.O. Box 1911
Santa Barbara, California 93116-1911

This book is printed on acid-free paper ∞

Manufactured in the United States of America

Contents

Introduction

Detective and crime fiction novels are in a mature phase—veteran writers showing how it's done, new writers elbowing at the edges of convention. The traditional model of the Sam Spade private investigator has lost some ground to the hardened but sympathetic police professional (particularly British) and the talented amateur with an unusual background.

The last decade has seen mystery writers emphasize character, emotion, and setting over puzzle, plot, or graphic violence, though hardly shortchanging those last. Whodunit is important, but the struggles of the protagonist to find the perpetrator—and perhaps overcome some personal entanglement—engages the readers.

There are myriad subgenres that thrive in the amateur detective category. There are culinary and legal and medical mysteries and archaeology and journalism and academic and religious mysteries. Stretching the field in both directions are historical mysteries and urban fantasies—and an occasional chick lit. There are crime solvers with the latest scientific equipment at their fingertips—the forensics specialists—and there are the ill-equipped, sometimes bumbling civilians. All get their man. Or woman. And they do so in all parts of the North American continent, Europe, Australia, and occasionally Asia and Africa.

Besides the private eye in the Philip Marlowe mold, in today's mysteries there are unlicensed but just as qualified individuals such as Lawrence Block's former cop Matt Scudder or Janet Evanovich's bail bondswoman Stephanie Plum.

The category of antihero largely covers those on the other side of the law, from killers for hire (Block's Keller, for example) or killers for whim (Jeff Dorsey's Dexter).

This guide zeroes in on 100 writers, selected from probably 10 times that number who are active today. Writers well known in the mystery field with a bent for relentless pace and action are to be found in a companion volume, *100 Most Popular Thriller and Suspense Authors* (Libraries Unlimited, 2009). This series of books is meant to help librarians and secondary level students learn more about popular authors and their work.

This work focuses on contemporary (alive and writing) writers with continuing series. If a favorite writer is missing, check *The 100 Most Popular Genre Fiction Authors* (Libraries Unlimited, 2005) for profiles of Mary Higgins Clark, Dick Francis, Elmore Leonard, P. D. James, Sara Paretsky, Robert B. Parker, Ruth Rendell, Stuart Woods, and other established keystones. Walter Moseley is featured in that volume and in *The 100 Most Popular African American Authors* (Libraries Unlimited, 2006), along with another 15 black writers of crime and mystery tales.

That clears the decks to offer a broad sampling of some of the genre's busiest writers today and to offer a feel of where the field is at as we enter the second decade of the 2000s.

Entries list the author's birth date and location, genres, and benchmark series or series character. Entries are mostly based on sound secondary sources and provide biographies of the authors, a look at their popular works or series, and a list of their works. Bibliographical entries show where the information came from, in case the reader is interested in pursuing a specific subject.

Susan Wittig Albert

Maywood, Illinois
1940

Amateur Detective, Culinary Mystery,
Historical Mystery
Benchmark Series: China Bayles

Susan Hoermann/Evergreen Studios

About the Author and the Author's Writing

Susan Wittig Albert writes as many as three mystery novels a year. Each takes at most 72 days to complete. She anticipates no major changes to her drafts, and she line edits only when she sends them off to her publishers.

"I chose to write genre fiction because I wanted to make my living writing and thought genre fiction was a better bet," she said in an interview for Cozy Mystery.

The author was born in Maywood, Illinois, in 1940. When she was a teenager, she had some early writing success with a sale to *Jack 'n Jill* magazine. Today she lives in Texas, writes full time, is married to William Albert, and has three children from a previous marriage.

In 1967 she received a B.A. from the University of Illinois and in 1972 a Ph.D. from the University of California, Berkeley. She worked as an instructor and professor at the University of San Francisco and the University of Texas at Austin, making her way up to associate dean of the graduate school at the latter university by 1977. From 1979 to 1981, she was dean at Sophie Newcomb College in New Orleans, then graduate dean at Southwest Texas State University in San Marcos, Texas, from 1981 to 1982. She was also vice president for academic affairs, 1982 to 1986. At the same time, from 1981 to 1987, she was a professor of English at the school.

Albert tired of the internal politics and abandoned academia to become a full-time writer in 1987. She gained a wide following for one contemporary and two historical mystery series. "I enjoy the multiple challenges of writing books in a series," she told *Contemporary Authors*, "developing characters over time and trying circumstances, creating multi-leveled plots that link several books, and keeping the themes and ideas fresh."

Albert modeled one of her protagonists, China Bayles, somewhat on her structured, logical, mildly egotistical self. The series began with *Thyme of Death* in 1992. Bayles abandoned her career as a lawyer (as the author, also, left hers) to become an herbalist and coproprietor, with her friend Ruby Wilcox, of an herb shop and tearoom in Pecan Springs, Texas. A typical case, *Dead Man's Bones* (2005), puts Bayles on the scent of a 30-year-old crime that appears to be linked to a modern-day killing. The books include recipes for fans of the culinary arts.

Albert initially considered her audience to be primarily feminist-thinking women on either coast. "[Bayles's] investigative skills make her a leader among female sleuths," said a *Publishers Weekly* reviewer. But by the 1990s, Albert realized that her following included a lot of people who liked to garden, so she boosted that element of her novels. She also sanded down some of Bayles's rougher edges so as to appeal more to an older readership.

The author and her husband teamed on a second, Victorian series, issued under the Robin Paige byline. They decided to work together while still dating. She asked his advice while writing a Nancy Drew mystery. "He told me what I needed to know, and I thought, 'Hey, this is the guy for me!' We collaborated on over 60 young adult novels, from 1986 to 1992," she said in a *Mysterious Musings* interview.

The Robin Paige books are set a century ago and are about Kate Ardleigh Sheridan, who writes so-called penny dreadful books. They are also about Sir Charles Sheridan, who is keenly interested in forensic science. The two characters marry in the first book, *Death at Bishop's Keep* (1994). That series ended after a dozen books.

Research is important to Albert's writing, even in the China Bayles books. "Albert's love of historic research comes shining through in this novel [*Wormwood*], which offers a fascinating portrait of the Shaker way of life," said reviewer Judy Coon in *Booklist* in 2009.

It is easier to write fiction with a present-day setting, Albert told interviewer Laura Strathman Hulka, "since this is my culture, my time, and the research burden is substantially less. But I love the more formal English of Victorian/Edwardian England, and I always learn so much with every book. I enjoy doing both. Actually, I love doing whatever I'm currently doing, which at the moment is one of the Cottage Tales."

The Cottage Tales use the real-life children's book author Beatrix Potter as their central character. These are more a puzzle than a crime series: "Readers should not expect a traditional mystery as there is no murder; instead, there is a series of intrigues to be untangled by the tactful Miss Potter," said Judy Coon in *Booklist*, in recommending *The Tale of Briar Bank* (2008).

The author's most recent series, Darling Dahlias, is set in the 1930s and features women crime solvers who live in a small, Depression-beset town in Alabama.

Far from being a hindrance, the challenges of her various series have been a plus in keeping her writing juices flowing, the author told journalist Beth Jones. "Each of my books is different in tone, nature of concepts, and metaphoric constructs. I go for as much diversity as possible."

Works by the Author

China Bayles Series

Thyme of Death (1992)

Witches' Bane (1993)

Hangman's Root (1994)

Rosemary Remembered (1995)

Rueful Death (1996)

Love Lies Bleeding (1997)

Chile Death (1998)

Lavender Lies (1999)

Mistletoe Man (2000)

Bloodroot (2001)

Indigo Dying (2002)

An Unthymely Death and Other Garden Mysteries (2003) stories

A Dilly of a Death (2004)

Dead Man's Bones (2005)

Bleeding Hearts (2006)

The China Bayles Book of Days (2006) nonfiction

Spanish Dagger (2007)

Nightshade (2008)

Wormwood (2009)

Holly Blues (2010)

Mourning Glory (2011)

Cottage Tales of Beatrix Potter Series

The Tale of Hill Top Farm (2004)

The Tale of Holly How (2005)

The Tale of Cuckoo Brow Wood (2006)

The Tale of Hawthorn House (2007)

The Tale of Briar Bank (2008)

The Tale of Applebeck Orchard (2009)

The Tale of the Oat Cake Crag (2010)

Darling Dahlias Series

The Darling Dahlias and the Cucumber Tree (2010)

The Darling Dahlias and the Naked Ladies (2011)

Victorian Series, with Bill Albert, writing as Robin Paige

Death at Bishop's Keep (1994)

Death at Gallows Green (1995)

Death at Daisy's Folly (1997)

Death at Devil's Bridge (1998)

Death at Rottingdean (1999)

Death at Whitechapel (2000)

Death at Epsom Downs (2001)

Death at Dartmoor (2002)

Death at Glamis Castle (2003)

Death in Hyde Park (2004)

Death at Blenheim Palace (2005)

Death on the Lizard (2006)

The author has also written more than 60 juvenile novels, including several Nancy Drew mysteries, under the house name Carolyn Keene. She has also written nonfiction.

For Further Information

Coon, Judy, *The Tale of Briar Bank* review, *Booklist*, Sept. 15, 2008.

Coon, Judy, *Wormwood* review, *Booklist*, May 1, 2009.

Dead Man's Bones review, *Publishers Weekly*, Mar. 21, 2005.

Hulka, Laura Strathman, Susan Wittig Albert interview, MyShelf.com, June 2008, http://www.myshelf.com/aom/08/albert.htm/ (viewed Sept. 18, 2009).

Jones, Beth, "Author shares stories," *Hartford City News-Times*, Nov. 27, 2004.

Susan Wittig Albert entry, Contemporary Authors, http://galenet.galegroup.com/servlet/BioRC/ (viewed Sept. 18, 2009).

Susan Wittig Albert interview, Cozy Mystery, http://www.cozy-mystery.com/Susan-Wittig-Albert-Interview.html/ (viewed Sept. 19, 2009).

Susan Wittig Albert interview, *Mysterious Musings*, Aug. 3, 2007, http://juliabuckley.blogspot.com/2007/08/susan-wittig-albert.html/ (viewed Sept. 18, 2009).

Susan Wittig Albert website, http://www.susanalbert.com/about.shtml/ (viewed Sept. 18, 2009).

Donna Andrews

Yorktown, Virginia
Date not revealed

Amateur Detective
Benchmark Series: Meg Langslow

About the Author and the Author's Writing

Meg Langslow and Michael, her boyfriend, go together to buy an old house. Its former owner never threw anything away, as the couple quickly discovers in Donna Andrews's 2005 mystery *Owls Well That Ends Well*. Their solution: hold a huge tag sale and let the neighbors cart stuff away. All goes fine until someone opens a trunk and finds the body of an antiques dealer inside. Life might go on and the police might solve the murder except that Michael is up for tenure and a professor who holds a key vote is one of the suspects. Meg must find the real killer, and fast. She must also get rid of all the rest of that junk.

Donna Andrews "playfully creates laughable, wacky scenes that are the backdrop for her criminally devious plot," said a reviewer in *Romantic Times Book Review*.

Andrews was born in Yorktown, Virginia. She majored in English and drama at the University of Virginia. For two decades, she worked for a communications firm in the Washington, D.C., area. She now lives in Reston, Virginia.

A voracious reader of fantasy and science fiction in her youth, she particularly enjoyed mystery fiction while she was a college student, so she decided to try her hand at that genre. She credits her corporate communications career with giving her a solid grounding in writing; it also gave her the discipline to try fiction. She has two draft science fiction novels still in a drawer. The third proved to be the charm.

Enamored of a Walter R. Brooks's children's book *Freddy the Detective*, in which the pig reads a Sherlock Holmes tale and decides to become a private eye, she wrote a mystery called *Murder with Peacocks*. She submitted the finished manuscript to the Malice Domestic/St. Martin's Press Best First Traditional Mystery contest, and her entry won. When it came out in 1999, it also garnered Agatha, Anthony, Barry, and *Romantic Times* honors for best first mystery. Her career was off to a strong start—and writing became her full-time job in 2001.

Andrews has taken advantage of the flexibility of cozy mysteries, placing her main characters in a variety of settings, from a holiday parade (*Cockatiels at Seven*) to an eXtreme Croquet tournament (*No Nest for the Wicket*) to a Porfira, Queen of the Jungle, fan convention (*We'll Always Have Parrots*). Although the awards shifted slightly—*Crouching Buzzard, Leaping Loon* received the Toby Bromberg Award for Excellence for the Most Humorous Mystery in 2003—they kept coming in. Her books are funny, her characters quirky—the fact that Meg is a blacksmith and sculptor by profession gives a hint of what to expect.

Humorous crime writing requires a delicate hand. Things can be funny to some people but not funny to others. "Some of the worst writing I see from good writers happens when they make the mistake of thinking they can just dash off something light and funny—that because it's light, it will also be easy," she said in an interview with G. M. Mailliet.

Andrews kept the light touch but added a science fiction element with her second series, in which the detective is Turing Hopper, an artificial intelligence personality (think of her as a computer brain), who helps her private investigator friend Tim solve mysteries. In the first book, *You've Got Murder*, which nabbed an Agatha Award for best mystery in 2002, a technician is the victim of a hit-and-run driver.

The author came up with the idea for her second series while working in Washington, "partly inspired by her experience serving as a translator between the marketing and systems departments at her day job," according to her website.

She has written several short stories and is active with Sisters in Crime, working with members of the Chesapeake chapter to bring out three collections.

"One thing I like about short stories is that you can experiment with different voices in them," she said to Sandra Parshall. Her first story, for Dana Stabenow's *The Mysterious North*, "was not humorous at all—it was dark, with a little bit of woo-woo."

So pretty much anything goes for this ambitious writer.

Works by the Author

Meg Langslow Series

Murder with Peacocks (1999)

Murder with Puffins (2000)

Revenge of the Wrought Iron Flamingos (2001)

Crouching Buzzard, Leaping Loon (2003)

We'll Always Have Parrots (2004)

Owls Well That Ends Well (2005)

No Nest for the Wicket (2006)

The Penguin Who Knew Too Much (2007)

Cockatiels at Seven (2008)

A Murder Hatched (2008) omnibus

Six Gees A-slaying (2008)

Swan for the Money (2009)

Stork Raving Mad (2010)

The Real Macaw (2011)

Turing Hopper Series

You've Got Murder (2002)

Click Here for Murder (2003)

Access Denied (2004)

Delete All Suspects (2005)

Contributor

The Mysterious North, edited by Dana Stabenow (2002), includes "An Unkindness of Ravens"

Death Dines In, edited by Claudia Bishop and Dean James (2005), includes "Birthday Dinner"

Powers of Detection: Stories of Mystery and Fantasy, edited by Dana Stabenow (2006), includes "Cold Spell"

Unusual Suspects, edited by Dana Stabenow (2008), includes "Spellbound"

Wolfsbane and Mistletoe, edited by Charlaine Harris and Toni L. P. Kelner (2008), includes "Haire of the Beast"

Editor

Chesapeake Crimes, with Barb Goffman and Marcia Talley (2004), includes "Night Shades"

Chesapeake Crimes 2, with Maria Y. Lima (2005)

Chesapeake Crimes 3, with Marcia Talley (2008)

For Further Information

Donna Andrews web page, http://www.donnaandrews.com/ (viewed July 29, 2009).

Malliet, G. M., Donna Andrews interview, InkSpot, http://midnightwriters.blog spot.com/2007/11/interview-with-donna-andrews-part-i.html/ (viewed July 29, 2009).

Owls Well That Ends Well review, *Romantic Times,* http://www.romantictimes.com/books_review.php?book=25506/ (viewed July 5, 2009).

Parshall, Sandra, Donna Andrews interview, Poe's Deadly Daughters, http://poes deadlydaughters.blogspot.com/2007/07/donna-andrews.html/ (viewed July 29, 2009).

Nancy Atherton

Greg Taylor

Chicago, Illinois
Date not disclosed

Amateur Detective, Paranormal Mystery,
Culinary Mystery
Benchmark Series: Aunt Dimity

About the Author and the Author's Writing

Nancy Atherton's Aunt Dimity mysteries are so cozy that Lori Shepherd, the heroine, sometimes solves the puzzle even before there's a murder. In *Aunt Dimity Slays the Dragon* (2009), the heroine and her gentle ghostly advisor, Aunt Dimity, typically figure out the source of a series of accidents that threaten the success of a Renaissance Faire in her adopted small English town of Finch. Aunt Dimity, an old friend of Lori's late mother, has left her estate to Lori. Now she writes messages to Lori in a blue journal—messages that help her solve mysteries.

Because of the specter, the books are considered paranormal. Because of the recipes, they are considered culinary. Because of the skilled characterizations, they are widely popular.

"The refreshing thing here," said *Booklist* reviewer Judy Coon of *Dragon*, "is that Lori manages to solve the puzzle before anyone really does die—the best kind of 'bloodless' mystery."

Aunt Dimity's Christmas (1999), likewise, drew praise from *Publishers Weekly*: "Though Atherton's novel requires a hefty suspension of disbelief, her charming characters and heartwarming narrative will make believers out of most readers. . . . Atherton offers a glimpse of the finer side of human nature."

Except for the second book, *Aunt Dimity and the Duke*—which follows a different character, Emma Porter, a computer analyst who also hears from Aunt Dimity—the stories focus on Lori, who at one point marries lawyer Bill Willis and, by the fourth book, has begun a family (twins) and relocated to England (although she often travels—for example, in *Aunt Dimity Goes West*, to a log cabin in American cowboy country).

Nancy Atherton, the author of these books, was born in Chicago, to a family including five brothers and two sisters. She still lives in rural Illinois. After graduating from the University of Chicago in 1989, she did some postgraduate study. She worked as a librarian and also as a proofreader and copyeditor and has held jobs at a ski lodge and a dude ranch. She is an avid traveler.

Atherton didn't visit Great Britain until she was 19 years old. "And I've been there many times since," she said on her website, "traveling from Land's End to John O'Groats by rail, automobile, bicycle, hiking book, and thumb. I've had hypothermia on the top of

Mount Snowden, food poisoning in London, and a root canal (my first!) in Haslemere, Surrey."

Atherton never expected to take up writing as a career. She read the usual animal and juvenile mystery series in her youth and today is fond of writers such as Georgette Heyer, P. D. James, and Terry Pratchett, to name just three. It took her two years to complete her first manuscript, which sold within a few weeks after her agent sent it around to publishers.

Her major challenge was to make sense of an amateur detective having the freedom or authority to poke her nose into things. "Having to clock in and clock out wouldn't be interesting. So they have to marry someone rich or be a crime writer (because we know they don't work). Or they can inherit money so they can do the things we want to read about. I think inheritance is a standard trope for freeing up characters to do cool things," she said in a Cozy Library interview.

Atherton has written all of her books from the same cluttered office. She finds music or television distracting; therefore she works in silence, to better hear what's going on in her stories.

The author based her Lori Shepherd character largely on herself (except for the inheritance), but Aunt Dimity came out of the blue. Atherton has said she doesn't believe in ghosts and that Aunt Dimity was in great measure drawn from the many people she has come across in the course of her life. Atherton delights in meeting people and getting to know them. By the same token, her made-up characters have their own personalities and, she has said, despite her efforts, they generally take the story on their own course. Her method of writing with little or no outline can make writing a book more time-consuming, but she says that not knowing the ending makes the effort more interesting to her.

Atherton disdains most writing advice. "It seems to me that there are as many ways to write as there are writers," she said in a Novel Journey interview, "so a rule book, if it existed, would have to contain so many disparate and contradictory rules that it would be entirely useless."

Works by the Author

Aunt Dimity Series

Aunt Dimity's Death (1992)

Aunt Dimity and the Duke (1994)

Aunt Dimity's Good Deed (1996)

Aunt Dimity Digs In (1998)

Aunt Dimity's Christmas (1999)

Aunt Dimity Beats the Devil (2000)

Aunt Dimity Detective (2001)

Aunt Dimity Takes a Holiday (2003)

Aunt Dimity Snowbound (2004)

Aunt Dimity and the Next of Kin (2005)

Aunt Dimity and the Deep Blue Sea (2006)

Aunt Dimity Goes West (2007)

Aunt Dimity, Vampire Hunter (2008)

Aunt Dimity Slays the Dragon (2009)

Introducing Aunt Dimity, Paranormal Detective (2009) omnibus, first two books in the series

Aunt Dimity Down Under (2010)

Aunt Dimity and the Family Tree (2011)

Contributor

Naked Came the Farmer, with Terry Bibo, Steven Burgauer, Dorothy Cannell, David Everson, Philip José Farmer, Joseph Flynn, Julie Kistler, Jerry Klein, Bill Knight, Tracy Knight, Garry Moore, and Joel Steinfeldt (1998)

For Further Information

Aunt Dimity's Christmas review, *Publishers Weekly*, Sept. 20, 1999.

Coon, Judy, *Aunt Dimity Slays the Dragon* review, *Booklist*, Jan. 1, 2009.

Nancy Atherton interview, Cozy Library, http://www.cozylibrary.com/default.aspx?id=20/ (viewed Sept. 24, 2009).

Nancy Atherton interview, Novel Journey, http://noveljourney.blogspot.com/2007/12/mystery-author-nancy-atherton.html/ (viewed Sept. 24, 2009).

Nancy Atherton profile, Who Dunnit, http://www.who-dunnit.com/authors/139/ (viewed Sept. 24, 2009).

Nancy Atherton website, http://www.aunt-dimity.com/ (viewed Sept. 24, 2009).

Donald Bain

Mineola, New York
1935

Amateur Detective, Police Procedural
Benchmark Series: Murder, She Wrote

Richard Koser

About the Author and the Author's Writing

Donald Bain has used so many aliases in his life, one would think he was hiding out in a witness protection program. A ghost writer for dozens of novels, Bain has written others under several pen names.

His first huge success was written under a double pen name; it was *Coffee, Tea, or Me?* by "Trudy Baker and Rachel Jones," a light, spicy look at the adventures of two airline hostesses. In the introduction to a 2003 reprint, the author said,

> Little did I know in 1967 that the book I was writing with a title lifted from a lame old
> joke would go on, along with its three sequels, to sell more than five million copies,
> be translated into a dozen languages, cause anxious mothers to forbid their daughters
> from becoming stewardesses, [and] spawn airline protest groups.

Bain has written more than 100 novels in crime (with two Toma books, based on a television series), western (nine novels under the pseudonym J. D. Hardin about a former Rough Rider named Fargo), and other genres.

For two decades and through more than 30 books, Bain has built a steady following. In a conversation with Mary Kennedy for Examiner.com, the author explained,

> My niche has been writing the tie-in novels based upon one of America's most beloved
> TV shows, *Murder She Wrote*. I get credit on these books along with Jessica Fletcher,
> who exists only as a TV character played by Angela Lansbury.

Bain has been so successful at bringing to life the characters created by others that the International Association of Media Tie-in Writers named him its first Grand Master in 2006.

Jessica Fletcher is a spinsterish character who calls Cabot Cove, Maine, her home. She was featured in a CBS-TV series that aired from 1984 to 1996 and continues in syndication. A typical cozy plot, in *A Slaying in Savannah* (2008), finds the heroine racing to solve the murder of Wanamaker Jones, who was killed decades earlier at a New Year's Eve party. If she can find the perpetrator, she stands to inherit $1 million from Jones's one-time fiancee Tillie Mortelaine.

The books come relatively effortlessly to the author, who has collaborated on them with his wife, Renee Paley-Bain, since the 13th in the series.

"When I first got the gig, I watched a lot of episodes," Bain told interviewer Brian Koonz of *News-Times*. "But apparently, I didn't watch enough of them." He described Jessica Fletcher as driving a car in one of the books. Fans knew she rode a bicycle and didn't know how to drive. "The fans really let me have it. Now, it's the ultimate compliment when a reader tells me it sounds just like Jessica Fletcher on the page."

Bain was born in Mineola, New York, in 1935 and now lives in Danbury, Connecticut. In 1957 he graduated from Purdue University with a degree in speech and communications. After working in broadcasting in Texas and New York, he became cohost of a radio show with Long John Nebel. He is also a jazz musician and has taught at the college level.

Bain was a writer/director for Peckham Productions and a public relations executive with McCann-Erickson and American Airlines. As a consultant to PanAm Airlines, he helped promote air travel through a national campaign. One of his most difficult professional assignments, he has said, was writing a speech for PanAm's chairman, with the right amounts of information, compassion, and outrage, in the wake of the bombing of Flight 103 over Lockerbie, Scotland.

There are pluses and minuses to writing tie-in books. The pluses include an already established audience. The minuses include an inflexibility in the character. In the case of Jessica Fletcher, a property owned by Universal Studios, the owners keep a tight rein. Universal wouldn't let Bain have Fletcher give a kiss to her old friend George Sutherland. But "I have a private pilot's license and thought it would be nice for Jessica to have one, too, and to be able to fly a plane. I never heard a peep from Universal," he told interviewer John Valeri.

While some disdain tie-in writing, Bain has heralded his accomplishments in a biography, *Murder HE Wrote,* published by his alma mater. (Purdue designated him a Distinguished Alumnus in 2003.)

The most popular book in the Murder She Wrote series has been *Murder on the QE2* (1997). When Bain and his wife, working up a recent plot, wanted to set it in the Museum of Natural History in New York, the publisher nudged them in another direction. Thus Jessica Fletcher is booked to give a lecture on the *Queen Mary 2* in *The Queen's Jewels* (2010).

The Bains don't stint on research. They traveled to London and came back on the *Queen Mary 2*. "Naturally, we squeezed in plenty of research, walking the length and breadth of the ship with tape recorder in-hand. And we were privileged to spend time with the QM2's charming captain, Nick Bates, who is never without a humorous story," Bain said on his website.

The travails of research!

Works by the Author

Murder, She Wrote Series, "with Jessica Fletcher"

Gin and Daggers (1989)

Manhattans and Murder (1994)

Brandy and Bullets (1995)

Martinis and Mayhem (1995)

Rum and Razors (1995)

A Deadly Judgment (1996)

A Palette for Murder (1996)

The Highland Fling Murders (1997)

Murder on the QE2 (1997)

A Little Yuletide Murder (1998)

Murder in Moscow (1998)

Knock 'Em Dead (1999)

Murder at the Powderhorn Ranch (1999)

Trick or Treachery (2000)

Blood on the Vine (2001)

Murder in a Minor Key (2001)

Provence—to Die For (2002)

You Bet Your Life (2002)

Destination Murder (2003)

Majoring in Murder (2003)

Dying to Retire (2004)

A Vote for Murder (2004)

The Maine Mutiny (2005)

Margaritas and Murder (2005)

A Question of Murder (2006)

Three Strikes and You're Dead (2006)

Coffee, Tea, or Murder (2007)

Panning for Murder (2007)

Murder on Parade (2008)

A Slaying in Savannah (2008)

A Fatal Feast (2009)

Madison Avenue Shoot (2009)

Murder Never Takes a Holiday (2009)

Nashville Noir (2010)

The Queen's Jewels (2010)

Skating on Thin Ice (2011)

As Jack Pearl Toma Series, with David Toma

The Airport Affair (1975)

The Affair of the Unhappy Hooker (1976)

As Mike Lundy

Baby Farm (1987)

Raven (1987)

As Nick Vasile

Sado Cop (1976)

A Member of the Family (1993)

Bain has written fiction under the bylines Trudy Baker and Rachel Jones, J. D. Hardin, Joni Moura and Jackie Sutherland, Kathy Cole and Donna Bain, Cornelius Wohl, Laura Mills and Pauline Gurlick, Janet McMillan and Mitzi Sims, Joan Wood, Teri Palmer, Mike Lundy, Pamela South, Lee Jackson, and Stephanie Blake. He has said that contractually he is unable to acknowledge an additional two dozen ghostwritten novels. He has also written nonfiction under his own and other names.

For Further Information

Bain, Donald. *Murder HE Wrote: A Successful Writer's Life*. West Lafayette, IN: Purdue University Press, 2006.

Donald Bain profile, International Association of Media Tie-in Writers, http://www. iamtw.org/about.html/ (viewed Aug. 7, 2009).

Donald Bain profile, New American Library, http://nalauthors.com/author88/ (viewed Aug. 7, 2009).

Donald Bain website, http://www.donaldbain.com/ (viewed Aug. 7, 2009).

Kennedy, Mary, "Why I Love Jessica Fletcher: A Conversation with Donald Bain," Examiner.com, May 10, 2009, http://www.examiner.com/x-10591-Crime-Fiction-Examiner~y2009m5d10-Why-I-love-Jessica-Fletcher-a-conversation-with-Donald-Bain/ (viewed Aug. 7, 2009).

Koonz, Brian, "Sometimes, a Word is Worth a Thousand Pictures," *News-Times*, Nov. 6, 2008.

Madison Avenue Shoot review, *Publishers Weekly*, Feb. 23, 2009.

Valeri, John, "Unmasking Donald Bain: The Man behind the Murder, She Wrote Books," Examiner.com, http://www.examiner.com/x-3859-Hartford-Books-Examiner~y2009m5d11-Unmasking-Donald-Bain-The-man-behind-the-Murder-She-Wrote-book-series-Part-1/ (viewed Aug. 7, 2009).

Linda Barnes

Detroit, Michigan
1949

Private Detective, Amateur Detective
Benchmark Series: Carlotta Carlyle

Lynne Wayne

About the Author and the Author's Writing

Should you hail a Green and White Taxi in Boston and the driver turns out to be a 6-foot, 1-inch redhead, ask if she's divorced, plays blues guitar, has a cat and a parakeet, and shares a house with a ditzy artist. If she says yes, then she is no doubt Linda Barnes's private eye Carlotta Carlyle. If she's in a hurry, she's probably on a case and you might want to grab the next hack.

Carlyle was a police officer for six years and now only drives a cab when she doesn't have a paying client for her private investigation business. The character first appeared in "Lucky Penny," an Anthony Award–winning short story, and soon graduated to a novel. By then the author had already written four books in an amateur detective series featuring Michael Spraggue, a wealthy actor and former private detective. "Because I had chosen to make Spraggue an amateur, I had the continuing problem of involving him legitimately in his cases," the author said in the *St. James Guide to Crime and Mystery Writers.* "I solved this by killing off many of his friends and relatives. His subsequent depression became difficult to deal with and I sought a new hero."

Barnes chose a female character—one blogger derogatorily suggested she was put together from a MadLibs exercise—and a first-person voice. Fans would say so what, they love her. And unlike Spraggue, Carlyle has a cluster of friends and co-workers who have endured. Besides Roz, her eccentric housekeeper tenant, there's gruff Gloria, the G&W dispatcher; Sam Gianelli, her son-of-a-mafioso boyfriend; Mooney, her partner before she turned in her gold badge; and Paolina, her Little Sister.

If it seems a jumble, Barnes makes it work, in the view of *New York Times Book Review*'s Marilyn Stasio, who said in describing *Steel Guitar* (1991):

> The seemingly irrelevant details of Carlotta's history and life are brought together with skill and subtlety. This lady is not merely a feminized representative of the hard-boiled school, a P.I. with a past and an attitude . . . she is a woman of wit and gravity, compassion and toughness, a heroine worth spending time with.

The author was born in Detroit, Michigan, in 1949. She graduated from Boston University with a B.F.A. cum laude in 1971. She taught theater at Chelmsford High School and the Lexington public schools, both in Massachusetts. She and her husband, Richard Allen Barnes, have one son. They live near Boston.

Barnes put a lot of herself into Carlyle. "Carlotta and I both grew up in Detroit. We have the same grandmother and the same shoe size," she told Stephen Anable of *Publishers Weekly*. "I wanted somebody who knew her way around the block, who was big enough to hold her own in physical disputes, and somebody who did not always get justice."

Barnes purposely gave her character great mobility, so that she could legitimately be in various ethnic neighborhoods of Boston and could reasonably befriend and become mentor to a Colombian girl.

The author has said characters often come to her first as voices. "When I begin to write, I start with voice. Once I hear the character, I visualize the character," she said in a conversation on the Jungle Red website. "Then I physicalize the character: how does he walk; what does she eat for breakfast; when does she smile and why." If it sounds something like method acting, it is. Barnes once aspired to become a Shakespearean actress. The closest she came was teaching as well as writing and producing two award-winning plays, *Wings* and *Prometheus*.

As her series have progressed, Barnes has come up with ways to push her characters. *Heart of the World* (2006), for example, takes place mostly in Colombia. "One of the dangers of a series is complacency. I'd already placed Carlotta in a wide variety of situations in the Boston/Cambridge area. She'd proved her mettle, so I wanted to haul her out of her comfort zone. Of course, that meant moving me out of my comfort zone as well," she told *Library Journal*'s Andi Schecter.

For a change of pace, she and some 20 fellow members of International Thriller Writers collaborated on a joint novel featuring former war crimes investigator Harold Middleton. It is titled *Watchlist*.

Barnes intends to continue to nudge the limits of detective fiction. Carlyle "is my 'mirror held up to nature,' my reflection of a changing society. As a teen, I read mystery novels about stalwart men who lived by a code of justice," she said on her website. "And that's Carlotta's mission, really, to demand, determine, and occasionally, mete out justice on her own."

Works by the Author

Carlotta Carlyle Series

A Trouble of Fools (1987)

The Snake Tattoo (1989)

Coyote (1990)

Steel Guitar (1991)

Snapshot (1993)

Hardware (1995)

Cold Case (1997)

Flashpoint (1999)

The Big Dig (2000)

Deep Pockets (2004)

Heart of the World (2006)

Lie Down with the Devil (2008)

Michael Spraggue Series

Blood Will Have Blood (1981)

Bitter Finish (1982)

Dead Heat (1984)

Cities of the Dead (1985)

Contributor

Sisters in Crime, edited by Marilyn Wallace (1989), includes "Lucky Penny"

Modern Treasury of Great Detective and Murder Mysteries, edited by Ed Gorman (1996), includes "Lucky Penny"

Oxford Book of American Detective Stories, edited by Tony Hillerman and Rosemary Herbert (1997), includes "Lucky Penny"

Two of the Deadliest, edited by Elizabeth George (2009), includes "Catch Your Death"

The Shamus Winners: America's Best Private Eye Stories, Vol. 1, 1982–1995 (2010) edited by Robert J. Randisi, includes "Lucky Penny"

Watchlist: A Serial Thriller, with Brett Battles, Lee Child, David Corbett, Jeffery Deaver, Joseph Finder, Jim Fusilli, John Gilstrap, James Grady, David Hewson, David Liss, Gayle Lynds, John Ramsey Miller, P. J. Parrish, and Ralph Pezzullo (2010)

For Further Information

Anable, Stephen, "Dirt Beneath the Big Dig," *Publishers Weekly*, Oct. 14, 2002.

Barnes, Linda, "Carlotta and Me," *Giallo Magazine,* http://lindabarnes.com/excerpt_essay.html/ (viewed Sept. 24, 2009).

Linda Barnes interview, Jungle Red, http://www.jungleredwriters.com/2008/08/on-linda-barnes-and-carlotta-carlyle.html/ (viewed Sept. 24, 2009).

Linda Barnes profile, Who Dunnit, http://www.who-dunnit.com/authors/115/ (viewed Sept. 24, 2009).

Linda Barnes website, http://lindabarnes.com/ (viewed Sept. 24, 2009).

Semple, Linda, and Ted Hertel, Linda Barnes entry, *St. James Guide to Crime & Mystery Writers*, fourth edition, edited by Jay P. Pederson. Detroit: St. James Press, 1996.

Shechter, Andi, "LJ Talks to Linda Barnes," *Library Journal*, June 13, 2006.

Stasio, Marily, *Steel Guitar* review, *New York Times Book Review*, Nov. 3, 1991.

Stasio, Marilyn, *The Big Dig* review, *New York Times Book Review*, Nov. 3, 2002.

Trouble of Fools review, GoodReads, http://www.goodreads.com/book/show/459015.A_Trouble_of_Fools/ (viewed Sept. 25, 2009).

M. C. Beaton (Marion Chesney)

Glasgow, Scotland
1936

Police Procedural, Amateur Detective, Historical Mystery
Benchmark Series: Hamish Macbeth

About the Author and the Author's Writing

In *Death of a Witch*, we read:

Police Constable Hamish Macbeth, heading home to his police station in the village of Lochdubh in Sutherland, heaved a sigh of relief. He stopped for a moment by the side of the road and rolled down the car window. He was driving a battered old Rover, manufactured before the days of power steering and electronic windows.

A humble man, indeed, is the rural Scottish officer, as readers meet him in the 25th entry in M. C. Beaton's long-running series. But Macbeth is humble by design; he masks his abilities and his intellect, so that he won't be promoted out of his comfortable setting to a more urban environment.

Macbeth is one of two popular mystery series characters created by Beaton—the other is Agatha Raisin. Beaton is not a real person. It is a pseudonym used by Marion Chesney. Chesney wrote a string of Regency romances under her real name and has written as Ann Fairfax, Jennie Tremaine, Helen Crampton, and Charlotte Ward. She has also used her own name for the Lady Rose Summer series of Edwardian mysteries. But it is as Beaton that she is best known to mystery readers.

Beaton was born in Glasgow, Scotland, in 1936. She worked as a fiction buyer for a bookseller, John Smith's in Glasgow, when the opportunity arose to review a play for the *Glasgow Daily Mail*. She liked writing and soon became a journalist with *Scottish Field*, theater critic with the *Scottish Daily Express* in Glasgow, and chief reporter with the *Daily Express* in London.

The author has cited numerous influences, ranging from John Buchan and Dorothy L. Sayers to Agatha Christie, Josephine Tey, and Marjory Allingham.

But it was her mother's love of Jane Austen's novels and her own fondness for Georgette Heyer that persuaded her to start writing love stories.

"I moved to the States after marrying Middle East Correspondent Harry Scott Gibbons. I had been reading a lot of Regencies and criticizing them and he urged me to write one."

She didn't write just one, she wrote dozens.

She was ready for a change of scene when, vacationing in northern Scotland, she looked around her and realized she had a perfect setting for a classic crime novel.

The strengths of the Macbeth crime novels are, indeed, setting as well as character.

As to setting, Connie Fletcher in a *Death of a Witch* review in *Booklist* noted, "Lochdubh has a ridiculously high homicide rate for a tiny village, but it provides readers with a great deal of atmospheric fun."

The author acknowledged in a Newsvine interview that

> I sometimes feel guilty about using the same Highland setting as there have been about two murders in Sutherland in the past 100 years. But I would never move Hamish from his Highland location. That is the escape for the reader.

As to character, particularly her constable hero, Beaton told Connie Fletcher in an interview for *Booklist* that "Hamish Macbeth represents the nicer part of the Highland character and is based on several people I have known. A lot of Agatha is me, although I would never dream of being so rude."

Agatha Raisin is the crusty heroine of books set in the Cotswolds, where the author and her husband now reside. Raisin is retired from the publicity field. But, we read in *A Spoonful of Poison* (2008), she "found that inactivity did not suit her and so had started up her own private detective agency. Now that it was successful, however, she wished she had more time to relax."

Publishers Weekly said of *A Spoonful of Poison*, "Beaton's sly humor enhances the cozy-style plotting."

The author has not abandoned Regency romances; *Emily Goes to Exeter* (2011) is the first of a new, non-mystery series, Traveling Matchmaker, featuring Hannah Pym. The "mystery" is whether she will succeed in arranging a marriage for spoiled Emily Freemantle and aristocrat Lord Ranger Harley.

Beaton's characters populate an enclosed world and she herself lives in the country, but she has adapted well enough to the times. "Best gift ever in the eighties was a word processor," she said on the Agatha Raisin website. "I used to type out my books which was back-breaking work involving sore shoulders and Tipp-Ex [correction fluid]. When I got my first Amstrad [personal computer], I felt like an overworked Victorian seamstress who had just been handed a sewing machine."

Works by the Author

The Skeleton in the Closet (2001)

Hamish Macbeth Series

Death of a Gossip (1985)

Death of a Cad (1987)

Death of an Outsider (1988)

Death of a Perfect Wife (1989)

Death of a Hussy (1990)

Death of a Snob (1991)

Death of a Prankster (1992)

Death of a Glutton (1993)

Death of a Travelling Man (1993)

Death of a Charming Man (1994)

Death of a Nag (1995)

Death of a Macho Man (1996)

Death of a Dentist (1997)

The Casebooks of Hamish Macbeth (1998), includes *Death of a Gossip* and *Death of a Cad*

Death of a Scriptwriter (1998)

Death of an Addict (1999)

A Highland Christmas (1999)

Death of a Dustman (2001)

Death of a Celebrity (2002)

Death of a Village (2003)

Death of a Poison Pen (2004)

Death of a Bore (2005)

Death of a Dreamer (2006)

Death of a Maid (2007)

Death of a Gentle Lady (2008)

Death of a Witch (2009)

Death of a Valentine (2010)

Death of a Chimney Sweep (2011)

Agatha Raisin Series

Agatha Raisin and the Quiche of Death (1992)

Agatha Raisin and the Vicious Vet (1993)

Agatha Raisin and the Potted Gardener (1994)

Agatha Raisin and the Walkers of Dembley (1995)

Agatha Raisin and the Murderous Marriage (1996)

Agatha Raisin and the Terrible Tourist (1997)

Agatha Raisin and the Wellspring of Death (1998)

Agatha Raisin and the Witch of Wyckhadden (1999)

Agatha Raisin and the Wizard of Evesham (1999)

Agatha Raisin and the Fairies of Fryfam (2000)

Agatha Raisin and the Love from Hell (2001)

Agatha Raisin and the Day the Floods Came (2002)

Agatha Raisin and the Case of the Curious Curate (2003)

Agatha Raisin and the Haunted House (2003)

The Deadly Dance (2004)

Agatha Raisin and the Perfect Paragon (2005)

Love, Lies and Liquor (2006)

Kissing Christmas Goodbye (2007)

Agatha Raisin and a Spoonful of Poison (2008)

Introducing Agatha Raisin (2008), includes *Vicious Vet* and *Quiche of Death*

There Goes the Bride (2009)

Busy Body (2010)

Contributor

Very Merry Mysteries, with Charlotte MacLeod and Margaret Maron (1999)

The author has also written historical romances under her own name, Marion Chesney, and as Ann Fairfax, Helen Crampton, Charlotte Ward, and Jennie Tremaine. She uses the M. C. Beaton name for a Regency series, Traveling Matchmaker.

Adaptations in Other Media

Hamish Macbeth mystery series (BBC, 1995)

For Further Information

Agatha Raisin web page, http://www.agatharaisin.com/ (viewed July 17, 2009).

Butki, Scott, "Interview with Author M. C. Beaton," Newsvine, May 1, 2007, http://sbutki.newsvine.com/_news/2007/05/01/675418-interview-with-author-mc-beaton/ (viewed July 30, 2009).

Fletcher, Connie, *Death of a Witch* review, *Booklist*, Dec. 1, 2008.

Fletcher, Connie, M. C. Beaton interview, *Booklist*, May 1, 2006.

M. C. Beaton interview, Euro Crime, July 13, 2007, http://eurocrime.blogspot.com/2007/07/m-c-beaton-interview.html/ (viewed July 17, 2009).

Spoonful of Poison review, *Publishers Weekly*, Aug. 4, 2008.

Stasio, Marilyn, "Murder Least Foul: The Cozy, Soft-Boiled Mystery," *New York Times Book Review*, Oct. 18, 1992.

Cara Black

Laura Skayhan

Chicago, Illinois
1951

Private Detective
Benchmark Series: Aimée Leduc

About the Author and the Author's Writing

Aimée Leduc has short spiky hair. She keeps her Beretta in the spoon drawer. Her Bichon Frise is named Miles Davis. She runs a computer security firm. Her partner, René Friant, is height-challenged. And she lives in Paris.

Is mystery writer Cara Black's series character Leduc a little offbeat? *Mais oui.* Reviewer Donna Liquori, writing in the *Times-Union,* would have it no other way. Black approaches each new book

> looking forward to the company of an independent woman, who is not without flaws—she's always quitting smoking, is attracted to bad boys and is usually trying to figure out how to pay the bills. And Aimée's Paris is a treat.

There's an overwhelming European flavor to Black's books, but the author is pure American. She was born in Chicago in 1951, to a Francophile family. She grew up in California and attended a French Catholic school. She had an opportunity, at a young age, to travel to France, and was taken with the culture. She received bachelor's and master's degrees from San Francisco State University, the last in 1982. She married photography bookseller Jun Ishimuro; they have one child. She worked as a teacher and director for a preschool before writing her first novel.

"I always wanted to be a writer," she told Timothy Peters for *Publishers Weekly,* "but never wanted to do the hard work to become one." Then, as a fan of the French novelist Romain Gary, she visited the writer in Paris and came away persuaded: "This is the writing life." Yet several years passed before she sat down to write *Murder in the Marais* (1999), about her investigative Parisienne.

Among her other influences, she has said, are the French crime writer Ló Malet, P. D. James, Philip Kerr, and John le Carré. As the Aimée Leduc series has progressed, Black has made it a point to take each one into a different arrondissement. This has required further visits to Paris, of course, and a fair amount of research. In a conversation with Marion Nowak of *Bonjour Paris,* she said, "When I am in Paris, I crawl under buildings, dig around in my friends' attics, explore the restrooms in old cafés . . . you name it. I've even gone into the little-known tunnels in the Palais Royal."

The prowling provides details that make the novels ring. That's her impetus to keep exploring new places. "Each part of Paris is a totally unique world, with its own flavor," she said in a Paris Intrigue interview. "Usually I read something in the newspaper or hear about an event in France, and that inspires my research. I always start with the exciting feeling that there's a story out there to share."

When she is exploring Paris, Black sometimes encounters the unexpected, as on a day in the Sentier when she missed a bus and began to walk. As she told interviewer Eleanor Beardsley,

> There were all these hookers standing on the street. Then there were these men pushing these big barrels of clothing into the courtyards of these 17th-century *hotels particu-liers*, into the basement where there were sweat shops. And I just loved this dichotomy of what was going on.

Black pulled together a lot of characteristics to come up with her heroine. "She's thinner, taller than me. I always have her doing things I'm scared to do. Climb ropes—I'm afraid of heights. I have her deal with rodents—I'm afraid of mice and rats," she told *San Francisco Chronicle* staff writer Edward Guthmann. "She does things on the computer I can't."

The author amplified, in an interview on the Paris Through Expatriate Eyes website:

> I couldn't write as a Frenchwoman because I'm not French. (Aimée is half French, half American). She's neither fish nor fowl. She doesn't belong in French society and she doesn't belong in American society. Her father was a flic (cop) her mother left the family. She's kind of out there.

Black has an engaging style, although she said in a *Library Journal* Q&A with Barbara Hoffert that she doesn't concentrate on style when writing. If anything, she takes a page from poets, and favors the light touch. "If a scene is about revealing character, setting the place, and giving atmosphere, it's best to show, not tell. As Chekhov said, 'Don't tell me the moon is shining, show me moonlight glinting on a piece of broken glass.'"

Works by the Author

Aimée Leduc Series

Murder in the Marais (1999)

Murder in Belleville (2000)

Murder in the Sentier (2002)

Murder in the Bastille (2003)

Murder in Clichy (2005)

Murder in Montmartre (2006)

Murder on the Ile Saint-Louis (2007)

Murder in the Rue de Paradis (2008)

Murder in the Latin Quarter (2009)

Murder in the Palais Royal (2010)

Murder in Passy (2011)

Contributor

Interrogations, edited by Jon Jordan (2003)

My Sherlock Holmes: Untold Stories of the Great Detective, edited by Michael Karland (2003)

A Second Helping of Murder: More Diabolically Delicious Recipes from Contemporary Mystery Writers, edited by Robert Weibezahl (2007)

Paris Noir: Capital Crime Fiction, edited by Maxim Jakubowski (2008)

For Further Information

Beardsley, Eleanor, "In Paris, a Mystery Writer Whose Name Is 'Noir,'" NPR, http://www.npr.org/templates/story/story.php?storyId=111513882/ (viewed Dec. 13, 2009).

Cara Black web page, http://www.carablack.com/ (viewed Dec. 13, 2009).

"A Conversation with Cara Black," Paris through expatriate eyes. http://www.paris-expat.com/interviews/interview_cb.html/ (viewed Dec. 13, 2009).

Guthmann, Edward, "Murders Most Parisian, Brought to You by Cara Black," *San Francisco Chronicle*, April 5, 2007.

Hoffert, Barbara, "Q&A: Cara Black," *Library Journal*, Nov. 1, 2007.

Jones, Scott, "A Chat with Cara Black," Crime Online. http://www.crimeonline.net/viewtopic.php?t=39/ (viewed Dec. 13, 2009).

Liquori, Donna, "The Detective I Want to Be," *Albany Times-Union* (New York), Jan. 10, 2010.

Nowak, Marion, Cara Black interview, *Bonjour Paris*, Apr. 2003, http://carablack.com/interview.html/ (viewed Dec. 13, 2009).

Peters, Timothy, "She Loves Paris," *Publishers Weekly,* Dec. 15, 2008.

Teisch, Jessica, "Paris Intrigue: An Interview with Cara Black," *Bookmarks*, http://www.bookmarksmagazine.com/paris-intrigue-interview-cara-black/jessica-teisch/ (viewed Dec. 13, 2009).

Teisch, Jessica, "Paris Intrigue, Part II: Another Interview with Cara Black," *Bookmarks*, spring 2009, http://www.bookmarksmagazine.com/paris-intrigue-part-ii-another-interview-cara-black-spring-2009/jessica-teisch/ (viewed Dec. 13, 2009).

Lawrence Block

Buffalo, New York
1938

Private Detective, Legal Mystery,
Rogue Detective
Benchmark Series: Matt Scudder

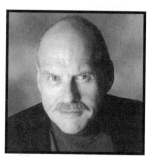

Courtesy of the author

About the Author and the Author's Writing

Could you imagine Lawrence Block as a science fiction writer, instead of a recipient of the Mystery Writers of America Grand Master Award as well as the Crime Writers Association Cartier Diamond Dagger Award for lifetime achievement?

"The first year I started writing professionally," he told *January Magazine*'s Kevin Burton Smith, "I actually wrote a science-fiction story and it wound up in a best-of-the-year collection. But remarkably, I never got another idea for a science-fiction story."

Lawrence Block, of course, gravitated to a life of crime—crime novel writing, that is—with a stable of stellar series characters, the newest on the scene being a loner, a stamp-collecting hired gun named Keller. One seldom thinks of paid assassins as having interesting personalities, but Block begs to differ. "It seems to me he has both roots and a conscience," he said in a Bookslut interview. "They're just a little different from most people, and he's learned to cope with them differently."

The author was born in Buffalo, New York, in 1938. He took English, history, and other classes at Antioch College from 1955 to 1959 but dropped out to pursue his writing. Divorced, with three daughters (and two granddaughters), he married Lynne Wood in 1983.

From 1957 to 1958, he worked as an editor for the Scott Meredith literary agency, and from 1964 to 1966, as an editor for a Whitman Publishing coin collecting periodical. He taught at Hofstra University in 1981. He conducted his Write for Your Life seminars on the East Coast from 1983 to 1988. The rest of the time he has been a freelance writer.

Block's first crime story was "You Can't Lose" for *Manhunt* in 1958. Perfecting his craft, he wrote pulpish stories for digests and men's magazines and publishers of lurid paperbacks—his way to learn the craft and be paid for it. He still writes short stories (*Enough Rope* collects the first 84), even as his novels have a large following.

Block's imagination has produced several ongoing series. Evan Tanner, who since he was wounded in Korea has lost his ability to sleep, supports himself by writing term papers for college students and traveling the world in support of political causes. Matthew Scudder is a recovering alcoholic, a retired police officer who wasn't where he should have been when his partner was shot. Now he solves crimes on his own hook. Bernie Rhodenbarr is a bibliophile and gentleman thief. Keller, as we already know, is a lonely hitman. Chip Harrison is girl-hungry assistant to the large detective Leo Haig. And Martin Ehrengraf is a lawyer who never loses a case—no matter what he has to do.

"I tend to find anti-heroes more interesting than white knights," Block told Katy Kelly of *USA Today*. In fact, he makes it his mission to lure his readers into liking his characters. "It seems to me there's nothing terribly challenging about making a reader like Alan Alda. Everybody likes Alan Alda."

Block travels extensively between books; thus, when he does write, he writes intensely. He frequently writes in seclusion, at a hotel or a writer's colony.

"I don't know that it's effortless," he said of his writing style in an interview with Tom Callahan for *The Writer*, "but there is not that much conscious effort involved. My feeling about writing is that most of the hard work gets done on an unconscious level anyway."

Block does minimal research. For the Tanner series, in which the protagonist hopped from Canada to Latvia to Afghanistan to Africa, "I would get hold of a certain amount of real data but beyond that I would just fake my way through it with an atlas and an encyclopedia," he told a BookEnds interviewer. He writes without an outline—making the Burglar books, with their intricate plots, the hardest to do.

"Except in the light books—Bernie, Chip—I never set out to be funny," Block told Ali Karim for *SHOTS* magazine. "It's my experience that, if I create clever characters, they're going to say some amusing things now and then." His Scudder books are particularly dark, and while Block admits that some readers find they have lightened in tone, to his thinking, except that the hero is going to AA and is now married, his tales are if anything more violent and troubling.

Block embraces New York City's whir and jangle. He uses the city for the setting of most of his books (Tanner and Keller being frequent travelers).

Most fictional characters stay the same age throughout a series. But Block's Scudder books, with their gritty realism, obliged the author to make his characters grow and change. Block observed to journalist Claire E. White, "I couldn't have him *not* altered by the experiences he would undergo in one book. So things just happened to him, and he's changed and aged, even as you and I."

Block has no issue with being cast as a mystery writer. "I think the mystery is getting more respect than it used to," he said in an *Armchair Detective* interview, "both commercially and critically, so one is less apt to feel, you know, a stepchild."

Works by the Author

Fiction

Babe in the Woods (1960), as by William Ard (Lou Largo Series)

The Specialists (1960)

Campus Tramp (1961), as by Andrew Shaw, reprinted as by Lawrence Block (2010)

Death Pulls a Doublecross (1961), retitled *Coward's Kiss* (1987)

Killing Castro (1961), as by Lee Duncan, reissued 2009 as by Lawrence Block

Markham: The Case of the Pornographic Photos (1961), retitled *You Could Call It Murder* (1987)

Mona (1961), retitled *Sweet Slow Death* (1986), retitled *Grifter's Game* (2004)

Pads Are for Passion (1961), as by Sheldon Lord, reissued 2008 as *A Diet of Treacle* by Lawrence Block

$20 Lust (1961), published pseudonymously, retitled *Cinderella Sims* as by Block (2003)

The Girl with the Long Green Heart (1963)

Deadly Honeymoon (1967)

After the First Death (1969)

Such Men Are Dangerous (1969), as by Paul Kavanagh, reissued as by Lawrence Block

Ronald Rabbit Is a Dirty Old Man (1971)

The Triumph of Evil (1971), as by Paul Kavanagh, reissued as by Lawrence Block

Not Comin' Home to You (1974), as by Paul Kavanagh, reissued as by Lawrence Block

Ariel (1980)

Code of Arms, with Harold King (1981)

Into the Night, with Cornwell Woolrich (1987)

Random Walk (1988)

Dead Honeymoon (2003)

Small Town (2003)

Lucky at Cards (2007)

Getting Off: A Novel of Sex & Violence (2011), as Jill Emerson

Bernie Rhodenbarr Series

Burglars Can't Be Choosers (1977)

The Burglar in the Closet (1978)

The Burglar Who Likes to Quote Kipling (1979)

The Burglar Who Studied Spinoza (1980)

The Burglar Who Painted Like Mondrian (1983)

The Burglar Who Traded Ted Williams (1994)

The Burglar Who Thought He Was Bogart (1995)

The Burglar in the Library (1997)

The Burglar in the Rye (1999)

The Burglar on the Prowl (2004)

Evan Tanner Series

The Canceled Czech (1966)

The Thief Who Couldn't Sleep (1966)

Tanner's Twelve Swingers (1967)

Two for Tanner (1967), as *The Scoreless Thai* (2001)

Here Comes a Hero (1968), as *Tanner's Virgin* (2003)

Tanner's Tiger (1968)

Me Tanner, You Jane (1970)

Tanner on Ice (1998)

The Scoreless Thai (2007)

John Keller Series

Hit Man (1999)

Hit List (2000)

Hit Parade (2006)

Hit and Run (2008)

Keller in Dallas (2010 for Kindle), novelette

Matthew Scudder Series

In the Midst of Death (1976)

The Sins of the Fathers (1976)

Time to Murder and Create (1976)

A Stab in the Dark (1981)

Eight Million Ways to Die (1982)

When the Sacred Ginmill Closes (1986)

Out on the Cutting Edge (1989)

A Ticket to the Boneyard (1990)

A Dance at the Slaughterhouse (1991)

A Walk among the Tombstones (1992)

The Devil Knows You're Dead (1993)

A Long Line of Dead Men (1994)

Even the Wicked (1997)

Everybody Dies (1998)

Hope to Die (2001)

All the Flowers Are Dying (2005)

A Drop of the Hard Stuff (2011)

Collections

Sometimes They Bite (1983)

Like a Lamb to Slaughter (1984)

Some Days You Get the Bear (1993)

By the Dawn's Early Light and Other Stories (1994)

Ehrengraf for the Defense (1994)

Collected Mystery Stories (1999)

One-Night Stands (1999)

The Lost Cases of Ed London (2001)

Enough Rope: Collected Stories (2002), expanded as *Collected Mystery Stories*

One-Night Stands and Lost Weekends (2008), short stories

Contributor

Alfred Hitchcock Presents: Once Upon a Dreadful Time, edited by Alfred Hitchcock (1964)

The Late Unlamented and Other Tales of Evil, edited by Alfred Hitchcock (1967)

Alfred Hitchcock Presents: A Month of Mystery, edited by Alfred Hitchcock (1969)

Murders on the Half-Skull, edited by Alfred Hitchcock (1970)

Alfred Hitchcock Presents: Terror Time, edited by Alfred Hitchcock (1972)

Best Detective Stories of the Year—1975, edited by Allen J. Hubin (1975)

The Year's Best Mystery and Suspense Stories—1977, edited by Edward D. Hoch (1977)

The Year's Best Mystery and Suspense Stories—1978, edited by Edward D. Hoch (1978)

Alfred Hitchcock Presents: The Master's Choice, edited by Alfred Hitchcock (1979)

Alfred Hitchcock's The Best of Mystery (1980)

The Best of Ellery Queen 2 (1982)

Alfred Hitchcock's A Choice of Evils, edited by Elana Lore (1983)

Alfred Hitchcock's Borrowers of the Night, edited by Cathleen Jordan (1983)

Ellery Queen's Crimes and Punishments, edited by Eleanor Sullivan (1984)

The Eyes Have It, edited by Robert J. Randisi (1984)

The Year's Best Mystery and Suspense Stories—1984, edited by Edward D. Hoch (1984)

Chapter and Hearse, edited by Marcia Muller (1985)

The Year's Best Mystery and Suspense Stories—1985, edited by Edward D. Hoch (1985)

Alfred Hitchcock's Tales of Terror, edited by Eleanor Sullivan (1986)

101 Mystery Stories, edited by Bill Pronzini (1986)

The Year's Best Mystery and Suspense Stories—1986, edited by Edward D. Hoch (1986)

Ellery Queen Masters of Mystery (1987)

Mystery Scene Reader 1, edited by Ed Gorman (1987)

Prime Suspects, edited by Bill Pronzini (1987)

The Year's Best Mystery and Suspense Stories—1987, edited by Edward D. Hoch (1987)

Alfred Hitchcock: Portraits of Murder (1988)

Ellery Queen's Media Favorites, edited by Eleanor Sullivan (1988)

The Mammoth Book of Private Eye Stories, edited by Bill Pronzini (1988)

The Second Black Lizard Anthology of Crime Fiction, edited by Ed Gorman (1988)

American Detectives, edited by Martin H. Greenberg (1989)

Ellery Queen's 11 Deadly Sins, edited by Eleanor Sullivan (1989)

Felonious Assaults, edited by Bill Pronzini (1989)

Justice for Hire, edited by Robert J. Randisi (1990)

The New Edgar Winners (1990)

Dark Crimes (1991)

The Perfect Murder, with Sarah Caldwell, Tony Hillerman, and Jack Hitt (1991)

Scarlet Letters (1991)

Hardboiled (1992)

High Adventure (1992)

Murder Takes a Holiday (1992)

Crimes of Passion (1993)

Dark Crimes 2 (1993)

Monsters in Our Midst (1993)

Murder on Main Street (1993)

The King Is Dead: Tales of Elvis Post-Mortem (1994)

Murder on Trial (1994)

Bad Behavior (1995)

Blowout in Little Mans Flats (1995)

Murder by the Book (1995)

Murder Is My Business (1995)

Murder Most Medical (1995)

Night Screams (1995)

No Alibi (1995)

The Eyes Still Have It (1996)

First Cases (1996)

Win, Lose or Die (1996)

American Pulp (1997)

Best American Mystery Stories 1997, edited by Robert B. Parker (1997)

First Cases 2 (1997)

Funny Bones (1997)

Hot Blood: Crimes of Passion (1997)

Law and Order (1997)

Love Kills (1997)

Mystery's Most Wanted (1997)

The Plot Thickens (1997)

Whydunit (1997)

Best American Mystery Stories 1998, edited by Sue Grafton (1998)

The Best of the Best (1998)

Cutting Edge (1998)

Murder for Revenge (1998)

Batman's Helpers (1999)

Best American Mystery Stories 1999, edited by Ed McBain (1999)

First Cases 3 (1999)

Best American Mystery Stories of the Century, edited by Otto Penzler and Tony Hillerman (2000)

Creme de la Crime (2000)

Master's Choice 2 (2000)

Murder among Friends (2000)

Over the Edge (2000)

World's Finest Mystery and Crime Stories, edited by Edward Gorman (2000)

Blood, Threat & Fears (2001)

Century of Great Suspense Stories, edited by Jeffrey Deaver (2001)

Death by Horoscope (2001)

Flesh & Blood (2001)

Murder Most Postal (2001)

Murder on the Ropes (2001)

Murderer's Row (2001)

Speaking of Lust (2001)

A Century of Noir (2002)

Most Wanted, edited by Robert J. Randisi (2002)

Mothers and Sons (2002)

Murder in the Family (2002)

Murder Is My Racquet (2002)

Murder on the Ropes: Original Boxing Mysteries, edited by Otto Penzler (2002)

World's Finest Mystery and Crime Stories: Third Annual Collection, edited by Ed Gorman (2002)

Death by Horoscope, edited by Anne Perry (2003)

World's Finest Mystery and Crime Stories: Fourth Annual Collection, edited by Ed Gorman and Martin H. Greenberg (2003)

Greatest Hits, edited by Robert Randisi (2005)

Men from Boys, edited by John Harvey (2005)

Terror's Echo (2005)

Transgressions, edited by Ed McBain (2005)

Murder at the Foul Line, edited by Otto Penzler (2006)

Murder in the Rough, edited by Otto Penzler (2006)

The Shamus Winners: America's Best Private Eye Stories, Vol. 1, 1982–1995, edited by Robert J. Randisi (2010)

Editor

Murder on the Run (1998)

Death Cruise: Crime Stories on the Open Sea (1999)

Master's Choice (1999)

Great Mystery Series: 11 of the Best Mystery Short Stories from Alfred Hitchcock's and Ellery Queen's Mystery Magazines, with Mary Higgins Clark and Ralph McInerny (2000)

Opening Shots (2000)

The Best American Mystery Stories 2001 (2001)

Opening Shots 2 (2001)

Speaking of Greed (2001)

Speaking of Lust (2001)

Writers Share Their First Published Stories (2001)

Speaking of Wrath (2002)

Blood on Their Hands (2003)

Manhattan Noir (2006)

Manhattan Noir 2: The Classics (2008)

Written as Chip Harrison, Chip Harrison Series

No Score (1970)

Chip Harrison Scores Again (1971)

Make Out with Murder (1974), published in England as *The Five Little Rich Girls*

The Topless Tulip Caper (1975)

A/K/A/ Chip Harrison (1984), as by Lawrence Block, reprints second two books

Introducing Chip Harrison (1984), as by Lawrence Block, reprints first two books

The Affairs of Chip Harrison (2001), omnibus

Block also wrote early paperback erotica under the names Lesley Evans, Sheldon Lord, Andrew Shaw, and Jill Emerson and nonfiction books including writing how-tos. He has also collected introductions and afterwords for *Introducing Myself and Others* for Kindle.

Motion Pictures Based on the Author's Works

Nightmare Honeymoon (1973), based on *Deadly Honeymoon*

Eight Million Ways to Die (1986), based on the novel

Burglar (1987), based on the series

The author also provided stories for *Tales of the Unexpected, Alfred Hitchcock Presents, Spine Chillers,* and *Tilt.* He wrote a screenplay for *My Blueberry Nights* (2007).

For Further Information

"Interview with Lawrence Block," BookSluts, Feb. 2006, http://www.bookslut.com/ features/2006_02_007786.php/ (viewed Sept. 25, 2009).

Karim, Ali, "Lawrence Block Talks to Shots about his Latest Novel, *Small Town*," *SHOTS*, http://www.shotsmag.co.uk/SHOTS%2018/Lawrence%Block%20 Interview.htm/ (viewed May 16, 2003).

Kelly, Katy, "Lawrence Block, Mystery Man," *USA Today* (Oct. 13, 1998).

Lawrence Block interview, BookEnds, http:62.173.217.bookends/chat/block.asp?
   TAG=&CID=/ (viewed April 5, 2003).

Lawrence Block website, http://www.lawrenceblock.com/ (viewed Sept. 30, 2009).

Meyer, Adam, "Telling Lies for Fun and Profit: An Interview with Lawrence Block,"
   The Armchair Detective (spring 1994).

Seels, James T., ed. *Lawrence Block Bibliography 1958–1993*. Royal Oak, Mich.:
   Airtight Seels Allie Production, 1993.

Smith, Kevin Burton, "A Year on the Block," *January Magazine,* http://januarymaga
   zine.com/profiles/lblock.html/ (viewed Sept. 25, 2009).

"Those Sexy Vintage Sleaze Books," http://vintagesleazepaperbacks.wordpress.
   com/2009/08/30/warm-willing-by-jill-emerson-lawrence-block-midwood-
   books/ (viewed Sept. 25, 2009).

Tribute to Lawrence Block, special issue, *Mystery Scene* No. 74 (2002).

White, Claire E., "A Conversation with Lawrence Block," Writers Write (Oct.–Nov.
   2001), http://www.writerswrite.com/journal/nov01.block2.htm/ (viewed May 16,
   2003).

Giles Blunt

Windsor, Ontario
1952

Police Procedural
Benchmark Series: John Cardinal

Matthew Plexman
Photography

About the Author and the Author's Writing

> Behind the snubnose .38 that was pointed at him stood the youngest gunman Cardinal
> had ever seen—blond hair cropped close to the skull, pale fuzz on the cheeks and chin.
> He wore a houndstooth sports jacket, as if trying to impersonate an older man.

His adversary was, indeed young, but he was also a Royal Canadian Mounted Police officer. The day wasn't off to a good start for detective John Cardinal, at this point one of Algonquian Bay Police Department's less than finest, in author Giles Blunt's taut crime novel *The Delicate Storm* (2008), which won the Crime Writers of Canada Arthur Ellis Award. In the swirl of what turns out to be the winter's fiercest snowstorm, Cardinal and Lise Delorme, his Francophone partner, pursue a cold-blooded killer whose handiwork was discovered at a remote trapper's cabin.

Blunt skillfully weaves full-bodied characters through a puzzling crime and a relentless environment, in his Cardinal novels.

The author lists Graham Greene, John Le Carré, and Martin Cruz Smith among his favorite authors, in no small part because of their rich depictions of locale. "I wanted to create a similarly strong sense of place," he said on his Random House web page, "I could have done New York, but we have so many crime stories set there. I could have done Toronto. But I thought that Northern Ontario was a region that hadn't been given its due in fiction."

Blunt knows the area firsthand, having been born in Windsor, Ontario, in 1952, of parents "so English that the space on their passports for citizenship could only be filled in British Beyond Belief. They had colorful accents and amusing habits and never allowed themselves to be influenced by Canadians. Consequently I lived in England at home and Canada at school," he says on his website.

When he was eight, he penned a few pages of an Enid Blyton–type adventure, marking his future path. He attended a Catholic high school, Scollard Hall, then Algonquin Composite. He received a B.A. in 1975 from the University of Toronto. While Blunt was in college, Samuel Beckett influenced his several attempts at writing short stories. Blunt married Janna Eggebeen, a college administrator.

He relocated to New York City, where he was a bartender and a room service waiter before he landed a two-year contract with television producers Grosso-Jacobson to write screenplays (including the pilot for *Diamonds*). His first book, *Cold Eye* (1989), is set against the New York art scene. He cowrote with Robert Nathan one episode of *Law & Order*, but when no new assignments came, he decided to write novels, this time with a Canadian setting. After 22 years below the 49th parallel, he returned to Toronto to live.

Blunt's own multinational background (not to mention his brief time as a social worker in Ontario) gave him something of an outsider's perspective with which to shape his fictional protagonists.

"In Blunt's dark world, even the seemingly well-meaning are eyed with suspicion, for demons lurk in places civilized souls least expect," said *Booklist* reviewer Allison Block of *By the Time You Read This* (2006).

Blunt has said that he was cautious not to block out Cardinal, Delorme, and other running characters too deeply, as he wanted them to come alive and to determine their own interests and motives.

"If you decide your character is a forty-seven-year-old, divorced, gay sociologist who collects stamps and plays the didgeridoo you will almost certainly find it makes no sense for him to do what he does in the story," he said in interview with Scott Butki. "Whereas if you let what he does partly dictate the characteristics you give him you'll end up with a better fit." He may do character thumbnails, but only to get started, he said.

The character Lise Delorme first appears with a secret secondary assignment: investigate Cardinal's potential involvement with drug runners. As it turns out, Cardinal is clear of that charge, though he has a different, deep secret that plagues him throughout the books. Too, his wife suffers from severe depression, has been hospitalized, and is carefully trying to reassemble her life.

The author's novels can be dark, but they aren't without humor. There's a remarkably inept criminal in *The Delicate Storm* and a likeable miscreant in *Forty Words for Sorrow*. For the books with themes of child pornography or suicide, there's not much room for levity. But "I get a lot of letters from people whose lives have been touched by manic depression, and they are enormously moved to have it described accurately," he said in a Poe's Deadly Daughters interview.

Blunt is a thorough researcher. For *Forty Words for Sorrow* and *The Delicate Storm*, he said, in a Crime Factory interview, that he had interviewed everyone from Mounties and New York and North Bay police to hydro workers and physicians.

> Basically people love to talk about their work. The trick is to find someone who talks well, then you can get really lucky. CSIS [Canadian Security Intelligence Service] was the only agency that wasn't all that cooperative, but you tend to expect that from a spy outfit.

With each novel he's written, Blunt has gained more attention. "The pulsing, tightly plotted narrative [of *Black Fly Season*] again shows why Blunt should be considered among the new practitioners of crime drama's elite," said a reviewer in *Publishers Weekly*.

Blunt has jumped to the fore of Canadian and, for that matter, all English-language crime fiction.

Works by the Author

Cold Eye (1989)

No Such Creature (2008)

Breaking Lorca (2009)

John Cardinal Series

The Delicate Storm (2000)

Forty Words for Sorrow (2000)

Black Fly Season (2005)

By the Time You Read This (2006), also titled *The Fields of Grief*

Crime Machine (2010)

The author has also written scripts for television series, including *Night Heat, Diamonds, Street Legal,* and *Law & Order.*

For Further Information

Black Fly Season review, *Publishers Weekly*, May 9, 2005.

Block, Allison, *By the Time You Read This* review, *Booklist*, Dec. 15, 2006.

Butki, Scott, "Interview with Giles Blunt," Newsvine.com, Aug. 21, 2007, http://sbutki.newsvine.com/_news/2007/08/21/910802-interview-with-giles-blunt-author-of-by-the-time-you-read-this/ (viewed Aug. 23, 2009).

"Canada Calling: Giles Blunt," Poe's Deadly Daughters, http://poesdeadlydaughters.blogspot.com/2007/07/canada-calling-giles-blunt.html/ (viewed Aug. 22, 2009).

Elliott, Julie, *No Such Creature* review, *Library Journal*, April 1, 2009.

Fletcher, Connie, *Forty Words for Sorrow* review, *Booklist*, May 1, 2001.

Giles Blunt interview, Random House Canada, http://www.randomhouse.ca/catalog/display.pperl?isbn=9780679314318&view=auqa/ (viewed Aug. 23, 2009).

Giles Blunt web page, http://www.gilesblunt.com/ (viewed Aug. 22, 2009).

Honeybee, David, Giles Blunt interview, Crime Factory, Oct. 27, 2003, http://www.crimefactory.net/cfOLM-001j.htm/ (viewed Aug. 23, 2009).

Gail Bowen

Eric Eggertson

Toronto, Ontario
1942

Amateur Detective, Academic Mystery
Benchmark Series: Joanne Kilbourn

About the Author and the Author's Writing

Gail Bowen learned to read when she was three, while walking through Prospect Cemetery on St. Clair Avenue in Toronto and reading the tombstones. That was appropriate, as now, in her dozen murder mysteries featuring academic heroine Joanne Kilbourn, Bowen has begun to fill a cemetery, however imaginary.

Born Gail Bartholomew in Toronto in 1945, the award-winning author (Crime Writers of Canada's Arthur Ellis Award for Best Novel, *A Colder Kind of Death*, in 1995 and Derrick Murdock Award for her contribution to Canadian crime writing in 2009) overcame childhood polio. She received a B.A. degree from the University of Toronto. Her master's thesis at the University of Waterloo was about Canadian author Robertson Davies. She was a graduate student at the University of Saskatchewan until 1979.

Bowen taught extension courses in several places in Saskatchewan and for 10 years taught at the Saskatchewan Indian Federated College. She was an instructor from 1976 to 1979 at the University of Saskatchewan in Saskatoon and from 1979 to 1985 at the Gabriel Dumont Institute in Regina. She was also a lecturer at the University of Regina, 1979 to 1985, then, tenured in 1986, she became assistant professor of English until 1997, when she became an associate professor of English and department head. She has now retired from teaching but spent 2008 as Mystery Writer in Residence at the Toronto Reference Library. She and Ted Wren Bowen, her researcher husband, live in Regina.

Bowen's first taste of fiction writing was *1919: The Love Letters of George and Adelaide* (1987), a novella she wrote with Ron Marken, describing the post–World War I years as seen through the experiences of three characters who meet at a nursing home. She has also written a half dozen plays, adapted *Peter Pan* and other works for the stage, and adapted *Doctor Doolittle* for CBC telecast. She has also written radio plays and an animated film script.

For her first full-length fiction, Bowen created an academic heroine. The character Joanne Kilbourn is also a political columnist and journalist, as the occasion merits. Widowed, as the series progresses she makes new friends and eventually marries Zach Shreve, a paraplegic criminal lawyer.

During a panel discussion at the Festival of Words at Moose Jaw, Saskatchewan, in 2009, the author said that over her career as a mystery writer, she has seen Canadian characters come into sharper focus. "One of the biggest changes in our writing is [that] it now reflects our Canadian population," she said, yielding a more accurate picture of problems faced by a variety of Canadians.

Bowen is among many Canadian mystery writers who are no longer shy about their northern settings and have won a strong reader following in the United States and other countries as well as in Canada. The first six of her Kilbourn novels were adapted for Canadian telefilms and have been broadcast internationally. Actress Wendy Crewson played the heroine.

As of this writing, Bowen has no interest in leaving her series to try other characters. "I have always been drawn to the development of characters," she said in a Mystery Fanfare interview, describing her own reading and "the sense of a real and changing world that a series offers. As a writer, the luxury of having 3,500 pages in which to develop the character of my protagonist and the people who share her life is seductive."

Bristling at the suggestion that mysteries are by nature lesser works, she has stated firmly that writers of mysteries more than hold their own in the world of literature.

Critics have agreed. "Bowen has a hard eye for the way human ambition can take advantage of human gullibility," said a *Publishers Weekly* reviewer of *A Killing Spring* (1997), "insight which makes this a compelling novel as well as a gripping mystery."

The author does her own research, often gleaning factual information through Internet sources but relying on personal observation to shape and examine her characters.

She lists Rex Stout, Carl Hiaasen, and Ruth Rendell as only a few of her favorite mystery writers. She has met Rendell but has ignored that writer's suggestion not to allow characters to age. Joanne Kilbourn encounters issues of getting older at the same time the author does.

In a MysteryBooks.ca interview, Bowen did offer her own advice to budding writers:

> Because of my voracious and totally indiscriminate reading, I knew what I liked in a mystery: a strong central protagonist with whom it was a pleasure to spend time; a vivid sense of place; and a problem (not necessarily a plot problem) that would engage my mind.

Obviously her legion of readers agree.

Works by the Author

Joanne Kilbourn Series

Deadly Appearances (1990)

Murder at the Mendel (1991), also titled *Love and Murder*

The Wandering Soul Murders (1992)

A Colder Kind of Death (1994)

A Killing Spring (1996)

Verdict in Blood (1998)

Burying Ariel (2000)

The Glass Coffin (2002)

The Early Investigations of Joanne Kilbourn (2004), includes first three novels

The Last Good Day (2004)

The Endless Knot (2006)

The Further Investigations of Joanne Kilbourn (2006), includes second three novels

The Brutal Heart (2008)

The Nesting Dolls (2010)

Contributor

Toronto Noir (2008), includes "The King of Charles Street West"

Adaptations in Other Media

The first six Kilbourn books were made into made-for-television movies in Canada and distributed internationally.

Bowen has also written plays, teleplays and radio dramas. Her novella "Love You to Death," was one of four inaugural titles in the Rapid Reads series from Raven Books.

For Further Information

"Cool Canadian Crime: Gail Bowen," Mystery Fanfare, July 6, 2009, http://my steryreadersinc.blogspot.com/2009/07/cool-canadian-crime-gail-bowen.html/ (viewed Aug. 26, 2009).

Dewar, Colin, "Questions Posed to Festival Writers: Why Do Mysteries Matter?" *Moose Jaw Times Herald*, July 18, 2009, http://www.mjtimes.sk.ca/index. cfm?sid=270384&sc=15/ (viewed Aug. 26, 2009).

Gail Bowen biography, Crime Writers of Canada. http://www.crimewriterscanada. com/bowen-gail (viewed Aug. 26, 2009).

Gail Bowen biography, Famous Canadians, http://www.canadaka.net/modules. php?name=Famous_Canadians&action=viewperson&person=270/ (viewed Aug. 26, 2009).

Gail Bowen interview, MysteryBooks.ca, http://www.mysterybooks.ca/catalog/dis play.pperl?isbn=9780771014680&view=auqa/ (viewed Aug. 26, 2009).

Gail Bowen website, http://www.gailbowen.com/whats_new/ (viewed Aug. 26, 2009).

Killing Spring review, *Publishers Weekly*, April 7, 1997.

Rhys Bowen

Bath, England
1941

Police Procedural, Amateur Detective,
Historical Mystery
Benchmark Series: Molly Murphy

Robin Burcell

About the Author and the Author's Writing

There aren't many mystery series set in Northern Wales, so Rhys Bowen knew she had a novel place for her crime series, featuring Constable Evan Evans. She made up the community of Llanfair, based on childhood memories of staying with relatives there. But "It is based on several villages around Mount Snowdon in North Wales, rather than one specific village," she revealed in a Mystery One interview. "I didn't want the local people to recognize themselves. However, I had to put it in a real valley, as the paths up Mt. Snowdon are important. Now all the locals know where it is."

Llanfair is a quaint village populated with so many members of the Evans family they are known by their professions. Evans the Law, for example. Evans the Meat. Evans the Milk. Evans the Post. But quaint goes only so far, and Llanfair also has a killer, whether an Evans or not. The constable has to find out who murdered three hikers on Mount Snowdon. The first of the cozy series, *Evans Above*, came out in 1997, and nine sequels have followed so far.

"I can't really take credit for having created him," the author said of Evan Evans. "He just walked into my head one day. He's young and has been maturing during the first books. He's the sort of bloke you'd like to date, or your daughter to bring home."

Bowen wanted to explore another setting, New York City, and another, earlier time period, just after 1900. Therefore, in 2001, she began a new series about Molly Murphy with *Murphy's Law*. Molly has fled Ireland, having killed a would-be rapist. But barely has she reached Ellis Island when she becomes a likely suspect in a new murder.

"I started writing the Molly books after a visit to Ellis Island when I was so moved by what I saw and felt that I had to set a book there," the author said in a Book-Club-Queen interview. "After the first book I focused on various pieces of New York history— the abuses in the garment industry, the anarchist movement and let a story evolve as I sent Molly into those situations." Bowen said she does minimal outlining, preferring to let her characters drive the story.

The Molly novels are edgier than the Evanses, and for a third series, Bowen went for lightness. A minor member of British royalty in 1930s England, Lady Victoria Georgiana Charlotte Eugenie, nicknamed Georgie, first turns up in *Her Royal Spyness* (2007). She's 34th in line to the crown and has absolutely no money, so she has plenty of room to explore opportunities—such as working as a maid to avoid an arranged marriage. By the second book, as the author explained in a Novel Journey conversation, her hapless heroine is babysitting visiting German Princess Hanni, who speaks English like a character from a gangster movie, lifts things she wants from store displays, and flirts recklessly with men. Oh, and our heroine is also solving an unexpected killing.

If interesting characters and fascinating settings seem to come easily to the author, you don't know the least of it. Rhys Bowen is an alias. She's actually Janet Quin-Harkin, a veteran staff member of the BBC who has written more than 100 young adult novels under her real name.

The writer was born in Bath, England, in 1941. She attended an all-girls school and sold her first short story when she was 16. She received a B.A. degree with honors from the University of London. She was a folk musician and sang in nightclubs with Al Stewart and Simon and Garfunkel. She worked for BBC in London in various capacities, including radio script-writer and studio manager, before relocating to Sydney to work for Australian Broadcasting. In 1966 she emigrated to the United States to settle with her husband, John Quin-Harkin, in San Francisco. She helped a textbook company develop new readers for urban children. She began to write children's books, then novels for teenagers in popular series including the Sugar and Spice books about bubbly Chrissy, a cheerleader from Iowa who comes to live with her ballet dancer cousin Cara in California. She also wrote a few television tie-in books and historical novels. Then she took the new name and began a new career shaping crime novels. So far, it looks like that was a good move. *Evan's Gate* was nominated for an Edgar and *Murphy's Law* won an Agatha award, certainly evidence that Bowen knows her stuff.

In a Novel Journey interview, Bowen offered this advice to writers: "Never write something because you think it's hot or trendy or will sell easily. You have to write where your heart is. Passionate writing shows."

Works by the Author

Constable Evan Evans Series

Evans Above (1997)

Evan Help Us (1998)

Evanly Choirs (1999)

Evan and Elle (2000)

Evan Can Wait (2001)

Evans to Betsy (2002)

Evan Only Knows (2003)

Evan's Gate (2004)

Evan Blessed (2005)

Evanly Bodies (2006)

Molly Murphy Series

Murphy's Law (2001)

Death of Riley (2002)

For the Love of Mike (2003)

In Like Flynn (2005)

Oh Danny Boy (2006)

In Dublin's Fair City (2007)

Tell Me, Pretty Maiden (2008)

In a Gilded Cage (2009)

The Last Illusion (2010)

Bless the Bride (2011)

Royal Spyness Series

Her Royal Spyness (2007)

A Royal Pain (2008)

Royal Flush (2009)

Royal Blood (2010)

Contributor

Unholy Orders (2000), includes "The Seal of the Confessional"

Mayhem in the Midlands (2001), includes "Do Have a Cup of Tea"

Blood on Their Hands (2003), includes "Doppelganger"

Death Dines In (2004), includes "Proof of the Pudding"

Sherlock Holmes: The Hidden Years (2004), includes "The Case of the Lugubrious Manservant"

The World's Finest Mystery and Crime Stories: Fifth Annual Collection (2004), includes "Doppelganger"

Fifty Years of Crime and Suspense (2006), includes "Voodoo"

A Merry Band of Murderers (2006), includes "If I Had Wings"

The author has also written children's books and young adult novels in the Sweet Dreams, On Our Own, and other series under her real name, Janet Quin-Harkin. And she has written historical novels for adults: *Madam Sarah* (1990) and *Amazing Grace* (1993).

For Further Information

"Rhys Bowen: A Little Slice of Evan," Crescent Blues, http://www.crescentblues.com/4_1issue/bowen.shtml/ (viewed Feb. 4, 2010).

Rhys Bowen interview, Book-Club-Queen, http://www.book-club-queen.com/rhys-bowen.html/ (viewed Feb. 4, 2010).

Rhys Bowen interview, Mystery One Bookstore, http://www.mysteryone.com/old site/RhysBowenInterview.htm/ (viewed Feb. 4, 2010).

Rhys Bowen interview, Novel Journey, Aug. 4, 2008, http://noveljourney.blogspot. com/2008/08/author-interview-rhys-bowen.html/ (viewed Feb. 4, 2010).

Rhys Bowen website, http://www.rhysbowen.com/ (viewed Feb. 4, 2010).

C. J. Box

Casper, Wyoming
1959

Police Procedural
Benchmark Series: Joe Pickett

About the Author and the Author's Writing

By the time C. J. Box was shaping his mystery novel *Open Season* (2001)—his first novel to find a publisher, after several unsuccessful tries with other manuscripts—he had a ready main character in mind: a game warden.

"Joe Pickett is a Wyoming game warden who loves his family, his low-paying job, and his frontier code of right and wrong," Box told a Readers Digest Select Editions interviewer. "He finds himself constantly in the middle of contentious environmental issues and vicious criminality and tries to put things right."

Charles James Box was born in Casper, Wyoming, in 1959. By his high school years, he was already taken with writing as a potential career and successfully applied for a journalism scholarship. In 1981 he graduated from the University of Denver with a B.A. in mass communications. Box has worked as a ranch hand, fishing guide, survey crewman, journalist, manager of travel development for Wyoming Travel Commission, and CEO and president of Rocky Mountain International Corp. He and his wife, Laurie, have three daughters and live near Cheyenne.

Box's first job, as a reporter for the *Sun*, a newspaper in Saratoga, Wyoming, gave him an opportunity to encounter and absorb the small things of rural life and, quite often, also to get outdoors. One time, while on a side job escorting fishermen to a likely spot, he observed on the river bank, observing him, a red-shirted game warden—ever alert, ever vigilant.

Box later met and interviewed that game warden about a poaching arrest. Their visit was in the official's home, with the warden's family buzzing around. Box has said on his website that

> Here was a man who was in charge of enforcing the law in a district that stretched 1,500 square miles. He did it without a real office, or a staff, or a supervisor. Virtually alone, he went out into that rough country every day with only his Labrador as his partner and backup.

Thus, Joe Pickett came to life.

Character is one element of Box's success. Two others are setting and regional morality.

"The Wyoming high country is a palpable presence here; its ruggedness plays a crucial role in the story," said Bill Ott in reviewing Box's *Open Season* for *Booklist*, "and its grandeur is continually set against the venality of most human concerns. The endangered-species theme . . . is explored with impressive complexity and no shortage of villains on all sides of the issue."

But this isn't just *any* great outdoors, as the author told interviewer Tamara Chapman, it's one

> shaped, and sometimes distorted, by the passions of so many advocates and oppositionists. Think fans and foes of the Endangered Species Act, the Clean Water Act and the Environmental Protection Agency. . . . Think larger-than-life characters with outsized carbon footprints or inflexible agendas.

Box addresses issues with balance, which is not to say that he is neutral. He's just pragmatic; the main aim of his novel is to tell a story and entertain, not to preach from a soapbox.

"Writing beautifully about the mountain West and its people, Box takes care to present both sides of the controversial issue of hunting," noted *Publishers Weekly* in reviewing *Blood Trail* (2008).

Recently Box has accelerated his writing output with alternating freestanding novels. The first, *Blue Heaven*, was a popular success and has been optioned for a motion picture.

"There are themes, formats, and characters that just won't work in a series format," the author said in a conversation with Keir Graff of *Booklist*, "and I wanted to stretch myself. Plus, I hoped readers who may think of the Joe Pickett books as huntin' and fishin' books—which they aren't—might give *Blue Heaven* a try and be surprised."

Box doesn't expect to stray from his proven niche.

"People who are battling each other at night at the Forest Service meeting, or whatever, are all having breakfast at the same diner in the morning," he told Jeff Salamon of the *American-Statesman*. "I think if I can accurately portray that, then it keeps the tension up even more so than in an urban novel."

Box produces about 1,000 words a day, five days a week, and apparently has plenty of stories in him. "I've always got about five ideas ahead of me," he said in *Mystery Scene*.

> Which one I'm going to go with depends on the logical arc of the storyline. The tough thing is to keep the characters and the series fresh. I hope I've done this by moving Joe around and giving him a new job and circumstances.

Works by the Author

Blue Heaven (2008)

Three Weeks to Say Goodbye (2009)

Back of Beyond (2011)

Joe Pickett Series

Open Season (2001)

Savage Run (2002)

Winterkill (2003)

Trophy Hunt (2004)

Out of Range (2005)

In Plain Sight (2006)

Free Fire (2007)

Blood Trail (2008)

Below Zero (2009)

Nowhere to Run (2010)

Cold Wind (2011)

Contributor

Meeting Across the River (2005)

America's Best Mystery Stories (2006)

For Further Information

Blood Trail review, *Publishers Weekly*, March 17, 2008.

Chapman, Tamara, "Mystery Man," University of Denver magazine, summer 2009, http://www.du.edu/magazine/archive/2009/02/Mystery_Man.html/ (viewed July 23, 2009)

C. J. Box interview, Readers Digest Select Editions, http://www.cjbox.net/features/readers-digest-select-editions-c.j.box/ (viewed July 8, 2009).

C. J. Box website, http://www.cjbox.net/ (viewed July 8, 2009).

Graft, Keir, "This Cowboy Has Issues," *Booklist*, May 1, 2005.

Ott, Bill, *Open Season* review, *Booklist*, May 1, 2001.

Salamon, Jeff, "Mystery Genre at Home on the Range," *American-Statesman*, June 14, 2009.

Wagner, Hank, "Law of the West: An Interview with C. J. Box," *Mystery Scene*, summer 2007.

Rita Mae Brown

Hanover, Pennsylvania
1944

Amateur Detective
Benchmark Series: Mrs. Murphy

About the Author and the Author's Writing

Mystery novelist Rita Mae Brown's first novel is decidedly not a cozy mystery, such as the Mrs. Murphy puzzlers that she is well known for today. *Rubyfruit Jungle* (1973) is a coming-of-age novel about Molly Bolt's family/social tangles as she was growing up in a poor family in the South. This work, one of the first to deal frankly with lesbianism, became a bestseller.

The author was born in Hanover, Pennsylvania, in 1944, and adopted by Ralph and Julia Ellen Brown. She attended the University of Florida and received an associate's degree from Broward Junior College in 1965, followed by a B.A. from New York University in 1968. The same year she received a cinematography certificate from New York School of Visual Arts.

In 1969 and 1970, she worked as photo editor for Sterling Publishing in New York City. She was a sociology lecturer at Federal City College in Washington, D.C., for a year after that. At the same time, she was a research fellow with Institute for Policy Studies in Washington, D.C., from which she received her Ph.D. in 1976. In 1973, she taught at Goddard College in Vermont. She founded or cofounded a number of gay rights organizations, was on the board of directors of the Sagaris school, and served as president of American Artists Inc. in Charlottesville, Virginia.

Brown went through a very public relationship breakup with tennis player Martina Navratilova and had a relationship with author Fannie Flagg, as she discusses in her memoir, *Rita Will* (1997). She told *Time* magazine interviewer Andrea Sachs she doesn't believe in straight or gay designations. "I think we're all degrees of bisexual. There may be a few people on the extreme if it's a bell curve who really truly are gay or really truly are straight."

In the *Time Out Chicago* conversation, Brown said that she first took up writing because she loved the way litanies sounded in church. She found joy in poetry. And her studies of Latin and Greek gave her a solid grounding in language. She wrote more novels. Her ability with words took her to Hollywood, where a Writers Guild strike curtailed her potential career. On the advice of Sneaky Pie, her cat, she decided to write a mystery.

Wish You Were Here (1990), for which Sneaky Pie is credited as coauthor, heroine Mary Minor Haristeen, postmaster of Crozet, Virginia, and owner of a cat named Mrs. Murphy and a Welsh Corgi named Tucker, sets out to solve the killing of a contractor (his body parts are found in a cement mixer) and a store owner (who was tied to a railroad track just before a train came through). "Brown's lively characterization brings merchants and first-family Virginians alive with affection and verve," *Publishers Weekly* said, adding that the conversations between the animal characters were reasonably credible. In a review of another Mrs. Murphy effort, *Whisker of Evil* (2004), "Witty dialogue will bring a smile to readers' faces as the animals outsmart the humans," wrote Claudia Moore in *School Library Journal*.

Brown delights in her Virginia surroundings. "The best thing about central Virginia is the people," she said in a Bookreporter interview. "They're funny, eccentric, even, always ready for a good time and deeply compassionate. Don't listen to what they say. Watch what they do."

Brown, a confirmed horsewoman, polo player, and fox hunter (she is master of the hounds at Oak Ridge Fox Hunt Club), used Virginia's foxhunting country as background for a series of crime tales featuring Sister Jane, master of the hunt. In the sixth book, *Hounded to Death* (2008), the death of a vile breeder of hounds and of a well-reputed horse veterinarian takes the heroine on a wild chase for clues and suspects. Praising the book, *Booklist* reviewer Jessica Moyer observed, "Clever and snappy dialogue between humans and animals is interspersed with more philosophical discussions on the value of human and animal life."

Brown greatly values animal life. She asked on her website,

> What I have done that I care about is I have cherished life. I've rescued by now hundreds of cats, dogs, foxes and hounds, and found homes for them. Too many stay here, so I am wearing the same dress and shoes I wore twenty years ago. So what?

Works by the Author

The Hand (1971)

Rubyfruit Jungle (1973)

In Her Day (1976)

Southern Discomfort (1982)

Sudden Death (1983)

High Hearts (1986)

Venus Envy (1993)

Dolley: A Novel of Dolley Madison in Love and War (1994)

Riding Shotgun (1996)

Alma Mater (2001)

A Nose for Justice (2010)

Mrs. Murphy Series, written with Sneaky Pie Brown

Wish You Were Here (1990)

Rest in Pieces (1992)

Murder at Monticello; or, Old Sins (1994)

Pay Dirt (1995)

Murder, She Meowed (1996)

Murder on the Prowl (1998)

Cat on the Scent (1999)

Sneaky Pie's Cookbook for Mystery Lovers (1999)

Pawing through the Past (2000)

Claws and Effect (2001)

Catch as Cat Can (2002)

The Tail of the Tip-Off (2003)

Three Mrs. Murphy Mysteries: Wish You Were Here/Rest in Pieces/Murder at Monticello (2003)

Whisker of Evil (2004)

Three More Mrs. Murphy Mysteries in One Volume: Pay Dirt/Murder, She Meowed/ Murder on the Prowl (2005)

Cat's Eyewitness (2006)

Sour Puss (2006)

The Third Three Mrs. Murphy Mysteries in One Volume (2007)

Puss 'n Cahoots (2008)

Santa Clawed (2008)

Purrfect Murder (2009)

Cat of the Century (2010)

A Nose for Justice (2010)

Hiss of Death (2011)

Runnymede Series

Six of One (1978)

Bingo (1988)

Loose Lips (1999)

The Sand Castle (2008)

Jane Arnold Foxhunting Series

Hotspur (2002)

Outfoxed (2002)

Full Cry (2003)

The Hunt Ball (2005)

The Hounds and the Fury (2007)

Hounded to Death (2008)

The Tell-Tale Horse (2008)

Contributor

I'd Kill for That, with Jennifer Crusie, Linda Fairstein, Lisa Gardner, Heather Graham, Kay Hooper, Katherine Neville, Anne Perry, Kathy Reichs, Julie Smith, and Tina Wainscott (2004)

Adaptations in Other Media

Murder She Purred: A Mrs. Murphy Mystery (television movie, 1998)

The author has also written several screenplays, including *Slumber Party Massacre* (1982) and *Mary Pickford: A Life on Film* (1997). Her collection of poems, *The Hand That Cradles the Rock,* came out in 1971.

For Further Information

Brown, Rita Mae. *Animal Magnetism: My Life with Creatures Great and Small*. New York: Ballantine, 2009.

Brown, Rita Mae, *Rita Will: Memoir of a Literary Rabble-Rouser*. New York: Bantam, 1997.

Castellanos, Marie, "An Interview with Rita Mae Brown, "Catholic Lesbians, http://cclonline.org/index.php?id=52/ (viewed Oct. 22, 2009).

Erbentraut, Joseph, "Rita Mae Brown: A Rebel with Plenty Cause," *Edge*, April 23, 2009, http://www.edgechicago.com/index.php?ch=entertainment&sc=books&sc2=&sc3=&id=90311/ (viewed Oct. 22, 2009).

Heidemann, Jason A., "Straight Talker: Author Rita Mae Brown Shoots from the Hip," *Time Out Chicago*, Sept. 4, 2008.

Justis, Janet, "Interview with Rita Mae Brown," *The Homestead*, Nov. 6, 2003, http://scholar.lib.vt.edu/ejournals/VALib/v50_n1/justis.html/ (viewed Oct. 22, 2009).

Moore, Claudia, *Whisker of Evil* review, *School Library Journal*, Sept. 2004.

Moyer, Jessica, *Hounded to Death* review, *Booklist*, Aug. 1, 2008.

Rita Mae Brown interview, Bookreporter.com, April 2, 2004, http://www.bookreporter.com/authors/au-brown-rita-mae.asp/ (viewed Oct. 22, 2009).

Rita Mae Brown website, http://www.ritamaebrown.com/content/index.asp/ (viewed Oct. 22, 2009).

Sachs, Andrea, "Rita Mae Brown: Loves Cats, Hates Marriage," *Time*, March 18, 2008.

Wish You Were Here review, *Publishers Weekly*, Sept. 21, 1990.

Ken Bruen

Ken Bruen with daughter Grace. Photo: Phyl Kennedy

Galway, Ireland
1951

Police Procedural; Private Detective
Benchmark Series: Jack Taylor

About the Author and the Author's Writing

Ken Bruen's Galsworthy investigator Jack Taylor—to call him private would glorify his reluctant, hit-or-miss, way-off-the-radar inquiries—has been ousted from the Guards (Garda Siochana, the elite police force), become an alcoholic and drug abuser, gone on and off the wagon, and suffered broken relationships, beatings, and other indignities. That he's in any shape to recount his stories is a miracle, and avid readers are grateful—particularly once they know something of the author's own life story.

Bruen was born in Galway, Connacht, Ireland, in 1951. Somewhat withdrawn and bookish as a lad, he found comfort in conceiving wild adventure tales of faraway places. "I grew up in a house where books and reading were regarded as not only a waste of time but a waste of money," he said in Otto Penzler's *The Lineup*.

He studied at St. Joseph's College and earned a Ph.D. in metaphysics from Trinity College, Dublin. For 25 years he taught English as a second language. He visited some of those places he had dreamed of as a youth. He traveled to Africa, Asia, and South America.

Those dreams of youth became all too vivid when he was newly arrived in Rio de Janeiro in 1979. He became involved in a scuffle in a barroom, after which he was arrested, tried, and convicted. "The situation changed his life," Steve Hintz wrote in *Irish American Post*.

> Horrific months of being imprisoned followed. The extended physical and emotional trial allowed him to see how low the human condition can plummet. This ordeal and the healing that took place after his release helped to shape Bruen into becoming an outstanding novelist.

Tired of seeing what he considered second-rate literary novels by others receive acclaim, he set about to become a writer himself. He had written poetry. A fondness for Samuel Beckett's works taught him to be economical with words. Jim Thompson, James Ellroy, Walter Moseley, and Ed McBain showed him how to shape plots. His own experiences gave him dark themes to explore. He was ready.

Bruen wrote three crime novels before he introduced Jack Taylor in *The Guards* (2001). Moping around most days in a barroom, with a modest reputation as a "finder,"

Taylor accepts Ann Henderson's plea to find her missing daughter. As it turns out, she is one of several young women who have gone missing. Though he relies on genre conventions (such as a hero who loves to read), Taylor, in the view of a *Publishers Weekly* reviewer, "gets away with it thanks to his novel setting, the Irish seacoast city of Galway, and unusual characters." "The writing is less hard-boiled than lyrical," said Craig Shufelt in his *Library Journal* assessment, "with a definite edge that perfectly fits the story."

Add to Bruen's personal challenges his wife's experience with breast cancer and his daughter's Down's syndrome (both of which showed up in his Taylor plots). Is it any wonder that empathy comes through in Bruen's lean yet lyrical prose? Prose that has won Edgar, Shamus, and other awards?

Bruen began a second series, set in London and featuring Detective Inspector Tom Brant. *The McDead* (2001), typically, finds Brant in pursuit of whoever killed his precinct chief inspector's brother. "Fans of British procedurals and noir novels will savor every speck of grit in this unrelenting crime novel," Wes Lukowsky wrote in a review for *Booklist*.

"I write Brant to chill me out and Taylor to torment meself," Bruen said in a "Things I'd Rather Be Doing" conversation. "Brant is pure fun, Taylor is me disgusted with our new rich Ireland."

Bruen and Jason Star have written another series with peculiar characters. Among these are Max Fisher, a New York businessman who hires a hitman to remove his wife so he can be free to pursue an affair with Angela Petrakos. *Bust* (2006) was followed by sequels in which the protagonist takes to crime (*Slide*) and ends up in prison (*The Max*).

Stepping up his writing pace has only given Bruen increased confidence.

"Writing can be a pretty discouraging business," the author said on Askaboutwriting.net, "but for me when I am writing and it is going well, it's the best feeling in the world. When it's going well it's a great buzz."

Works by the Author

Shades of Grace (1993)

Martyrs (1994)

The Hackman Blues (1997)

Her Last Call to Louis MacNeice (1997)

Rilke on Black (1997)

London Boulevard (2001)

Dispatching Baudelaire (2004)

Murder by the Book (2005), chapbook

American Skin (2006)

Once Were Cops (2008)

Tower, with Reed Farrel Coleman (2009)

Inspector Brant Series

A White Arrest (1998)

The McDead (2000)

Taming the Alien (2000)

Blitz (2002)

Vixen (2003)

The White Trilogy (2003), omnibus including first three titles

The Dead Room (2005), chapbook

Calibre (2006)

Ammunition (2007)

Jack Taylor Series

The Guards (2001)

The Killing of the Tinkers (2002)

The Magdalen Martyrs (2003)

The Dramatist (2004)

Priest (2006)

Cross (2007)

Sanctuary (2008)

The Devil (2010)

Max Fisher and Angela Petrakos Series, with Jason Starr

Bust (2006)

Slide (2007)

The Max (2008)

Collections

Funeral: Tales of Irish Morbidities (1992)

Sherry: And Other Stories (1994)

Time of Serena-May and Upon the Third Cross: A Collection of Short Stories (1995)

A Fifth of Bruen: Early Fiction of Ken Bruen (2006)

Contributor

Brooklyn Noir (2004), includes "Fade to . . . Brooklyn"

The Cocaine Chronicles (2005), includes "White Irish"

Editor

Dublin Noir (2006)

Her Last Call to Louis McNeice and *London Boulevard* were adapted for film.

Adaptations in Other Media

London Boulevard (announced), based on the novel.

For Further Information

Graff, Keir, *Priest* review, *Booklist*, Feb. 15, 2007.

Guard review, *Publishers Weekly*, Nov. 25, 2002.

Hintz, Stevem, "Galway Writer Bruen Shows His Grace," *Irish American Post*, Feb./Mar. 2004.

Ken Bruen interview, Askaboutwriting.net, Oct. 2004, http://www.askaboutwriting.net/kenbruena.htm/ (viewed Aug. 20, 2009).

Ken Bruen Monday interview, Things I'd Rather Be Doing, Jan. 28, 2009, http://www.tirbd.com/2007/01/monday-interview-ken-bruen.html/ (viewed Aug. 20, 2009).

Ken Bruen website, http://www.kenbruen.com/ (viewed Aug. 20, 2009).

Lukowsky, Wes, *The McDead* review, *Booklist*, May 1, 2001.

Ó Conghaile, Pól, "To Hell and Back," *Irish Echo*, Mar. 2005, http://www.irishecho.com/newspaper/story.cfm?id=14593/ (viewed Aug. 20, 2009).

Penzler, Otto, ed. *The Lineup: The World's Greatest Crime Writers Tell the Inside Story of Their Greatest Detectives*. New York: Little, Brown, 2009.

Sanctuary review, *Publishers Weekly*, Mar. 23, 2009.

Shufelt, Craig, *The Guard* review, *Library Journal*, Dec. 2002.

James Lee Burke

Houston, Texas
1936

Police Procedural, Amateur Detective, Legal Mystery
Dave Robicheaux Series

About the Author and the Author's Writing

James Lee Burke has put his own brand on crime fiction, not to mention southern literature. "His action plays out in the dark heart of the Louisiana bayou, so that although Burke follows in the footsteps of such writers as Raymond Chandler and Ross Macdonald," in the view of journalist Lucretia Stewart; "the exotic, sweltering atmosphere of the bayou means the novels have a very different sensibility."

Burke's launch as a writer was shaky. He wrote three books for three publishers. He quit for 13 years, but when he finally made another attempt, this time at a crime novel, his work was nominated for a Pulitzer Prize.

Burke found his voice and his literary persona with Dave Robicheaux, who first appeared in *The Neon Rain* (1987). Robicheaux is a 14-year member of the New Orleans Police Department in that story of violence, corruption, drugs and illegal arms. Robicheaux and his half brother Jimmie were raised by their father, a commercial fisherman and offshore derrick man. A recovering alcoholic, the hero periodically faces new demons.

"The writing is beautiful, as always," observed *Publishers Weekly* of *Last Car to Elysian Fields*.

Born in Houston, Texas, on December 5, 1936, Burke grew up on the Texas–Louisiana Gulf Coast. He read an occasional Mickey Spillane novel but otherwise avoided mysteries. He attended the University of Southeastern Louisiana Institute at Lafayette, then earned B.A. (1959) and an M.A. (1960) from the University of Missouri at Columbia.

The author taught English and worked as a reporter, oil company landman and pipeliner, land surveyor, social worker on Los Angeles's Skid Row, U.S. Forest Service truck driver in the Dan'l Boone National Forest, and U.S. Job Corps instructor.

In 1960 Burke married Pearl Pai Chu. They have four children and homes in Missoula, Montana, and New Iberia, Louisiana. He describes himself politically as a Jeffersonian liberal. Avocational interests include fishing, weightlifting, sports, and bluegrass music.

Burke's fictional Cajun hero has gone through severely stressful episodes in the course of the series—an alcoholic who is frequently haunted by memories of the Vietnam War, he quits the police force in the very first book. In the course of the series, he encounters right-wing retired generals, drug-smuggling Nicaraguans, a Mafia boss, and assorted psychopaths and thugs. He also meets and falls in love with social worker Anne Ballard.

It is Burke's intention that the individual books be self-contained, each with its own theme and plotting. "The challenge is to encapsulate events and characters out of the past in such a way that the reader is familiar with the larger story, without being repetitive," he told interviewer Dave Weich for Powells.com. "That's what art is."

Burke considers *Black Cherry Blues* his breakthrough novel—the one, as he told Steven Womack for *The Armchair Detective*, that allowed him to become a full-time writer. It is a rough and violent book, but the author "always indicates to the reader that violence is a failure, that it represents the failure of everything that is decent and good in human beings."

Burke also has a second series, featuring Billy Bob Holland. *Cimarron Rose*, the first in the series, "is about redemption," Burke told Alden Mudge for BookPage. "All of us have mistakes in our past we need to address. In Billy Bob's case, it's the fact that he killed his best friend, L. Q. Navarro. It was an accident, but it is the reason Billy Bob is where he is when the book begins."

Burke thrives on the mystery genre.

"I think all good narration contains an element of mystery and suspense," Burke told interviewer Scott Butki. "If it didn't, if the storyline were predictable, we would have no interest in reading it. I think the 'crime novel' has replaced the sociological novel of the 1930s."

As to his Louisiana setting, Burke expects to never exhaust its possibilities. He told interviewer Nicholas Wroe, "Faulkner said he'd never be able to exhaust that tiny postage stamp of Mississippi where he was from. I've got a slightly larger postage stamp, but so far as I can tell, everything I need seems to be within it."

Burke writes nearly every day. "I have never thought of my vocation as work," he wrote in the *New York Times* in 2002.

> I never had what is called writer's block, nor have I ever measured the value of what I do in terms of its commercial success. I also believe that whatever degree of creative talent I possess was not earned but was given to me by a power outside myself, for a specific purpose, one that has little to do with my own life.

Works by the Author

Half of Paradise (1965)

To the Bright and Shining Sun (1970)

Lay Down My Sword and Shield (1971)

Two for Texas (1983)

The Lost Get-Back Boogie (1986)

White Doves at Morning (2002)

Rain Gods (2009)

Feast Day of Fools (2011)

Dave Robicheaux Series

The Neon Rain (1987)

Heaven's Prisoners (1988)

Black Cherry Blues (1989)

A Morning for Flamingoes (1990)

A Stained White Radiance (1992)

In the Electric Mist with Confederate Dead (1993)

Dixie City Jam (1994)

Burning Angel (1995)

Cadillac Jukebox (1996)

Sunset Limited (1998)

Purple Cane Road (2000)

Jolie Blon's Bounce (2002)

Last Car to Elysian Fields (2003)

Crusader's Cross (2005)

Pegasus Descending (2006)

The Tin Roof Blowdown (2007)

Swan Peak (2008)

The Glass Rainbow (2010)

Billy Bob Holland Series

Cimarron Rose (1997)

Heartwood (1999)

Bitterroot (2001)

In the Moon of Red Ponies (2004)

Collections

The Convict and Other Stories (1985)

Jesus Out to Sea: Stories (2007)

Contributor

Best American Short Stories of 1986 (1986)

The 2007 Pushcart Anthology (2007)

Adaptations in Other Media

Heaven's Prisoners (1996), motion picture

Two for Texas (1998), motion picture

In the Electric Mist (2009), French motion picture

For Further Information

Burke, James Lee, "Seeking a Vision of Truth, Guided by a Higher Power," *New York Times* (Dec. 2, 2002).

Butki, Scott, "Interview with Mystery Writer James Lee Burke," Newsvine, June 3, 2007, http://sbutki.newsvine.com/_news/2007/06/03/753507-interview-with-mystery-writer-james-lee-burke-part-1/ (viewed Dec. 16, 2009).

James Lee Burke interview, Orion Publishing Group, http://www.orionbooks.co.uk/QandA.aspx?id=4559&catID=2/ (viewed Dec. 16, 2009).

James Lee Burke web page, *http://www.jamesleeburke.com/* (viewed Dec. 16, 2009).

Last Car to Elysian Fields review, *Publishers Weekly* (Aug. 11, 2003).

Mudge, Alden, James Lee Burke interview, BookPage, http://www.bookpage.com/9708bp/firstperson2.html/ (viewed April 5, 2003).

Stewart, Lucretia, "Nothing but the Sleuth," *Daily Mail*, Aug. 30, 2002.

Weich, Dave, James Lee Burke interview, Powells.com, http://www.powells.com/authors/burke.html/ (viewed Dec. 16, 2009).

Womack, Steve, "A Talk with James Lee Burke," *Armchair Detective* (spring 1996).

Wroe, Nicholas, "After the Storm," *The Guardian*, Nov. 17, 2007, http://www.guardian.co.uk/books/2007/nov/17/featuresreviews.guardianreview14/   (viewed Dec. 16, 2009).

Jan Burke

Houston, Texas
1953

Amateur Detective, Journalism Mystery,
Paranormal
Benchmark Series: Irene Kelly

Julie Dennis Brothers Photography

About the Author and the Author's Writing

Jan Burke was managing a manufacturing plant when she wrote the first chapters of her debut mystery novel, *Goodnight Irene* (1993).

Born Jan Fischer in Houston, Texas, in 1953, she had moved with her family to California. She majored in history at California State University at Long Beach, earning her B.A. in 1978. She then wrote a Sunday column for the *Long Beach Press-Telegram*. But with few prospects for a job in the history field, she went to work for her father's company, which was later bought out by a conglomerate. In 1988 she married musician Timothy Burke.

Having admired the writing of Dashiell Hammett, Josephine Tey, Peter O'Donnell, Dorothy Dunnett, and Captain Marryat, among others, Burke set about writing a novel featuring investigative journalist Irene Kelly. She says she found Lawrence Block's books about the writing craft helpful. Her first two chapters sat in a drawer for quite a while, not reaching the standard she had set for herself. When finally a manuscript was finished, she overcame momentary discouragement at finding an agent and sent the pages to a contact in Simon and Schuster's sales department. That person steered the book to the top of the editorial slush pile, and Burke landed a three-book contract.

Goodnight, Irene sets Kelly on the trail of the killer of her friend O'Connor. The weapon was a bomb, secreted in a package. "She writes with remarkable sensitivity about the physical and spiritual reactions of people terrorized by cold-blooded killers," said *Publishers Weekly*, "and her gift for characterization somewhat compensates for her still-rudimentary pacing skills."

Burke polished her pacing skills and followed her best instincts as she added to the Kelly series. Among aspects that set it apart from other series are Kelly's marriage to a police detective. At first, she said in a Writers Write interview with Claire E. White, she meant Frank Harriman to simply serve as the obligatory cop in the background, supply information, harass the heroine, but blend in. However,

> Every time I had the two of them on the page together, the sparks were flying. Gradually, it dawned on me that I should give them their way. There was lots of conflict built into their situation, which is always a plus in fiction writing.

But the conflict brought the obligation to fully realize the characters, to make them distinct and more interesting.

The character of Irene is drawn from the author's imagination and experience. Once Burke could hear Kelly's voice, she could comprehend the character. And critics appreciated the strong character.

Typically, Rex E. Klett, reviewing *Bloodines* for *Library Journal* in 2004, said, "In-depth characterization, dynamic storytelling, and wonderful prose makes this essential for most mystery collections."

Also strong in the Irene Kelly books is the setting, the fictional Las Piernas, near Los Angeles. Of course, coastal California cities are a dime a dozen in crime fiction. So Burke mapped it out as being the size of Long Beach, with features of Venice Beach and South Bay as well as a zoo and the made-up Angelus Hotel.

Burke writes from a home office in southern California. She juggles her craft with a number of volunteer commitments, including support of the Crime Lab Project, "a nonprofit I started to help support forensic science labs," she said in a *Publishers Weekly* interview in 2008. "I began meeting families of murder victims and thinking about the subject of death and loss."

Over the years, Burke has nurtured her craft, and it shows. For *Bones*, she won the 2000 Mystery Writers of America Edgar Award for best novel. She has departed from the Kelly novels long enough to write stand-alone novels (including 2008's *The Messenger*, which has paranormal elements) and short stories. Of the latter, she said on her Web website,

> I love writing short stories, both because I am a fan of the form as a reader and because they give me a chance to stretch as a writer. "The Man in the Civil Suit," for example, is comedic and quite different in style from my contemporary novels.

Works by the Author

Unharmed (1996), chapbook

Eighteen (2002), collection

Nine (2002)

The Messenger (2009)

Irene Kelly Series

Goodnight, Irene (1993)

Sweet Dreams, Irene (1994)

Dear Irene (1995)

Remember Me, Irene (1996)

A Fine Set of Teeth (1997), chapbook

Hocus (1997)

Liar (1998)

Bones (1999)

Flight (2001)

Bloodlines (2005)

Kidnapped (2006)

Disturbance (2011)

Contributor

Malice Domestic 6, edited by Elizabeth Foxwell (1997), includes "Mea Culpa"

Crime Through Time II: Historical Mystery Short Stories, edited by Miriam Grace Monfredo and Sharan Newman (1998), includes "A Man of My Stature"

Death Cruise: Crime Stories on the Open Seas, edited by Lawrence Block (1999), includes "Miscalculation"

Irreconcilable Differences, edited by Lia Matera and Martin Greenberg (1999), includes "An Unsuspected Condition of the Heart"

Crime through Time III: Historical Mystery Short Stories, edited by Sharan Newman and Miriam Grace Monfredo (2000), includes "The Haunting of Carrick Hollow"

Malice Domestic 9 (2000), includes "The Man in the Civil Suit"

The World's Finest Mystery & Crime Stories, Second Annual Collection, edited by Ed Gorman (2001), includes "The Man in the Civil Suit" and "The Abbey Ghosts"

The Sunken Sailor, with Simon Brett, Dorothy Cannell, Margaret Coel, Deborah Crombie, Eilen Dreyer, Carolyn Hart, Edward Marston, Francine Mathews, Sharan Newman, Alexandra Ripley, Walter Satterthwait, Sarah Smith, and Carolyn Wheat (2004)

Murder Most Crafty, edited by Maggie Bruce (2006), includes "Call It Macaroni"

Creature Cozies, edited by Jill Morgan (2005), includes "Lost and Found"

Murder at the Race Track, edited by Otto Penzler (2006), includes "Zuppa Inglese"

For Further Information

Goodnight, Irene review, *Publishers Weekly*, Jan. 11, 1993.

Hall, Melissa Mia, "PW Talks with Jan Burke: Walking into the Dark Forest," *Publishers Weekly*, Nov. 24, 2008.

Jan Burke website, http://www.janburke.com/about.php/ (viewed Dec. 16, 2009).

Klett, Rex E., *Bloodlines* review, *Library Journal,* Dec. 1, 2004.

Parker, T. Jefferson, Jan Burke interview Mystery Readers International, http://www.mysteryreaders.org/athomeburke.html/ (viewed Dec. 16, 2009).

White, Claire E., "A Conversation with Jan Burke," Writers Write, http://www.writerswrite.com/journal/jul98/burke.htm/ (viewed Dec. 16, 2009).

Jim Butcher

Toledo, Ohio
1971

Private Detective, Paranormal
Benchmark Series: Dresden Files

About the Author and the Author's Writing

This will take a little explaining. Harry Blackstone Copperfield Dresden is a Chicago private detective. He's also a wizard. He doesn't have the best control of his powers, but he's well intentioned. He wears a duster and carries a .44 revolver. When he faces a being beyond his abilities to best, he relies on a posse of friends, among them Special Investigations Lt. Karrin Murphy, who has no paranormal abilities but is nevertheless one tough cookie. She's often assigned to puzzling cases that involve the unexplained. Thus her frequent contact with Dresden. There are also Bob, the air elemental; Molly Carpenter, Dresden's apprentice, who dabbles in dark magic; and William Borden, the engineer who's also a werewolf.

In *White Night* (2007), typically, this motley crew investigates a series of minor wizard killings, of which Dresden's brother Thomas is the likely perpetrator. A *Publishers Weekly* reviewer, in praising the novel, explained,

> As a Warden of the White Council, at war with both the Red Court of blood-drinking vampires and the White Court of psychic vampires, Harry has to go into action, including a battle with ghouls on the lakefront that turns into a gripping flashback of another encounter with ghouls some years before in New Mexico.

Solidly on the fantasy shelves in libraries and bookstores, author Jim Butcher's mind-spinning forays into the supernatural have also caught the attention of mystery readers. He based his hero on Sherlock Holmes, after all. And on Merlin. And Spider-Man. And Scooby-Doo.

The author was born in Independence, Missouri, in 1971. He received a bachelor of arts degree from the University of Oklahoma. He is married and has one son. He has worked variously as a sales rep, restaurant manager, computer support technician, and horse wrangler while trying to jump start his writing career.

How he became a professional writer has as many plot twists as one of his novels.

He skipped high school classes one day and was present when Margaret Weis, author of the DragonLance fantasy books, gave a talk. Maybe, he thought, he would become a writer too. He wrote a manuscript. He was 19. He wrote another, and a third. He rewrote the first one and then conceived a fourth. He took a writing class and wrote the first Dresden story. The next semester, he wrote the second. The third was well under way when he began to look for an agent. He ran into repeated dead ends until he began to attend fantasy fan conventions and seek out agents. Eventually an agent took him on, and six months later he had a contract with Roc. (Apparently, he said, the tipping factor was that he had three manuscripts already done.)

The moral of the story, the author said on his website, is you have to work to learn the craft. "You have to have the attitude of a successful writer," he said. "Rejection shouldn't discourage you. It's just part of the day, like a thunderstorm or a car horn. It happens. It isn't personal."

Part of that hard work goes into landing a publisher and building and sustaining an audience is research. Everything Butcher knows about magic he learned from books—shaped to his particular needs. "I didn't want Dresden to be a mystic, shamanistic wizard. I wanted him to be a plumber, a carpenter, and engineer. Only instead of working with water, wood, or physics, he was working with magic," he said in a Bitten by Books interview.

Butcher expects the series to run to at least 20 books and has an idea of how things will come to a spectacular climax. "Some things I can see from planning way ahead of time, and some things I don't see until I'm actually at the keyboard writing things," Butcher told a Crescent Blues interviewer. "What I try and do is make sure that the events that happen in each book are discrete to themselves."

The Dresden series has caught on with readers and has been turned into a graphic novel, a role-playing game, and a 12-episode SciFi Channel television series.

Butcher has meanwhile developed a second, more traditional horses-and-swords fantasy series, the Codex Alera books, published by Ace Books.

Should a biographer someday want to tackle his story, Butcher told Powell's Books, he has a ready title: "How to Slay Dragons, Catch Unicorns, Break into Publishing, and Do 101 Other Impossible Things, or . . . The Little Author That Could."

Works by the Author

Codex Alera Series

Furies of Calderon (2004)

Academ's Fury (2005)

Cursor's Fury (2006)

Captain's Fury (2007)

Princeps' Fury (2008)

First Lord's Fury (2009)

Dresden Files Series

Fool Moon (2000)

Storm Front (2000)

Grave Peril (2001)

Summer Knight (2002)

Death Masks (2003)

Blood Rites (2004)

Dead Beat (2005)

Wizard for Hire (2005), includes *Storm Front, Fool Moon,* and *Grave Peril*

Proven Guilty (2006)

Wizard at Large (2006), includes *Blood Rites* and *Dead Beat*

Wizard by Trade (2006), includes *Summer Knight* and *Death Masks*

White Night (2007)

Wizard Under Fire (2007), includes *Proven Guilty* and *White Night*

Backup: A Story of the Dresden Files (2008)

Small Favor (2008)

Welcome to the Jungle (2008), graphic novel with Ardian Syaf

Storm Front, Vol. 1 (2009), graphic novel

Turn Coat (2009)

Changes (2010)

Fool Moon, Vol. 1 (2010), graphic novel

Side Jobs: Stories from the Dresden Files (2010)

Storm Front, Vol. 2 (2010), graphic novel

Ghost Story (2011)

Contributor

My Big Fat Supernatural Wedding, with L. A. Banks, Rachel Caine, P. N. Elrod, Esther Friesner, Lori Handeland, Charlaine Harris, Sherrilyn Kenyon, and Susan Krinard (2006)

Many Bloody Returns (2007)

My Big Fat Supernatural Honeymoon, with Kelley Armstrong, Rachel Caine, P. N. Elrod, Caitlin Kittredge, Marjorie M. Liu, Katie MacAlister, Lilith Saintcrow, and Ronda Thompson (2007)

Blood Lite, with Kelley Armstrong, Charlaine Harris, and Sherrilyn Kenyon (2008)

Mean Streets, with Simon Green, Kat Richardson, and Thomas E. Sniegoski (2009)

Strange Brew (2009)

Dark and Story Knights, edited by P. N. Elrod (2010), includes "Even Hand"

Spider-Man Series

The Darkest Hours (2006)

Adaptations in Other Media

The Dresden Files (Sci-Fi Channel, 2007)

For Further Information

Cullen, Ian, Jim Butcher interview, SciFi Pulse, http://scifipulse.net/?tag=jim-butcher/ (viewed Dec. 3, 2009).

Jim Butcher interview, Powell's Q&A, http://www.powells.com/ink/butcher.html/ (viewed Dec. 2, 2009).

Jim Butcher interview, Bitten by Books, http://bittenbybooks.com/?p=6529/ (viewed Dec. 3, 2009).

Jim Butcher website. http://www.jim-butcher.com/ (viewed Dec. 2, 2009).

Murray, Frieda, *First Lord's Fury* review, *Booklist*, Nov. 1, 2009.

Smith, Teri, "Jim Butcher: 'Longshot' Makes Good," Blue Crescent, http://www.crescentblues.com/7_4issue/int_butcher.shtml/ (viewed Dec. 2, 2009).

White Night review, *Publishers Weekly*, Feb. 26, 2007.

Laura Childs

Location and date not disclosed

Amateur Detective
Benchmark Series: Tea Shop Mysteries

Robert J. Poor

About the Author and the Author's Writing

Melody Mayfeldt, a jeweler, believes in the supernatural. She's an eager helper when an old New Orleans mansion is being temporarily set up as a haunted house for a horror fan convention. But it was not a ghost but a human being who was responsible for smashing Melody in the head and throwing her from a third-floor window—of that, her friends Carmela Bertrand, proprietor of the Memory Mine scrapbook shop, and her pal Ava Grulex are sure. All this happens in *Tragic Magic* (2009), the eighth in Laura Childs's popular Scrapbooking mystery series.

Carmela's friend Detective Edgar Babcock is assigned to the case, and with the help of the two women he narrows the small circle of suspects to one.

A similar ethereal angle confronts Theodosia Browning, proprietor of the Indigo Tea Shop, in another Childs series. *The Jasmine Moon Murder* (2004), the first of the novels to appear in hardcover, typically revolves around the death of a cardiologist during a Ghost Crawl in Charleston, South Carolina. As Theodosia pursues her clues, she offers a few culinary tips, "enough scrumptious descriptions of teas and baked goods to throw anyone off the killer's scent," commented *Library Journal*'s reviewer Rex E. Klett.

Childs has a third series, this one featuring three amateur sleuths. The Cackleberry Club Café proprietors, Suzanne, Petra, and Toni, all recently single again, are adept cooks and caterers. They are also crime solvers by avocation. The thornier the puzzle in their town of Kindred, the better for these forty-something heroines. In *Eggs Benedict Arnold* (2009), for example, they figure out who had it in for Ozzie Driesden, the funeral director.

One might expect it to be a handful for Childs to juggle these continuing characters as she keeps all three series alive. Hardly. Childs, whose real name is Geraldine "Gerry" Schmitt, in previous years was a writer and producer for several national advertising agencies. She was CEO and creative director for her own firm, Mission Critical Marketing. She wrote and produced dozens of television commercials. In other words, she's used to being busy.

On her website she explains how she became a writer of cozy mysteries:

I wrote four screenplays, got one read by Paramount, but never actually sold one. I then turned to writing mysteries. After I'd produced two manuscripts, the planets seemed to align, and I got very lucky with a great agent and a visionary editor.

The upshot was, within a few years she sold her agency and became a writer full time.

She lists Stephen King, John Sanford, Robert Crais, and Mary Higgins Clark as among her favorite fiction writers. In fact, it was when she attended a Mystery Writers of America symposium featuring Clark that she became determined to take up a new career. Her first book was selected by the Literary Guild.

Childs explains she tries to write 2,000 words a day and completes a book in three or four months. She lets them percolate, then rereads the manuscripts, adding details and developing characters as needed. She credits watching the TV shows *The Twilight Zone* and *Alfred Hitchcock Presents* with her cue to add bits of irony and humor wherever she can in the novels.

She is adept at creating credible backgrounds for her books. *Oolong Dead* (2009), for example, impressed *Booklist* reviewer Judy Coon: "Charleston emerges in Childs' series as a beautiful old city imbued with culture and filled with uniquely warm characters."

Characters, Childs finds, are a cinch. "Characters just seem to pop into my head," she said in a Mystery Lovers Corner interview. "People always ask if I do index cards or plan intricate bios. I can't imagine doing anything that studied. To me writing is about intuition and gut instinct—you've got to sit back and let the characters speak to you."

It goes without saying that the final piece, the plot, comes naturally to the author, who told the Fresh Fiction website:

> I try to combine well-written prose with a carefully thought out plot and thin sprinkle in lots of twists and tension. Also, I try to make my books extremely character-driven. I want readers to think of my characters as dear friends they want to stay in touch with.

The author and her husband, Robert J. Poor, a professor of Asian art history, live near Minneapolis, where she quietly brews ideas for new Tea Shop crimes.

Works by the Author

Cackleberry Club Series

Eggs in Purgatory (2008)

Eggs Benedict Arnold (2009)

Bedeviled Eggs (2010)

Scrapbooking Series

Keepsake Crimes (2003)

Bound for Murder (2004)

Photo Finished (2004)

Death by Design (2006), omnibus

Motif for Murder (2006)

Frill Kill (2007)

Death Swatch (2008)

Tragic Magic (2009)

Fiber & Brimstone (2010)

Tea Shop Series

Death by Darjeeling (2001)

Gunpowder Green (2002)

The English Breakfast Murder (2003)

Shades of Earl Grey (2003)

The Jasmine Moon Murder (2004)

Chamomile Mourning (2005)

Blood Orange Brewing (2006)

Dragonwell Dead (2007)

The Silver Needle Murder (2008)

Oolong Dead (2009)

The Teaberry Strangler (2010)

Scones & Bones (2011)

For Further Information

Coon, Judy, *Oolong Dead* review, *Booklist*, March 15, 2009.

Klett, Rex E., *The Jasmine Moon Murder* review, *Library Journal*, Sept. 1, 2004.

Laura Childs interview, Mystery Lovers Corner, http://www.sleuthedit.com/Laura Childs/Interview.html/ (viewed Jan. 9, 2010).

Laura Childs interview, Sharon's Cozy Corner, http://freshfiction.com/page.php?id=2118/ (viewed Jan. 9, 2010).

Laura Childs website, http://www.laurachilds.com/faq.html/ (viewed Dec. 9, 2010).

Tragic Magic review, *Publishers Weekly*, Aug. 24, 2009.

Ann Cleeves

Hereford, England
1954

Police Procedural, Amateur Detective
Benchmark Series: Shetland Island
Quartet

About the Author and the Author's Writing

In 2006 Ann Cleeves received the Crime Writers Association's Duncan Lawrie Dagger for best crime novel for *Raven Black*, her 19th novel. The honor, in a competitive field, left her speechless. Literally. She woke up the morning of the awards ceremony, unable to speak more than a squeak. She had a bad cold and had spoken too much to her library staff the day before. Her editor accepted the dagger on her behalf.

While she may have briefly lost her voice, Cleeves has never been at a loss for words since she first embarked on a writing career in 1986 with *A Bird in the Hand*, the first of the George and Molly Palmer-Jones puzzlers.

The author was born in 1954 in Hereford, England. She graduated from Liverpool University in 1979, two years after her marriage to Tim Cleeves. She worked as a child care officer for Camden Social Services in London from 1973 to 1975, was a bird observatory cook on Fair Isle, Scotland, for a year, and then worked in the auxiliary Coast Guard from 1977 to 1981. From 1981 to 1983 she was a probation officer in Wirral and Cheshire, England. And she raised two daughters.

Her first writing was nonfiction, an essay about a coastal island near Wirral coauthored with her husband for a travel book. Tim Cleeves works for the Royal Society for the Protection of Birds.

When she turned to crime, the author made good use of her knowledge of birds and birding. The Palmer-Jones books use as a background the competitive world of life-listers, indefatigable birders who go anywhere and everywhere to extend their species counts. Cleeves eventually went on to create other series, including one featuring Inspector Ramsey.

"Ann Cleeves always writes in a crisp economical style," in the view of critic Martin Edwards. "She is rare among modern crime writers in concentrating on rural settings."

She pays close attention to detail, and lovingly shapes her characters, even the unlovable ones. "I identify with all my characters when I write them, even, or perhaps especially, the less attractive ones," she said in a conversation with Julian Maynard-Smith. "Writing's a bit like acting, I think. You have to believe you're the person you're writing, stand in their shoes and get inside their head."

Cleeves has written a few stand-alone novels, though she so enjoyed the main character in one that she felt compelled to make a second visit. That character was Detective Inspector Vera Stanhope, who first appeared in *Crow Trap* in 1999. "I was quite cross that even feminist writers always write young and beautiful central characters," the author said in an interview on the Pan Macmillan website.

> They also seem to have lots of energy, be very fit and can run without looking ridiculous. Vera is middle-aged, overweight and a spinster. She deeply regrets not having a partner or children. She can't run and she drinks too much.

And as it turns out, Stanhope's two later book appearances caught the attention of ITV producers, who featured her in a two-hour drama based on *Hidden Depths* in 2010. (Actress Brenda Blethyn, one has to say, doesn't quite fit Cleeves's description of her character, but no matter, she captured the spirit.)

The author's latest series is a quartet set on a remote Shetland Island. *Red Bones*, the third in the series, finds Inspector Jimmy Perez on the scent of a shooter. The case becomes complicated when a body turns up at an archaeological site, leading to connections with a World War II resistance movement.

What is the secret of this successful writer? Cleeves revealed some of her creative process in a *Mystery News* interview:

> I never plot in advance. I never know ahead of time who the murderer is. That means quite a lot of rewriting. By the time I'm about a third of the way through, I've got this fairly hazy idea about more or less how it's going to end, but sometimes that changes right at the last chapter.

How better to keep the audience in suspense?

Works by the Author

The Sleeping and the Dead (2002)

Burial of Ghosts (2003)

Inspector Ramsay Series

A Lesson in Dying (1990)

Murder in My Back Yard (1991)

A Day in the Death of Dorothea Cassidy (1992)

Killjoy (1993)

The Healers (1995)

The Baby Snatcher (1997)

Palmer-Jones Series

A Bird in the Hand (1986)

Come Death and High Water (1987)

Murder in Paradise (1989)

A Prey to Murder (1989)

Sea Fever (1991)

Another Man's Poison (1993)

The Mill on the Shore (1994)

High Island Blues (1996)

Shetland Island Quartet

Raven Black (2006)

White Nights (2008)

Red Bones (2009)

Blue Lightning (2010)

Vera Stanhope Series

The Crow Trap (1999)

Telling Tales (2005)

Hidden Depths (2007)

Silent Voices (2011)

Contributor

Northern Blood, edited by Martin Edwards (1992), includes "A Winter's Tale"

Northern Blood 2, edited by Martin Edwards (1995), includes "The Harmless Pursuits of Archibald Stamp"

The Murder Squad Anthology, edited by Martin Edwards (2001), includes "Sad Girls" and "The Plater"

Crime in the City, edited by Martin Edwards (2002), includes "A Rough Guide to Tanga"

Green for Danger, edited by Martin Edwards (2003), includes "Games for Winter"

Crime on the Move, edited by Martin Edwards (2004), includes "Owl Wars"

Phantoms at the Phil, edited by Chaz Brenchley (2005), includes "The Midwife's Assistant"

Adaptations in Other Media

Hidden Depths (ITV dramatization, 2010), based on the novel

The author also wrote *Catching Birds*, a short Border TV film.

For Further Information

Ann Cleeves interview, Pan Macmillan, http://www.panmacmillan.com/displayPage. asp?PageID=4759/ (viewed Feb. 17, 2010).

Ann Cleeves website, http://www.anncleeves.com/ (viewed Feb. 17, 2010).

Edwards, Martin, "Ann Cleeves: A Profile," TW Books, http://www.twbooks.co.uk/crimescene/acleevesme.html/ (viewed Feb. 17, 2010).

Kaczmarek, Lynn, "Ann Cleeves: On the Shetland Islands," *Mystery News*, Oct./Nov. 2008.

Maynard-Smith, Julian, Ann Cleeves conversation, *SHOTS*, 2006. http://www.shotsmag.co.uk/interviews2006/a_cleeves/a_cleeves.html/ (viewed Feb. 17, 2010).

Red Bones review, *Publishers Weekly*, July 20, 2009.

Max Allan Collins

Muscatine, Iowa
1948

Police Procedural, Police Forensics,
Private Detective, Historical Mystery,
Amateur Detective, Criminal
Benchmark Series: Nate Heller

Bamford Studio

About the Author and the Author's Writing

Max Allan Collins's library is jammed, with one shelf holding his novelizations of popular television series (*CSI*) and motion pictures (*U.S. Marshals*), another his comic strip (Dick Tracy) and comic book (Ms. Tree) tales; a third holds his original crime (Quarry) and detective (Nate Heller) series. His collaborations with his favorite author, the late Mickey Spillane, on new Mike Hammer cases, are starting a shelf of their own, alongside the collaborations with his wife, Barbara Collins.

The author averages a rigorous three novels a year, with no letup in sight. And he still has time to script independent films.

Collins was born in Muscatine, Iowa, in 1948. He graduated from Muscatine Community College and the University of Iowa, from which he received an M.F.A. in 1972. He was a professional musician off and on, a journalist, and an instructor, until he began to write fiction full time in 1972. His first crime novel, featuring a professional thief named Nolan, turned into a series.

"I've been trying to write since I was in Junior High," Collins said in a Spiderweb interview in 1982,

> and starting in ninth or tenth grade, I wrote seven full-length books before I sold one. They're mostly Spillane, with maybe a little Ian Fleming. Then, when I was about twenty, I discovered Richard Stark [Donald E. Westlake] and Parker, and the idea of the thief as protagonist.

When his publisher asked for a second book featuring the hard-nosed antihero Nolan with a kid sidekick, Collins first asked Westlake if he objected. Westlake gave his blessing, and more Nolan books followed. Next came Quarry books, about a professional assassin, and Mallory books, about a young writer and amateur detective.

Longest running of his original novels is the Nate Heller series, set in the Prohibition era.

"The Heller novels are designed to be traditional private eye stories in the Hammett/Chandler/Spillane manner," Collins said in a Mystery One interview, "using this style and voice to explore crimes and mysteries of the twentieth century. Nate Heller is a 'private eye witness' to major events (and particularly crimes)."

The Heller books require considerable research, much of it done by longtime associate George Hagenauer.

"The characters, historical and fictional, come delightfully to life," in the view of *Publishers Weekly*. In a review of *Angel in Black* (2001), it said that "Collins paints a web of interconnections in a tightly woven plot and posits a radical solution to a crime that still resonates in literature and movies."

Collins has been nominated 15 times for Private Eye Writers of America Shamus awards and has won for *True Detective* (1983) and *Stolen Away* (1991).

With artist Terry Beatty, he produced what became the longest-running private detective comic book, featuring Ms. Michael Tree, who inherits an investigation agency when her husband is murdered. The character appears intermittently, with four independent publishers and also DC comics, from 1981 to 1993. She also appears in a prose novel, *Deadly Beloved*, in 2009.

In another collaboration, this time with Matthew Clemens, Collins also writes books about former sheriff, now host of the TV show *Crime Seen*, J. C. Harrow.

Collins's graphic novel *Road to Perdition* (with artist Richard Piers Rayner, 1998), about a syndicate enforcer during the Great Depression, was made into the award-winning motion picture featuring actor Tom Hanks. Collins also wrote the film novelization and sequels.

Cofounder of the International Association of Media Tie-In Writers, Collins was, not surprisingly, given the nickname "the novelization king" by Entertainment Weekly. Several of his prose versions of movies—such as *Saving Private Ryan, Air Force One,* and *The Mummy*—have made it onto the *USA Today* bestseller list.

Living what was dream come true for a Spillane fan, Collins got to know the late author and was entrusted with his incomplete manuscripts when Spillane died in 2006. Their collaborative *The Goliath Bone* came out in 2008.

"I suppose I should say I'm intimidated," Collins told Carol Memmott of *USA Today*, "but I took Mickey Spillane books as vitamins when I was a kid. I was born to do this, and Mickey trusted me."

Works by the Author

Novels

Midnight Haul (1986)

Tough Tender (1991)

In the Line of Fire (1993)

Maverick (1994)

Waterworld (1995)

Daylight (1996)

Mommy (1996)

Air Force 1 (1997)

Mommy's Day: Mommy 2 (1998)

Saving Private Ryan (1998)

U.S. Marshals (1998)

Regeneration, with Barbara Collins (1999)

U-571: A Novel (2000)

Murder, His and Hers, with Barbara Collins (2001)

Windtalkers (2001)

I Spy (2002)

The Scorpion King (2002)

Johnny Dynamite (2003)

Bombshell, with Barbara Collins (2004)

Two for the Money (2004)

American Gangster (2007)

Deadly Beloved (2007)

Bones/Temperance Brennan Series, with Kathy Reichs

Buried Deep (2006)

Crime Seen Series, with Matthew Clemens

You Can't Stop Me (2010)

No One Will Hear You (2011)

Criminal Minds Series

Jump Cut (2007)

Finishing School (2008)

Killer Profile (2008)

CSI: Crime Scene Investigation Series

Double Dealer (2001)

Sin City (2002)

Body of Evidence (2003)

Cold Burn (2003)

Serial (2003)

Bad Rap (2004)

Demon House (2004)

Grave Matters (2004)

Binding Ties (2005)

Killing Game (2005)

Snake Eyes (2006)

Mortal Wounds (2007), includes *Double Dealer, Sin City,* and *Cold Burn*

CSI: Miami Series

Florida Getaway (2003)

Heat Wave (2004)

Dark Angel Series

Before the Dawn (2002)

After the Dark (2003)

Skin Game (2003)

Dick Tracy Series

Dick Tracy (1990), film novelization

Dick Tracy and the Nightmare Machine (1991)

Dick Tracy Goes to War (1991)

Dick Tracy Meets His Match (1992)

Dick Tracy: The Collins Casefiles, three volumes (2003–2005)

Disaster Series

The Titanic Murders (1999)

The Hindenburg Murders (2000)

The Pearl Harbor Murders (2001)

The Lusitania Murders (2002)

The London Blitz Murders (2004)

The War of the Worlds Murder (2005)

Eliot Ness Series

Butcher's Dozen (1987)

The Dark City (1987)

Bullet Proof (1988)

Murder by the Numbers (1989)

Jack and Maggie Starr Series

A Killing in Comics (2007)

Strip for Murder (2008)

Mallory Series

No Cure for Death (1983)

The Baby Blue Rip-Off (1982)

Kill Your Darlings (1984)

A Shroud for Aquarius (1985)

Nice Weekend for a Murder (1986)

Mike Hammer Series, with Mickey Spillane

The Dead Street (2007)

The Goliath Bone (2008)

King of the Weeds (2009)

The Big Bang (2010)

Kiss Her Goodbye (2011)

Ms. Tree Series

Files of Ms. Tree, Vol. 1 (1984), graphic novel

Files of Ms. Tree, Vol. 2 (1985), graphic novel

Ms. Tree (1988), graphic novel

Deadly Beloved (2007)

Mummy Series

The Mummy (1998)

*The Mummy Return*s (2001)

The Mummy: Tomb of the Dragon Emperor (2008)

Nate Heller Series

True Detective (1983)

True Crime (1984)

The Million Dollar Wound (1986)

Neon Mirage (1988)

Dying in the Post-War World (1991)

Stolen Away (1991)

Carnal Hours (1994)

Blood and Thunder (1995)

Damned in Paradise (1996)

Flying Blind: A Novel about Amelia Earhart (1998)

Majic Man: A Nathan Heller Novel (1999)

Angel in Black (2001)

Kisses of Death (2001), short stories

Chicago Confidential (2002)

Bye Bye Baby (2010)

Nightstalker Series

Kolchak: The Night Stalker, with Elaine Bergstrom, Peter David, Mark Dawidziak, P. N. Elrod, Ed Gorman, C. J. Henderson, Stuart M. Kaminsky, Brett Matthews, and Robert E. Weinberg (2003)

The Night Stalker Chronicles (2005)

Nolan Series

Bait Money (1973)

Blood Money (1973)

Fly Paper (1981)

Hard Cash (1981)

Hush Money (1981)

Scratch Fever (1982)

Spree (1987)

Mourn the Living (1988)

Two for the Money (2004), includes *Bait Money* and *Blood Money*

NYPD Blue Series

Blue Beginning (1995)

Blue Blood (1997)

On the Road to Perdition Series (graphic novels)

Oasis (2003)

Sanctuary (2003)

Detour (2004)

Quarry Series

Quarry (1976), also titled *The Broker*

Quarry's Deal (1976), also titled *The Dealer*

Quarry's List (1976), also titled *The Broker's Wife*

Quarry's Cut (1977), also titled *The Slasher*

Primary Target (1987)

Quarry's Greatest Hits (2003)

The Last Quarry (2006)

The First Quarry (2008)

Quarry in the Middle (2009)

Quarry's Ex (2011)

Road to Perdition Series

Road to Perdition (1998)

Road to Purgatory (2004)

Road to Paradise (2005)

Trash 'n' Treasures Mystery Series, with Barbara Collins

Antiques Roadkill (2006)

Antiques Maul (2007)

Antiques Flee Market (2008)

X-Files Series

I Want to Believe: X-files Movie Novelization (2008)

Contributor

The Shamus Winners: America's Best Private Eye Stories, Vol. 1, 1982–1995 edited by Robert J. Randisi (2010), includes "Dying in the Post-War World"

Editor

Private Eyes, with Mickey Spillane (1988)

Dick Tracy: The Secret Files, with Martin H Greenberg (1990)

Murder Is My Business, with Mickey Spillane (1994)

Vengeance Is Hers, with Mickey Spillane (1997)

Too Many Tomcats and Other Feline Tales of Suspense, with Barbara Collins (2000)

Flesh and Blood: Erotic Tales of Crime and Passion, with Jeff Gelb (2001)

A Century of Noir: Thirty-Two Classic Crime Stories, with Mickey Spillane (2002)

Flesh and Blood: Dark Desires, with Jeff Gelb (2002)

Creature Features, with Barbara Collins (2003)

Flesh and Blood: Guilty as Sin; Erotic Tales of Crime and Passion, with Jeff Gelb (2003)

My Lolita Complex: And Other Tales of Sex and Violence, with Matthew V. Clemens (2006)

Written as by Patrick Culhane

Black Hats (2007)

Red Sky in Morning (2008)

As an independent filmmaker, Collins wrote and directed *Mommy* (1996) and *Mommy's Day* (1997) for Lifetime and wrote *The Expert* (1995) for HBO World Premiere. He has also written and edited nonfiction books.

For Further Information

Angel in Black review, *Publishers Weekly*, Feb. 26, 2001.

Davenport, Colin, Max Allan Collins interview, CSI Files, http://www.csifiles.com/interviews/max_allan_collins.shtml/ (viewed Sept. 3, 2009).

Max Allan Collins website, http://www.maxallancollins.com/ (viewed Sept. 3, 2009).

Max Allan Collins interview, Crime Scene NI, http://crimesceneni.blogspot.com/2008/11/mini-interview-max-allan-collins.html/ (viewed Sept. 3, 2009).

Max Allan Collins interview, *January Magazine,* http://www.januarymagazine.com/profiles/collins.html/ (viewed Sept. 3, 2009).

Max Allan Collins interview, Mystery One, http://www.mysteryone.com/MaxAllanCollinsInterview.htm/ (viewed Sept. 3, 2009).

Max Allan Collins Unofficial Appreciation Page, http://maxfan.tripod.com/ (viewed Sept. 3, 2009).

Max Collins interview, *Spiderweb* No. 1, winter 1982.

Memmott, Carol, "Friend Hammers out Spillane Novel," *USA Today*, Oct. 9, 2008.

Ott, Bill, *The First Quarry* review, *Booklist,* Aug. 1, 2008.

Susan Conant

Massachusetts
1946

Amateur Detective, Culinary Mystery
Benchmark Series: Dog Lover's Mysteries

About the Author and the Author's Writing

Write what you know, aspiring writers are often told. In 1988 Susan Conant became coordinator for the Alaskan Malamute Protection League of Massachusetts. So it should be no surprise to learn that she also wrote her first mystery novel that year, *A New Leash on Death* (1989), a crime story featuring a dog—a malamute, in fact.

The author was born in northeastern Massachusetts in 1946. Her father raised show dogs; his pointer was New England Field Trial Champion in the 1930s. In 1968, Conant graduated from Radcliffe College; in the same year she married clinical psychologist Carter Umbarger, who maintains a private practice in Cambridge. She received an Ed.D. in human development from Harvard University in 1978 and worked as an educational researcher for a decade. Then she started to write mysteries.

All Shots (2007), typically, is set in Massachusetts and finds Holly Winter, Malamute trainer and author of a column for *Dog Life* magazine, stumbling on the body of a woman who has in her possession papers that identify her as Holly Winter. Then she finds a living and breathing Holly Winter. And it all becomes a big case of confusion and identity theft. "Conant includes a lot of insider doggy details," said the *Publishers Weekly* review, "and lovingly depicts Holly's interactions with her malamutes, Kimi, Rowdy and a young pup Sammy. Sammy and Rowdy's courageous defense of Holly when the killer catches up to her will have dog lovers cheering."

Conant is also writing a series of culinary mysteries with her daughter, Jessica Conant-Park. *Turn Up the Heat* (2008), the third Gourmet Girl case, sets heroine Chloe Carter in quest of whoever killed a waitress named Leandra in the back of a refrigerated fish truck. "This mother–daughter writing team combines a nicely detailed Back Bay setting with plenty of insights into the restaurant business, its kitchen characters, table-service staff, purveyors, and guests," praised Mark Knoblauch in *Booklist*.

Mother–daughter writing teams are atypical in publishing. Jessica Conant-Park, whose husband Bill Park is an executive chef, said that she devours chick-lit. Susan Conant does too, but she also adores Jane Austen, the classic mysteries of Margery Allingham, and the contemporary procedurals of Reginald Hill. Mother and daughter share a love of fine food, however, and, as Susan Conant said on the Berkley Prime Crime website,

> We are also only children. Our writing process allows each of us considerable independence. Maybe we fit the stereotype of the only child in the sense that we are happier when we are taking turns than we are when we have to share.

Jessica Conant-Park explained to Once Upon a Romance how they came up with the idea for *Steamed* (2006): "My mother and I plotted the book together over the phone, resulting in six phone calls a day and numerous e-mails back and forth to plan out the mystery part of the book." They created a 25-page outline that was flexible enough to allow creative diversions as they did the actual writing.

Not biased against cats, Conan began what she expected to be a companion Cat Lover's Series with *Scratch the Surface* (2005). Conant "takes the opportunity to poke gentle fun at some of the conventions of the cozy genre," said *Publishers Weekly*, which further called the book "side-splittingly funny and very clever."

Then, as she related in a Trashionista interview in 2007, "I was outlining my second cat lover's mystery, but Holly Winter's malamutes leapt in and shoved the casts aside, so I am writing my nineteenth dog lover's mystery."

Works by the Author

Scratch the Surface: A Cat-Lover's Mystery (2005)

Holly Winter Dog Mystery Series

A New Leash on Death (1989)

Dead and Doggone (1990)

A Bite of Death (1991)

Paws Before Dying (1991)

Bloodlines (1992)

Gone to the Dogs (1992)

Black Ribbon (1994)

Ruffly Speaking (1994)

Stud Rites (1996)

Animal Appetite (1997)

The Barker Street Regulars (1998)

Evil Breeding (1999)

Creature Discomforts (2000)

The Wicked Flea (2002)

The Dogfather (2003)

Bride and Groom (2004)

Gaits of Heaven (2006)

All Shots (2007)

Brute Strength (2011)

Gourmet Girl Series, with Jessica Conant-Park

Steamed (2006)

Simmer Down (2007)

Turn Up the Heat (2007)

Fed Up (2009)

Cook the Books (2010)

For Further Information

All Shots review, *Publishers Weekly*, Sept. 10, 2007.

"Five Questions with Jessica Conant-Park and Susan Conant, Berkley Prime Crime, http://berkleysignetmysteries.com/content.php?id=32/ (viewed Nov. 11, 2009).

Jessica Conant-Park interview, Once Upon a Romance, July 2006, http://www.once uponaromance.net/JessicaParkInterview.htm/ (viewed Nov. 11, 2009).

Knoblauch, Mark, *Turn Up the Heat* review, *Booklist*, March 15, 2008.

Scratch the Surface review, *Publishers Weekly*, May 9, 2005.

Susan Conant interview, Trashionista, http://www.trashionista.com/2007/06/author-intervie-1.html/ (viewed Nov. 11, 2009).

Susan Conant website. http://conantparkmysteries.googlepages.com/abouttheau thors/ (viewed Nov. 11, 2009).

John Connolly

Hugh Glynn

Dublin, Ireland
1968

Private Detective
Benchmark Series: Charlie Parker

About the Author and the Author's Writing

John Connolly's road to publication with his first novel—featuring Charlie Parker, a New York City police detective wrenched by the murder of his wife and daughter and in relentless pursuit of the killer—was a slow one. And that, after all, wasn't so bad.

It took him five years to find a publisher for *Every Dead Thing* (1998), and in the interim his hero grew. The author told interviewer Judith Spelman, for *Writing Magazine,*

> When I began writing it I was only about 22 going on 23, but by the time it was published I was nearly 30. He had all that time to gestate and I had found the things that were wrong so I think he was a fuller character.

John Connolly was born in Ireland, in Dublin's Rialto section, in 1968. After earning a B.A. degree in English from Trinity College in Dublin and an M.A. in journalism from Dublin City University in 1993, he worked random jobs as a bartender and government laborer. Then he became a journalist and author.

Connolly devoured American crime fiction, from Ed McBain to James Lee Burke and Ross Macdonald. Thus, when he looked for an alternative to newspaper writing, he decided to put together his own crime novel. And he set it in the United States. He says on his web page that

> American crime fiction seemed much more concerned with the victims, with the possibility that it was society, or the institutions of the law, or, in Macdonald's case, the sins of the fathers and the impact of family history that was responsible for what happened.

Parker is a haunted hero, guilty that he was in a bar, drinking, the night his wife and child died. Typically, in *The Lovers* (2009), the hero is now a private investigator. He's a PI, that is, until the state of Maine suspends his license and he has to take a job tending bar in Portland. He decides to take on his own case—to find out why his father, who had been a New York City police officer, had killed two young people and then killed himself. "It's a sentimental journey, filled with painful memories for the conflicted hero," said *Booklist* reviewer Thomas Gaughan. "The trip also offers the first hint of some kind of spectral evil that, inevitably, Charlie must confront and destroy."

Spirits and specters weave in and out of Connolly's cases. On his website, the author asserts that he employs the supernatural because he doesn't believe that fiction can be truly realistic.

Criminals are unusually despicable. "I was very influenced by Ian Fleming," the author said in a *January Magazine* interview. "He was one of the first adult writers I read, if you can call Fleming an 'adult writer.' Seriously, he did carve out some very grotesque villains in his career."

Even Connolly's recurring secondary characters, Angel and Louis, have rough edges, though they afford a degree of comic relief. They serve a secondary purpose as role models for Parker, sources of wisdom when it comes to making compromises, according to the author.

Connolly wondered, in an essay for Otto Penzler's *The Lineup*, "if part of the appeal of mystery fiction is its capacity to give us answers and solutions that we don't always get in real life."

In a departure from the Parker books, Connolly has begun to write free-standing books, including 2009's young adult novel *The Gates*, which has an 11-year-old protagonist. "If anything I'm more honest in writing for younger readers, because they won't put up with any nonsense at all, and they're smarter than a lot of adults, writers or non-writers give them credit for," Connolly said in a conversation with Dick Donahue of *Publishers Weekly*.

The author's advice to anyone who wants to write? Just do it. "I still find writing hard," he said in an interview for Bestsellers World,

> and there are days when it's difficult to get anything done. . . . Take it to the finish, then go back. And don't tell anyone that you're writing, and don't ask anyone close to you to judge your work. Keep it quiet.

Works by the Author

Bad Men (2003)

Nocturnes (2004), short stories

The Book of Lost Things (2006)

The Gates (2009)

Charlie Parker Series

Every Dead Thing (1998)

Dark Hollow (2000)

The Killing Road (2002)

Every Dead Thing/Dark Hollow (2003), omnibus

The Black Angel (2005)

The Unquiet (2007)

The Reapers (2008)

The Lovers (2009)

The Whisperers (2010)

The Burning Soul (2011)

For Further Information

Donahue, Dick, John Connolly interview, *Publishers Weekly*, Oct. 5, 2009.

Gaughan, Thomas, *The Lovers* review, *Booklist*, May 15, 2009.

John Connolly interview, *Bestsellers World*, Aug. 25, 2002, http://www.bestseller sworld.com/interviews-connollyjohn.htm/ (viewed Nov. 27, 2009).

John Connolly website, http://www.johnconnollybooks.com/meet.php/ (viewed Nov. 27, 2009).

Johnson, Paul, "Criminal Conversations in Dublin," *SHOTS*, March 25, 2002, http://www.shotsmag.co.uk/Criminal%20Conversations%20in%20Dublin.htm/ (viewed Nov. 27, 2009).

Karim, Ali, "On the Road to Redemption with John Connolly," *January Magazine,* 2003, http://www.januarymagazine.com/profiles/johnconnolly.html/ (viewed Nov. 27, 2009).

Penzler, Otto, ed. *The Lineup: The World's Greatest Crime Writers Tell the Inside Story of Their Greatest Detectives*. New York: Little, Brown, 2009, http://www.johnconnollybooks.com/interviews_isleofman.php/ (viewed Nov. 27, 2009).

Quirk, John, "An Interview with John Connolly," *Isle of Man Examiner*, June 2003.

Spelman, Judith, "Meet John," *Writing Magazine*, Oct.–Nov. 2003.

Thomas H. Cook

Fort Payne, Alabama
1947

Police Procedural, Amateur Detective
Benchmark Series: Frank Clemons

About the Author and the Author's Writing

Mystery writer Thomas H. Cook works within the genre but also elbows its boundaries. An Edgar Award recipient for best novel for *The Chatham School Affair* in 1996, Cook observed in an interview with Jordan Foster, for *Publishers Weekly*,

> It's always a struggle, what you call yourself. I think it can be snooty to define yourself as something other than a crime writer. I've written mainstream fiction. But essentially I write about people in crisis, and crime is usually what propels that crisis.

The author was born in Fort Payne, Alabama, in 1947, but now splits his time between New York City and Cape Cod. He and his wife, Susan Terner, have one son. He was educated at Georgia State College, from which he received a B.A. in 1969, and Hunter College of the City University of New York, where he received an M.A. in 1972. He received a Ph.D. from Columbia University in 1976.

Before he became a full-time fiction writer in 1981, Cook was an advertising executive with U.S. Industrial Chemicals in New York from 1970 to 1971 and a clerk/typist for the Association for Help of Retarded Adults in New York from 1973 to 1975. From 1978 to 1981 he taught English and history at Dekalb Community College in Clarkston, Georgia. He was a contributing editor and book review editor with *Atlanta* magazine from 1978 to 1982.

Cook wrote his first novel, *Blood Innocents* (1980), while still in graduate school. He circulated it without an agent and it quickly found a publisher. It is a police procedural and, setting a tone for his later works, was as much about the moral challenges to his main character as the pursuit of the criminal.

His next book, *The Orchids* (1982), was commended for its more literary qualities. Cook wrote more procedurals and books featuring an ex-cop turned private detective, Frank Clemons.

But Cook wasn't pleased with the Clemons trilogy. "These books were very much in the tradition of the classic detective story," he said in a *January Magazine* interview.

> I found that I didn't like my main character very much after a while. He was sad and boring and I hated spending time with him. He was very close to the line of self-pity, and that is a line that can't be crossed.

Cook favors atmosphere over plot haste. He falls through the cracks of puzzle crafters and thriller writers. He's interested in individuals, in surroundings, in personal history. He often incorporates elements of classic mythology in his works.

"I never really know what my books are going to be about," he told Crime Time's Michael Carlson. "It would probably be easier to go with a sure-fire formula, but I just can't work that way." He admitted that his rebellion against formula makes his books harder to market in the United States, though he has a very substantial following in France, England, and Japan.

"In my literary novels I would like to help bring back what I think of as the 'meditative novel,'" the author told Contemporary Authors, "that is, the work with a quiet, reasoned, and highly reflective voice."

He returns to familiar themes, such as the abduction or killing of an offspring, in *Red Leaves* (2005) and *The Fate of Katherine Carr* (2009). "I think the loss of a child is one of the most profound experience of human life," he said in an interview with Julia Buckley. "I can think of nothing that could propel an individual or a family into a more heightened state of crisis."

In spite of his use of recurrent themes, Cook enjoys the freedom of creating new characters with each novel. He's empowered by his maverick stance on genre.

"When a reader feels that a writer is moved by the situation and really cares about the people," he told journalist Robert Dahlin of *Publishers Weekly*, "the book gains a resonance, which can create the sense of a crossover book. It can interest readers of general fiction as well as those who like to read mysteries."

As he continues to investigate new directions in his writing, Cook never fails to keep his readers turning the pages in anticipation.

Works by the Author

Blood Innocents (1980)

The Orchids (1982)

Tabernacle (1983)

Elena (1986)

Streets of Fire (1989)

The City When it Rains (1991)

Evidence of Blood (1991)

Mortal Memory (1993)

Breakheart Hill (1995)

The Chatham School Affair (1996)

Instruments of the Night (1998)

Places in the Dark (2000)

The Interrogation (2002)

Moon over Manhattan, with Larry King (2002)

Taken (2002)

Into the Web (2004)

Peril (2004)

Red Leaves (2005)

The Murmur of Stones (2006), also titled *The Cloud of Unknowing*

Master of the Delta (2008)

A Thomas H. Cook Omnibus (2008)

The Fate of Katherine Carr (2009)

The Last Talk with Lola Faye (2010)

The Quest for Anna Klein (2011)

Frank Clemons Series

Sacrificial Ground (1988)

Flesh and Blood (1989)

Night Secrets (1990)

Contributor

Best American Mystery Stories of 1999 (1999), includes "Fatherhood"

Dangerous Women: Original Stories from Today's Greatest Suspense Writers, edited by Lorenzo Carcaterra (2005), includes "What She Offered"

On a Raven's Wing: New Tales in Honor of Edgar Allan Poe, edited by Stuart Kaminsky (2009)

Editor, with Otto Penzler

Best American Crime Writing (2002)

Best American Crime Writing (2003)

Best American Crime Writing (2004)

Best American Crime Writing (2005)

The author has also written true crime books.

For Further Information

Buckley, Julia, "Thomas H. Cook on The Whims of Fate, The Artistic Imagination, and The Saddest Places on Earth," Poe's Deadly Daughters, May 23, 2009, http://poesdeadlydaughters.blogspot.com/2009/05/thomas-h-cook-on-whims-of-fate-artistic.html/ (viewed Oct. 14, 2009).

Carlson, Michael, "Thomas H. Cook: My Characters Are Fighting Inevitability," *Crime Time*, http://www.crimetime.co.uk/community/mag.php/showarticle/1353/ (viewed Oct. 14, 2009).

Dahlin, Robert, Thomas H. Cook profile, *Publishers Weekly*, Oct. 19, 1998.

Foster, Jordan, "Master of Crisis and Crime," *Publishers Weekly*, April 7, 2008.

Karim, Ali, "The Great Unknown Psst! Thomas H. Cook," *January Magazine,* Sept. 11, 2009, http://januarymagazine.com/2009/09/interview-thomas-h-cook.html (viewed Oct. 14, 2009).

Thomas H. Cook interview, Kacey Kowars Show, Jan. 26, 1005/ http://www.kaceykowarsshow.com/authors/cook.html/ (viewed Oct. 14, 2009).

Thomas H. Cook profile, Contemporary Authors Online, Biography Resource Center, http://galenet.galegroup.com/servlet/BioRC/ (viewed Oct. 14, 2009).

Patricia Cornwell

Miami, Florida
1956

Police Procedural
Benchmark Series: Dr. Kay Scarpetta

About the Author and the Author's Writing

If she didn't invent the forensics crime novel, Patricia Cornwell nevertheless sent it charging onto the bestseller lists and has dominated the subgenre of crime fiction since her debut book *Postmortem* (1991), the first of the series to feature Dr. Kay Scarpetta. That novel earned the author Edgar, John Creasey, Anthony, and Macavity awards—plus a Prix du Roman d'Adventure.

Technical aspects of her novels oblige the author to keep up with the latest in crime-solving methods. In *The Scarpetta Factor* (2009), she said on her website, she rode with the pros. "I'm describing what I saw. I spent a lot of time visiting various facilities and having their equipment and procedures explained in detail." There was one exception: "no, I certainly didn't 'ride' with the bomb squad."

Patricia Daniels was born in 1956 in Miami, Florida. Her parents divorced when she was seven, and Patricia and two siblings moved with their mother to North Carolina. In 1979, she received a B.A. in literature from Davidson College. She married Charles Cornwell in 1980. A decade later they divorced.

Patricia was a crime reporter for the *Charlotte Observer* in North Carolina from 1979 to 1981. She wrote a biography of Ruth Bell Graham, the wife of the Rev. Billy Graham, in 1983.

From 1985 to 1991, Cornwell worked as a computer analyst in the office of the chief medical examiner of Richmond, Virginia. She went to medical school lectures, attended trials, and did library medical research. She witnessed autopsies but found them difficult to bear. "Especially the smells. People don't know that about me, they assume I find it easy or entertaining. I don't get used to it," she said in an interview with *The Telegraph*'s Nigel Farndale.

Chief Medical Examiner Scarpetta and Detective Sergeant Pete Marino, in their debut appearance, pursue a serial killer who has brutalized and strangled three women in their own bedrooms.

In 1997 the author began a second series featuring Police Chief Judy Hammer of Charlotte. Massachusetts State Investigator Winston Garano heads the at-risk team in a third Cornwell series, which began with *At Risk* (2006).

Cornwell has modeled some of her characters on real people, including Senator Orrin Hatch of Utah, Chief Medical Examiner Marcella F. Fierro of Virginia, and forensic anthropologist William Bass, but Scarpetta herself is all fabrication. Or perhaps she is Cornwell herself. Discussing *The Last Precinct* in an iVillage interview, the author said the story reveals a lot about the heroine.

I've done so much research on Kay that, by revealing so much of her, you'll find out more about me. I feel that I fight injustice in my writing. I try to be a scribe to the real people out there who are trying to keep us safe.

In 1995 Cornwell herself faced unwanted publicity when an FBI agent attempted to kill his wife after coming to suspect that she had had a brief lesbian affair with Cornwell. According to Galina Espinoza's profile of the author in *People Weekly*, being forced into the spotlight also forced Cornwell to create "the 'thick skin' she needs to stand up to her critics," particularly those who came to disparage her research for the nonfiction *Portrait of a Killer: Jack the Ripper—Case Closed* (2002).

In *Portrait of a Killer*, Cornwell concludes that painter Walter Sickert was the 1880s London serial killer. Many researchers on Jack the Ripper mocked her methods and her findings. Though she obviously relished the detective work—and purportedly spent an estimated $6 million of her own money in the investigation—Cornwell, with some relief, has since reentered the imaginary world and the writing more Scarpetta and Garano cases.

Works by the Author

Judy Hammer and Andy Brazil Series

Hornet's Nest (1997)

Southern Cross (1999)

Isle of Dogs (2001)

Dr. Kay Scarpetta Series

Body of Evidence (1991)

Postmortem (1991)

All That Remains (1992)

Cruel & Unusual (1993), first of Gault trilogy

The Body Farm (1994), second of Gault trilogy

From Potter's Field (1995), last of Gault trilogy

Cause of Death (1996)

Three Complete Novels (1997), includes *Postmorten, Body of Evidence,* and *All That Remains*

Unnatural Exposure (1997)

Point of Origin (1998)

Black Notice (1999)

The Last Precinct (2000)

Blow Fly (2003)

Trace (2004)

Predator (2005)

Book of the Dead (2007)

Scarpetta (2008)

The Scarpetta Collection, Vol. 1 (2009), includes *Postmortem* and *Body of Evidence*

The Scarpetta Factor (2009)

Port Mortuary (2010)

Winston Garano Series

At Risk (2006)

The Front (2008)

Cornwell contributed to *The Writing Life: Writers on How They Think and Work*, edited by Marie Arana (2003). She also wrote the nonfiction *Coroner's Journal: Forensics and the Art of Stalking Death* (2007), with Louis Cataldie, and *Portrait of a Killer: Jack the Ripper—Case Closed* (2002).

For Further Information

Beahm, George. *The Unofficial Patricia Cornwell Companion: A Guide to the Bestselling Author's Life and Work*. New York: St. Martin's Minotaur, 2002.

Espinoza, Galina, with Diane Herbst, "Killer Instinct: Author Patricia Cornwell Thinks She Has Unmasked a Notorious Serial Killer. Critics Say She Doesn't Know Jack," *People Weekly* Dec. 9, 2002.

Farnsdale, Nigel, "Killer Queen: Patricia Cornwell Interview," *The Telegraph*, Nov. 16, 2009.

Feole, Glenn L., and Don Lasseter. *The Complete Patricia Cornwell Companion*. New York: Berkley Books, 2005.

Herbert, Rosemary, "All That Remains," *The Armchair Detective,* fall 1992.

Muller, Adrian, Patricia Cornwell entry, *St. James Guide to Crime & Mystery Writers*, fourth edition, edited by Jay P. Pederson. Detroit: St. James Press, 1996.

"Patricia Cornwell: Kay and I Went through the Same Pain," iVillage, http://www.ivillage.com/books/intervu/myst/articles/0,11872,240795_192641,00.html/ (viewed May 13, 2003).

Patricia Cornwell website. http://www.patriciacornwell.com/q-and-a (viewed Jan. 28, 2010).

Peter Corris

Irina Dunn

Stawell, Victoria, Australia
1942

Police Procedural
Benchmark Series: Cliff Hardy

About the Author and the Author's Writing

Cliff Hardy has been the go-to man to solve complicated crimes in Australia for some three decades. The licensed private investigator had served in the army, studied law, and honed his skills as an insurance investigator. His clients aren't always society's top notch, but Hardy relishes a challenge.

In his novel *The Dying Trade* (1980), Peter Corris borrowed generously from the Hammett–Chandler–Macdonald school of private-eye fiction when he brought Hardy to life to find the missing twin sister of a real estate heiress.

In a Crime Down Under conversation, the author said

> I wrote *The Dying Trade* just to see if I could write the kind of recreational fiction I most enjoyed reading at that time. . . . I enjoyed the actual writing so much that I wrote the second book that became *White Meat* and made a start on the third.

Corris quickly mastered the heartbeat of the private detective with a conscience. He captured the appropriate setting as well. According to Maxim Jakubowski of *St. James Guide to Crime & Mystery Writers,*

> The steamy mean streets of Sydney emerge as an unforgettable locale, blowsy, rough, vital, and corrupt, but still sprawling, indolent and beautiful in the way the Los Angeles of yesteryear was in the Lew Archer books of Ross Macdonald or Chandler's Philip Marlowe tales.

Born in Stawell, Victoria, Australia, in 1942, Corris received a B.A. from the University of Melbourne and an M.A. from Monash University. He subsequently completed requirements for a Ph.D. from Australian National University. He and his wife, Jean Bedford, live near Sydney and have three daughters.

Corris worked as an instructor at several universities and also as a researcher and writer. He was literary editor of the *National Times* in 1980 and 1981. Trained as a historian, he wrote several nonfiction books, beginning with *Aborigines and Europeans in Western Victoria* (1968). Although he has written novels in three other series—featuring former detective Luke Dunlop, government agent Ray "Creepy" Crawley and his sidekick Huck, and old-time amateur actor Richard Browning—he has particularly remained faithful to Cliff Hardy.

It took Corris five years to write the first Hardy manuscript and find a publisher. Hardy was initially a harder drinker and a rude character. Although the author denies that he is depicting himself in the Hardy books, the two evolved along similar lines.

"I stopped smoking about one or two books in," he said in a Matilda interview, "Cliff stopped smoking. I started jogging and trying to take better care of myself five or six books in. Cliff starts exercising. I try to keep alcohol consumption down. Likewise, Cliff cuts down his drinking."

Corris works in both the novel and short-story format with Hardy. Of the collection *Saving Billie* (2005), *Booklist* reviewer David Pitt commented, "Hardy's resourcefulness apparently knows no bounds. The stories are uniformly strong, proving that Corris is as proficient with the short form as he is with the full-length novel."

The number of plot ideas Corris generates may reflect how deep the character is within him. "I'm conscious more and more these days that I'm rehearsing the books in between the writing sessions," he said in *The Age*. "I'm much more aware now than I used to be that I'm going through a dialogue and scenes for the books when I'm at the gym or walking the dog."

If this sounds as if the author can't get away from his work, it's true. However, he sees it all as part of his obligation, now a very comfortable obligation. "I believe that my only talent is as a storyteller," he told *Contemporary Authors*. "I am suspicious of experimental writing and originality. Various personal concerns, such as a dislike of religion and conservative politics and an interest in sports and literature, surface in my books, but I try to amuse, not instruct."

Works by the Author

The Winning Side (1989)

The Gulliver Fortune (1990)

Naismith's Dominion (1991)

Wimmera Gold (1994)

Blood Brothers (2008)

Cliff Hardy Series

The Dying Trade (1980)

White Meat (1981)

The Marvelous Boy (1982)

The Empty Beach (1983)

Heroin Annie: And Other Cliff Hardy Stories (1984)

The Big Drop: And Other Cliff Hardy Stories (1985)

Make Me Rich (1985)

Deal Me Out (1986)

The Greenwich Apartments (1986)

A Cliff Hardy Collection (1987), omnibus

The January Zone (1987)

The Man in the Shadows (1988)

Man in the Shadows and Other Stories (1988)

O'Fear (1989)

Aftershock (1991)

Wet Graves (1991)

Beware of the Dog (1992)

Burn: And Other Stories (1993)

Matrimonial Causes (1993)

Casino (1994)

Forget Me If You Can: Cliff Hardy Stories (1997)

The Washington Club (1997)

The Reward (1998)

The Black Prince (1999)

The Other Side of Sorrow (1999)

Lugarno (2001)

Salt and Blood (2002)

Master's Mates (2003)

The Coast Road (2004)

Taking Care of Business (2004)

Saving Billie (2005)

The Undertow (2006)

Appeal Denied (2007)

The Big Score: Cliff Hardy Cases (2007)

Open File (2008)

Deep Water (2009)

Torn Apart (2010)

Ray "Creepy" Crawley Series

The Baltic Business (1988)

The Kimberley Killing (1989)

The Cargo Club (1990)

The Azanian Action (1991)

The Japanese Job (1992)

The Vietnam Volunteer (2000)

Luke Dunlop Series

Set Up (1992)

Cross Off (1993)

Get Even (1994)

Richard Browning Series

Beverly Hills Browning: From Tapes among the Papers of Richard Browning (1987)

Box Office Browning (1991)

Browning in Buckskin: From the Tapes and Papers of Richard Browning (1991)

Browning P.I. (1992)

Browning Battles On (1993)

Browning without a Cause (1995)

Adaptations in Other Media

The Empty Beach (1995), film
   The author has also written many nonfiction books of history, sports, and biography.

For Further Information

Cuope, Stuart, "Crime and the Corris Factor," *The Age*, Aug. 30, 2003, ttp://www.theage.com.au/articles/2003/08/27/1061663846146.html/ (viewed Sept. 24, 2009).

Coupe, Stuart, *Peter Corris: A Biography*. Australia: Unwin & Allen, 1998.

Jakubowski, Maxim, Peter Corris profile, *St. James Guide to Crime & Mystery Writers*, fourth edition, edited by Jay P. Pederson. Detroit: St. James Press, 1996.

Middlemiss, Perry, "Peter Corris Interview," Matilda, http://www.middlemiss.org/matilda/2009/04/peter-corris-interview.html/ (viewed Sept. 24, 2009).

Peter Corris interview, Crime Down Under, http://afterdarkmysweet.blogspot.com/2008/03/australian-crime-fiction-snapshot-peter_07.html/ (viewed Sept. 24, 2009).

Peter Corris profile, Contemporary Authors, http://galenet.galegroup.com/servlet/BioRC/ (viewed Sept. 24, 2009).

Peter Corris web page, http://www.petercorris.net/ (viewed Sept. 24, 2009).

Bill Crider

Mexia, Texas
1941

Police Procedural, Private Detective,
Amateur Detective, Academic Mystery,
Westerns, Horror
Benchmark Series: Sheriff Dan Rhodes

Judy Crider

About the Author and the Author's Writing

Bill Crider has written mystery, crime, western, horror, espionage, and young adult novels steadily since the late 1980s—so many books in several series that it is surprising to learn that writing was not his first career choice.

"When I was in the fifth grade, I was sure I was going to be a Major League baseball player," he said on his website. "The fact that I had 20/200 vision, lousy coordination, and poor bat speed, plus the fact that it takes me about five minutes to run the bases, pretty much put an end to that idea."

In high school, he settled on a second career option: to teach and write. That he handily achieved.

Crider was born in Mexia, Texas, in 1941. He received a B.A. from the University of Texas at Austin in 1963, an M.A. from North Texas State University in 1966, and a Ph.D. from the University of Texas in 1972. In 1965 he married Judy Stutts. They have two children and live in Alvin, Texas. Crider taught high school English in Corsicana, Texas, for two years before he joined the English faculty at Howard Payne University for a dozen years. He then joined Alvin Community College and, during the 19 years before he retired in 2002, served as department chairman.

Crider wrote his dissertation on the hard-boiled crime novels of Raymond Chandler and Dashiell Hammet. He enjoys reading horror and gritty crime novels by John D. MacDonald, Charles Williams, Vin Packer, and Day Keene, but his writing falls into the category of comfortable if not cozy.

Consider the Dan Rhodes books, Crider's earliest and longest-running series. The sheriff–hero solves crimes in rural Clearview, Texas. The small town and its denizens are as much a feature of the books as the crimes. *Murder Among the O.W.L.S.* (2007), for instance, finds Rhodes investigating the death, apparently due to accidental fall, of Helen Harris, a 70-year-old member of the Older Women's Literary Society (O.W.L.S.). "The laconic lawman brings his dry wit and down-home sensibilities to bear on the investigation," said *Texas Monthly* reviewer Mike Shea. "One could fault Crider for the happy sheen he applies to the mystery genre, but that would be to miss the point entirely."

To read a Sheriff Dan Rhodes novel is to learn whether he has been successful in keeping his wife, Ivy, in the dark about his latest yen for fast food; to see how long his dispatcher Hack and jailer Lawton can keep useful information from him; whether his deputy, Ruth Grady, will show up in time to rescue him from a severe beating at the hands of some miscreant or other; or what the latest Gold Medal paperback novel Clyde Ballinger, the undertaker, is reading.

In discussing another Rhodes entry, *Murder in Four Parts* (2009), *Booklist* reviewer Wes Lukowsky says that "Rhodes is a keen, wryly observant and nonjudgmental investigator. He sees the humor as well as the pain in the lives we lead—a combination that makes for an entertaining entry in a very likable series."

Crider's first venture into writing a series novel arose as a result of a friend's invitation. They produced a Nick Carter, Killmaster paperback that came out in 1981. Crider then wrote stand-alone westerns and a handful of horror novels under the pen name Jack MacLane. And he wrote dozens of short stories, some featuring his series characters, such as Rhodes or college professor Carl Burns or Sally Good.

In a Mystery One Bookstore conversation, the author said,

> Both Carl and Sally are English department chairs, and both of them remind me a little of me. Some of the experiences they have, and some of the student papers they grade, are awfully close to reality. The murders, of course, are all made up.

Crider partnered with television weatherman Willard Scott to craft two crime novels featuring Stanley Waters, a TV weatherman (naturally). "Crider captures the subtle jealousies, affections and motives only small towns can offer," said *Booklist* reviewer Wes Lukowsky of *Murder in the Mist* (1999). With Clyde Wilson, he has written two novels featuring Houston private eye Ted Stevens.

He has written three Mike Gonzo tales for young adult readers and one juvenile novel based on the popular Public Television character Wishbone. *We'll Always Have Murder* (2003) has as the main character the actor Humphrey Bogart.

Crider's private detective Truman Smith mostly fishes and reads Faulkner on Galveston Island in Texas, taking cases only as necessary. *Publishers Weekly* reviewer Sybil Steinberg said of *Dead on the Island* (1991), "Crider has created another well-drawn protagonist, this time a moody, introspective PI in the finest tradition, who works in a seamy city smoldering with old and dangerous secrets."

Crider, who is a regular writer of book reviews for print and electronic media, is a student of the mystery novel form. "I like and read all kinds, the tough guy stuff and the cozies," he said in an interview with Steve Hockensmith of writerinterviews. "Maybe it's the plotting. I became an English teacher because I love stories, and to me, that meant tales with a beginning, a middle, and an end. Mysteries never let me down in that regard."

Works by the Author

Galveston Gunman (1988)

Ryan Rides Back (1988)

A Time for Hanging (1989)

Medicine Show (1990)

A Vampire Named Fred (1990)

Blood Marks (1991)

The Texas Capitol Murders (1992)

Outrage at Blanco (1998)

Texas Vigilante (1999)

We'll Always Have Murder (2003)

Carl Burns Series

One Dead Dean (1988)

Dying Voices (1989)

A Dangerous Thing (1994)

Dead Soldiers (2004)

Sally Good Series

Murder Is an Art (1999)

A Knife in the Back (2002)

A Bond with Death (2004)

Sheriff Dan Rhodes Series

Too Late to Die (1986)

Shotgun Saturday Night (1987)

Cursed to Death (1988)

Death on the Move (1989)

Evil at the Root (1990)

Booked for a Hanging (1992)

Murder Most Fowl (1994)

Winning Can Be Murder (1996)

Death by Accident (1997)

A Ghost of a Chance (2000)

A Romantic Way to Die (2001)

Red, White, and Blue Murder (2003)

A Mammoth Murder (2006)

Murder among the O.W.L.S. (2007)

Of All Sad Words (2008)

Murder in Four Parts (2009)

Murder in the Air (2010)

Stanley Waters Series, with Willard Scott

Murder under Blue Skies (1998)

Murder in the Mist (1999)

Ted Stevens Series, with Clyde Wilson

Houston Homicide (2007)

Mississippi Vivian (2010)

Truman Smith Series

Dead on the Island (1991)

Gator Kill (1992)

When Old Men Die (1994)

The Prairie Chicken Kill (1996)

Murder Takes a Break (1997)

Collection

The Nighttime Is the Right Time (2000)

Contributor

Fourteen Vicious Valentines, edited by Rosalind Greenberg, Martin Greenberg, and Charles Waugh (1988), includes "My Heart Cries for You"

Westeryear, edited by Edward Gorman (1988), includes "Wolf Night"

The Nighttime Is the Right Time (1991)

Obsessions, edited by Gary Raisor (1991), includes "Franklin and the Can of Whup-Ass"

Cat Crimes, edited by Ed Gorman and Martin Greenberg (1992), includes "Buster," featuring Dan Rhodes

Cat Crimes II, edited by Ed Gorman and Martin Greenberg (1992), includes "The New Black Cat"

Cat Crimes III, edited by Ed Gorman and Martin Greenberg (1992), includes "Cat Burglar"

Christmas Stalkings, edited by Charlotte MacLed (1992), includes "The Santa Claus Caper"

Dark at Heart, edited by Joe and Karen Lansdale (1992), includes "An Evening Out with Carl"

Cat Crimes IV, edited by Carol-Lynn Waugh and Martin Greenberg (1993), includes "Code Red: Terror on the Mall"

Santa Clues, edited by Carol-Lynn Waugh and Martin Greenberg (1993), includes "The Night Before Christmas," featuring Carl Burns

Cat Crimes V, edited by Ed Gorman and Martin Greenber (1994), includes "Cap'n Bob and Gus"

Celebrity Vampires, edited by Martin Greenberg (1994), includes "King of the Night"

Dark Destiny, edited by Ed Kramer (1994), includes "But I See the Bright Eyes"

Murder for Father, edited by Martin Greenberg (1994), includes "Blest Be the Ties"

Murder for Mother, edited by Martin Greenberg (1994), includes "A Matter of the Heart," featuring Truman Smith

The Mysterious West, edited by Tony Hillerman (1994), includes "Who Killed Cock Rogers?," featuring Dan Rhodes

Partners in Crime, edited by Elaine Raco Chase (1994), includes "See What the Boys in the Locked Room Will Have"

Women on the Edge, edited by Martin Greenberg (1994), includes "Death's Brother"

Cat Crimes VI, edited by Ed Gorman and Martin Greenberg (1995), includes "How I Found a Cat, Lost True Love and Broke the Bank at Monte Carlo"

City of Darkness Unseen, edited by Erin Kelley and Stewart Wieck (1995), includes "Assault on Treasure Island"

Murder Most Delicious, edited by Ed Gorman (1995), includes "Gored," featuring Dan Rhodes

The Splendor Falls, edited by Erin Kelley (1995), includes "Jack of Thieves"

Truth Until Paradox, edited by Staley Krause and Stewart Wieck (1995), includes "Dreamseeker"

Werewolves, edited by Martin Greenberg (1995), includes "The Nighttime Is the Right Time"

Cat Crimes on Holiday, edited by Martin Greenberg and Ed Gorman (1996), includes "The Easter Cat"

The Fatal Frontier, edited by Ed Gorman and Martin Greenberg (1996), includes "The Hanging of Chick Dupree"

Holmes for the Holidays, edited by Martin Greenberg (1996), includes "The Adventure of the Christmas Ghosts"

Murder Most Irish, edited by Ed Gorman, Larry Segriff, and Martin Greenberg (1996), includes "The Rose of Tralee"

White Houser Horrors, edited by Martin Greenberg and Ed Gorman (1996), includes "The Ghost and Mr. Truman"

Pawn of Chaos: Tales of the Eternal Champion, edited by Stewart Wieck (1997), includes "The Captive Soul"

Urban Nightmares, edited by Jo Sherman (1997), includes "What a Croc!"

Best of the American West II, edited by Ed Gorman and Martin Greenberg (1998), includes "Wherever I Meet with a Deck of Cards"

How the West Was Read II, edited by Bob Randisi (1998), includes "I Am a Roving Gambler"

Midnight Louie's Pet Detectives, edited by Carole Nelson Douglas (1998), includes "El Lobo Rides Alone"

More Holmes for the Holidays, edited by Martin Greenberg, Lon L. Lellenberg, and Carol-Lynn Waugh (1998), includes "The Adventure of the Christmas Boar"

Once Upon a Crime, edited by Ed Gorman and Martin Greenberg (1998), includes "It Happened at Grandmother's House"

Cat Crimes Through Time, edited by Ed Gorman, Martin Greenberg, and Larry Segriff (1999), includes "Tinseltown Follies of 1948"

The New Adventures of Sherlock Holmes, edited by Martin Greenberg, Carol-Lynn Waugh, and Jon L. Lellenberg (1999), includes "The Adventure of the Venomous Lizard"

Till Death Do Us Part (1999), includes "At the Hop," cowritten with Judy Crider

The Blue and the Gray Undercover, edited by Ed Gorman (2001), includes "Belle Boyd, the Rebel Spy"

Death by Horoscope, edited by Anne Perry (2001), includes "Out Like a Lion"

Death Dines at 8:30, edited by Claudia Bishop and Nick DiChario (2001), includes "Chocolate Moose," featuring Dan Rhodes

Murder in Baker Street, edited by Martin Greenberg, Jon Lellenberg, and Daniel Stashower (2001), includes "The Case of the Vampire's Mark"

Murder, Mayhem and Mistletoe, with Terence Faherty, Wendi Lee, and Aileen Schumacher (2001)

Murder Most Celtic, edited by Martin Greenberg (2001), includes "One of Our Leprechauns Is Missing"

For a Few Stories More, edited by Joe R. Lansdale (2002), includes "Jail Bait"

Damned Near Dead: An Anthology of Geezer Noir, edited by Duane Swierczynski (2006)

Editor

Damn Near Dead 2: Live Noir or Die Trying, with Charlaine Harris (2010)

Written as by Jack MacLane

Goodnight Moon (1988)

Keepers of the Beast (1988)

Blood Dreams (1989)

Goodnight Moom (1989)

Just Before Dark (1990)

Rest in Peace (1990)

Written as by Nick Carter Killmaster Series

The Coyote Connection (1981), with Jack Davis

The author has also written one Wishbone juvenile novel and three Mike Gonzo books.

For Further Information

"Bill Crider," *Who Done It?* July–Aug. 2008.

Bill Crider interview, Mystery One Bookstore, http://www.mysteryone.com/JonCrid erInterview.htm/ (viewed Aug. 28, 2009).

Bill Crider profile, Contemporary Authors Online, http://galenet.galegroup.com/serv let/BioRC/ (viewed Aug. 7, 2009).

Bill Crider website. http://www.billcrider.com/ (viewed Aug. 28, 2009).

Hockensmith, Steve, Bill Crider interview, Writerinterviews, http://writerinterviews. blogspot.com/2008/03/bill-crider.html/ (viewed Sept. 2, 2009).

Lukowsky, Wes, *Murder in Four Parts* review, *Booklist*, Feb. 15, 2009.

Lukowsky, Wes, *Murder in the Mist* review, *Booklist*, Jan. 1, 1999.

Shea, Mike, *Murder Among the Owls* review, *Texas Monthly*, Jan. 2007.

Steinberg, Sybil, *Dead on the Island* review, *Publishers Weekly*, April 12, 1991.

Deborah Crombie

Dallas, Texas
1952

Police Procedural
Benchmark Series: Duncan Kincaid and
Gemma James

Steve Ullathorne

About the Author and the Author's Writing

"This atmospheric novel is as much a splendid depiction of London's Notting Hill Road district as it is a harrowing murder mystery," praised Connie Fletcher in her *Booklist* review of *And Justice There Is None* (2002). Author Deborah Crombie, she continued, "weaves the café and pub owners and the stall keepers in Notting Hill Market into the story, giving it a feeling of groundedness that many contemporary mysteries lack."

Would you be surprised to know, then, that Crombie is a native Texan?

Born in Dallas in 1952, the author grew up in suburban Richardson. She learned to read at an early age, thanks to the attention of her maternal grandmother, a retired teacher. In 1976 she graduated from Austin College with a B.S. in biology. After taking part in a Rice University Publishing Program, she traveled to England and lived in Edinburgh, Scotland, and Chester, England, with her first husband, Peter Crombie, until 1981. Deborah had been an anglophile from an early age and, as a teen, had devoured British mysteries. Living in Britain was a dream come true. She took delight in exploring the city and countryside. She worked in newspaper advertising and at the family business (manufacturer's representatives for theatrical concessions). And in 1993 she wrote her first book, while raising her daughter. She now lives with her second husband, Rick Wilson, a policeman, in McKinney, Texas.

Crombie's first of what are now more than a dozen novels features a team of crime solvers, New Scotland Yard Detective Superintendent Duncan Kincaid and Sergeant Gemma James. In their first outing, *A Share in Death* (1993), Kincaid, a bachelor, is attempting to vacation in Yorkshire when he nearly witnesses a murder (an electrocution in a Jacuzzi) and intrudes upon the local investigation. James, meanwhile, a single mom, is still on the job in London and provides remote backup as needed for Kincaid to narrow in on the killer.

The author told Anne Dingus of *Texas Monthly* that she "set out to write a very traditional mystery, with a closed circle of suspects. And I insisted on fair play—the reader should have every clue the detective has."

To keep her settings current, Crombie "reads English newspapers cover to cover, watches British television, and goes with her notebooks to coffee shops" when she makes periodic visits, she said in an AudioFile interview. "People-watching and eavesdropping on conversations are enormously helpful. That, plus all the reading I do, I hear the speech patterns in my head."

When deeper research is required, she dives in with no qualms. "I love doing research," she told Contemporary Authors. "The trick is in not getting carried away, not losing sight of the story in a muddle of detail. What the reader gets is usually only the tip of the iceberg."

In *Where Memories Lie* (2008), the police team investigates a series of apparent accidents that claim the lives of individuals associated with a London auction house. "Crombie raises the suspense by alternating the contemporary story, which includes news of Gemma's mother's battle against cancer, with flashbacks to the investigation of [an] unsolved murder in 1952," a *Publishers Weekly* reviewer commented.

With her series well established, Crombie said on her web page that she now has a good idea where her characters are headed over the next couple of books. When she wrote the first entry, she didn't anticipate that Kincaid and James would become romantically involved. "Some [characters] have developed in unexpected ways," she said, "so that by the end of the book I've found it necessary to change the plot to accommodate those changes. And some of my minor characters have been known to run away with things, which is always great fun."

All of which keeps readers coming back for more.

Works by the Author

Duncan Kincaid and Gemma James Series

A Share in Death (1993)

All Shall Be Well (1994)

Leave the Grave Green (1995)

Mourn Not Your Dead (1996)

Dreaming of the Bones (1997)

Kissed a Sad Goodbye (1999)

A Finer End (2001)

And Justice There Is None (2002)

Now May You Weep (2003)

In a Dark House (2004)

Water Like a Stone (2006)

Where Memories Lie (2008)

Necessary as Blood (2009)

Where Memories Lie (2010)

No Mark Upon Her (announced)

Contributor

The Sunken Sailor, with Simon Brett, Jan Burke, Dorothy Cannell, Margaret Coel, Eileen Dreyer, Carolyn Hart, Edward Marston, Francine Mathews, Sharan Newman, Alexandra Ripley, Walter Satterthwait, Sarah Smith, and Carolyn Wheat (2004)

For Further Information

Deborah Crombie profile, Contemporary Authors Online, http://galenet.galegroup.com/servlet/BioRC/ (viewed Aug. 31, 2009).

Deborah Crombie website, http://www.deborahcrombie.com/ (viewed Sept. 2, 2009).

Dingus, Anne, "Briterature," *Texas Monthly*, Nov. 1997.

Fletcher, Connie, *And Justice There Is None* review, *Booklist*, Aug. 2002.

Henschel, S. J., "Talking with Deborah Crombie," AudioFile, http://www.audiofilemagazine.com/features/A1650.html/ (viewed Sept. 2, 2009).

A Share in Death review, *Publishers Weekly*, Dec. 14, 1992.

Where Memories Lie review, *Publishers Weekly*, June 2, 2008.

Mary Daheim

Seattle, Washington
1937

Amateur Detective
Benchmark Series: Bed & Breakfast

About the Author and the Author's Writing

Author Mary Daheim was itching to get away from the past, so she asked the publisher of her historical romances to take a look at a manuscript for a contemporary mystery. Instant new career.

Daheim, a native of Seattle, Washington, was born in 1937. She took to storytelling early on—by making crude pictures—as a tot. An only child with chronic physical ailments, she was often obliged to entertain herself, she has said. She devoured books as a teen, particularly Cherry Ames juveniles.

"She realized that by becoming a journalist she could accomplish two things: (1) Ask people embarrassing questions in the name of her profession; (2) support herself until she published a book," according to Mystery Lovers Corner.

So Daheim earned a B.A. from the School of Communications at the University of Washington, Seattle, in 1960. She married David C. Daheim, a college professor, and they raised three daughters, who are now grown. She worked as a communications expert with Northwest Bell, other telecommunications companies, and banks. In 1983 she wrote her first novel, *Love's Pirate* (1983), a period romance.

Daheim thrives on research. "I've always written, never wanted to do anything else," she told Contemporary Authors. "I use the historical romance to inform, entertain, and amuse. I like research and do a lot of it. I consider myself a storyteller, not a novelist."

After four paperback originals for the publisher Avon and three for Harlequin, she settled comfortably into the cozy mystery genre with two series.

The first of her Bed & Breakfast books is *Just Desserts* (1991). (The titles often employ puns.) The heroine, Judith McMonigle, is readying her Hillside Manor Inn for the arrival of carpet-sweeper magnate Otto Broadie and his clan. The guests have a rollicking first night, until their hired fortune teller, Madame Gushenka, turns up dead. Her tea was laced with insecticide. McMonigle has more cleaning up to do than she had anticipated, but she won't let the crime go unsolved. She recruits friend Joe Flynn, a policeman, to lure the killer into the open.

Daheim makes the claim, reasonably, to have started the Bed & Breakfast subgenre.

She came by her research easily enough; her family's first experience in a B&B was in Victoria, British Columbia, and they've sampled a good many in the American Northwest.

For her curious offering of characters, Daheim looked no further than her own family. As she said in an About.com interview,

> Judith, for example, was indeed married to a 400-pound man who blew up at the age of 49 and left her a widow with a son named Mike. She went home to live with her mother, who is the basis for Gertrude. Those things have actually happened.

Daheim's second series, the Emma Lord series, also set in Washington, has another amateur female detective, Emma Lord, and begins with *Alpine Advocate* (1992). (The titles are alphabetical.) Lord has been publisher–editor of a weekly newspaper, the *Alpine Advocate*, for a year, and she is yet to land a really big story. But be careful what you wish for. Mark Doukas is murdered. He's the grandson of wealthy Neeny Doukas, who keeps his lips tight to a prying newswoman.

"What begins with an innocent story about the murdered man, ends with Emma conducting the most interesting, and probably the last, interview of her career from the wrong end of a .38," according to a publisher's blurb. A *Publishers Weekly* reviewer found a later series entry, *Alpine Kindred*, full of "witty one-liners and amusing characterizations." What more can fans ask for?

With the 16th book in the series, *The Alpine Pursuit* (2005), the books began to appear in hardcover.

Alpine was once a real town. "I never saw Alpine, but my parents, grandparents and other relatives and friends called the town their home for many years," the author said on her webpage. "The stories and anecdotes handed down were a fascinating testimonial to the hearty souls who lived in this isolated mountain aerie before and after the First World War."

The author has brought the small towns alive with comfortable characters and rich stories—and a dead body now and then.

Works by the Author

Emma Lord Series

The Alpine Advocate (1992)

The Alpine Betrayal (1993)

The Alpine Christmas (1996)

The Alpine Decoy (1994)

The Alpine Escape (1995)

The Alpine Fury (1995)

The Alpine Gamble (1996)

The Alpine Hero (1996)

The Alpine Icon (1998)

The Alpine Journey (1998)

The Alpine Kindred (1999)

The Alpine Legacy (1999)

The Alpine Menace (2000)

The Alpine Nemesis (2001)

The Alpine Obituary (2002)

The Alpine Pursuit (2005)

The Alpine Quilt (2005)

The Alpine Mysteries Omnibus (*The Alpine Advocate/The Alpine Betrayal/The Alpine Christmas*) (2006)

The Alpine Recluse (2006)

The Alpine Scandal (2007)

The Alpine Traitor (2008)

The Alpine Uproar (2009)

The Alpine Vengeance (2011)

Bed & Breakfast Mystery Series

Just Desserts (1991)

Fowl Prey (1992)

Holy Terrors (1992)

Bantam of the Opera (1993)

Dune to Death (1993)

A Fit of Tempera (1994)

Major Vices (1995)

Auntie Mayhem (1996)

Murder, My Suite (1996)

Nutty as a Fruitcake (1996)

September Mourn (1997)

Snow Place to Die (1998)

Wed and Buried (1998)

Legs Benedict (1999)

Creeps Suzette (2000)

A Streetcar Named Expire (2001)

Suture Self (2002)

Silver Scream (2003)

Hocus Croakus (2004)

Dead Man Docking (2005)

This Old Souse (2005)

Saks & Violins (2007)

Scots on the Rocks (2007)

Vi Agra Falls (2008)

Loco Motive (2010)

Contributor

Jessica Fletcher Presents . . . Murder, They Wrote (1997)

Motherhood Is Murder, with Carolyn G. Hart, Jane Isenberg, and Shirley Rousseau (2003)

Sugarplums and Scandal, with Cait London, Dana Cameron, and Suzanne Macpherson (2006)

Daheim is also the author of six historical romances, including *Love's Pirate* (1983).

For Further Information

Alpine Kindred review, *Publishers Weekly*, Dec. 14, 1998.

Arneson, Elizabeth, "Interview with Mary Daheim," About.com, http://bandb.about.com/od/murder/a/mary_daheim.htm/ (viewed July 8, 2009).

"Mary Daheim," Fresh Fiction for Today's Reader, http://freshfiction.com/author.php?id=533/ (viewed July 17, 2009).

"Mary Daheim: Once a Snoop, Always A . . . ," Mystery Lovers Corner, http://www.sleuthedit.com/MaryDaheim/MaryDaheim.html/ (viewed July 17, 2009).

Mary Daheim entry, Contemporary Authors Online, Reproduced in Biography Resource Center, Gale, 2009, http://galenet.galegroup.com/servlet/BioRC/ (viewed July 17, 2009).

Mary Daheim webpage, http://www.authormarydaheim.com/ (viewed July 8, 2009).

Barbara D'Amato

Grand Rapids, Michigan
1938

Private Detective, Police Procedural
Benchmark Series: Cat Marsala

About the Author and the Author's Writing

Readers of Barbara D'Amato novels have come to expect a pleasant variety in theme and setting with each new book. In *Killer.app* (1996), for instance, a Cat Marsala story, a computer programmer named Sheryl Birch tumbles onto a conspiracy within SJR Data-Systems to break into hospital records in Chicago. *Hard Road* (2001), the private detective and her nephew, Jeremy, attend the Chicago Oz Fest and witness two murders—and go on the run to elude the killers.

Details of the real-life story of Bruno Bettelheim, head of the Orthogenic School in Chicago, who told parents of autistic children that their cold approach to child rearing was the cause of their offsprings' affliction, so angered D'Amato that she created his fictional counterpart and made him the victim in *Death of a Thousand Cuts* (2004).

"It seemed horribly cruel to me that he [Bettelheim] would destroy families on what was no more than speculation," D'Amato said in a BookBrowse interview. "I had thought for years that I would write a book like this some day."

The author was born in Grand Rapids, Michigan, in 1938 and grew up in a Boston suburb. She attended Cornell University. In 1958 she married Anthony D'Amato, a law professor; they have two sons. She graduated from Northwestern University in 1971 with a B.A. and received her M.A. the following year. She has worked at a range of jobs, from assistant surgical orderly to carpenter for a stage magic show to researcher for a law office. She has taught mystery writing and been president of Mystery Writers of America (1999–2000) and Sisters in Crime International.

Her first experience writing was a cooperative venture with her husband, crafting two-act musical comedies (*The Magic Man*, 1974, among them) performed in Chicago. Her research into the Dr. John Branion murder case resulted in an episode of *Unsolved Mysteries* (which originally ran on NBC-TV).

Beyond that, she has written crime fiction in the Gerritt De Graaf (beginning in 1980), Cat Marsala (beginning in 1989), and Suze Figueroa and Norm Bennis (beginning in 1996) series.

D'Amato makes great use of the Chicago setting. "Chicago has absolutely everything," the author said in a *Booklist* interview with journalist Connie Fletcher. "It's a beautiful city. It has architecture you'll never see anywhere else. And it has a lot of places to hide. . . . You can also blend in. Chicago has every ethnic neighborhood known to man."

D'Amato doesn't rely on her own experiences in the city. She does considerable research for each new book. In the case of *Hard Luck* (1992), in which she wanted one of the characters to be pushed off the roof of City Hall, she looked further—and that turned out to be a good thing. A roof barrier would have prevented precisely the crime she was going to present. Change of plot. The ninth floor worked.

Tree plantations figured in her novel *Hard Christmas* (1995). "I realized I'd been driving past Christmas tree farms all my life and never knew basic things about growing the trees," she told interviewer Sarah Wisseman. She found a handy murder weapon: the particularly sharp blades growers use to shape their trees.

While she's not preachy about it, D'Amato sees to it that her readers go away from her novels with a little extra lore. As she said in an interview on the Come Unity website,

One of my big hopes with [*White Male Infant*] is that people who read it would take a good look at the possibility of unethical adoption agencies. Of course my main hope is that people would realize how many babies around the world will have no family and in many cases no life unless we do something.

As to her sometimes unorthodox murder methods, "I have a nasty imagination!" she joked to Pat Koch of *Publishers Weekly.* "Seriously, I take an idea, say, where the purpose is to stop the person's breath, and think of the various ways that could be done. If it's unpleasant, that's even more evocative."

Works by the Author

White Male Infant (2002)

Death of a Thousand Cuts (2004)

Foolproof, with Jeanne M. Dams and Mark Richard Zubro (2009)

Other Eyes (2011)

Cat Marsala Series

Hardball (1989)

Hard Tack (1991)

Hard Luck (1992)

Hard Women (1993)

Hard Case (1994)

Hard Christmas (1995)

Hard Bargain (1997)

Hard Evidence (1999)

Hard Road (2001)

Gerritt De Graaf Series

The Hands of Healing Murder (1980)

The Eyes on Utopia Murders (1981)

Suze Figueroa and Norm Bennis Series

Killer.app (1996)

Good Cop, Bad Cop (1998)

Help Me Please (1999)

Authorized Personnel Only (2000)

Writing as Malacai Black (reissued as by Barbara D'Amato)

On My Honor (1989)

Collection

Of Course You Know That Chocolate Is a Vegetable and Other Stories (2000), includes two Marsala stories and six Bennis/Figueroa stories

Contributor

Cat Crimes (1991), includes "The Lower Wacker Hilton"

Sisters in Crime 4 (1992), includes "Stop Thief!"

The Year's 25 Finest Crime and Mystery Stories, second edition (1993), includes "Stop Thief!"

Danger in D.C. (1993), includes "Freedom of the Press"

Deadly Allies 2 (1994), includes "If You've Got the Money, Honey, I've Got the Crime"

Partners in Crime (1994), includes "Soon to Be a Minor Motion Picture"

Celebrity Vampires (1995), includes "I Vant to Be Alone"

Crimes of the Heart (1995), includes "Hard Feelings"

Malice Domestic 5 (1996), includes "Shelved"

Detective Duos (1997), includes "Stop Thief!"

First Cases 2, edited by Robert Randisi (1997), includes "See No Evil"

August is a Good Time for Killing (1998), includes "Freedom of the Press"

First Lady Murders, edited by Nancy Pickard (1999), includes "Dolley Madison and the Staff of Life"

Crème de la Crime (2000), includes "Of Course You Know That Chocolate Is a Vegetable"

Death Dines at 8:30 (2002), includes "Steak Tartare"

On My Honor (2004), includes "Steak Tartare"

Sisters on the Case: Celebrating Twenty Years of Sisters in Crime (2007), includes "Steak Tartare"

Editor

Great Writers & Kids Write Mystery Stories, with Brian D'Amato (1996), includes "Too Violent"

The author and her husband have also scripted stage musicals.

For Further Information

Authorized Personnel Only review, *Publishers Weekly*, Nov. 20, 2000.

Barbara D'Amato interview, Bookbrowse, http://www.bookbrowse.com/author_ interviews/full/index.cfm?author_number = 783/ (viewed Nov. 12, 2009).

Barbara D'Amato website. http://www.barbaradamato.com/ (viewed Nov. 12, 2009).

Fletcher, Connie, "The *Booklist* Interview: Barbara D'Amato," *Booklist*, May 1, 2003.

Johnson, Pam, "*Hard Road* Review," *School Library Journal*, Feb. 2002.

Killer.app review, *Publishers Weekly*, Feb. 26, 1996.

Koch, Pat, "PW Talks with Barbara D'Amato," *Publishers Weekly*, Nov. 20, 2000.

Martin, Allison, "An Interview with Barbara D'Amato Author of 'White Male Infant,'" Come Unity, http://www.comeunity.com/adoption/adopt/interview-damato. html/ (viewed Nov. 12, 2009).

Wisseman, Sarah, "Interview with Barbara D'Amato, Sarah Wisseman, Mystery Author," July 24, 2007, http://sarahwisseman.blogspot.com/2007/07/interview-with-barbara-damato.html/ (viewed Nov. 12, 2009).

Diane Mott Davidson

Honolulu, Hawaii
1949

Amateur Detective, Culinary Mystery
Benchmark Series: Goldy Schulz

About the Author and the Author's Writing

Just because her mystery novels feature a caterer—Goldy Bear Schulz, proprietor of Goldilocks' Catering in Aspen Meadows, Colorado—doesn't mean the books are your typical cozies, insists author Diane Mott Davidson. Once she gets her teeth into a case, Schulz is a tenacious, adept crime solver, the author said. And as more of the heroine's background has been revealed in the series, readers have come to realize that she has very noncozy issues, not the least of them being a former husband who was abusive.

The author was born in Honolulu, Hawaii, in 1949. She grew up in Charlottesville, Virginia, and married James Davidson, an electrical engineer, in 1969. They have three children. She attended Wellesley College and received a double B.A. in art history and political science from Stanford University in 1970. She received an M.A. in art history from Johns Hopkins University in 1976 and then studied at Bishop's School of Theology and the Iliff School of Theology. She has been a teacher in public school and Episcopal Sunday school. Davidson has also volunteered as a rape counselor and a tutor at a juvenile correctional facility. She has been a political activist and is a licensed lay preacher in the Episcopal Church. She has also served on the Episcopal Church's Diocesan Board of Examining Chaplains for a decade. As of this writing, Davidson lives in Evergreen, Colorado.

The determined Davidson wrote three manuscripts before one sold. She initially wanted to be a literary writer and wrote several short stories and a couple of novels. An editor at St. Martin's Press suggested that she work up the elements of a crime and make it a full-fledged mystery novel.

With her youngest son in preschool, Davidson joined a writers group. She made daily visits to a local eatery and wrote. "It was both a café and a catering business," she said in *People Weekly*, "and I became fascinated watching the people and the money they would pay for a catered dinner."

At this point Davidson knew she had the background for her crime solver heroine. But she took nothing for granted. She devoured Julia Child's books about French cooking. She volunteered with the caterer and learned what it was like to serve a hundred people at a wedding or fundraiser or political gathering. She interviewed policemen with the Jefferson County Sheriff's Department to learn more about professionals and their routines. The bonus recipes in her books come from her own kitchen experiences.

In *The Cereal Murders* (1993), the third in the Goldy Schulz series, Goldy is 31 years old and is raising Archie, her 12-year-old son. She is divorced from Dr. John Korman, whom she refers to as The Jerk, and has a new romantic interest (and eventual husband), police detective Tom Shulz.

"The book proves to be a light but delicious combination of unique personalities, first-rate recipes and sustained suspense," said *Publishers Weekly*, "with only a surfeit of red herrings for leftovers."

Fourteen books and an Anthony Award from Bouchercon later, she is one of the leading practitioners of the culinary mystery. And sometimes they are edgy mysteries as well.

For example, the tone is darker in *Double Shot* (2004), in which Goldy's venal ex, paroled early from his jail sentence for underhanded business dealings, comes back into her life. But only for a brief time. Someone kills him, and Goldy is the prime suspect.

Davidson touches on the subject of spousal abuse and might have gone further in expressing her outrage had her editor allowed. Then another opportunity arose for her to discuss the topic. To celebrate the 150th anniversary of Denver, the *Rocky Mountain News* commissioned fiction writers to use the city as a setting for new stories. Davidson wrote the short story "Beginnings" and delved into Goldy's earlier days, her experiences as an abused wife, and her transformation into a self-sufficient, independent woman.

The author told reporter Patti Thorn of *Rocky Mountain News*,

> I absolutely wanted to convey a sense of hope in this story, because so many movies and novels just end with this terribly downbeat denouement. . . . I think it's in the book of Proverbs where you have the quotation, "Without a vision, the people perish." And so that's what she gets in this story.

In *Double Shot*, Davidson looks at the relationship between Goldy and Tom and Tom's depression when he fails to solve a case.

The author had a conversation with a Denver police officer about what it was like to think of oneself as a failure. "The detective talked about withdrawing from those around him. He had seen people who died young, died in accidents, people losing children—all this was helpful in bringing out Tom's feelings and Goldy's helplessness at reaching out to him," the author told journalist Cynthia Bowan.

So no, Diane Mott Davidson's mysteries are not your typical cozies. But they're darned good novels.

Works by the Author

Goldy Schulz Series

Catering to Nobody (1990)

Dying for Chocolate (1992)

The Cereal Murders (1993)

The Last Suppers (1994)

Killer Pancake (1995)

The Main Corpse (1996)

The Grilling Season (1997)

Prime Cut (1998)

Tough Cookie (2000)

Sticks and Scones (2001)

Chopping Spree (2002)

Double Shot (2004)

Dark Tort (2006)

Sweet Revenge (2007)

Fatally Flaky (2009)

Crunch Time (2011)

Contributor

A Dozen in Denver, with Margaret Coel, Pam Houston, Sandra Dallas, Nick Arvin, Joanne Greenberg, Connie Willis, Manuel Ramos, Arnold Grossman, Robert Greer, Laura Pritchett, and Robert Pogue Ziegler (2009), includes "Beginnings"

For Further Information

Bowan, Cynthia, "A Recipe for Crime: Interview with Diane Mott Davidson," Chef2 Chef Culinary Portal, http://74.125.93.132/search?q=cache:ms0axnRHAioJ: www.chef2chef.net/features/cynthia/article/2004–11.htm+Diane+Mott+David son+interview&cd=6&hl=en&ct=clnk&gl=us/ (viewed Oct. 2, 2009).

Cereal Murders review, *Publishers Weekly*, Sept. 20, 1993.

Diane Mott Davidson web page, Random House, http://www.harpercollins.com/ author/microsite/about.aspx?authorid=25347/ (viewed Oct. 2, 2009)

Fatally Flaky review, *Publishers Weekly*, Feb. 23, 2009.

Pour-El, I., *Double Shot* review, *Library Journal*, May 1, 2005.

Sanz, Cynthia, "Murder on the Menu," *People Weekly*, Sept. 30, 1996.

Steinberg, Sybil, *Catering to Nobody* review, *Publishers Weekly*, June 29, 1990.

Thorn, Patti, "A Dozen on Denver: Interview with Author Diane Mott Davidson," *Rocky Mountain News*, Nov. 3, 2008.

Paul C. Doherty

Middlesborough, England
1946

Private Detective, Historical Mystery
Benchmark Series: Hugh Corbett
Medieval Mysteries

About the Author and the Author's Writing

Paul C. Doherty thinks he knows something history doesn't when it comes to the death of England's King Edward II. Doherty, according to his website, has long wanted to petition the Privy Council to open the king's tomb in Gloucester Cathedral, as he believes that it contains not the king's body but that of an imposter. The real Edward II escaped imprisonment and lived his last years in exile in Italy, or so Doherty claims.

Whether that aspiration comes to fruition, Doherty put his theory to paper for his first novel, *The Death of a King* (1985), and was pleased with the result.

Doherty told interviewer Michael Shankland,

> I tend to regard historical fiction as speculative history. In other words, it allows you to experience, to theorize as well as to create an imaginative environment for the theorizing to take place. I began writing historical fiction because I wished to speculate in my novel *The Death of a King* about the possible fate of Edward II.

As Doherty well knew, there is no shortage of historical crimes, murders, and puzzles to be brushed off and rerendered as mystery novels. He came upon many of his ideas while writing his thesis for Oxford University. "One of the fascinating things I came across," he told Don Herron of *Publishers Weekly,* "were all these horrible crimes hidden away in the records of the court, which cried out to be written about. . . . [I]t's very important to convince your reader that what you're writing about is actually based on fact."

Writing historical crime novels has largely been a backup career for Doherty, who works by day as a school headmaster. Born in 1946 in Middlesborough, England, he attended Liverpool University from 1968 to 1972 and received a first class honors degree. At Exeter College, Oxford, he earned B.A., D.Phil., and Ph.D., the last in 1977. He studied for the Catholic priesthood at Durham for three years but left to become a teacher and, since 1981, has been school administrator at Trinity Catholic School. He met his future wife, Carla Lynn Corbitt, at Exeter. They have six children and live near Epping Forest, between London and Essex.

Once he began writing, Doherty was prolific, averaging three novels a year in both freestanding and series form and set in the Middle Ages, ancient Greece, Italy, Egypt, and elsewhere. The books have appeared under his name and, until the last few years, under several pseudonyms.

The author has written of Brother Athelstan, a Dominican friar; and (as Michael Clynes) of Roger Shallot, right hand to Cardinal Wolsey and Henry VII; as Ann Dukthas, he has written of Nicholas Segalla, a time traveler in 16th-century Europe; finally, as C. L. Grace, he has written of Kathryn Swinbrokke, a physician in 15th-century Canterbury.

If it strains credulity to find a woman detective in olden times, it shouldn't. Doherty knows his facts. "In 1322 Edward II hired Mathilda of Westminster (London's most skilled physician) to keep an eye on his health and particularly provide safeguards against poisons (everyone wanted Edward II dead, including the wife!)," Doherty explained in a *SHOTS* magazine conversation.

Besides providing sufficient details to make his settings real, Doherty said he is cognizant of anachronistic language. He avoids it.

Nor is he simply content to create a puzzle and glide to a solution. He often devises locked-room riddles. "I think it's like a game of chess," he said in a conversation with Don Herron for *Publishers Weekly*. "If I kill somebody, what I do is try and pass the death off as an accident, or too impossible to solve, and that's the real challenge that faces the investigator."

With all these series set in different times and on different continents, does he ever become confused? On the contrary, he told Herron, each culture is so distinct—some are leisurely and rich, some are fast-paced and violent—he quickly becomes immersed in his settings and characters.

To interviewer Nickie Fleming of Historical Fiction, he said,

> I only write what I have researched. Accordingly, I don't get confused. For an Egyptian novel, I try and get myself into the mindset, conjure up the images and contrasts of Ancient Egypt, the heat of the day, the cold of the night, their fascination with death and its rituals etc.

And there remain plenty of records to inspire more books. He has researched, he has said, such arcane documents as the records of tomb robbing in ancient Egypt through the Papyrus Salt 1234 in the British Library.

The longest-running of Doherty's series has featured Hugh Corbett, clerk to Edward I and holder of the Secret Seal. Corbett's first appearance was in *Satan in St. Mary's* (1986), when he took on the investigation of a murder, possibly by a Satanist cult. His recent outing, *The Magician's Death* (2009), was said by *Booklist* reviewer Margaret Flanagan to have a mystery to match that in Dan Brown's *The Da Vinci Code*. "Corbett has his work cut out for him as he attempts to unravel a labyrinthine plot to destroy Edward's secret chancery of royal spies. The always reliable Doherty delivers another complexly constructed, authentically detailed historical whodunit."

Literature, not history, inspired one series, takeoffs on Geoffrey Chaucer's *Canterbury Tales*. *A Haunt of Murder* (2008), told by the clerk of Oxford, is characteristically Doherty, as a *Publishers Weekly* reviewer opined: "Evoking the medieval world through sparing use of period detail and language, veteran British author Doherty weaves an intricate and suspenseful tale sure to please both longtime fans and newcomers."

Works by the Author

The Death of a King: A Medieval Mystery (1985)

Prince Drakulya (1986)

Dove amongst the Hawks (1990)

The Fate of Princes (1990)

The Masked Man (1991)

The Haunting (1997)

The Rose Demon (1997)

The Soul Slayer (1998)

The Plague Lord (2002)

The Death of the Red King (2006)

Amerotke Series

The Mask of Ra (1998)

The Horus Killings (1999)

The Anubis Slayings (2000)

The Slayers of Seth (2001)

The Assassins of Isis (2004)

The Poisoner of Ptah (2007)

The Spies of Sobeck (2008)

Ancient Rome Series

Domina (2002)

Murder Imperial (2003)

The Song of the Gladiator (2004)

The Queen of the Night (2006)

Murder's Immortal Mask (2008)

Canterbury Tales/Nicholas Chirke Series

An Ancient Evil, Being the Knight's Tale (1994)

A Tournament of Murders, Being the Franklin's Tale (1997)

Ghostly Murders, Being the Priest's Tale (1998)

A Tapestry of Murders, Being the Man of Law's Tale (1998)

A Haunt of Murder (2003)

The Hangman's Hymn: The Carpenter's Tale of Mystery and Murder as He Goes on a Pilgrimage from London to Canterbury (2004)

Egyptian Mystery Series

An Evil Spirit out of the West (2003)

The Season of the Hyaena (2005)

The Year of the Cobra (2006)

Hugh Corbett Series

Satan in St. Mary's (1986)

The Crown in Darkness (1988)

Spy in Chancery (1988)

The Angel of Death (1989)

Murder Wears a Cowl (1992)

The Prince of Darkness (1992)

The Assassin in the Greenwood (1993)

The Song of a Dark Angel (1994)

Satan's Fire (1995)

The Devil's Hunt (1996)

The Demon Archer (1999)

The Treason of the Ghosts (2000)

Corpse Candle (2001)

The Magician's Death (2004)

The Waxman Murders (2006)

Nightshade (2008)

The Mysterium (2010)

Mathilde of Westminster Series

The Cup of Ghosts (2005)

The Poison Maiden (2007)

The Darkening Glass (2009)

Dark Tower (announced)

Matthew Jenkyn Series

The Whyte Harte (1988)

The Serpent Amongst the Lilies (1990)

Mystery of Alexander the Great Series

The House of Death (2000)

The Godless Man (2002)

The Gates of Hell (2003)

Templars Series

The Templar (2007)

The Templar Magician (2009)

Contributor

Past Poisons: An Ellis Peters Memorial Anthology of Historic Crime (2005)

Written as by Anna Apostolou, Alexander the Great Series

A Murder in Macedon (1997)

A Murder in Thebes (1998)

Written as by Michael Clynes, Sir Roger Shallot Series

The White Rose Murders (1991)

The Poisoned Chalice (1992)

The Grail Murders (1993)

A Brood of Vipers (1994)

The Gallows Murders (1995)

The Relic Murders (1996)

Written as by Ann Dukthas, Nicholas Segalla Series

A Time for the Death of a King (1994)

The Prince Lost to Time (1995)

The Time of Murder at Mayerling (1996)

In the Time of the Poisoned Queen (1998)

Written as by C. L. Grace, Kathryn Swinbrooke Series

A Shrine of Murders (1993)

The Eye of God (1994)

The Merchant of Death (1995)

The Book of Shadows (1996)

Saintly Murders (2001)

A Maze of Murders (2003)

Written as by Paul Harding, Brother Athelstan Series

The Nightingale Gallery (1991)

The House of the Red Slayer (1992), also titled *The Red Slayer*

Murder Most Holy (1992)

The Anger of God (1993)

By Murder's Bright Light (1994)

The House of Crows (1995)

The Assassin's Riddle (1996)

The Devil's Domain (1998)

The Field of Blood (1999)

The House of Shadows (2003)

For Further Information

Flanagan, Margaret, *Magician's Death* review, *Booklist*, May 1, 2009.

Fleming, Nickie, Paul Doherty interview, Historical Fiction, Feb. 12, 2007, http://www.nickiefleming.com/html/latest_interview.php/ (viewed Oct. 15, 2009).

Haunt of Murder review, *Publishers Weekly*, Dec. 22, 2008.

Herron, Don, "Lots of History, with Mystery: PW Talks with Paul Doherty," *Publishers Weekly*, July 28, 2003.

Paul Doherty interview, *SHOTS*, http://www.shotsmag.co.uk/Paul%20Doherty.htm/ (viewed Oct. 15, 2009).

Paul Doherty website. http://www.paulcdoherty.com/ (viewed Oct. 15, 2009).

Shankland, Michael, Paul Doherty interview, Historical Novels Society, http://www.historicalnovelsociety.org/solander%20files/doherty.htm/ (viewed Oct. 15, 2009).

Tim Dorsey

Indiana
1941

Rogue Detective
Benchmark Series: Serge A. Storms

Janine Dorsey

About the Author and the Author's Writing

If you're ever driving the Florida interstates, don't, whatever you do, let road rage overcome you. If you encounter a tall, thin, dark-haired man with deep blue eyes with a fondness for bottled water and catfish—Serge A. Storms—and his stoned sidekick who seems to have only one name, Coleman, watch out! Consider what happens to a man in *Atomic Lobster* (2008): He ends up dangling from an overpass, clinging to life, only thanks to Coleman's strength.

Storms and Coleman are on a road trip in Tim Dorsey's 10th novel in a series. And while they aren't reluctant to dispatch the deserving, they mostly want to be left alone. Unfortunately, ex-con Tex McGraw has revenge on his mind, American and Mexican drug dealers are at odds over their distribution agreement, a stripper named Rachael hates being insulted and a group of grandmothers . . . well, you get the idea. The characters make the books.

According to a reviewer on the Mysterious Reviews website,

> Serge may be a cold-blooded killer, but he's a compassionate one. Those that are condemned to die deserve it (in his universal role as prosecutor, defense attorney, judge, and jury), but he usually gives them an opportunity to live albeit at some, often considerable, cost. It's all quite fascinating to read and oddly compelling.

And yes, the goings on are a bit odd. "While Dorsey's brand of comedy isn't for the faint of heart," said a reviewer for *Publishers Weekly*, "this fast-moving, raucous tale delivers its usual punch while gleefully skewering everyone and everything along the way."

Tim Dorsey was born in Indiana in 1941. He moved to Riviera Beach, Florida, at an early age—so early, in fact, that the Sunshine State has permeated his being. He attended Auburn University on an ROTC scholarship and graduated in 1983 with a B.S. in transportation. He edited the student newspaper at Auburn and after college, for four years, worked as police and court reporter for the *Alabama Journal*. In 1987 he moved to the Tampa Tribune as a general assignment reporter, then covered politics in Tallahassee. He was night metro editor from 1994 to 1997. In 1999 he left the newspaper to write fiction full time. He and his wife, Janine, and two daughters live in Tampa.

Dorsey views Florida with the same warped sense of humor as authors Carl Hiassen and Dave Barry, with a touch of the humanity of John D. MacDonald. The Sunshine State is the perfect setting, he told BookPage, because "the real-life criminals are so darn plentiful and stupid."

How did he come up with Serge Storms? He simply wanted to create a ruthless villain in *Florida Roadkill* (1999), he said in an interview with Craig Rogers.

> I kept working on him, making him criminally insane, and having him kill people. After I finished, I realized that I had revealed something about myself. I realized that Serge had killed people that I really don't like! Child molesters, people who exploit the elderly. Bad guys. I was subconsciously killing off people I hate.

Storms, of course, isn't your typical serial killer. He's keenly interested in history and is an encyclopedia of Florida trivia. And his favorite ice cream treat is a Nutty Buddy. He's more outgoing and perhaps more huggable than Jeff Lindsay's Dexter.

Nuclear Jellyfish (2009), said critic Philip Booth in the St. Petersburg Times, is an "entertaining addition to a collection of books that, in the long run, may well be viewed as valuable if unconventional treasure troves of all things Florida."

Dorsey doesn't take his books entirely seriously, of course. In a Powell's Q&A, he said "The books' satire also provides a cathartic vent to keep me sane in my home state, which I love too much to ever leave, while thinking I'm crazy for staying."

Even if you're not driving on a Florida interstate, beware Serge and Coleman. They're addictive.

Works by the Author

Serge A. Storms Series

Florida Roadkill (1999)

Hammerhead Ranch Motel (2000)

Orange Crush (2001)

Triggerfish Twist (2002)

The Stingray Shuffle (2003)

Cadillac Beach (2004)

Torpedo Juice (2005)

The Big Bamboo (2006)

Hurricane Punch (2007)

Atomic Lobster (2008)

Nuclear Jellyfish (2009)

Gator A-Go-Go (2010)

Electric Barracuda (2011)

For Further Information

Atomic Lobster review, Mysterious Reviews, http://www.mysteriousreviews.com/mystery-book-reviews/dorsey-atomic-lobster.html/ (viewed Sept. 18, 2009).

Atomic Lobster review, *Publishers Weekly*, Dec. 3, 2007.

Bancroft, Colette, "With Serge at the Wheel, All Is Well," *St. Petersburg Times*, Jan. 20, 2008.

Booth, Philip, "Toxic Twosome: A Serial Killer (with a Few Standards) and His Sidekick Meet a Gang of Jewel Thieves," *St. Petersburg Times*, Jan. 25, 2009.

Rogers, Craig, "Meet Author Tim Dorsey," *Gulfscapes Magazine,* http://www.gulfscapes.com/tim_dorsey.html/ (viewed Sept. 9, 2009).

Serge A. Storms web page, http://www.gulfscapes.com/serge_a_storms.html/ (viewed Sept. 9, 2009).

Tim Dorsey interview, BookPage, http://www.bookpage.com/0502bp/meet_tim_dorsey.html/ (viewed Sept. 9, 2009).

Tim Dorsey interview, Powells Q&A, http://www.powells.com/ink/dorsey.html/ (viewed Sept. 9, 2009).

Tim Dorsey web page, http://timdorsey.com/ (viewed Sept. 9, 2009).

James D. Doss

Reading, Pennsylvania
1939

Police Procedural
Benchmark Series: Charlie Moon

About the Author and the Author's Writing

In James D. Doss's *The Widow's Revenge* (2009), Apache woman Loyola Montoya, who has a reputation as an eccentric, is bothered by witches—witches lurking the woods near her home. She telephones Charlie Moon, the seven-foot-tall rancher and part-time Ute tribal investigator, for help. But Moon reaches her isolated Colorado farm too late. A kitchen fire has destroyed the house and killed Montoya. Did the kerosene lamp fall? Or was it murder? Moon—with an assist from FBI agent Lila Mae McTeague and Police Chief Scott Parris and even Moon's Aunt Daisy Perika, a shaman—faces an increasingly violent case, including challenges posed by the executives of an oil company.

Doss began to write his popular mystery novels when he was 55 years old and still on the technical staff of Los Alamos National Laboratory in New Mexico. Retired since 1999, he now lives in a small cabin near Taos and travels to many of the locations that appear in his books.

The author was born in Reading, Pennsylvania, in 1939 and grew up in nearby Kentucky. He earned a B.A. from Kentucky Wesleyan College in 1964 and an M.S. in electrical engineering from the University of New Mexico in 1969. He went to work for Los Alamos in 1964. He has also been an adjunct instructor in radiology and surgery at the University of New Mexico School of Medicine, having developed thermal methods of treating tumors and other medical innovations. He holds 14 patents.

The author has said that he once had thoughts of studying to become an archaeologist. When he started his first novel, *The Shaman Sings* (1994), he wanted to set it in southern Colorado but had no expectation that he would have Native Americans at center stage. But minor Indian characters showed so much spunk, he knew he had to give them stronger focus. And he had to do some homework. He started with the Los Alamos library and its books about Utes and came upon the pitukupf, a mystical oracle figure. He was hooked. He had to learn more. He ended up devising a character who could speak to this mystic.

"And so that's where Daisy Perika came in," he said in a Twilight Lane interview. "And then, near the end, it was necessary to have a Ute policeman show up. And that's where Charlie Moon appeared, practically in the last chapter. And that's how it started."

A reviewer for *Publishers Weekly* liked that first book, commenting: "Science and mysticism, ghosts and hard-edged cop work combine to stunning effect."

Doss is accustomed to being compared with the late Tony Hillerman, or Margaret Coel. But there's a difference, he points out: Neither of those writers delves into the mysticism the way he does. Charlie Moon, a modern-day Indian, is very skeptical. But Daisy Perika has no doubts about her beliefs.

And, given Doss's longevity as a mystery writer, readers appreciate learning more.

"Doss is long past the time when he needs to be compared to Tony Hillerman," *Booklist*'s David Pitt wrote of *Three Sisters* (2007). "Doss is a powerful force in his own right and deserves equal recognition."

In doing his research, the author has gone to reservations and spoken with many Indians. He's determined to get the details right. Although, in the case of the sundance, which he wrote about in *The Shaman's Game* (1998), he inadvertently learned that there is a way in which the sundancer's power can be taken at a critical time. Rather than reveal the truth (and betray a confidence), he devised an alternate way someone could have taken this power.

Doss finds story ideas in unlikely places. "It can be something someone says to me, about something interesting that happened to them," he said in a New Mystery Reader interview. "At other times, I'll read an interesting newspaper article. In *Grandmother Spider* [2001], one harrowing scene is based upon something that happened in the middle of the night at my mountain cabin."

It's little wonder *Publishers Weekly* has twice named his novels as best books of the year in their category.

Works by the Author

Charlie Moon Series

The Shaman Sings (1994)

The Shaman Laughs (1995)

The Shaman's Bones (1997)

The Shaman's Game (1998)

The Night Visitor (1999)

Grandmother Spider (2001)

White Shell Woman (2002)

Dead Soul (2003)

The Witch's Tongue (2004)

Shadow Man (2005)

Stone Butterfly (2006)

Three Sisters (2007)

Snake Dreams (2008)

The Widow's Revenge (2009)

Dead Man's Tale (2010)

For Further Information

James D. Doss interview, New Mystery Reader, http://www.newmysteryreader.com/James_D._Doss.htm/ (viewed Dec. 13, 2009).

James D. Doss profile, Contemporary Authors, http://galenet.galegrou.com/servlet/ BioRC/ (viewed Sept. 17, 2009).

James D. Doss web page, HarperCollins, http://www.harpercollins.com/authors/ 16295/James_D_Doss/index.aspx/ (viewed Dec. 16, 2009).

Pitt, David, *Three Sisters* review, *Booklist*, July 1, 2007.

Rowen, John, *The Shaman's Bones* review, *Booklist*, Aug. 1997.

Shaman Sings review, *Publishers Weekly*, Dec. 20, 1993.

Snake Dreams review, *Publishers Weekly*, Sept. 15, 2008.

Taylor, Art, James D. Doss interview, Twilight Lane, http://www.mysterynet.com/ doss/author.shtml/ (viewed Sept. 17, 2009).

Taylor, Art, James D. Doss interview, Twilight Lane. http://www.mysterynet.com/ doss/author.shtml (viewed Dec. 13, 2009).

Carole Nelson Douglas

Sam Douglas

Everett, Washington
1944

Amateur Detective, Historical, Cat,
Paranormal
Benchmark Series: Irene Adler

About the Author and the Author's Writing

Few villains in Arthur Conan Doyle's Sherlock Holmes canon earned the violin-playing detective's respect. Even fewer women. Irene Adler impressed (and outsmarted) the wizard of Baker Street in "A Scandal in Bohemia," bidding him a cheery "goodnight" before he knew she'd gotten the best of his clever scheme to protect the reputation of the King of Bohemia.

Adler was too good a character to let sail into the sunset, and Carole Nelson Douglas brought her back for new adventures.

"My Irene Adler is as intelligent, self-sufficient and serious about her professional and personal integrity as Sherlock Holmes, and far too independent to be anyone's mistress but her own," the author said in Contemporary Authors. "She also moonlights as an inquiry agent while building her performing career, so she is a professional rival of Holmes's rather than a romantic interest."

Carole Nelson was born in 1944 in Everett, Washington. She received a B.A. from the College of St. Catherine (now the University of St. Catherine) in 1966. The next year, she married Sam Douglas, an artist. She worked for the *St. Paul Pioneer Press & Dispatch* as a reporter and feature writer from 1967 to 1983, then as a page designer and editorial writer for the opinion pages, 1983 to 1984. She sold *Amberleigh* (1980), a paperback original novel, to Jove, and *Six of Swords* (1982), a fantasy, as well as its sequels, to Del Rey Books. Douglas became a full-time fiction writer in 1984.

The author told interviewer Ed Gorman that she wrote *Amberleigh,* which she described as a postfeminist Gothic, while still in college, to counter the weak women characters she had found in Gothic fiction. "Since then I've merrily reformed the fiction genres, reinventing women as realistic protagonists. Of course, creating true women means creating true men as partners and co-protagonists."

In a review of *Spider Dance* (2004), which Douglas has said may be the last in the series, *Publishers Weekly* noted, "Witty, fast-paced and meticulously researched, this sepia-tinted Victorian confection also reflects a contemporary sensibility as it ponders religious fanaticism and the challenges of a female celebrity living by her own rules."

Douglas had incorporated animals in her writing since her first novel—there was an Irish wolfhound in *Amberleigh* and a King Charles spaniel in *Fair Wind, Fiery Star*

(1981), the next historical. So it's no surprise that she began to write about Midnight Louie, the 20-pound black tomcat with the wit of Damon Runyon. The cat was based on a true-life cat who made his home at a motel and truly munched on the fish in the reflecting pond. The motel owners had no use for the cat, a stray, but a sympathetic woman retrieved and cared for it—and Douglas interviewed both woman and cat for a story for the St. Paul newspaper she worked for at the time. Douglas later came to own a number of cats, including one she named Midnight Louie Jr.

Midnight Louie first appeared in the romantic suspense novels *Crystal Days* and *Crystal Nights* (1990). As she explained in a Crescent Blues interview,

> I just moved Louie and his carp pond to the abandoned (fictional) Joshua Tree hotel on the Las Vegas Strip, which was remodeled into the (fictional) Crystal Phoenix, the classiest hotel in Vegas, with Midnight Louie in lace as "unofficial house dick."

Louie lives with Nicky Fontana and Van Von Rhine in these stories. When they first came out, each paperback contained two stories, as Douglas's manuscripts were severely truncated by the editor. Douglas eventually took back the rights and issued them in restored, slightly revised editions from Five Star as the "Cat and a Playing Card" series.

Midnight Louie made his hardcover debut in *Catnap* in 1992. This time he had moved on to become companion to Temple Barr, a public relations specialist with a missing ex, a stage magician known as The Mystifying Max Kinsella, and a possible new boyfriend, Matt Devine, a radio self-help guru. A female police lieutenant, C. R. Molina, makes frequent appearances for good measure. And this time, the series found its voice and its audience, with annual appearances. The author has said that she envisions the series as running to 27 books; thus she has woven a few threads through the books that will reach resolution only at the last.

Meanwhile, Midnight Louie's adventures take some interesting directions. *Cat in a Sapphire Slipper* (2008), for instance, takes the action to a Nevada brothel, where a prostitute has been murdered. "Douglas explores the campy, lighter side of 'chicken ranches' at the same time she exposes their seamier aspects," said a *Publishers Weekly* reviewer.

"All of Douglas's novels use a mainstream matrix to blend elements of mystery or fantasy with contemporary issues and psychological realism," said a writer on the Fantastic Fiction website. "A literary chameleon with an agenda, Douglas has reinvented the roles of women in a variety of fiction forms."

Douglas burrows deep for her information. For an earlier novel, *Cat in a Midnight Choir* (2002), in which someone is killing strippers, the author (a Texas resident) interviewed several strippers in the Dallas/Fort Worth area. "I got such a complete picture of the culture and the strippers from visiting backstage," she told interviewer M. M. Hall. "I was literally watching these women display abusive backgrounds, and yet there's a certain toughness and survival ability that's very admirable."

But it's the cat aspect that has generated one of the more unusual marketing strategies in mystery publishing. Douglas and her publisher have organized Midnight Louie Adopt-a-Cat events in cooperation with bookstores, humane societies, and the ASPCA. One Dallas event resulted in the placement of 20 cats and the sale of 30 books, according to *Publishers Weekly*.

Douglas merged her interests in crime fiction and fantasy with a new series featuring Delilah Street, Paranormal Investigator, in 2007.

"I like writing popular and genre fiction because it's so influential: it forms attitudes that shape society," the author said on her website.

Works by the Author

Cat and a Playing Card Series

The Cat and the King of Clubs (1999)

The Cat and the Queen of Hearts (1999)

The Cat and the Jack of Spades (2000)

The Cat and the Jill of Diamonds (2000)

Delilah Street, Paranormal Investigator Series

Dancing with Werewolves (2007)

Brimstone Kiss (2008)

Vampire Sunrise (2009)

Silver Zombie (2010)

Irene Adler Series

Good Morning, Irene (1990), also titled *The Adventuress* (2003)

Good Night, Mr. Holmes (1990)

Irene at Large (1992), also titled *A Soul of Steel*

Irene's Last Waltz (1994), also titled *Another Scandal in Bohemia*

Chapel Noir (2001)

Castle Rouge (2002)

Femme Fatale (2003)

Spider Dance (2004)

Midnight Louie Series

Catnap (1992)

Pussyfoot (1993)

Cat on a Blue Monday (1994)

Cat in a Crimson Haze (1995)

Cat in a Diamond Dazzle (1996)

Cat with an Emerald Eye (1996)

Cat in a Flamingo Fedora (1997)

Cat in a Golden Garland (1997)

Cat on a Hyacinth Hunt (1998)

Cat in an Indigo Mood (1999)

Cat in a Jeweled Jumpsuit (1999)

Cat in a Kiwi Con (2000)

Cat in a Leopard Spot (2001)

Cat in a Midnight Choir (2002)

Cat in a Neon Nightmare (2003)

Cat in an Orange Twist (2004)

Cat in a Hot Pink Pursuit (2005)

Cat in a Quicksilver Caper (2006)

Cat in a Red Hot Rage (2007)

Cat in a Sapphire Slipper (2008)

Cat in a Topaz Tango (2009)

Cat in an Ultramarine Scheme (2010)

Contributor

Cat Crimes II, edited by Martin H. Greenberg (1992), includes "Maltese Double Cross," featuring Midnight Louie

Danger in D.C.: A Treasury of Cat Mysteries (1993), includes "Sax and the Single Cat," featuring Midnight Louie

Malice Domestic II, edited by Mary Higgins Clark (1993), includes "Parris Green," featuring Irene Adler

Probable Cause, with Carolyn Banks, William Bernhardt, and Jon L Breen (1993)

Year's 25 Finest Crime and Mystery Stories (1993), includes "Maltese Double Cross," featuring Midnight Louie

Dreamspun Christmas, edited by Marilyn Campbell (1994), includes "Christmas Magic"

Mysterious West (1994), includes "Coyote Peyote," featuring Midnight Louie

Angel Christmas, edited by Mary Balough (1995), includes "Catch a Falling Angel"

Celebrity Vampires (1995), includes "Dracula on the Rocks," featuring Irene Adler

Malice Domestic IV, edited by Carolyn G. Hart (1995), includes "Dirty Dancing"

Year's 25 Finest Crime and Mystery Stories (1995), includes "Coyote Peyote," featuring Midnight Louie

Great Writers and Kids Write Mysteries (1996), includes "Dog Collar," featuring Midnight Louie

Holmes for the Holidays, edited by Martin H. Greenberg (1996), includes "The Thief of Twelfth Night," featuring Irene Adler

Rivals of Dracula, edited by Robert Weinburg (1996), includes "Dracula on the Rocks," featuring Irene Adler

Year's 25 Finest Crime and Mystery Stories (1996), includes "Dirty Dancing"

Cat Crimes for the Holidays (1997), includes "lä lä lä lä Cthuloui!," featuring Midnight Louie

First Cases II, edited by Robert J. Randisi (1997), includes "Parris Green," featuring Irene Adler

Mystery's Most Wanted (1997), includes "Dirty Dancing"

Wild Women, edited by Melissa Mia Hall (1997), includes "Cold Turkey"

Cat Crimes Through Time, edited by Martin H. Greenberg (1998), includes "Mummy Case," featuring Midnight Louie

Crime Through Time II (1998), includes "Mesmerizing Bertie," featuring Irene Adler

Year's 25 Finest Crime and Mystery Stories (1998), includes "Cold Turkey"

Fathers and Daughters, edited by Jill Morgan (1999), includes "Shadows of My Father"

Past Lives, Present Tense, edited by Elizabeth Ann Scarborough (1999), includes "Night Owl"

Felonious Felines, edited by Carol Gorman and Ed Gorman (2000), includes "Sax and the Single Cat," featuring Midnight Louie

Forever Texas, edited by Mike Blakely and Mary Elizabeth Goldman (2000), includes "Texas Bound"

World's Finest Mystery and Crime Stories, edited by Ed Gorman and Martin H. Greenberg (2000), includes "Mummy Case," featuring Midnight Louie

Death Dance, edited by I. Trevanian (2002), includes "Dirty Dancing"

Much Ado About Murder, edited by Anne Perry (2002), includes "Those Are Pearls That Were His Eyes"

Death Dines In (2003), includes "License to Koi," featuring Midnight Louie

Something Fishy (2003, self-published), illustrated reprint of "lä lä lä lä Cthuloui!," featuring Midnight Louie

Death by Dickens, edited by Anne Perry (2004), includes "Scrogged: A Cyber Christmas Carol"

Creature Cozies (2005), includes "Junior Partner in Crime," featuring Midnight Louie

Thou Shalt Not Kill: Biblical Mystery Stories, edited by Anne Perry (2005), includes "Strangers in a Strange Land"

Coyote Peyote (2006, self-published), illustrated edition

Deadly Housewives, edited by Christine Matthews (2006), includes "Lawn and Order"

Poe's Lighthouse, edited by Christopher Conlon (2006), includes "The Riches There That Lie," featuring Midnight Louie

More Tales of Zorro, with Kage Baker, Matthew Baugh, Johnny D. Boggs, Keith R. A. DeCandido, Win Scott Eckert, Jennifer Fallon, Alan Dean Foster, Craig Shaw Gardner, Joe Gore, Joe R. Lansdale, and Timothy Zahn (2009)

Tails of Wonders and Imagination: Cat Stories, edited by Ellen Datlow (2010), includes "Coyote Peyote"

Editor

Marilyn: Shades of Blonde (1997), includes "Sunset: A Monologue in One Act"

Midnight Louie's Pet Detectives (1998), includes "Baker Street Irregular," featuring Irene Adler and Midnight Louie

White House Pet Detectives: Tales of Crime and Mystery at the White House from a Pet's Eye View (2002), includes "Sax and the Single Cat," featuring Midnight Louie

The author has also written fantasy works in the Sword and Circlet, Probe, and Talis-woman series. Her first books were *Amberleigh* (1980), *Fair Wind, Fiery Star* (1981), and *Six of Swords* (1982). *Crystal Days* and *Crystal Nights* both came out in 1990.

For Further Information

Carole Nelson Douglas profile, Contemporary Authors Online, http://galenet.gale group.com/servlet/BioRC/ (viewed Aug. 31, 2009).

Carole Nelson Douglas profile, Fantastic Fiction, http://www.fantasticfiction.co.uk/d/carole-nelson-douglas/ (viewed Sept. 2, 2009).

Carole Nelson Douglas website, http://www.carolenelsondouglas.com/ (viewed Sept. 2, 2009).

Cat in a Sapphire Slipper review, *Publishers Weekly*, July 7, 2008.

Dahlin, Robert, "This Promotion Is the Cat's Meow," *Publishers Weekly*, Oct. 20, 1997.

Gorman, Ed, "Pro-File: Carole Nelson Douglas," Gormania, http://edgormanrambles. blogspot.com/2006/02/pro-file-carole-nelson-douglas.html/ (viewed Sept. 2, 2009).

Nine+ Lives of Carole Nelson Douglas, Crescent Blues, http://www.crescentblues. com/1_2_issue/douglas.shtml/ (viewed Sept. 2, 2009).

Spider Dance review, *Publishers Weekly*, Nov. 29, 2004.

Aaron Elkins

Bob Lampert

Brooklyn, New York
1935

Police Procedural, Forensics, Amateur
Detective
Benchmark Series: Gideon Oliver

About the Author and the Author's Writing

Aaron Elkins figures it hasn't hurt that he has set several of his Gideon Oliver crime series in offshore lands such as Switzerland or Italy or Alaska as well as the United States. Foreign rights sales have always been strong.

And he's made sure, in each instance, to visit with the local police to learn something of their procedures.

In an interview with Carlo Vennarucci of Italian-mysteries.com, the author said:

> My approach is always that [if] I'm writing a book that's going to be set in this area, the police will be in it. I'm on the side of the police, they never look stupid in my books and I want to make sure I don't write anything silly that's so wrong that people laugh at it. So police always like to do what they can.

His method didn't work, he added, in Egypt and Tahiti, where, perhaps for language reasons, he couldn't explain his intentions well enough.

Aaron Elkins was born in Brooklyn, New York, in 1935. He earned a B.A. from Hunter College in 1956 and did graduate studies at the University of Wisconsin in Madison from 1957 to 1959. In 1960 he received one M.A. from University of Arizona and another from California State University in Los Angeles in 1962. The University of California at Berkeley granted him an Ed.D. in 1976. He has two sons from a first marriage and has been married to Charlotte Trangmar since 1972.

Trained as an anthropologist, Elkins worked in a number of governmental and educational positions. He lectured in anthropology, psychology, and business at the University of Maryland at College Park, European Division, in Heidelberg, West Germany, from 1976 to 1978 and then lectured at the same institution in business from 1984 to 1985. He worked for the U.S. Office of Personnel Management in San Francisco as a management analyst from 1979 to 1980. In 1984, two years after his first novel appeared, he became a full-time writer but continued to lecture at California State University and other institutions.

When Elkins set out to write a mystery, he knew he wanted to add an instructional element. A longtime fan of mysteries, he "especially enjoy[s] books by authors who teach me something about subjects that they themselves know and obviously love—books, for example, by Jonathan Gash, or Dick Francis, or Tony Hillerman," he said in *St. James Guide to Crime & Mystery Writers*. "Those are the kinds of books I try to write."

To help with the details, when he uses overseas locales, he has relied on a journal he kept while teaching at NATO bases in England, Germany, Holland, Spain, and Sicily.

Elkins finds that his home base on the Olympic Peninsula of Washington state is where he's most comfortable doing his writing. He sometimes works out plot ideas while riding a Clallam Transit bus. "I think well, I plot well, when I'm moving along," the author told journalist Diane Urban de la Paz. A ride along the shore of Crescent Lake frees his thinking. "Looking at the water, my mind floats freer," he said.

The author's recent *Skull Duggery* (2009) is set at a dude ranch in Oaxaca, Mexico, where Oliver and his wife, Julie, anticipate a restful vacation—but, of course, end up helping a local police department figure out the identity of a mummified corpse.

Elkins has twice launched new crime series. Chris Norgren books are about a retired museum curator, created when the author was having trouble coming up with new Gideon Oliver ideas. After he started the Norgren books, he won an Edgar for Best Mystery Novel for the Gideon book *Old Bones* (1987) and five episodes of Oliver stories on *Monday Night Mystery* on ABC-TV. His publisher insisted that forensics were a hot subgenre, so Elkins keeps close to the tried and true.

Elkins's wife, Charlotte, came up with the idea for the Lee Ofstead books. The heroine is a young professional (barely) golfer who is frequently distracted from improving her scorecards by murder investigations. A fan of P. G. Wodehouse golf stories, Charlotte Elkins persuaded her husband to take golf lessons with her. She writes the first drafts.

"I'm sort of the in-house editor," Elkins explained to Amanda Smith of *Publishers Weekly*. "I'm really not that good with ideas—it takes me a year to write a book—but with her ideas on the page, I enjoy polishing the words."

Loot (1999), a stand-alone novel about the search for the art plundered by Nazis during World War II, took Elkins in a new direction, to critical acclaim. The author "uses his low-key narrative voice, personably erudite central characters, and historically intriguing plot to enthrall readers," in the view of Susan Clifford of *Library Journal*.

To Elkins, life as a mystery novelist is an unexpected delight. "It never occurred to me that I could be a writer myself until a few years ago. Until then, I had classed novelists with opera singers or baseball players, or movie stars—extraordinary people who inhabited some other world than mine," he said in *Contemporary Authors*.

Aaron Elkins—novelist of another world, the world of crime and crime solving.

Works by the Author

Loot (1999)

Turncoat (2002)

The Worst Thing (2011)

Chris Norgren Series

A Deceptive Clarity (1987)

A Glancing Light (1991)

Old Scores (1993)

Gideon Oliver Series

Fellowship of Fear (1982)

The Dark Place (1983)

Murder in the Queen's Armes (1985)

Old Bones (1987)

Curses! (1989)

Icy Clutches (1990)

Make No Bones (1991)

Dead Men's Hearts (1994)

Twenty Blue Devils (1997)

Skeleton Dance (2000)

Good Blood (2004)

Where There's a Will (2005)

Unnatural Selection (2006)

Little Tiny Teeth (2007)

Uneasy Relations (2008)

Skull Duggery (2009)

Lee Ofsted Series, with Charlotte Elkins

A Wicked Slice (1989)

Rotten Lies (1995)

Nasty Breaks (1997)

Where Have All the Birdies Gone? (2004)

On the Fringe (2005)

Adaptations in Other Media

Gideon Oliver segments, *Monday Mystery Movie* (ABC-TV, 1989) based on the character

For Further Information

Aaron Elkins profile, Contemporary Authors Online, http://galenet.galegroup.com/servlet./BioRC/ (viewed Oct. 21, 2009).

Aaron Elkins website. http://www.aaronelkins.com/ (viewed Oct. 21, 2009).

Carter, Dale, updated by Phyllis Bown, Aaron J. Elkins entry, *St. James Guide to Crime & Mystery Writers*, fourth edition, edited by Jay P. Pederson. Detroit: St. James Press, 1996.

Clifford, Susan, *Loot* review, *Library Journal*, Jan. 1999.

De la Paz, Diane Urban, "'Looking Out at the Water, My Mind Floats Freer': How Author Aaron Elkins Is Inspired to Write Best-sellers," *Peninsula Daily News,* http://www.peninsuladailynews.com/article/20080730/NEWS/807300309/ (viewed Oct. 21, 2009).

Ott, Bill, *Where Have All the Birdies Gone?* review, *Booklist*, Nov. 145, 2004.

Skull Duggery review, *Publishers Weekly*, July 27, 2009.

Smith, Amanda, "Charlotte & Aaron Elkins: A Marriage Shaped by Murder," *Publishers Weekly*, Nov. 27, 1995.

Vennarucci, Carlo, Aaron Elkins interview, Italian-mysteries.com, Oct. 17, 2003, http://italian-mysteries.com/elkins-interview.html/ (viewed Oct. 21, 2009).

James Ellroy

Los Angeles, California
1948

Private Detective
Benchmark Series: Underworld USA

About the Author and the Author's Writing

James Ellroy's Los Angeles noir novels draw rich praise from reviewers. Katherine A. Powers, writing in the *Boston Sunday Globe* about *Blood's a Rover* (2009), for example, said,

> The plot grows slowly, but the prose comes on full tilt, a 1950s-cadenced rat-a-tat-tat. Drenched in racial insult, passage after passage slams onto the page like a hail of bullets, and you're often forced to go back to examine the blood spatter to take in what just happened.

If that sounds daunting to one first encountering Ellroy, it's justified. The author hammers his readers with short, declarative sentences to navigate vine-snarled plots, twisted characters, and fascinating cases.

"The plotting is fiendish and intricate," Richard Rayner raved in *The Hartford Courant*, also discussing *Blood's a Rover*. "This [novel] involves the usual Ellroy catalogue of rogue cops, shakedown artists, faked-up FBI reports and real-life political figures seen in mental and physical undress."

The author was born Lee Earle Ellroy in Los Angeles in 1948. His mother, Jean Hilliker, was a nurse, his father an accountant. They divorced. When his mother, who had custody of Lee, was mysteriously murdered in 1958, the boy went to live with his father. He never overcame the shock of his mother's death, and in 1996 teamed with retired Los Angeles detective Bill Stoner to try to solve the crime. They failed, as he reported in the nonfiction *My Dark Places* (1996).

He was expelled from high school and took an early discharge from the army. His father died. In the late 1960s he was in and out of trouble for intoxication and shoplifting; he was imprisoned for several months. In 1977, he was hospitalized with pneumonia; it proved a turning point. He joined Alcoholics Anonymous.

During the late 1970s and early 1980s, Ellroy worked in a variety of low-paying jobs, including golf caddy. A copy of Jack Webb's novel *The Badge*, a history of the Los Angeles police department, engrossed him, as did the story of the 1947 real-life murder, also unsolved, of another woman, Elizabeth Short, aka the Black Dahlia. He wrote a private eye novel, *Brown's Requiem* (1981), which, like his later books, appeared under the name James Ellroy. His second novel, *Clandestine* (1982), loosely based on his mother's murder, was nominated for an Edgar Award.

The four books that make up the L.A. Quartet garnered Ellroy wide critical attention. He has never let up in his mission. In a Salon interview with Laura Miller, he said,

> I will be a better writer. I will take the risk, will write the book that takes longer, the book that will destroy genre strictures. The book that might not be as magnanimously praised as the books of lesser [writers] who adhere to genre strictures.

He eventually found his life story—his mother's violent death—a distraction as he worked through and beyond that theme in his fiction. "Every interview with me, every television performance, every journalist's piece written contains references to my mother and often to the Black Dahlia, and their symbiosis," he told *Interview* in 2008. "I write political books now that are set outside of Los Angeles, and I'm tired of telling the story, and I would like to grant my mother and Elizabeth Short a piece of denied disclosure."

Although Ellroy may be seen as working in the Hammett–Chandler tradition, he disdains the comparison. He told Salon interviewer Laura Miller that he finds their detective heroes too self-pitying. He said there have been no new takes on the tired genre.

Ellroy has taken refuge in the bygone eras of the 1940s and 1950s and at times has employed two researchers to compile background for his novels. *Blood's a Rover* required a remarkable 2,397-page outline, he told *Mystery Scene*. "You want to buttress your period sense with as much fact as you can without appearing overly factualized," he said in an Identity Theory interview. "One of the ways that I do this in *The Cold Six Thousand* is that the book is written largely in the language of racism, because it is seen from the perspective of racist characters bent on enforcing a racist agenda."

The past informs the present and the future. "I like to live in the big moments of history," the author said to Colette Bancroft of the *St. Petersburg Times*, "in the private infrastructure of public events. I'm going back in time to rewrite history to my specifications."

In a turn unusual among crime writers, Ellroy finally faced his demons head-on in 2010 with *The Hilliker Curse: My Pursuit of Women,* a memoir that probes deep into his shattered childhood and his relentless drive to untangle troubled relationships and find himself. Potent reading.

Works by the Author

Brown's Requiem (1981)

Clandestine (1982)

Silent Terror (1986), also titled *Killer on the Road*

Hollywood Nocturnes (1994), titled *Dick Contino's Blues and Other Stories* in Great Britain

Crime Wave: Reportage and Fiction from the Underside of L.A. (1999)

Destination: Morgue! L.A. Tales (2004), stories and essays

L.A. Quartet

The Black Dahlia (1987)

The Big Nowhere (1988)

L.A. Confidential (1990)

White Jazz (1992)

The Dudley Smith Trio: Big Nowhere, L.A. Confidential, White Jazz (1999)

Lloyd Hopkins Trilogy

Because the Night (1984)

Blood on the Moon (1984)

Suicide Hill (1985)

L.A. Noir (1998) omnibus

Underworld USA Trilogy

American Tabloid (1995)

The Cold Six Thousand (2001)

Blood's a Rover (2009)

Editor

The Best American Mystery Stories 2002 (2002)

The Best American Noir of the Century, with Otto Penzler (2010)

Nonfiction

The Badge: True and Terrifying Crime Stories That Could Not Be Presented on TV, from the Creator and Star of Dragnet, with Jack Webb (2005)

Adaptations in Other Media

Cop (1988)

Fallen Angels (Showtime, 1992), episode "Since I Don't Have You," adapted by Steven A. Katz

L.A. Confidential (1997)

Brown's Requiem (1998)

Dark Blue (2002)

Stay Clean (2002)

Feast of Death (Showtime, 2003)

The Black Dahlia (2006)

Land of the Living (2008)

Street Kings (2008)

White Jazz (2009)

For Further Information

Bancroft, Colette, "Hooked on Crime," *St. Petersburg Times*, Sept. 14, 2006.

Birnbaum, Robert, James Ellroy interview, Identitytheory.com, 2001, http://www.identitytheory.com/people/birnbaum13.html/ (viewed Oct. 1, 2009).

Ellroy, James. *The Hilliker Curse: My Pursuit of Women*. New York: Knopf, 2010.

Ellroy, James. *My Dark Places*. New York: Knopf, 1996.

Hubbard, Kim, and Stanley Young, "Telltale Heart: A Writer Confronts His Murdered Mother's Ghost," *People Weekly*, Nov. 25, 2006.

James Ellroy interview, *Interview*, October 2006,

James Ellroy website. http://www.ellroy.com/ (viewed Oct. 1, 2009).

McDonald, Craig, "Demon Dog Unleashed," *Mystery Scene* 111 (2009).

Miller, Laura, "Edipus Wrecks," Salon.com, December 1996, http://www.salon.com/dec96/interview961209.html/ (viewed Oct. 1, 2009).

Powers, Katherine A., "Forging History—One Contract Hit at a Time," *Boston Sunday Globe*, Sept. 20, 1009.

Rayner, Richard, "Murder, Power, Sex, Lingo. . . ," *Hartford Courant*, Sept. 27, 2009.

Earl W. Emerson

Tacoma, Washington
1948

Private Detective
Benchmark Series: Thomas Black

About the Author and the Author's Writing

Earl W. Emerson is paid to do the research for his popular Mac Fontana crime novels; he's a lieutenant with the Seattle Fire Department.

In *The Dead Horse Paint Company* (1997), for example, Fontana, a former fire inspector who is now chief of the small-town department in Staircase, Washington, responds to a car fire at Snoqualmie Pass. There's a body in the trunk—that of the former fire chief Edgar Callahan. Callahan was chief when the department lost nine of its members in the deadly blaze at the Dead Horse Paint Company. Did someone hold a grudge?

"Fontana relives the night of the fire in vivid, effective flashbacks and sifts through the rubble of broken lives to find a killer as Emerson constructs a brooding, engaging tale of personal and professional conflict," said a *Publishers Weekly* reviewer.

Earl W. Emerson was born in Tacoma, Washington, in 1948. He attended Principia College in 1966 and 1967 and the University of Washington, Seattle, in 1967 and 1968. He married Sandra Evans in 1968; they have three children. Before joining the Seattle Fire Department in 1978, he worked as a writer.

Emerson initially found it jarring to mix careers. When he was on duty, on one of his 24-hour shifts, he said, in an interview with Lynn Kaczmarek of *Mystery News*,

> I'd come in and everybody's yelling . . . and there was all this hoo-rah about the fire they had last night, and we gotta get this ready on the rig 'cuz it isn't yet and then the bell would hit and off you'd go . . . and then I'd go home and I couldn't unwind.

Eventually he found a way to refocus when he was away from the station, leading him to launch his Thomas Black private detective series. *The Rainy City* (1984), his first book, took a while to land a publisher. But once he got going, Emerson garnered a Shamus award and an Edgar nomination.

Black is a former cop who becomes a no-nonsense investigator for private clients. *The Portland Laugher* (1994) finds him following Philip Bacon, the man who is engaged to lawyer Kathy Birchfield. Black is in love with Birchfield. He is also thrilled that he might find some dirt on the man. Meanwhile, there's a killer at large in the city—a killer who maniacally calls authorities to taunt them.

147

To heighten the mood, Emerson relies on a recurring goof, Snake Slezak, Black's friend. To vary the mood, Emerson had Black and Birchfield become husband and wife.

"Now [I have] two ongoing male and female characters, who have shared much, are fun to write about in a completely different way. I think they are sexier. Despite what Hollywood portrays," Emerson said in an interview with Alan Egerton Ball, adding that "marriage is always sexier than a single life."

To take a different direction, Emerson created his second character, Mac Fontana.

"There are few writers in any genre who can sustain a narrative at such breakneck speed," said *Booklist*'s Dennis Dodge in reviewing *Primal Threat* in 2007. That book, about a weekend gone awry for a group of buddies who have escaped into Washington's Cascade Mountains only to be assaulted by a psycho and his wacked allies, is typical of Emerson's move into thriller mode.

The author is comfortable with the departure from his usual urban settings. As he said to blogger Jonathan Mayberry,

> I think that, to a large degree, plot rises out of place. Things happen because of place. The nature of the conflicts that drive the story is often shaped by place. Think of *Gone with the Wind*. Couldn't have happened in Columbus, Ohio.

As professional as Emerson has become as a writer and as familiar with firefighting as he is, incendiary scenes are among his most difficult to write. "There is no part of my firefighting novels that I give more scrutiny to than the fire scenes," he said in a Q&A on his website. "I would hazard to say that the house fire in *Into the Inferno* [2003] got three times as many rewrites as any other single section of the book. Maybe thirty-five rewrites."

That was in part because he knew, with his reputation, that there would be a lot of volunteer and professional firefighters in his audience, and the book had to be letter perfect—which it was.

Works by the Author

Fill the World with Phantoms (1979)

Vertical Burn (2002)

Into the Inferno (2003)

Pyro (2004)

The Smoke Room (2005)

Firetrap (2006)

Primal Threat (2008)

Mac Fontana Series

Black Hearts and Slow Dancing (1988)

Help Wanted: Orphans Preferred (1990)

Morons and Madmen (1993)

Going Crazy in Public (1996)

The Dead Horse Paint Company (1997)

Thomas Black Series

The Rainy City (1984)

Nervous Laughter (1985)

Poverty Bay (1985)

Fat Tuesday (1987)

Deviant Behavior (1988)

Yellow Dog Party (1991)

The Portland Laugher (1994)

The Vanishing Smile (1995)

The Million-Dollar Tattoo (1996)

Deception Pass (1997)

Catfish Cafe (1998)

Cape Disappointment (2009)

For Further Information

Ball, Alan Egerton, "Mysteries to Set the Page on Fire: A Cautionary Conversation with Earl Emerson," *FFWD Weekly,* 1997, http://www.ffwdweekly.com/Issues/1997/0130/book1.html/ (viewed Oct. 15, 2009).

Cape Disappointment review, *Publishers Weekly*, Dec. 8, 2008.

Dead Horse Paint Company review, *Publishers Weekly*, May 12, 1997.

Dodge, Dennis, *Primal Threat* review, *Booklist*, Dec. 1, 2007.

Earl Emerson website, http://www.earlemerson.com/ (viewed Oct. 15, 2009).

Kaczmarek, Lynn, "Earl Emerson: Writing Fire," *Mystery News*, June/July 2002, http://www.blackravenpress.com/Author%20pages/emerson.htm/ (viewed Oct. 15, 2009).

Mayberry, Jonathan, "Regional Mysteries and Thrillers," Jonathan Mayberry's Big Scary Blog, Sept. 21, 2009, http://jonathanmaberry.com/tag/earl-emerson/ (viewed Oct. 15, 2009).

Portland Laugher review, *Publishers Weekly*, Aug. 8, 1994.

Loren D. Estleman

Ann Arbor, Michigan
1952

Private Detective; Historical Mystery,
Rogue Detective, Westerns
Benchmark Series: Amos Walker

Deborah Morgan

About the Author and the Author's Writing

"I'm exactly like Walker: handsome, strong, courageous, and honest. Criminals blanch at the mention of my name and I shake women off my lapels like snow." Thus Loren D. Estleman described himself, tongue in cheek, to Mystaery One interviewer Jon Jordan. Estleman was comparing himself with his long-running private detective series character, Amos Walker. He might have given the same thumbnail portrait of Page Murdock, his western lawman, for the author is equally comfortable in both genres.

Switching between series, he told interviewer Steven Law, is "a kind of literary crop rotation. The variety preserves the challenge."

Estleman has no aspirations to become a literary writer. "I'm pretty popular with myself," he wrote in a letter, "but there are times, invariably when the writing isn't going well, when I wonder if anyone cares. But since at this point I couldn't hold down a real job to save myself or the mortgage, I push on."

Born in Whitmore Lake, near Ann Arbor, Michigan, in 1952, the son of a truck driver and a postal clerk, Estleman as a child watched *Gunsmoke* and *The Untouchables* on a black-and-white television set. His grandmother knew stories about Al Capone and told them to the author.

Estleman received a B.A. in literature and journalism from Eastern Michigan University in 1974. (Years later, in 2002, the university presented Estleman with an honorary doctorate in letters.)

Through 1980, he was a reporter or editor for the *Ypsilanti Press*, *Community Foto-News*, *Ann Arbor News,* and *Dexter Leader*.

His first novel, *The Oklahoma Punk*, came out in 1976, after 160 rejection slips. He followed that with more than 50 mysteries and westerns—all produced on a manual typewriter.

Estleman wrote the first of his long-running Walker books in 1980. "Amos goes with the flow," the author told Mary Ann Tennenhouse for *Publishers Weekly*. "Anything that happens in Detroit he's willing to embrace because it might bring him work. Like me, he has a love-hate relationship with the city so, as much fun as he has kicking apart what's wrong, he celebrates what's right."

Walker is a throwback. He has no cell phone, no Internet access. He lives alone, with his television set in the largely Polish community of Hamtramck. He solves crimes the old-fashioned way, on phone, on foot, and by direct contact. All of the conventions of the Raymond Chandler–style noir private detective novel are there, but very much with Estleman twists.

Estleman was at the heart of a 1980s resurrection in private detective fiction. "I am a stubborn old crock; whenever a publisher went cold, I walked and battered doors until someone let me and Walker in," he said in a *January Magazine* interview.

Estleman's characters are honest and realistic. "Amos Walker is a compendium of every police officer I have ever known and part of myself, or what I would like to be," he told *Armchair Detective* interviewer Keith Kroll, admitting that his fictional character is actually a little taller, slimmer, and better looking than he is. "He says on the spot what I think of on the elevator on the way down. For what it's worth, there's some of me in Amos Walker. I wish there were more of Amos Walker in me."

The author's Page Murdock is a deputy U.S. marshal called on in *Stamping Ground* (1980) to quell a blood reprisal in Cheyenne country, in *The High Rocks* (1979) to bring in for trial mountain man Bear Anderson, who is hiding in the Montana Bitterroot Mountains.

Peter Macklin, featured in another series, is a hit man, while Valentino is a film archivist and amateur crime solver. The Detroit books cover a rich period of crime and history in Michigan's biggest city.

Among the writers who came to inspire Estleman were Jack London, Edgar Allan Poe, W. Somerset Maugham, Ernest Hemingway, Raymond Chandler, and Edith Wharton.

Estleman averages two books a year. He is a methodical writer, generally spending six hours a day (or as long as it takes to finish five good pages) working at his craft, rewriting and polishing as he goes, "writing for the wastebasket" as he calls it, consuming many a cola as he works. He starts with the title and begins writing when he's come up with a story to go with it.

The author lives in Michigan with his wife, mystery novelist Deborah Morgan. Estleman is an avid collector of books—modern firsts and also reference books (about 15,000 titles)—and of movies (at least 1,300 titles).

Estleman has received national writing awards from the Private Eye Writers of America, the Western Writers of America, and the Cowboy Hall of Fame and has been nominated for others, including the Pulitzer Prize and the National Book Award.

Linda Fairstein said of Estleman that he is "one of the best American writers working today. Forget genre and categories. His characterizations are brilliant, his dialogue is dead-on, and his settings are backdrops for universal themes, whether a Detroit back alley or a Southwest corral."

Works by the Author

The Oklahoma Punk (1976), retitled *Red Highway* (1987)

The Hider (1978)

Aces and Eights (1981)

Mr. St. John (1983)

The Wolfer (1983)

This Old Bill (1984)

Gun Man (1985)

Bloody Season (1988)

Peeper (1989)

Sudden Country (1991)

Billy Gashade (1997)

The Rocky Mountain Moving Picture Association (1999)

The Master Executioner (2001)

Black Powder, White Smoke (2002)

The Undertaker's Wife (2005)

The Adventures of Johnny Vermillion (2006)

Gas City (2008)

Roy & Lillie (2010)

Amos Walker Series

Motor City Blue (1980)

Angel Eyes (1981)

The Midnight Man (1982)

The Glass Highway (1983)

Sugartown (1984)

Every Brilliant Eye (1985)

Lady Yesterday (1987)

Downriver (1988)

General Murders: Ten Amos Walker Mysteries (1988), short stories

Silent Thunder (1989)

Sweet Women Lie (1990)

Never Street (1996)

The Witchfinder (1998)

The Hours of the Virgin (1999)

A Smile on the Face of the Tiger (2000)

Sinister Heights (2002)

Poison Blonde (2003)

Retro (2004)

Nicotine Kiss (2006)

American Detective (2007)

Amos Walker's Detroit (2007), nonfiction

Amos Walker: The Complete Story Collection (2010)

The Left-Handed Dollar (2010)

Detroit Novels

Whiskey River (1990)

Motown (1991)

King of the Corner (1992)

Edsel (1995)

Stress (1996)

Jitterbug (1998)

Thunder City (1999)

Judge Isaac Parker Series

The Branch and the Scaffold (2009)

Page Murdock Series

The High Rocks (1979)

Stamping Ground (1980)

Murdock's Law (1982)

The Stranglers (1984)

City of Widows (1994)

White Desert (2000)

Port Hazard (2004)

The Book of Murdock (2010)

Peter Macklin Series

Kill Zone (1984)

Roses Are Dead (1985)

Any Man's Death (1986)

Something Borrowed, Something Black (2002)

Little Black Dress (2005)

Sherlock Holmes Series

Sherlock Holmes vs. Dracula: The Adventures of the Sanguinary Count (1978)

Dr. Jekyll and Mr. Holmes (1979)

Valentino Series

Frames (2008)

Alone (2009)

Valentino: Film Detective (announced), collection

Collections

The Best Western Stories of Loren D. Estleman, edited by Bill Pronzini and Martin H. Greenberg (1989), retitled *Hell on the Draw: The Best Western Stories of Loren D. Estleman* (1999)

People Who Kill (1993)

Attitude and Other Stories of Suspense (announced)

Play

Dr. and Mrs. Watson at Home (1987), in *The New Adventures of Sherlock Holmes*, edited by Martin H. Greenberg and Carol-Lynn Rössel-Waugh

Contributor

The Eyes Have It: The First Private Eye Writers of America Anthology, edited by Robert J. Randisi (1984)

Best of the West, edited by Joe R. Lansdale (1986)

The Mean Streets (1986)

The Year's Best Mystery and Suspense Stories 1986, edited by Edward D. Hoch (1986)

A Matter of Crime, edited by Matthew J. Bruccoli and Richard Layman (1987)

An Eye for Justice, edited by Robert J. Randisi (1988)

A Matter of Crime 3 (1988)

Raymond Chandler's Philip Marlowe, edited by Byron Preiss (1988)

Westeryear, edited by Edward Gorman (1988)

The Arizonans, edited by Bill Pronzini and Martin H. Greenberg (1989)

The Fatal Frontier (1989)

The New Frontier, edited by Joe R. Lansdale (1989)

Christmas Out West, edited by Bill Pronzini and Martin H. Greenberg (1990)

The Northwesterners, edited by Bill Pronzini and Martin H. Greenberg (1990)

Invitation to Murder (1991)

Deals with the Devil (1994)

For Crime Out Loud (1995)

Holmes for the Holidays, edited by Martin H. Greenberg, Jon L. Lellenberg, and Carol-Lynn Waugh (1996)

Homicide Hosts Presents (1996)

Best American Mystery Stories 1997, edited by Robert B. Parker (1997)

Western Hall of Fame Anthology, edited by Dale L. Walker (1997)

Best of the American West, edited by Ed Gorman and Martin H. Greenberg (1998)

Best of the American West II, edited by Ed Gorman and Martin H. Greenberg (1998)

The Fatal Frontier (1998)

Best American Mystery Stories 1999, edited by Ed McBain (1999)

Legend (1999)

More Holmes for the Holidays, edited by Martin H. Greenberg, Jon L. Lellenberg, and Carol-Lynn Waugh (1999)

The Night Awakens (2000)

The Shamus Game (2000)

Tin Star, edited by Robert J. Randisi (2000)

Murder on Baker Street, edited by Martin H. Greenberg, Jon L. Lellenberg, and Daniel Stashower (2001)

Mysterious Press Anniversary Anthology (2001)

Mysterious Press Anniversary Anthology: Celebrating 25 Years (2001)

Murder, My Dear Mr. Watson, edited by Martin H. Greenberg (2002)

Murder on the Ropes: Original Boxing Mysteries, edited by Otto Penzler (2002)

Westward: A Fictional History of the American West, edited by Dale L. Walker (2003)

The Shamus Winners: America's Best Private Eye Stories, Vol. 1, 1982–1995, edited by Robert J. Randisi (2010)

Editor

P.I. Files, with Martin H. Greenberg (1990)

Deals with the Devil, with Martin H. Greenberg and Mike Resnick (1994)

American West: Twenty New Stories from the Western Writers of America (2001)

For Further Information

Crider, Bill, Loren D. Estleman entry, *Twentieth-Century Western Writers*, second edition, edited by Geoff Sadler. Chicago: St. James Press, 1991.

Dundee, Wayne, "Estleman—Meeting the Challenges," *Hardboiled* 2 (1985).

Estleman, Loren D., "Twilight for High Noon: Today's Western," *The Writer*, July 1997.

Estleman, Loren D., "No Trap So Deadly: Recurring Devices in the Private Eye Story," *Alfred Hitchcock's Mystery Magazine,* Dec. 1983.

Estleman, Loren D., "Plus Expenses: The Private Eye as Great American Hero," *Alfred Hitchcock's Mystery Magazine*, Sept. 1983.

Estleman, Loren D., "The Road to *Never Street*," *Mystery Scene* 56 (1997).

Estleman, Loren D., "Westerns: Fiction's Last Frontier," *The Writer,* July 1981.

Jordan, Jon, "Interview with Loren Estleman," Mystery One, Oct. 12, 2001, http://www.mysteryone.com/interview.php?ID=723/ (viewed Sept. 17, 2010).

Kroll, Keith, "The Man from Motor City," *The Armchair Detective*, winter, 1991.

Loren D. Estleman website, http://www.lorenestleman.com/ (viewed Aug. 5, 2009).

Morgan, Deborah, Loren D. Estleman profile, http://www.lorenestleman.com/author.htm/ (viewed Apr. 20, 2003).

Pierce, J. Kingston, "Think Fast, Mr. Motown," *January Magazine,* http://january-magazine.com/profiles/estleman.html/ (viewed Aug. 5, 2009).

Raphael, Lev, "50 Years, 50 Books: Loren Estleman Reaches a Milestone with 'Poison Blonde,' His Latest Mystery with a Detroit Bent," *Detroit Free Press,* Apr. 7, 2003.

Tennenhouse, Mary Ann, "PW Talks with Loren D. Estleman," *Publishers Weekly*, Apr. 21, 2003.

Janet Evanovich

South River, New Jersey
1943

Amateur Detective
Benchmark Series: Stephanie Plum

About the Author and the Author's Writing

Janet Evanovich's wise-cracking, free-swinging bounty hunter heroine Stephanie Plum has ridden high on the bestseller charts for a decade and a half, the pride of chick-lit and mystery lovers.

"The appeal of Janet Evanovich's popular creation is that she's not much better than the average Jersey girl would be at nabbing criminals," observed reviewer Laura Miller of *Entertainment Weekly,* noting that Stephanie Plum doesn't know kung-fu, refuses to exercise, and eats recklessly.

Who would think the two writers she most credits with inspiring her heroine are Carl Barks and Robert B. Parker? "When I was a kid I read [Barks'] Donald Duck and Uncle Scrooge comics and I developed a love for the adventure story," she told interviewer Eve Tan Gee. "When I made the decision to move from romance to crime I read all the Parker books . . . He's such an incredible technician. He makes reading easy."

The author was born in South River, New Jersey, in 1943. "When I was a kid I spent a lot of time in LaLa Land. Lala Land is like an out-of-body experience—while your mouth is eating lunch your mind is conversing with Captain Kirk," she said on her web-site, by way of explaining her vivid plot imagination.

She studied art at Douglass College and married high school friend Peter Evanovich, at the time a doctoral candidate at Rutgers University. They moved frequently because of his navy postings. She worked as an office temp, waitress, insurance claims adjuster, and saleswoman of hospital supplies and used cars. Juggling parental and household respon-sibilities, she began to write. After 10 years, her manuscript for a romance novel landed with the Second Chance at Love imprint. She used the name Steffie Hall on that and a dozen subsequent romances, mostly for Bantam Loveswept.

"I wanted to write bigger books with more action, sort of like the movie Romancing the Stone," she told the reviewer for *Charlotte Austin Review*, "and I couldn't get any of the romance editors to give me a contract. So I took a year off and reinvented myself . . . Truth is, the Plum series is probably neither romance nor mystery. I think the Plum series is adventure."

She did her homework. "I got to be friends with a couple of bounty hunters and tried to figure out what kind of people they were," she told Adrian Muller for *Mystery Scene*. "It turned out that they flew by the seat of their pants, responding to all sorts of situations."

Plum's ensemble of southern New Jerseyites includes Lula, a former prostitute; Grandma Mazur, who hangs out at Stiva's Funeral Home; vice cop Joe Morelli; cousin Vinnie, who sends jobs from his bail bonding business her way; fellow bondsman and mentor Ranger; and Rex the hamster.

Evanovich's Plum novels sparkle with sassy wit and brisk verbal exchanges. To improve her ability in this area, she took improvisational acting classes.

Her unexpected touches of humor delight readers, and she shows no sign of letting up, this deep into the series. *Boston Globe* reviewer Rich Barlow commented, "The question each summer is whether the new book delivers more or fewer laughs than is par. *Finger Lickin' Fifteen* [2009] delivers more, earning it a thumbs-up and a beach pass."

The author is in no hurry to return to romances. "I prefer mystery for structural reasons," she said in an interview for BookBrowse. "I like writing in first person and it's more accepted in mystery. I write with a lot of humor and I think humor can get tedious so I prefer a short book, and again, this is more accepted in mystery."

Evanovich also likes to experiment. She ended *High Five* (1999) with a cliffhanger; readers had to wait until *Hot Six* (2000) to find out who Plum's new lover was. (One group of fans was so eager to find out, it bid more than $460 on the eBay Internet auction service for an advance reading copy.)

Evanovich, who now lives in Hanover, New Hampshire, spends long hours in her office overlooking the Connecticut River, seated at her computer, devouring Cheez Doodles and drinking Coke. She has a second series that grew from one of her earlier romances. She and friend and author Charlotte Hughes took *Full House* (2002), expanded it, and followed it with further stories. She has also launched a Plum character, Diesel, into his own series, and alternates longer Plum books with "lite" ones to appease readers who are anxious for more.

Is she comfortable in the writing life? The author answered in a BookPage interview, "Basically, I'm just a boring workaholic. I motivate myself to write by spending the money I make before it comes in."

Further, she told interviewer Jess Lourey, "I prefer writing to having written. I love the process, the isolation, the unique world I go into every morning. Once the book is off my desk it belongs to someone else."

As bestseller lists testify, her books belong to a lot of someone elses.

Works by the Author

Alexandra Barnaby Series

Metro Girl (2004)

Motor Mouth (2006)

Troublemaker 1, with Alex Evanovich and Joelle Jones (2010), graphic novel

Troublemaker 2, with Alex Evanovich and Joelle Jones (2010), graphic novel

Cate Madigan Series, with Leanne Banks

Hot Stuff (2007)

Diesel Series

Wicked Appetite (2010)

Stephanie Plum Series

One for the Money (1994)

Two for the Dough (1995)

Four to Score (1998)

Three to Get Deadly (1998)

High Five (1999)

Hot Six (2000)

One for the Money/Two for the Dough (2001)

Seven Up (2001)

Three Plums in One (2001)

Hard Eight (2002)

The Stephanie Plum Novels (2002)

Three to Get Deadly/Four to Score/High Five/Hot Six (2002)

Visions of Sugar Plums (2002)

To the Nines (2003)

Ten Big Ones (2004)

Eleven on Top (2005)

Hot Six/Seven Up/Hard Eight (2006)

Twelve Sharp (2006)

Lean Mean Thirteen (2007)

More Plums in One (2007)

Plum Lovin' (2007)

Seven Up/Hard Eight/To the Nines (2007)

Ten Big Ones/Eleven on Top/Twelve Sharp (2007)

Fearless Fourteen (2008)

Plum Lucky (2008)

Between the Plums (2009), omnibus

Finger Lickin' Fifteen (2009)

A Plum New Year (2009)

Plum Spooky (2009)

Sizzling Sixteen (2010)

Smokin' Seventeen (2011)

Max Holt Series, with Charlotte Hughes

Full House (2002), revision of title originally issued as by Steffie Hall

Full Tilt (2002)

Full Speed (2003)

Full Blast (2004)

Full Bloom (2005)

The Full Box (2006), omnibus

Full Scoop (2006)

Contributor

The Plot Thickens, edited by Mary Higgins Clark (1997), includes "The Last Peep"

The author has also written books in the Loveswept Romance, Loveswept/Elsie Hawkins, and Second Chance at Love series (as Steffie Hall).

For Further Information

Barlow, Rich, "Evanovich Formula Still Finger Lickin' Good," *Boston Globe*, July 15, 2009.

Evanovich, Janet. *Have You Met Stephanie Plum?* New York: St. Martin's Press, 2003.

Evanovich, Janet. *How I Write: Secrets of a Serial Fiction Writer*, with Ina Yalof. New York: St. Martin's Press, 2006.

Gee, Eve Tan, Janet Evanovich interview, Crime Time, http://www.crimetime.co.uk/interviews/janetevanovich.php/ (viewed Sept. 18, 2009).

Janet Evanovich interview, Bookbrowse, http://www.bookbrowse.com/index.cfm?page-author&authorID=232&view=interview/ (viewed June 30, 2003).

Janet Evanovich website, http://www.evanovich.com/ (viewed Sept. 18, 2009).

Lourey, Jess, Janet Evanovich interview, InkSpot, Oct. 5, 2008, http://midnight-writers.blogspot.com/2008/10/janet-evanovich-interview-by-jess.html/ (viewed Sept. 18, 2009).

Miller, Laura, "A Plum Assignment," *Entertainment Weekly*, July 18, 2003.

Muller, Adrian, "Janet Evanovich," *Mystery Scene* 54 (1996).

Nunn, P. J., Janet Evanovich interview, *Charlotte Austin Review,* http://www.collection.nk-bnc.ca/100/202/300/charlotte/2000/07–31/pages/interviews/authors/janetevanovich.htm/ (viewed June 30, 2003).

Wilson, Leah. *Perfectly Plum: An Unauthorized Celebration of the Life, Loves and Other Disasters of Stephanie Plum, Trenton Bounty Hunter*. Dallas, Tex.: Benbella Books, 2007.

Joanne Fluke

Minnesota
1943

Amateur Detective
Benchmark Series: Hannah Swensen

About the Author and the Author's Writing

Joanne Fluke has a recipe for just about anything—including a successful cozy murder mystery series.

The Minnesota-born author holds a degree in clinical psychology. She began her writing career in eighth-grade, she said on her website, completing weekly assignments—one-page short stories—for an English teacher. She has taught in public school, worked as a psychologist and as a musician, and has been an assistant to a private detective. She was also a short-order cook, an assistant in a flower shop, a party planner and caterer, and a computer consultant.

When Fluke decided to write for real, she sold a manuscript for a thriller, *The Stepchild* (1980), and wrote 33 romances, young adult novels, and nonfiction books before she told her agent she wanted to write a cookbook. He suggested a mystery novel instead.

"Mysteries are my first love," the author told interviewer Cathy Sova. "I've always loved puzzles and a good mystery is like a good puzzle. You're given the pieces and you have to put them together in a way that makes sense."

Fluke had first been exposed to mysteries as a young child; her babysitting grandmother always had the latest Perry Mason novel at hand.

The result was *The Chocolate Chip Cookie Murder* (2000), featuring Hannah Swensen, owner of a small-town bakery—a Minnesotan (naturally) with a flair for baking (much like the author) and a nose for prying facts out of bystanders and suspects.

Fluke has a deft hand with her small-town characters. They are made up, she said, but "They seem real to me," she said on her website. "Several times, when I've been writing from an outline, I've decided that I just can't let my character do what the outline says. The characters take on a life of their own. I feel as if I know everyone in Lake Eden."

Familiarity with Minnesota people and environs (even after the author had lived in southern California for several years) provides most of her research. The recipes, though, are another matter. "There's much more research involved in the Hannah Swensen series because of the recipes. I want to make sure they're perfect. I really lucked out by inheriting my grandmother's book of recipes, all hand-written and original," Fluke said in a conversation with Cathy Sova.

Her screenwriter husband (between them they have five children) takes an active role in helping test the recipes. He also reviews each novel's outline. "When I have a fairly detailed outline, I sit down again with my husband, who is very good at spotting holes in the plot," the author told Bookreporter. "Eventually I'm ready to do the actual writing, which takes several months. From start to finish takes the better part of a year."

The novelty of her characters and her setting, as well as her culinary theme, have propelled Fluke's series beyond regional popularity.

With all the tempting cakes and pastries coming from Hannah Swensen's kitchen, it's little surprise, by the 11th novel in the series, *Cream Puff Murder* (2009), the heroine is enrolled in a dieting program at Heavenly Bodies.

" 'Uh-oh,' Hannah breathed, giving a little shudder. The phrase *fitness coach* was not in her vocabulary," we read in the novel. "Even worse, the phrase *exercise program* brought back painful memories of mandatory calisthenics in elementary school gym class."

Little fear. The fitness instructor with the body to die for (and, unfortunately, a nasty attitude to match), Ronni Ward, naturally ends up a murder victim, her body found in a Jacuzzi.

So there's little chance that the series will take a new, aerobics direction. (In fact, the author has announced that a cookbook now in the works will include all of Hannah Swensen's published recipes and more.)

Works by the Author

Hannah Swensen Series

Chocolate Chip Cookie Murder (2000)

Strawberry Shortcake Murder (2001)

Blueberry Muffin Murder (2002)

Lemon Meringue Pie Murder (2003)

Fudge Cupcake Murder (2004)

Sugar Cookie Murder (2004)

Peach Cobbler Murder (2005)

Cherry Cheesecake Murder (2006)

Key Lime Pie Murder (2007)

Carrot Cake Murder (2008)

Cream Puff Murder (2009)

Plum Pudding Murder (2009)

Apple Turnover Murder (2010)

Gingerbread Cookie Murder (2010)

Devil's Food Cake Murder (2011)

Joanne Fluke's Lake Eden Cookbook: Hannah Swensen's Recipes from the Cookie Jar (2011), nonfiction

Contributor

Sugar and Spice, with Beverly Barton, Shirley Jump, and Fern Michaels (2006)

Candy Cane Murder, with Laura Levine and Leslie Meier (2007)

The author has written young adult novels, thrillers (including *The Stepchild*, published in 1980), and romances under her own name and as Jo Gibson and Kathryn Kirkwood.

For Further Information

Cream Puff Murder review, *Publishers Weekly*, Jan. 26, 2009.

James, Pamela, "Interview with Joanne Fluke," Mystery File, http://www.mystery file.com/Fluke/Interview.html/ (viewed Aug. 20, 2009).

Joanne Fluke interview, Bookreporter, http://www.bookreporter.com/authors/au-fluke-joanne.asp/ (viewed Aug. 20, 2009).

Joanne Fluke website, http://www.murdershebaked.com/ (viewed Aug. 20, 2009).

Knoblauch, Mark, *Carrot Cake Murder* review, *Booklist*, Mar. 15, 2008.

"Murder She Baked: Batter Chatter with Joanne Fluke," Cakespy.com, http://www.cakespy.com/2007/10/murder-she-baked-batter-chatter-with.html/ (viewed Aug. 20, 2009).

Sova, Cathy, Joanne Fluke interview, The Mystery Reader, http://www.themys teryreader.com/nf-fluke.html/ (viewed Aug. 20, 2009)

G. M. Ford

Everett, Massachusetts
1945

Private Detective, Journalism Mystery
Benchmark Series: Leo Waterman

About the Author and the Author's Writing

Yes, his name, Gerald M. Ford, sounds like that of an ex-president. And his chosen byline for two mystery series, G. M. Ford, is suggestive of a major automotive conglomerate. But the reader quickly passes that by to discover the writer's keen sense of character and sharp way with dialogue.

Ford was born in 1945 in Everett, Massachusetts. He earned a B.A. from Hawthorne College and an M.A. from Adelphi University. He received a second M.A., in political science, from the University of Washington in Seattle, where he now makes his home with his third wife and a son. Ford taught English at a public high school and at Rogue Community College in Grants Pass, Oregon, from 1972 to 1985. Until 1992, he worked as an instructor in the communications department at City University in Bellevue, Washington.

Having grown up with the Hardy Boys and Nancy Drew, having fallen in love with mystery novels after reading Rex Stout's Nero Wolfe series, having devoured classic writers including Ross MacDonald and John D. Macdonald, Ford created his own private eye character, Seattle-based Leo Waterman. Ford describes him as being a character assembled from John D. MacDonald's Travis McGee, Gregory McDonald's Fletch, a little of Ross McDonald's Lew Archer, and a dollop of Robert B. Parker's Spenser for good measure.

"He is a perpetual adolescent; his behavior is often dictated by the fact that he knows he's coming into serious amounts of money on his forty-fifth birthday," Ford told *January Magazine* interviewer J. Kingston Pierce.

In that same conversation, the author said he feels no compulsion to create a realistic hero, based on long and thorough research. As long as he doesn't make any major bloopers when it comes to procedure, as long as he has a good story, Ford's content.

Ford has populated the series books with a posse of secondary characters, bums, or rather "the Boys," who sometimes struggle to take over the books. For the same reason and because he does not yet feel comfortable portraying strong female characters, Ford has eased Waterman's pathologist girlfriend Rebecca out of the action.

"Ford conveys the larger-than-life suspects, rag-tag operatives, and exaggerated situations with delightful finesse," said *Library Journal* reviewer Rex E. Klett of *Slow Burn* (1998).

After a half-dozen entries, Ford found the need to write about someone else. In a Mystery One Bookstore interview, he said,

By that time you've subjected your protag to a wide array of indignities and probably used up most of the ideas you started with. In Leo's case I'd use up every drunk joke I'd ever heard and just felt like it was time to move on.

So he started the Frank Corso series. With a hero who writes true crime for a living, there was a broader opportunity for plot ideas. Too, Ford wrote the new books in the third person, allowing greater leeway in creating his plot threads. The hero didn't always have to be on stage.

Ford had ideas but not detailed outlines when he wrote his first books. As he moved to more complicated story lines, he found that he had to have a better idea, ahead of time, of where he was going, so he put more detail into his outlines. Leo Waterman solved cases through brute confrontation. Frank Corso, with a greater investigative arsenal, allowed for more complex cases.

Ford has said he learned a lot by observing fellow mystery authors. For instance, he noted Ross McDonald was always careful with secondary characters, often bringing them back in new roles later in a story.

Ford's recent *Nameless Night* (2008) is a nonseries novel that has given him the opportunity to further explore character—in this case, Paul Hardy, a man who has suffered traumatic injury and lost his memory, goes on a cross-country quest to avoid people who want to kill him, and to find out who he really is. "His first stand-alone novel provides a thrilling ride through the dark side of humanity," said Ken Bolton in *Library Journal*.

The novel represents a leap for Ford. "Comic crime is easier to write because it doesn't have to be as tightly plotted," he said on the PanMacmillan website. "Problem is that here in the states at least almost nobody with the exception of Janet Evanovich is making a good living at it. Humor is sufficiently subjective as to make writing funny a bit more dicey than writing thrillers."

Works by the Author

Nameless Night (2008), retitled *Identity* (2009)

Frank Corso Series

Fury (2001)

Black River (2002)

A Blind Eye (2003)

Red Tide (2004)

No Man's Land (2005)

Blown Away (2006)

Leo Waterman Series

Who in Hell Is Wanda Fuca? (1995)

Cast in Stone (1996)

The Bum's Rush (1997)

Slow Burn (1998)

Last Ditch (1999)

The Deader the Better (2000)

For Further Information

Bolton, Ken, *Nameless Night* review, *Library Journal*, Jan. 1, 2008.

Deader the Better review, *Publishers Weekly*, Jan. 17, 2000.

Dodge, Dennis, *Red Tide* review, *Booklist*, June 1, 2004.

G. M. Ford interview, Mystery One Bookstore, summer 2003, http://www.mystery one.com/GMFordInterview.htm/ (viewed Aug. 20, 2009).

G. M. Ford profile, Contemporary Authors Online, http://galenet.galegroup.com/ servlet/BioRC/ (viewed Aug. 7, 2009)

"An Interview with G. M. Ford," PanMacmillan website, http://www.panmacmillan. com/displayPage.asp?PageID=5783/ (viewed Aug. 20, 2009).

Kaczmarek, Lynn, G. M. Ford interview, *Mystery News*, August/September 2003.

Klett, Rex E., *Slow Burn* review, *Library Journal*, Feb. 1, 1998.

No Man's Land review, *Publishers Weekly*, June 13, 2005.

Pierce, J. Kingston, "Who in Hell Is G. M. Ford?" *January Magazine,* http://january magazine.com/profiles/gmford.html/ (viewed Aug. 20, 2009).

Earlene Fowler

Allen Fowler

Lynwood, California
1954

Amateur Detective
Benchmark Series: Benni Harper

About the Author and the Author's Writing

Since the title of each of Earlene Fowler's Albenia "Benni" Harper mystery novels takes its name from a quilt pattern, the handicraft is a convenient metaphor for the writing profession and the way she approaches it.

Quilt makers assemble shapes and colors of fabrics, arranging them into a pattern. "Every quilt tells an unspoken story about the quilter and people the quilter knows. Writers perform a similar task taking pieces of family history, people we've met, things we've read and heard, half-truths and out-and-out lies and turn the into stories," she said in a Crescent Blues interview.

The author was born Earlene Worley in Lynwood, California, in 1954. In 1973 she married Allen W. Fowler, an engineer. Her first novel was published in 1994, though by then she had been writing for several years, thanks to a creative writing class.

"I began writing short stories because it seemed doable. Of course they were rejected. I made that first crucial step in becoming a real writer—I realized I wasn't that good. My stories weren't up to the quality of what was being accepted," she told Cindy Tambourine for *Mystery News*.

Some 150 literary stories later, she attended a program put on by established mystery writers. And—as a lover of quilts, horses, and country-and-western music—she conceived of her heroine, a ranchwoman turned curator of a folk-art museum, and a supporting cast. She set her stories in the made-up town of San Celina, California, a skewed San Luis Obispo. Soon she had a contract for three novels with Putnam-Berkley Publishing.

The quilter/writer analogy fails when Fowler explains how she shapes her prose: mostly as she goes, with a barebones outline at best. Of necessity, she does a lot of editing and sometimes rewriting, but she prefers the spontaneity of this approach.

"Every writer has their own method of getting from A to Z and I believe, whatever it takes to get there, that's the right way to write a novel," she states on her website.

The results speak for themselves: four of her novels were nominated for Agatha Awards before a fifth, *Mariner's Compass*, won in 1999.

Some elements of the books grow from her upbringing in a largely Hispanic community (thus Benni's love interest, Police Chief Gabe Ortiz) and from her strong faith. Of the last, she told fellow mystery author Julia Spencer-Fleming, "When it feels logical to me for a person to think or act on spiritual matters, I put it in. I try not to preach, but just lay it out there."

In *Tumbling Blocks* (2007), Benni is pulling her hair out, unexpectedly caring for a friend's dog, still not done with Christmas shopping, and her mother-in-law about to show up any minute. So of course a puzzle is thrown her way when her boss, Constance Sinclair, insists she investigate the death of art patron Pinky Desmond. "Benni delves into the secrets of the town's elite with her usual flair, unraveling a plot that is as dangerous as the bulls on her father's ranch and as cozy as the quilts she reveres" said reviewer John Rowen in *Booklist*.

Fowler doesn't expect to run out of ideas for the Harper books, but she has changed course to write two stand-alone novels, including *The Saddlemaker's Wife* (2006), which allows her to explore the plight of Ruby Gavin, a young widow unprepared to learn secrets from her late husband's past.

Fowler lists southern writers such as Eudora Welty, Harper Lee, Flannery O'Connor, and James Lee Burke as having most influenced her writing. But it is the people around her who most inspire her: "People have always fascinated me," she told *Publishers Weekly*. "I just love hearing about people's lives. So it makes sense that my books and stories would be character-driven."

Works by the Author

The Saddlemaker's Wife (2006)

Love Mercy (2009)

Benni Harper Series

Fool's Puzzle (1994)

Irish Chain (1995)

Kansas Troubles (1996)

Goose in the Pond (1997)

Dove in the Window (1998)

Mariner's Compass (1999)

Seven Sisters (2000)

Arkansas Traveler (2001)

Steps to the Altar (2002)

Sunshine and Shadow (2003)

Benni Harper's Quilt Album: A Scrapbook of Quilt Projects, Photos and Never-before-Told Stories, with Margrit Hall (2004), includes short stories

Broken Dishes (2004)

Delectable Mountains (2005)

Tumbling Blocks (2007)

State Fair (2010)

Spider Web (2011)

Contributor

Murder on Route 66, with Carolyn Hart, J. A. Jance, and John Lutz (1999)

For Further Information

"Earlene Fowler: Down-home Murder," Crescent Blues, http://www.crescentblues. com/3_6issue/fowler.shtml/ (viewed Dec. 2, 2009).

Earlene Fowler web page, http://www.earlenefowler.com/ (viewed Dec. 2, 2009).

James, Dean, "The Importance of Family: PW Talks with Earlene Fowler," *Publishers Weekly*, Apr. 3, 2006.

Rowen, John, *Mariner's Compass* review, *Booklist*, Apr. 15, 1999.

Spencer-Fleming, Julia, "A Conversation with Earlene Fowler," The Narthex, http://www.juliaspencerfleming.com/Earlene-Fowler.html/ (viewed Dec. 2, 2009).

Tambourine, Cindy, "Earlene Fowler: Writing Quilted Mysteries," *Mystery News*, June/July 2009.

Margaret Frazer (Gail Frazer and Mary Pulver Kuhfeld)

Gail Frazer
Kewanee, Illinois
1946

Mary Pulver Kuhfeld
Terre Haute, Indiana
1943

Amateur Detective, Historical Mystery,
Police Procedural
Benchmark Series: Dame Frevisse

Justin Alexander

About the Author and the Author's Writing

"Margaret Frazer" is known for writing popular historical mystery novels. But Margaret Frazer has a history herself. She's a pen name, used for six Dame Frevisse books by Gail Frazer and Mary Pulver Kuhfeld, then continued by Frazer while Kuhfeld took a new name, Monica Pulver, to write a contemporary needlecraft mystery series.

And even that's not the whole story.

Gail Frazer and Mary Kuhfeld met through the Society for Creative Anachronism, whose members enjoy costumed re-creations of medieval British customs, events, and battles. Frazer and Kuhfeld hit it off and decided to pair their talents to write a book, *The Novice's Tale* (1992), about a Benedictine nun called Dame Frevisse, who lived at a priory called Saint Frideseide in Oxfordshire in the days of Thomas Chaucer (son of Geoffrey Chaucer).

Their second novel, *The Servant's Tale* (1993), was nominated for an Edgar Award, and their fourth, *The Bishop's Tale* (1994), was nominated for a Minnesota Book Award.

Gail Frazer was born in Kewanee, Illinois, in 1946. She is divorced and has two sons. She attended Beloit College, the University of Colorado, and the University of Oregon, majoring in archaeology. She has worked as a librarian, gift shop manager, television station researcher, and assistant matron at an English girls' school. She now lives in Elk River, Minnesota.

The Novice's Tale was Frazer's first published fiction. She long aspired to write straight historical novels, and historical crime novels were a close facsimile. "I started writing the mysteries when I went back to finish my Ph.D. In medieval history," she told interviewer Jeri Westerson. "There are so many holes in history that we simply don't have the information to fill. These make great sites for novels. And historians are all really detectives."

When Frazer collaborated with Mary Kuhfeld on the Dame Frevisse books for Jove, Frazer researched, plotted, and wrote the first draft; Kuhfeld did the second revision; and they then passed the manuscript back and forth until it was done. Frazer assumed the entire load when Kuhfeld left the partnership, and Frazer later spun off a character from the Dame Frevisse books—Joliffe the actor and spy—for his own crime cases.

Frazer thrives on the research. She described her collaboration with Kuhfeld this way: "Because I was writing the first drafts of all the novels, I had to really research medieval nunnery life. I could see how it could be a very fascinating fulfilling lifestyle for certain people," she said in a conversation with Joel Van Valin of Backyard Writer.

However, writing mysteries with medieval settings can be dicey when it comes to language, Frazer said, forcing the author to try to capture the sound of the times without confusing the reader. As she said on her website,

> Trying to hold to medieval vocabulary provides me with an insight into the time and keeps me from imposing alien concepts on the characters while giving readers a subtle sense of being *there*, instead of here, of being *then* instead of now.

Mary Monica Pulver was born in 1943 in Terre Haute, Indiana, and attended the University of Wisconsin. She was a journalist with the U.S. Navy for more than six years and is married to Albert W. Kuhfeld, a museum curator. They live in St. Louis Park, Minnesota. Her first professional sale was to *Alfred Hitchcock's Mystery Magazine* in 1983. With her husband, she wrote several Jack Hafner and Thor Nygaard police procedural short stories. Her first novel, *Murder at the War* (1987), was nominated for an Anthony as best first novel. She then wrote five police procedural mysteries for St. Martin's Press featuring Peter Brichter. These came out under her maiden name Mary Monica Pulver. Kuhfeld teamed with Gail Frazer for six books.

"I like the mystery genre because there is a strong element of morality in it," Kuhfeld told Contemporary Authors. "Good triumphs and wickedness is punished and all (or much) is well at the end. Both in writing and reading them one comes away with a feeling of something having been accomplished."

Kuhfeld accepted an invitation from an editor to write a mystery novel featuring needlecraft. She then left the Dame Frevisse partnership, and as Monica (her real middle name) Ferris (a popular carnival ride) wrote *Crewel World* (1999), the first of a continuing Betsy Devonshire series for Berkley Prime Crime.

Initially Margo Berglund, the proprietor of a needlework shop, was to be Kuhfeld's heroine. But as she did her research, the author said on her website,

> I found I didn't know nearly enough about needlepoint and counted cross stitch, or about running a small business, to carry her off. So I murdered Margot and brought in her sister Betsy, who is as ignorant as I am. It's been interesting.

Works by Gail Frazer and Mary Monica Pulver Kuhfeld Writing as Margaret Frazer

Dame Frevisse Series

The Novice's Tale (1992)

The Servant's Tale (1993)

The Bishop's Tale (1994)

The Outlaw's Tale (1994)

The Boy's Tale (1995)

The Murderer's Tale (1996)

Contributor

The Mammoth Book of Historical Detectives, edited by Mike Ashley (1995), includes "The Midwife's Tale" by Margaret Frazer

Shakespearean Whodunnits, edited by Mike Ashley (1997), includes "The Death of Kings" by Margaret Frazer

Works by Gail Frazer writing as Margaret Frazer, Dame Frevisse Series

The Prioress' Tale (1997)

The Maiden's Tale (1998)

The Reeve's Tale (1999)

The Squire's Tale (2000)

The Clerk's Tale (2002)

The Bastard's Tale (2003)

The Hunter's Tale (2004)

The Widow's Tale (2005)

The Sempster's Tale (2006)

The Traitor's Tale (2007)

The Apostate's Tale (2008)

"The Witch's Tale" (2010), Kindle edition, short story

Joliffe Series

A Play of Isaac (2004)

A Play of Dux Moraud (2005)

A Play of Knaves (2006)

A Play of Lords (2007)

A Play of Treachery (2009)

A Play of Piety (2010)

Margaret Frazer Tales

"Neither Pity, Love, nor Fear" (2010), Kindle edition, short story

"The Simple Logic of It" (2010), Kindle edition, short story

"Strange Gods, Strange Men" (2010), Kindle edition, short story

Contributor

Royal Whodunnits: Tales of Right, Royal Murder and Mystery, edited by Mike Ashley and P. C. Doherty (1999), includes "Neither Pity, Love, nor Fear" by Margaret Frazer

The Mammoth Book of Locked-Room Mysteries, edited by Mike Ashley (2000), includes "A Traveller's Tale" by Margaret Frazer

Murder Most Medieval: Noble Tales of Ignoble Demises, edited by Martin H. Greenberg and John Helfers (2000), includes "The Simple Logic of It" by Margaret Frazer

The Mammoth Book of More Historical Whodunnits, edited by Mike Ashley (2001), includes "Heretical Murder" by Margaret Frazer

Unholy Orders, edited by Serita Stevens (2002), includes "Volo te habere" by Margaret Frazer

Works by Mary Monica Pulver, Peter Brichter Series

Murder at the War (1987)

Ashes to Ashes (1988)

The Unforgiving Minutes (1988)

Original Sin (1991)

Show Stopper (1992)

Works by Mary Monica Pulver, writing as Monica Ferris, Betsy Devonshire Series

Crewel World (1999)

Framed in Lace (1999)

A Stitch in Time (2000)

A Murderous Yarn (2002)

Cutwork (2003)

Hanging by a Thread (2003)

Crewel Yule (2004)

Embroidered Truths (2005)

Patterns in Murder (2005) omnibus of first three novels

Sins and Needles (2006)

Knitting Bones (2007)

Thai Die (2008)

Blackwork (2009)

Sew Far, So Good (2009)

Buttons and Bones (2010)

Contributor

The Mammoth Book of Historical Detectives, edited by Mike Ashley (1995), includes "Ordeal by Fire" by Mary Monica Pulver

Shakespearean Whodunnits, edited by Mike Ashley (1997), includes "The Shrewd Taming of Lord Thomas" by Mary Monica Pulver

Royal Whodunnits: Tales of Right, Royal Murder and Mystery, edited by Mike Ashley and P. C. Doherty (1999), includes "To Whom the Victory?" by Mary Monica Pulver

Unholy Orders, edited by Serita Stevens (2002), includes "Father Hugh and the Kettle of St. Frideswide" by Mary Monica Pulver

Silence of the Loons Thirteen Tales of Mystery by Minnesota's Premier Crime Writers (2005), includes story by Monica Ferris

Murder Most Crafty: 15 All-New Stories of Criminal Handiwork and the Art of Deduction, edited by Maggie Bruce (2006), includes "Strung Out" by Monica Ferris and Denise Williams

For Further Information

Gail Frazer profile, Contemporary Authors Online, http://galenet.galegroup.comserv let/BioRC/ (viewed Dec. 10, 2009).

Margaret Frazer web page, http://berkleysignetmysteries.com/author157/ (viewed Dec. 10, 2009).

Margaret Frazer website, http://www.margaretfrazer.com/biography.html/ (viewed Dec. 10, 2009).

Mary Kuhfeld profile, Contemporary Authors Online, http://galenet.galegroup.com servlet/BioRC/ (viewed Dec. 10, 2009).

Mary Kuhfeld website, http://monica-ferris.com/Kuhfeld/kuhfeld.htm (viewed Dec. 10, 2009).

Monica Ferris web page, Berkley Prime Crime, http://berkleysignetmysteries.com/ author155/ (viewed Dec. 11, 2009).

Monica Ferris website, http://marykuhfeld.name/MeonFer.htm/ (viewed Dec. 10, 2009).

Van Valin, Joel, "A Medieval Interview with Margaret Frazer," Backyard Writer, http://www.whistlingshade.com/0501/frazer.html/ (viewed Dec. 10, 2009).

Westerson, Jeri, "Interview with Sharan Newman and Margaret Frazer," Getting Medieval, http://jeriwesterson.typepad.com/my_weblog/2006/08/interview_ with_.html/ (viewed Dec. 10, 2009).

Frances Fyfield

Derbyshire, England
1948

Amateur Detective, Legal Mystery
Benchmark Series: Sarah Fortune

About the Author and the Author's Writing

Critics laud Frances Fyfield's books. Susanna Yager in *The Telegraph*, for example, said of *The Art of Drowning* (2006): "It's a skillfully plotted story of revenge by one of our most elegant crime writers, piling on the suspense right up to the unpredictable climax."

Frances Fyfield, winner of the Duncan Lawrie Dagger from the Crime Writers' Association in 2008 for *Blood from Stone*, is best known under that name, though she began her literary career as Frances Hegarty. (Fyfield was her mother's maiden name, Hegarty was her father's name.)

She was born in Derbyshire, England, and read English at Newcastle University. She studied criminal law and worked for the Metropolitan Police and later the Crown Prosecution Service, and since 1975 she has been a solicitor. While she toyed with writing romance, her first and subsequent books have been police procedurals or suspense novels.

She has had two continuing series, one with London Crown Prosecutor Helen West and Detective Superintendent Geoffrey Bailey, another with Sarah Fortune, a private attorney.

A Clear Conscience (2001), one of the Helen West series, grows from a theme of domestic abuse. West's cleaning woman, Cathy, leading a dead-end life and mourning the murder of her brother, takes a bold step and leaves her violent husband, her situation intertwining with others to produce a tightly woven story. "*A Clear Conscience* should not be considered a police procedural but a character study in the human condition," posited reviewer Angel L. Soto. "The book is dark and disturbing, concentrating on the psyches of all the players involved in the story."

Fyfield can write fast-paced tales when she wants, but in *Blood from the Stone*, about the suicide of criminal defense lawyer Marianne Shearer, in the view of reader Luke Croll, she was also able to slow the pace.

> The use of the trial transcripts and the slow pace of the story-telling mean that the novel feels much longer than it actually is. This gives Fyfield plenty of time to delve into the protagonists' psyche, which she does by switching perspective often, telling the story from various characters' points of view.

The author's knowledge of ill circumstances and bad characters mostly comes from her work or her research, but keep in mind her remark that "I once worked on the meat pie assembly line in Landers Food Factory," she joked in an interview with *The Scotsman*.

Fyfield sometimes takes different approaches to presenting her crime stories. She alternates the perspectives of Helen West and Geoffrey Bailey in *Without Consent* (1996), for example.

"Helen and Bailey race to the solution, both from different angles, arriving approximately at the same time," reviewer Kay Black said. "Fyfield really knows how to portray the professionals and involves the reader in caring about them. That is the ultimate goal—these are all likeable characters, quirks and all."

Fyfield doesn't hesitate to assume a masculine perspective. "I find no difficulty in writing about a male character," she told Bookreporter. "They are human, after all."

It's not all courtroom or writing office for the author. "When I'm not working (which is as often as possible), I can be found in the nearest junk/charity shop or auction," she said on her website, "looking for the kind of paintings which enhance my life. Otherwise, with a bit of luck, I'm relaxing by the sea with a bottle of wine and a friend or two."

The author claims that Jane Austen's Emma is her favorite character, and author John Le Carré always gets her over rough ground when she's writing. She said that she finds her work is enriched by her reading. In a Crime Time conversation with Eve Tan Gee, she said,

> You always learn something from a good novel, because good novels, whatever their genre, are truthful about the human condition, however fantastical the fiction. Reading is a primary source of education; it refines concentration, understanding and compassion, and it underlines all the knowledge gained in so-called real life.

Works by the Author

Blind Date (1998)

Undercurrents (2000)

The Nature of the Beast (2001)

Seeking Sanctuary (2003)

The Art of Drowning (2006)

Blood from Stone (2008)

Cold to the Touch (2009)

Helen West Series

A Question of Guilt (1988)

Trial by Fire (1990), also titled *Not That Kind of Place*

Deep Sleep (1991)

Shadow Play (1993)

A Clear Conscience (1994)

Without Consent (1996)

A Helen West Omnibus (2002)

A Second Helen West Omnibus (2004)

Sarah Fortune Series

Shadows on the Mirror (1989)

Perfectly Pure and Good (1994)

Staring at the Light (1999)

Looking Down (2004)

Safer Than Houses (2005)

Sarah Fortune Omnibus (2007)

Written as by Frances Hegarty

The Playroom (1991)

Half Light (1992)

Let's Dance (1995)

Adaptations in Other Media

Trial by Fire (1999, TV movie)

The Blind Date (2000, TV movie)

Helen West (2002, British TV series)

For Further Information

Black, Kay, *Without Consent* review, The Mystery Reader, http://www.themys teryreader.com/fyfield-without.html/ (viewed Feb. 4, 2010).

Croll, Luke, *Blood from Stone* review, Reviewing the Evidence, http://www.review ingtheevidence.com/review.html?id=7432/ (viewed Feb. 4, 2010).

Frances Fyfield interview, Bookreporter, April 20, 2001, http://www.bookreporter. com/authors/au-fyfield-frances.asp/ (viewed Feb. 4, 2010).

Frances Fyfield website, http://www.francesfyfield.co.uk/ (viewed Feb. 4, 2010).

Gee, Eve Tan, "Frances Fyfield: The English Are Not What They Seem," Crime Time, http://www.crimetime.co.uk/features/francesfyfield.php/ (viewed Feb. 4, 2010).

"Interview: Francesa Fyfield, author," *The Scotsman*, Nov. 30, 2009, http://living. scotsman.com/books/Interview-Frances-Fyfield-Author.5865629.jp/ (viewed Feb. 4, 2010).

Soto, Angel L., *A Clear Conscience* review, Viewing the Evidence, http://www. reviewingtheevidence.com/review.html?id=2393/ (viewed Feb. 4, 2010).

Yager, Susannah, *The Art of Drowning* review, *The Telegraph*, July 25, 2006.

Elizabeth George

Warren, Ohio
1949

Police Procedural
Benchmark Series: Inspector Thomas Lynley

About the Author and the Author's Writing

Elizabeth George is American through and through. But she shares names with two British monarchs and she is one of the leading crafters of British mysteries.

"I chose the English style because I was interested in writing in what's called the great tradition of the British mystery—and that's a novel that's really an enormous tapestry," the author said in an *Armchair Detective* interview with Nancy-Stephanie Stone.

George's Inspector Thomas Lynley, as you might know, is not just British, he's an aristocrat, married to Lady Helen Clyde Lynley. The inspector's right hand is Detective Sergeant Barbara Havers. And a key friend and forensics guru is pathologist Simon St. James.

When she wrote her first mystery manuscript, in fact, George thought St. James would be the main character. She wrote five manuscripts and none found a home. So she revisited her premise, realized that the characters of Lynley and Havers had a certain chemistry and appeal, and gave them a case to solve. She sent it to an agent. The agent liked it and within weeks found her a publisher. *A Great Deliverance,* released in 1988, earned France's Grand Prix de Littérature Policière.

Elizabeth George was born in Warren, Ohio, in 1949. She graduated from Foothill Community College with an associate's degree in 1969; from University of California, Riverside, with a B.A. in 1970; and from California State University, Fullerton, with an M.S. in 1979. She taught English at the high school and community college levels. A longtime California resident, she and her second husband, Tom McCabe, a retired firefighter, live in Washington State.

As her series has gone on, George has not only kept the characters she started with (except for Lady Lynley, who was murdered in *A Place of Hiding* [2003]), she has at times given them more prominent roles and added new regulars.

"I hated books where the detectives are conveniently orphaned," she told Edie Gibson for *Mystery Scene*. "I've set a challenge for myself to give everyone relatives instead of having everyone dead. I want to be able to share them with readers."

Havers was at first very at much at odds with Lynley; as time has gone on, she has mellowed and grown as a character and their working relationship has shifted dramatically.

Plotting is a serious exercise for George. She has to know who the killer is before she starts writing. "I outline the plot beginning with the primary event that gets the ball rolling," she said in *Writer's Digest*. "Then I'll list the potentials that are causally related to what's gone before." The story is plotted out, but not so strictly, she said, that she can't make changes and discoveries.

Despite the outline, George has at times found that she had way too much plot. She said in *Pacific Northwest,*

> I usually spend two and a half years on a book, partly because I have to go to England for research during the writing and revision. I have a book coming out ... that I wrote 800 pages on before I realized it was too complicated and removed part, which will be the next novel already in draft form.

"Stylistically, I have always written more like a British or European writer than an American writer," the author said in a BookPage conversation. "Setting the books in England gives me much more leeway to do that, I think."

At least one reviewer has chided George for failing to keep up with the latest in police procedures, particularly technical ones. She countered in a Times Online interview that modern investigative methods at times involve way too much personnel. "It's best to know as little as possible, otherwise you'd have a cast of thousands and it would be dreadfully dull."

George is an advocate for new writers. She has taught creative writing since 1988 at colleges, universities, and writing retreats. She told interviewer Kathy Pohl,

> You can't teach somebody to be a creative artist, to have talent or passion, but you *can* teach somebody craft. Whether they can apply it in an artistic fashion, well, that's in the hands of the gods. But they can certainly learn what the craft if writing is.

As with her police characters, George becomes more skilled at her vocation with each case.

Works by the Author

Inspector Thomas Lynley Series

A Great Deliverance (1988)

Payment in Blood (1989)

Well-Schooled in Murder (1990)

A Suitable Vengeance (1991)

For the Sake of Elena (1993)

Missing Joseph (1994)

Playing for the Ashes (1995)

In the Presence of the Enemy (1996)

Deception on His Mind (1997)

In Pursuit of the Proper Sinner (1999)

A Traitor to Memory (2001)

A Place of Hiding (2003)

With No One as Witness (2005)

What Came Before He Shot Her (2006)

Careless in Red (2008)

This Body of Death (2010)

Collections

The Evidence Exposed (1990)

I, Richard (2002)

Editor

Crime from the Mind of a Woman (2002), also titled *A Moment on the Edge: 100 Years of Crime Stories by Women* (2004)

Two of the Deadliest: New Tales of Lust, Greed, and Murder from Outstanding Women of Mystery (2009)

Adaptations in Other Media

Inspector Lynley Mysteries (BBC, 2001–2007)

The author has also written the nonfiction *Write Away* (2004).

For Further Information

Easton, Valerie, "From California and Now Seattle, Elizabeth George Masters the British Mystery," Pacific Northwest, 2004, http://www.elizabethgeorgeonline. com/inprint/interview-pacificnw-2004.htm/ (viewed Dec. 11, 2009).

Elizabeth George interview, *Writer's Digest*, Feb. 2002.

Elizabeth George website, http://www.elizabethgeorgeonline.com/biography.htm/ (viewed Dec. 11, 2009).

Gibson, Edie, "Talking with Elizabeth George," *Mystery Scene* 25 (1990).

Macdonald, Jay, "The Other Side of the Story," BookPage, http://www.bookpage. com/0611bp/elizabeth_george.html (viewed Dec. 11, 2009).

Pohl, Kathy, "Demystifying the Writing Process," *The Writer*, June 2007.

Stone, Nancy-Stephanie, "Self-Schooled in Murder," *The Armchair Detective*, summer 1992.

Wheatley, Jane, "Interview with Elizabeth George, the Californian Crime Writer Who Looks to England for Inspiration," *Times Online,* June 12, 2008. http://entertain ment.timesonline.co.uk/tol/arts_and_entertainment/books/article4122668.ece (viewed Dec. 11, 2009).

Robert Goddard

Fareham, Hampshire, England
1954

Amateur Detective
Benchmark Series: Harry Barnett

About the Author and the Author's Writing

Stephen King discovered the mystery/suspense novels of Robert Goddard when he read one on his new Kindle. "Since then I've read eight more and have about seven to go. I'll parcel them out, because they're too good to gulp," he said in his *Entertainment Weekly* column. "There are missing heirs, stolen fortunes, mistaken identities, raffish con men, hot sex, and cold-blooded murder. These books have more twists than a box of macaroni."

Goddard, indeed, is well known in Great Britain for his artful plots and skillful twists. The books have gradually made their way to American shores to equal acclaim.

"Robert Goddard is a superb storyteller," said The Mystery Reader reviewer Jane Davis of *In Pale Battalions* (1988); "each novel surpasses the previous one. This latest effort is so good he could rest on his laurels without ever writing again."

The author was born in Fareham, Hampshire, England, in 1954, and today lives with his wife, Vaunda North, in Truro, Cornwall. He received a B.A. from Peterhouse in 1976, an M.A. in 1980. He did postgraduate study at the University of Exeter and then worked as a journalist and teacher. From 1978 to 1987 he was an administrator for the Devon County Council; then he left to write full time.

In Goddard's works, things that happened in the past often have consequences in the present. "I find the roots for my writing in my preoccupation with the impact of the past on the present," he told Contemporary Authors. "I was inspired to take up writing by a growing dissatisfaction with much contemporary literature in which I detect a growing rift between technique and meaning."

To overcome that rift, he develops very involved plots and tells his stories with opulent language and description.

"Many of Goddard's work explore the noble values of integrity, honor and self-sacrifice," critic Vickie Britton observed on Suite101.com. "Often the rather flawed hero must make a life-altering decision."

Goddard amplified on this in a Bookreporter interview: "I choose as a central character someone with a big stake in the story who generally has to discover just as much as the reader about the truth of what's happening. I then throw the problems raised by the plot at them, and see how they react, giving them as much independence from me as I can import."

Goddard has so far written three novels about Harry Barnett, a forced retiree who eats and drinks more than he should but has a way with sniffing out murderers. In *Never*

Go Back (2006), he reluctantly attends a 50th reunion of his old RAF squad. He knows he shouldn't have gone when the others start to die, one by one, at a killer's hand. Part of the solution comes from sorting out precisely how something long forgotten actually happened years ago. "Robert Goddard always does a good job presenting a tale that keeps the reader guessing and engaged," said reviewer Jane Davis.

"I guess I write suspense because that's the kind of book I always enjoy most as a reader," the author said in a Crime House conversation. "It's the genre that comes naturally to me." He further explained that he begins with a hook, whether it's a reunion or an art fraud or a kidnapping. "The settings follow from the historical elements in the story. Then I develop characters who I feel will carry it along and provide sympathetic points of view. Only after all that does the plot take detailed shape."

And that detailed shape includes setting as well as character. "Goddard describes the British countryside so clearly that one can easily imagine the scene in the mind's eye," said *Beyond Recall* reviewer Andy Plonka. "One scene which occurs in a tube station is depicted so accurately that a reader could find that exact spot."

Goddard has mastered the art of creating a comfort zone for his fans—then taking them well beyond with his dazzling tales of crime and solution.

Works by the Author

Past Caring (1986)

In Pale Battalions (1988)

Painting the Darkness (1989)

Take No Farewell (1991), also titled *Debt of Dishonour*

Hand in Glove (1992)

Closed Circle (1993)

Borrowed Time (1995)

Beyond Recall (1998)

Caught in the Light (1998)

Set in Stone (1999)

Sea Change (2000)

Dying to Tell (2001)

Days without Number (2003)

Play to the End (2004)

Sight Unseen (2005)

Name to a Face (2008)

Long Time Coming (2010)

Found Wanting (2011)

Harry Barnett Series

Into the Blue (1990)

Out of the Sun (1996)

Never Go Back (2006)

Adaptations in Other Media

Into the Blue (1997), television movie featuring John Thaw, based on the novel, airing on *Masterpiece Theater* in the United States

For Further Information

Britton, Vickie, "Mystery Writer Robert Goddard," Suite101.com, http://britishfiction.suite101.com/article.cfm/robert_goddard/ (viewed Jan 9, 2010).

Davis, Jane, *In Pale Battalions* review, The Mystery Reader, http://www.themysteryreader.com/goddard-pale.html/ (viewed Jan. 15, 2010).

Davis, Jane, *Never Go Back* review, The Mystery Reader, http://www.themysteryreader.com/goddard-never.html/ (viewed Jan. 15, 2010).

King, Stephen, "The Best Books of 2008," *Entertainment Weekly,* http://www.ew.com/ew/gallery/0,,20162677_20164091_20244426_10,00.html/ (viewed Jan. 15, 2010).

Plonka, Andy, *Beyond Recall* review, The Mystery Reader, http://www.themysteryreader.com/goddard-beyond.html/ (viewed Jan. 15, 2010).

Robert Goddard interview, Bookreporter, http://www.bookreporter.com/authors/au-goddard-robert.asp/ (viewed Jan. 9, 2010).

Robert Goddard interview, Crime House, http://www.thecrimehouse.com/interview-with-robert-goddard/ (viewed Jan. 9, 2010).

Robert Goddard profile, Contemporary Authors, http://galenet.galegrup.com/servlet/BioRC/ (viewed Jan. 8, 2010).

"Stephen King's New Discovery: Robert Goddard," *Los Angeles Times*, Nov. 17, 2008.

Ed Gorman

Carol Gorman

Cedar Rapids, Iowa
1941

Private Detective, Western, Horror
Benchmark Series: Sam McCain

About the Author and the Author's Writing

Crime fiction author Ed Gorman is busier than a one-eyed private detective trying to solve a locked-lounge murder at an international airport with 200 suspects and Homeland Security breathing down his neck. An exaggeration? Consider his several dozen novels, his Jack Dwyer private detective and Leo Guild cowboy series, his two-decades stint as editor of *Mystery Scene* magazine, his short stories, and his editing of more than 50 anthologies.

Gorman was born in 1941 in Cedar Rapids, Iowa. He graduated from Coe College in 1968. He and his second wife, novelist Carol Maxwell, have two sons. From 1968 to 1987 Gorman worked as an advertising copywriter and director of television commercials. Then he switched to writing fiction full time.

There is generally a dark element to Gorman's writing—bad things happening to good people—reflective of his troubled teenage years. "In the small cities where we lived," he said in a Crime Time interview, "I gravitated toward the outcasts, and that inevitably meant the criminals. I became a master thief. I could shoplift damned near anything." His salvation was a charge brought by police that he had stolen a large sum of money. He hadn't, but his lawyer suggested he cop a plea. The charges were dropped when the real criminal was identified. But Gorman took the message to heart: straighten up.

While still in advertising, Gorman wrote stories for men's magazines and small literary journals. "And I started dozens of novels—literally—over the years that I never finished," he said in an interview with Harry Shannon. "Then one morning before work—by that time I owned a small ad agency—I sat down and started a novel as a birthday gift for my 40th year." That one he not only finished, he place it with a publisher.

Motion pictures he watched while growing up also had an influence.

"Like many men who came back from the big war, my father was a fan of hardboiled films and westerns," the author told Dean Brierly. "I saw many of the noirs that interest us today when they were first released, but I was too young to understand them." The sense of despair that permeates the movie *Kiss Me Deadly* is one example of movies he saw and remembered.

Gorman names John D. MacDonald, Peter Rabe, and Graham Greene among his favorite authors as he was getting established, also Dean Koontz, Stephen King, Frederic Brown, Jack Kerouac, Chester Himes, and Richard Matheson.

He credits fellow author Max Allan Collins with having given him excellent advice: "Look at each chapter as a story and never look back until you've finished the book," Gorman said in a Saddlebums Western Review conversation. "Then worry about revisions."

To get established as a writer, Gorman wrote horror, suspense, and science fiction. And he indeed writes his novels straight through, five pages a day. He disdains rewriting. As a consequence, he has had to toss out several completed manuscripts that just didn't work. But the survivors have found an eager audience.

Gorman's current detective series character Sam McCain is the least successful lawyer in Black River Falls, Iowa, so he supplements his income as an investigator for Judge Esme Anne Whitney. *The Day the Music Died* (1999) has a story woven around rock musician Buddy Holly's last concert in 1959, before his fatal airplane crash. McCain solves not Holly's death but the murder of Judge Whitney's nephew's wife. The nephew, Kenny, is the chief suspect.

"Good stories are good stories," Gorman told a Dark Echo interviewer, "whatever their kind. I ask only one thing of the book I'm working on, that it keeps me interested. And that means characterization. It's what has made Stephen King the greatest mainstream dark suspense writer of all time—his people."

A lifelong reader, Gorman sees an inner reason for his love of writing. Writing, he said in Prime Crime, gives relief of his fears and anxieties. Of course, it also generates considerable anticipation and suspense in his readers.

Works by the Author

Grave's Retreat (1989)

Dark Trail (1990)

Night of Shadows (1990)

What the Dead Men Say (1990)

The Night Remembers (1991)

Robin: I, Werewolf, with Angelo Torres (1992), graphic novel

Shadow Games (1993)

The Sharpshooter (1993)

Trapped, with Dean Koontz (1993), graphic novel

Wolf Moon (1993)

The Marilyn Tapes (1994)

Black River Falls (1995)

Cold Blue Midnight (1995)

Out There in the Darkness (1995), chapbook

Cage of Night (1996)

The Fatal Frontier (1996)

Runner in the Dark (1996)

The Poker Club (1997)

Daughter of Darkness (1998)

The Silver Scream (1998)

Trouble Man (1998)

Famous Blue Raincoat (1999)

I Know What the Night Knows (1999)

Ride into Yesterday (1999)

Senatorial Privilege (1999)

Storm Riders (1999)

Lawless (2000)

Pirate's Plea (2000)

Snow White and the Eleven Dwarfs, with Edward D. Hoch (2000)

What Dead Man Say (2000)

Ghost Town (2001)

Cast in Dark Waters, with Tom Piccirilli (2002), chapbook

Rituals (2002)

Vendetta (2002)

Gun Truth (2003)

Lynched (2003)

Relentless (2003)

Branded (2004)

Two Guns to Yuma (2005)

Shoot First (2006)

A Knock at the Door (2007)

The Midnight Room (2009)

Cavalry Man Series

The Killing Machine (2005)

Moving Coffin (2007)

Dev Conrad Series

Sleeping Dogs (2008)

Stranglehold (2010)

Dev Mallory Series

Bad Money (2005)

Fast Track (2006)

Jack Dwyer series

New Improved Murder (1985)

Rough Cut (1985)

Murder in the Wings (1986)

Murder Straight Up (1986)

The Autumn Dead (1987)

A Cry of Shadows (1990)

Leo Guild Series

Guild (1987)

Death Ground (1988)

Blood Game (1989)

Robert Payne Series

Blood Moon (1994), also titled *Blood Red Moon*

Hawk Moon (1995)

Harlot's Moon (1998)

Voodoo Moon (2000)

Sam McCain Series

The Day the Music Died (1999)

Will You Still Love Me Tomorrow? (2000)

Wake Up Little Susie (2001)

Save the Last Dance for Me (2002)

Everybody's Somebody's Fool (2003)

Breaking Up Is Hard to Do (2004)

Fools Rush In (2007)

Ticket to Ride (2009)

Tobin Series

   Murder in the Aisle (1987)

   Several Deaths Later (1988)

Collections

   Best Western Stories of Ed Gorman (1992)

   Prisoners and Other Stories (1992)

   Criminal Intent: 1, with Marcia Muller and Bill Pronzini (1993)

   Dark Whispers (1993)

   Cages (1995)

   Moonchasers (1996)

   Famous Blue Raincoat (1999)

   Legend, with Judy Alter, Jane Candia Coleman, Loren D. Estleman, Elmer Kelton, Robert J. Randisi, and James Reasoner (1999)

   The Dark Fantastic (2001)

   The Long Silence After (2001)

   Such a Good Girl (2001)

   Crooks, Crimes, and Christmas, with Michael Jahn, Irene Marcuse, and Susan Slater (2003)

   The Long Ride Back (2004)

   Different Kinds Of Dead and Other Tales (2005)

   Different Kinds of Dead (2006)

   The End of It All: And Other Stories (2009)

   Noir 13 (2010)

Contributor

   Masques 3 (1989)

   Lovecraft's Legacy (1990)

   Riverworld Fool's Paradiser (1992)

   Borderlands 3 (1993)

   Confederacy of the Dead (1993)

   Monsters in Our Midst (1993)

   The Year's Best Fantasy and Horror Sixth Annual Collection (1993)

   Blue Motel: Narrow Houses, vol. 3 (1994)

   The Earth Strikes Back (1994)

Adventures of the Batman (1995)

Dark Love (1995)

Heaven Sent: 18 Glorious Tales of the Angels (1995)

More Phobias (1995)

Tales of the Batman (1995)

The Ultimate Alien (1995)

Diagnosis—Terminal: An Anthology of Medical Terror (1996)

The Fortune Teller (1997)

Robert Bloch's Psychos (1997)

The UFO Files (1997)

Alien Abductions (1999)

999 (1999)

Vampire Slayers: Stories of Those Who Dare to Take Back the Night (1999)

City of Night, with Dean Koontz (2005)

The Shamus Winners: America's Best Private Eye Stories, vol. 1, 1982–1995 (2010), edited by Robert J. Randisi, includes "Turn Away"

Editor

The Black Lizard Anthology of Crime Fiction (1987)

The Second Black Lizard Anthology of Crime Fiction (1988)

Stalkers, with Martin H. Greenberg (1989)

Night Kills (1990)

Under the Gun: Mystery Scene Presents the Best Suspense and Mystery, first annual collection, with Martin H. Greenberg and Robert J. Randisi (1990)

Cat Crimes, with Martin H. Greenberg (1991)

Dark Crimes (1991)

Invitation to Murder, with Martin H. Greenberg (1991)

Solved, with Martin H. Greenberg (1991)

Cat Crimes II, with Martin H. Greenberg (1992)

Cat Crimes III, with Martin H. Greenberg (1992)

Dark Crimes 2: Modern Masters of Noir (1992)

Danger in DC: Cat Crimes in the Nation's Capital (1993)

The Fine Art of Murder: The Mystery Reader's Indispensable Companion (1993)

Predators, with Martin H. Greenberg (1993)

Feline and Famous: Cat Crimes Goes Hollywood, with Martin H. Greenberg (1994)

A Modern Treasury of Great Detective and Murder Mysteries (1994)

Cat Crimes for the Holidays, with Martin H. Greenberg and Larry Segriff (1995)

Cat Crimes Takes a Vacation, with Martin H. Greenberg (1995)

Gunslinger and Nine Other Action-Packed Stories of the Wild West, with Bill Pronzini and Martin H. Greenberg (1995)

Night Screams, with Martin H. Greenberg (1995)

Woman on the Beat: Stories of Women Police Officers, with Martin H. Greenberg (1995)

Murder Most Irish (1996)

American Pulp (1997)

Love Kills (1997)

The UFO Files, with Martin H. Greenberg (1997)

The Year's 35 Finest Crime and Mystery Stories, with Martin H. Greenberg (1997)

The Best of the American West (1998)

Cat Crimes through Time, with Martin H. Greenberg and Larry Segriff (1998)

Once Upon a Crime (1998)

Future Crimes, with Martin H. Greenberg and John Helfers (1999)

Pure Pulp, with Bill Pronzini (1999)

The Year's 35 Finest Crime and Mystery Stories, with Martin H. Greenberg (1999)

Sleuths of the Century (2000)

Star Colonies, with Martin H. Greenberg and John Helfers (2000)

The Worlds Finest Mystery and Crime Stories (2000)

The Blue and the Gray Undercover (2001)

Desperadoes (2001)

Murder Most Feline: Cunning Tales of Cats and Crime (2001)

Pulp Masters, with Martin H. Greenberg (2001)

Such a Good Girl, and Other Crime Stories (2001)

Guns of the West, with Martin H. Greenberg (2002)

Kittens, Cats and Crime (2003)

Stagecoach (2003)

Texas Rangers, with Martin H. Greenberg (2004)

The World's Finest Mystery and Crime Stories V (2004)

The Adventures of the Missing Detective, and 25 of the Year's Finest Crime and Mystery Stories, with Martin H. Greenberg (2005)

Lone Star Law (2005)

The Deadly Bride and 19 of the Year's Finest Crime and Mystery Stories, with Martin H. Greenberg (2006)

The Widow of Slane and Six More of the Best Crime and Mystery Novellas of the Year, with Martin H. Greenberg (2006)

Wolf Woman Bay and Nine More of the Finest Crime and Mystery Novellas of the Year, with Martin H. Greenberg (2007)

Between the Dark and the Daylight, and 27 More of the Best Crime and Mystery Stories of the Year, with Martin H. Greenberg (2009)

The author has also written Trailsman western series novels under the house name Jon Sharpe.

For Further Information

Brierly, Dean, "Point Blank with Crime Novelist Ed Gorman," Cinemaretro, http://www.cinemaretro.com/index.php?/archives/293-DEAN-BRIERLY-INTER VIEWS-CRIME-NOVELIST-ED-GORMAN.html/ (viewed Dec. 11, 2009).

Dillon-Parkin, Peter, Ed Gorman interview, Crime Time, http://www.crimetime.co.uk/interviews/edgorman.html/ (viewed Dec. 11, 2009).

Ed Gorman website, http://www.newimprovedgorman.com/ (viewed Dec. 11, 2009).

Ed Gorman interview, DarkEcho Horror, http://www.darkecho.com/darkecho/archives/gorman.html/ (viewed Dec. 11, 2009).

Ed Gorman interview, Saddlebums Western Review, http://saddlebums.blogspot.com/2007/10/saddlebums-interview-ed-gorman.html/ (viewed Dec. 11, 2009).

Shannon, Harry, Ed Gorman interview, FeoAmante, http://www.feoamante.com/Stories/Inter_views/Gorman/edgor_pg1.html/ (viewed Dec. 11, 2009).

Sue Grafton

Louisville, Kentucky
1940

Private Detective
Benchmark Series: Kinsey Milhone

About the Author and the Author's Writing

Sue Grafton's series hero Kinsey Milhone is so real that people often assume she's simply the author putting herself on the page. But, aside from such obvious differences as Grafton being happily married and with grandchildren, they're quite a bit different in temperament. "Kinsey is also very undomesticated, whereas I am a little more so," Grafton said in a Pan Macmillan interview. "But it's all great fun, because I get to live through her—she's my alter ego and she does all this exciting stuff I don't get to do as a married lady!"

Sue Taylor Grafton was born in 1940 in Louisville, Kentucky. Her upbringing was unconventional, as her parents were alcoholics, she said in a *Mystery Scene* interview. "I grew up in a very dysfunctional situation. Sometimes I think it was a very perfect upbringing, because I was raised with a great deal of freedom. It was a very unstructured household, and I lived in my imagination."

She earned a B.A. in English literature with minors in humanities and fine arts from the University of Louisville in 1961. She also studied at Western Kentucky State Teachers College. Grafton married Steven F. Humphrey, a professor of philosophy, in 1978. She has three children by two earlier marriages.

Grafton worked as a hospital admissions clerk, cashier, and medical secretary before starting her writing career with two novels. She spent a decade in Hollywood writing television and motion picture scripts, then decided to break away.

She found the prospect of writing her first detective novel, *A Is for Alibi* (1982), daunting. "I was teaching myself how to write a mystery novel by reading every how-to I could get hold of," she told interviewer Dave Welch. "I was teaching myself California criminal law, private eye procedure, police procedure, anything that seemed relevant to the job. It took me five years to write A."

The author gained helpful insights about her craft from her father, Chip Warren Grafton, who wrote three mystery novels in the 1940s. "He taught me how to write with clarity and simplicity," she said in an interview with Bruce Taylor. "He said it was never my job to revise the English language or to play games with punctuation, spelling, or capitalization.

The mysteries are on a slower time track than the real world; *O Is for Outlaw*, for example, still has the heroine in 1986, before cellular telephones or the Internet. This may derive from Grafton's religious background; both sets of grandparents were Presbyterian missionaries. "The Presbyterians believe that in the mind of God there is no time, which makes sense," she said, with good humor, on the Writers Write website. "In God's mind, it's all over, beginning, middle and end, all through the end of time. If that is true, then I have already written these books, right? All I have to do is figure out what I've already said."

Grafton does not outline before she writes. She maintains a journal where she tries out some "what-ifs." She often discards more ideas than she keeps as she gets into the rhythm of a particular novel. Does this method of writing get her into plot conundrums? Yes. Is she a capable professional who can work her way through? Yes again.

She interviews cops, investigators, lawyers, coroners, and others and also reads widely to be able to create a solid background to her various plots and settings. While her character is in great part based on her own personality, Grafton said she works hard to maintain Milhone's perspective and not let hers take over. She doesn't know everything about her heroine's life; when she decided to write about Milhone's ex, Mickey Magruder, the author said she knew little more than that he was a police officer, a little older than Milhone, and that Milhone had walked out on their marriage. She learned the details only as they emerged in her writing.

What gives Milhone her great appeal, Grafton expects, is her real dimension. She has no college degree. She's a hard worker. She makes her own way. She pays her bills promptly. "Readers are convinced she's real," the author said in a 1996 interview, which appears on her website. "I don't idolize her; she isn't larger than life; she's human-sized. She makes mistakes."

What does she like about writing mysteries? "I love a well-structured story," she said in *The Writer* in 2002.

> I'm interested in what motivates an individual to do good or ill and I'm fascinated by the dark side of human nature. Basically, any mystery writer is both magician and moralist . . . two species of artist in short supply. Sometimes I claim I write because I put in an application at Sears and they've never called back.

As Grafton has progressed through the alphabet, readers have expressed concern that *Z is for Zero*—announced but not yet written—will be the end.

"I think it's their own abandonment issues," the author told *January Magazine*'s Linda Richards. "So I have to assure them: mother loves you and we're all going to be together forever."

Works by the Author

Fiction

Keziah Dane (1967)

The Lolly-Madonna War (1969)

Kinsey Milhone Series

    A Is for Alibi (1982)

    B Is for Burglar (1985)

    C Is for Corpse (1986)

    D Is for Deadbeat (1987)

    E Is for Evidence (1988)

    F Is for Fugitive (1989)

    G Is for Gumshoe (1990)

    H Is for Homicide (1991)

    Kinsey and Me (1991), short stories

    I Is for Innocent (1992)

    J Is for Judgment (1993)

    K Is for Killer (1994)

    L Is for Lawless (1995)

    M Is for Malice (1996)

    N Is for Noose (1998)

    Sue Grafton: Three Complete Novels A, B & C (1999), omnibus

    O Is for Outlaw (2001)

    P Is for Peril (2001)

    Sue Grafton: Three Complete Novels D, E & F (2001), omnibus

    Q Is for Quarry (2002)

    Sue Grafton: Three Complete Novels G, H & I (2002), omnibus

    "The Lying Game" (2003), short story in Land's End catalog

    R Is for Ricochet (2004)

    S Is for Silence (2005)

    T Is for Trespass (2007)

    U Is for Undertow (2009)

Anthologies

    Mean Streets, edited by Robert J. Randisi (1986)

    The Year's Best Mystery and Suspense Stories, edited by Edward D. Hoch (1987)

    An Eye for Justice, edited by Robert J. Randisi (1988)

    Criminal Elements, edited by Bill Pronzini (1988)

    Lady on the Case, edited by Marcia Muller (1988)

City Sleuths and Tough Guys, edited by David Willis McCullough (1989)

Deadly Doings, edited by Martin H. Greenberg (1989)

Match Me Sidney!, (1989)

Sisters in Crime, edited by Marilyn Wallace (1989)

Sisters in Crime 2, edited by Marilyn Wallace (1990)

Under the Gun, edited by Ed Gorman (1990)

Best American Mystery Stories 2000, edited by Donald E. Westlake (2000)

Best American Mystery Stories of the Century, edited by Otto Penzler and Tony Hillerman (2001)

Most Wanted, edited by Robert J. Randisi (2002)

The Shamus Winners: America's Best Private Eye Stories, vol. 1, 1982–1995, edited by Robert J. Randisi (2010)

Grafton alone and with Stephen F. Humphrey has written numerous teleplays. She has also written nonfiction, including *Writing Mysteries*.

For Further Information

Bing, Jonathan, "Sue Grafton: Death and the Maiden," *Publishers Weekly* (Apr. 20, 1998).

Chapman, Jeff, and John D. Jorgenson, eds., "Sue Grafton," in *Contemporary Authors New Revision Series*, vol. 55. Detroit: Gale Research, 1997.

Fish, Peter, "Gumshoe in Paradise," *Sunset* (Sept. 1999).

Geherin, David, "Sue Grafton," in *St. James Guide to Crime & Mystery Writers*, fourth edition. Detroit: St. James Press, 1996.

Goodman, Susan, " '2' Is for Bestsellers," *Writer's Yearbook 1996* (1996).

Grafton, Sue, "How I Write," *The Writer* (May 2002).

Kaufman, Natalie Hevener, and Carol McGinnis Kay. *G Is for Grafton: The World of Kinsey Milhone*. New York: Holt, 1997.

Nolan, Tom, "Seven Down and Nineteen to Go," *Mystery Scene* 72 (2001).

Richards, Linda, "G is for Grafton: Sue Grafton's Murderous Moments," *January Magazine,* http://www.januarymagazine.com/grafton.html/ (viewed Dec. 3, 2009).

Stasio, Marilyn, "Lady Gumshoes: Boiled Less Hard," *New York Times Book Review* (Apr. 28, 1985).

"Sue Grafton," in *Authors and Artists for Young Adults*, vol. 49. Detroit: Gale Group, 2003.

"Sue Grafton," in *The Mammoth Encyclopedia of Modern Crime Fiction*, edited by Mike Ashley. New York: Carroll & Graf, 2002.

Sue Grafton interview, Pan Macmillan, http://www.panmacmillan.com/displayPage. asp?PageID=4101/ (viewed Dec. 3, 2009).

Sue Grafton web page. http://www.suegrafton.com/ (viewed Dec. 3, 2009).

"Sue Grafton: M is for Mysteries," iVillager, http://www.ivillage.com/books/intervu/ myst/articles/0,,240795_39443.html/ (viewed July 27, 2003).

Taylor, Bruce, "G is for (Sue) Grafton," *The Armchair Detective* (winter 1989).

Welch, Dave, "S is for Sue Grafton," Powell's Books, http://www.powells.com/ authors/suegrafton.html (viewed Dec. 3, 2009).

White, Claire, E., "A Conversation With Sue Grafton," Writers Write, http://www. writerswire/com/journal/oct99/grafton.htm/ (viewed July 27, 2003).

Sarah Graves

Wisconsin
1951

Amateur Detective
Benchmark Series: Jacobia Tiptree

About the Author and the Author's Writing

Sarah Graves works with sandpaper and finish nails. And Sarah Graves works with nouns and verbs. Her vocation (writing) very much reflects her avocation (home renovation) in her successful series of Home Repair Is Homicide novels that feature Jacobia "Jake" Tiptree, an amateur with a hammer belt.

"Taking something apart—an old doorknob mechanism or five layers of wallpaper—is like doing the detective work," the author told *Boston Globe* interviewer Letitia Baldwin. "It reveals the nuts and bolts of a situation. Once you've got the information, putting whatever it is back together again is like recreating the original incident."

Had *McCall's* magazine accepted the story she sent it when she was seven, the author might have gotten off to a precocious career start. "It was about a squirrel lost in the woods," she said on her website. "The editors sent a form rejection letter, possibly because it was not very realistic for a squirrel to be lost in the woods."

Born Mary Squibb in Wisconsin in 1951 and now living in Eastport, Maine, with her musician husband John Graves, she worked as a respiratory therapist before deciding to relocate to New England and become a home renovator. Her first project was an 1823 Federal-style house. How far has she progressed? About as well as Jake Tiptree in the books.

Tiptree and Graves have quite a lot in common. As Andrea de Leon, on NPR, has noted,

> Tiptree would prefer to spend her time glazing windows or taking a sledge hammer to the ancient upstairs commode, but it wouldn't be a mystery book if someone didn't turn up dead—and quickly. And Graves wouldn't be a mystery writer if she couldn't spot means, motive, and opportunity as she drives around town.

Graves waited a couple of decades after her *McCall's* rejection before trying seriously to write fiction. Her road to publication was relatively brief, she has said. Her initial Tiptree book, *The Dead Cat Bounce* (which, she has admitted, is unfortunately titled, referring to a Wall Street trend but usually mistaken for animal cruelty) came out in 1998. "In her polished debut," *Publishers Weekly* said, "Graves blends charming, evocative digressions about life in Eastport with an intricate plot, well-drawn characters and a wry sense of humor."

Graves initially sets the stage this way: Tiptrees was a financial advisor in New York City until her marriage went sour. She then packed her teenage son Sam into her car and sought a new beginning in Maine. No sooner had she settled in and met a fun neighbor

197

Ellie White than a dead body turns up in her storeroom. As the series progresses, we learn that Tiptree's mother had died 35 years before, when she was a toddler. She confronts that old crime in later novels. In *A Face at the Window* (2008), Graves ups the ante, speeding the book's pace with thriller elements.

At the same time, Graves has kept in place all the characters her readers have come to expect. "The most rewarding part of writing a recurring character," she told Shannon McKenna of Bookreporter, "is the opportunity to find out a little more each time. Characters don't just tell all their secrets on the first date! They have to get comfortable with the writer before they'll confide much."

Graves writes detailed outlines for her books, but not so detailed that she doesn't have wiggle room once she gets deeply into the chapters. She assigns herself a set number of words to write each day and usually stops writing in midscene, but with a good idea of where she's going next.

She urges budding writers to read and read some more, and to write. "Join the toughest writing workshop that will take you, and listen to what the members tell you," she said in Novel Journey. "But don't follow any advice that makes your inner baloney detector go off."

Works by the Author

Home Repair Is Homicide Series

The Dead Cat Bounce (1998)

Triple Witch (1999)

Wicked Fix (2000)

Repair to Her Grave (2001)

Wreck the Halls (2002)

Unhinged (2003)

Mallets Aforethought (2004)

Tool & Die (2004)

Nail Biter (2005)

Trap Door (2006)

The Book of Old Houses (2007)

A Face at the Window (2008)

Crawlspace (2009)

Knockdown (2011)

For Further Information

"Author Sarah Graves Interviewed," Novel Journey, Feb. 13, 2009, http://novel journey.blogspot.com/2009/02/author-sarah-graves-interviewed.html/ (viewed Dec. 3, 2009).

Baldwin, Letitia, "Mysteries of Home Repair Maine Writer's 1823 Fixer-upper Is a Main Character in Her Novels," *Boston Globe*, June 17, 2004.

Book of Old Houses review, *Publishers Weekly*, Nov. 12, 2007.

De Leon, Andrea, "Small-town Murder in Sarah Graves' Eastport," NPR, July 14, 2008, http://www.npr.org/templates/story/story.php?storyId=92294115/ (viewed Dec. 3, 2009).

Dead Cat Bounce review, *Publishers Weekly*, July 20, 1998.

Kessel, Joyce, *A Face at the Window* review, *Library Journal*, May 1, 2009.

McKenna, Shannon, Sarah Graves interview, Bookreporter, http://www.bookreporter. com/authors/au-graves-sarah.asp/ (viewed Dec. 3, 2009).

O'Brien, Sue, *Trap Door* review, *Booklist*, Dec. 1, 2006.

Sarah Graves website, http://www.randomhouse.com/bantamdell/graves/ (viewed Dec. 3, 2009).

Kerry Greenwood

Footscray, Victoria, Australia
1954

Amateur Detective, Historical Mystery,
Culinary Mystery, Fantasy, Science
Fiction
Benchmark Series: Phryne Fisher

Vicki Jones

About the Author and the Author's Writing

Transplant Dorothy L. Sayers's Lord Peter Wimsey to another continent, change his gender, give her a stylish taste in fashion, keep her in the Roaring Twenties but provide an exotic boyfriend (perhaps the magical martial artist Lin Ghung) and you have—Phryne Fisher, crime-solving heroine of nearly 20 books in Australian writer Kerry Greenwood's popular fictional series.

Born in Footscray, Victoria, Australia, in 1954, Greenwood has been a folk singer, factory worker, translator, costume maker, and film director. She earned a law degree from Melbourne University in 1979 and has been a barrister and solicitor for Sunshine Legal Aid. Her successful novels—fantasy as well as mystery—have allowed her to curtail her professional activities to serving as an advocate in the Magistrates Court of the Victorian Legal Aid Commission.

Greenwood created a brassy character in order to stand out in the modest Australian market and attract attention in other English-speaking countries. Plus, the period had great appeal.

"Phryne is the product of the losses of the Great War," the author said in a Poe's Deadly Daughters interview—"the sudden elevation of women because there were few men, and she is bold but not impossible for that period. It's not as easy as it used to be to be bold in the twenty-first century."

Qualities that make Phryne (pronounced like shiny) distinctly Australian, Greenwood has said, include her disdain for authority and her unbridled interest in having a delightful time.

"Phryne is a hero, just like James Bond or The Saint, but with fewer product endorsements and a better class of lovers," she said on the Phryne Fisher website. "I decided to try a female hero and made her as free as a male hero, to see what she would do. Mind you, at that time I only thought there would be two books."

In another interview, with *Festival* online magazine, she elaborated, "I wanted her to be a heroine, but without all the difficulties Harriet Vane had." She modeled her character on her sister, Janet, noting wistfully, "It would be nice to be like Phryne."

Greenwood writes the novels in a flurry of research—typically three months' worth—and a white heat of writing—often an intense three weeks with little break. Distractions are few—and mostly come from the demands of the three cats in her household.

She has flown an airplane and parachuted from one. But she prefers earthbound activities, such as haunting secondhand bookstores to expand her collection of some 7,000 volumes.

Ideas for her books do not come from her work. "My kind of crime [at legal aid] is not fictional crime," she said in an interview on the Sydney Writers' Centre blog.

> I work down among the Magistrates' Courts. I get people who are no good at it—they fall through colorbond roofs when burgling houses and break their legs, they leave their healthcare card in the lock they are trying to slip, they etch their fingerprints into the panels of a burned car.

In addition, Greenwood strives for happier endings in her mysteries than usually occur in real life. She respects the conventions of detective storytelling.

In *Murder on a Midsummer Night* (2008), typically, the heroine juggles more than one case. She looks into an apparent suicide on St. Kilda beach and tries to find a lost heir to a fortune. "Greenwood keeps the action moving as swiftly as milady's Hispano-Suiza," said a reviewer for *Publishers Weekly*. "There's no quibbling with the author's ability to create a sybaritic piece of period escapism."

Greenwood has written novels about women of Greek mythology (three Delphic Women novels), young adult science fiction books (the Stormbringer series), and nonfiction. She has also created a second mystery series, featuring Corinna Chapman, proprietor of a bakery in Melbourne called Earthly Delights. These books, with a modern setting, include a character who enjoys eating her own creations.

In *Trick or Treat* (2007), Corinna, her apprentice Jason, and bakery staff Kylie and Goss are embroiled in a cauldron of trouble involving a competitor who has just moved in down the street, the arrival of her boyfriend's past lover, a gathering of witches, and a search for valuables stolen during World War II. Reviewer Harriet Klausner called it

> a superb amateur sleuth that deftly merges several mysteries with the Lonsdale Street neighborhood goings-on that impact the lead heroine and her friends. The story line is fast-paced from the first confection to the final confrontation as Kerry Greenwood bakes a delightful Australian tale with a terrific twist.

Greenwood has developed a strong following, though she is cautious not to bow to demands. "I write like I write and the fans like it (Goddess bless them)," she said in a Spaced Out Inc. interview. "But fandom is important. It's the biggest information exchange around and an excellent way to get recommendations from people who think like you do and like the same sort of books."

Any ideas for the brash Aussie heroine?

Works by the Author

Corinna Chapman Series

Earthly Delights (2004)

Heavenly Pleasures (2005)

Devil's Food (2006)

Trick or Treat (2007)

Forbidden Fruit (2009)

Phryne Fisher Series

Cocaine Blues (1989), also issued as *Death by Misadventure*

Flying Too High (1990)

Murder on the Ballarat Train (1991)

Death at Victoria Dock (1992)

The Green Mill Murder (1993)

Blood and Circuses (1994)

Ruddy Gore (1995)

Urn Burial (1996)

Raisins and Almonds (1997)

Death Before Wicket (1999)

Away with the Fairies (2001)

Murder in Montparnasse (2002)

The Castlemaine Murders (2003)

The Phryne Fisher Mysteries: Cocaine Blues / Flying Too High (2004)

Queen of the Flowers (2004)

Death by Water (2005)

Murder in the Dark (2006)

A Question of Death: An Illustrated Phryne Fisher Treasury (2007)

Murder on a Midsummer Night (2008)

Dead Man's Chest (2009)

Introducing the Honorable Phryne Fisher (2010), reprints first three novels

Collections

Recipes for Crime, with Jenny Pausacker (1995)

For Further Information

"Author Interview: Kerry Greenwood," Sidney Writers' Centre, http://thestoryso far.typepad.com/valeries_blog/2007/10/author-intervie.html/ (viewed Aug. 29, 2009).

"An Interview with Kerry Greenwood," Spacedoutinc, http://spacedoutinc.org/ DU-17/KerryGreenwoodInterview.html/ (viewed Aug. 29, 2009).

Kerry Greenwood website, Phrynefisher.com, http://www.phrynefisher.com/ (viewed Aug. 29, 2009).

Klausner, Harriet, *Trick or Treat* review, Genre Go Round reviews, http://genre goroundreviews.blogspot.com/2009/08/trick-or-treat-kerry-greenwood.html/ (viewed Sept. 2, 2009).

"Murder and Mayhem in Jazz Age Melbourne," Festivale.info, http://www.festivale. info/ffeatures/kerry.htm/ (viewed Aug. 29, 2009).

Murder on a Midsummer Night review, *Publishers Weekly*, May 11, 2009.

Parshall, Sandra, "Kerry Greenwood & the Fabulous Phryne Fisher," Poe's Deadly Daughters, http://poesdeadlydaughters.blogspot.com/2009/03/kerry-green wood-fabulous-phryne-fisher.html/ (viewed Aug. 29, 2009).

Robert O. Greer

Columbus, Ohio
1944

Private Detective, Amateur Detective,
Medical Mystery
Benchmark Series: C. J. Floyd

About the Author and the Author's Writing

Robert O. Greer is a professor of pathology, medicine, surgery, and dentistry. And he is a cattle rancher in Wyoming.

His fictional hero, C. J. Floyd, is an African American bail bondsman who wears a Stetson, smokes cheroots, and collects license plates.

Which makes both Greer and Floyd pretty interesting.

The author was born in Columbus, Ohio, in 1944, the son of educators. He grew up there and in Gary, Indiana. He majored in zoology, chemistry, and journalism at Miami University in Ohio, earning a B.A. in 1965. He then studied dentistry at Howard University. During the Vietnam War he was a medic with the Coast Guard. He earned a medical degree from Boston University, with a specialty in head and neck pathology. In 1974, he joined the University of Colorado Health Sciences Center, where he is a full professor and cancer researcher. He also has a private pathology practice. If that isn't sufficient, he founded and has edited the *High Plains Literary Review* since 1986. He and his wife, Phyllis, who also edited the *Review*, owned a ranch in Steamboat Springs, Colorado. After her death, he sold that ranch and purchased Triangle Long Bar ranch in southern Wyoming.

A fan of writers ranging from Mark Twain and Eudora Welty to Willa Cather and George Orwell, Greer adores the short story form. But with few markets for short prose, he shifted to the novel format when he began his C. J. Floyd books. The books brim with colorful characters, including old rodeo cowboys Dittier Atkins and Morgan Williams as well as Floyd's partner, a former Marine intelligence officer named Flora Jean Benson.

The writer centers his stories in Denver but often ventures into the modern West. "When I'm writing, I'm writing from a sense of place that doesn't get the same exposure that things east of the Hudson get," he told *Bloomsbury Review*. "That's part of why I write. I want to write about where I live and the places I love."

Each new novel begins with a concept. "Interestingly, neither the plot nor my characters come first," he told Cheryl's Book Nook, "especially since after twelve novels, I'm pretty much set with the characters. What usually comes first is a kernel of an idea. That idea then generally works itself into a plot that characters are placed within."

Some ideas grow from his day job. In *The Devil's Hatband* (1996), Floyd is hired to find a federal judge's missing daughter. It turns out she has become an eco-tourist who wants to destroy the cattle ranch industry. When she disappeared, she took valuable bio tech documents and Carson Technologies desperately wants them back.

With *Heat Shock* (2003), Greer introduced a new series character, half black, half Vietnamese Carmen Nguyen, who rides a motorcycle to work—as an emergency room physician in Denver. In the book, she reluctantly agrees to crusty Luke Redstone's dying request and looks to protect his flock of prizewinning fighting cocks from poachers, not expecting this would bring her into partnership with a river rafter and Gulf War veteran named Walter Rios and into conflict with a relentless businessman, Jack Kimbrough, who wants the birds for his genetic research.

Greer's standalone novel *Spoon* (2009) features Arcus Witherspoon, a restless cowboy who befriends the Darleys, Montana ranch owners who have yet to get over the untimely death of their son. The author found the novel a change of pace. "There was a bit of difference in the construction of the plot for *Spoon* than with one of my mysteries or medical thrillers," he said in *New West*. "With a mystery the writer has to drop clues along the way, insert red herrings, and all in all perform quite a bit of sleight of hand." In a mainstream novel, more character driven, he had greater opportunity to develop and explore personalities as well as a favorite theme of an outsider—in this case a man half-Indian, half-black—trying to fit in.

Readers of the Floyd series will recognize that drift. "I really wanted to deal with C. J.'s ability to integrate himself back into mainstream society after his service in Vietnam," Greer said in *Rocky Mountain News*, "so I dealt with the angst that he has as he tries to reset himself in society."

As he explores social themes, Greer hasn't lost sight of his primary mission: a good crime story.

Works by the Author

Limited Time (2000)

Isolation and Other Stories (2001)

Spoon (2009)

C. J. Floyd Series

The Devil's Hatband (1996)

The Devil's Red Nickel (1997)

The Devil's Backbone (1998)

Resurrecting Langston Blue (2005); Dr. Carmen Nguyen also appears

The Fourth Perspective (2006)

The Mongoose Deception (2007)

Blackbird, Farewell (2008)

First of State (2010)

Dr. Carmen Nguyen Series

Heat Shock (2003)

For Further Information

Kenney, Jay, "Renaissance Man, Western Writer; An Interview with Robert Greer," *Bloomsbury Review*, 2005, http://www.bloomsburyreview.com/Archives/2005/Robert%20Greer.pdf/ (viewed Dec. 17, 2009).

Robert O. Greer website, http://www.robertgreerbooks.com/author.html/ (viewed Dec. 17, 2009).

Shank, Jenny, "An Interview with Writer, Pathologist, Professor, and Rancher Robert Greer," *New West*, Nov. 27, 2009, http://www.newwest.net/topic/article/an_interview_with_writer_pathologist_professor_and_rancher_robert_greer/C39/L39/ (viewed Dec. 17, 2009).

"Talking with Dr. Robert Greer, Author of *Spoon*," Cheryl's Book Nook, Oct. 22, 2009, http://cherylsbooknook.blogspot.com/2009/10/talking-with-dr-robert-greer-author-of.html/ (viewed Dec. 17, 2009).

Thorn, Patti, "Interview with Author Robert Greer," *Rocky Mountain News*, Oct. 27, 2008.

Martha Grimes

Pittsburgh, Pennsylvania
1931

Private Detective, Amateur Detective,
Legal Mystery
Benchmark Series: Superintendent Richard Jury

Courtesy of the author

About the Author and the Author's Writing

Martha Grimes's rich imagery shines on her every page. Here, chosen at random, is a paragraph from the Richard Jury crime novel *The Anodyne Necklace* (1983):

> "They found her here," said Jury, stopping in front of the Evita poster, now further defaced by a long rip from the loose corner down through the center. One glittering arm was upraised; the other was off at the shoulder. Mustached and maimed, Evita still clung to the wall as, in real life, she must have clung to power.

Martha Grimes excels at the British mystery novel. But she is not British. She was born in Pittsburgh, Pennsylvania, in 1931. Her father died when she was six. She received a B.A and an M.A. from the University of Maryland. She taught at University of Iowa, Frostburg State College, and Montgomery College before becoming a full-time writer. Divorced, she lives in Washington, D.C., and she travels to England as often as she can.

Grimes submitted her first novel without an agent. A Little, Brown editor liked what he read and brought out *The Man with a Load of Mischief* (1981). Its title—as became a mark of the Scotland Yard Detective Superintendent Richard Jury series—took its name from a pub. "Before I started writing books, I didn't think one way or the other about pubs, but now I get violently attached to the name of a pub," she said on her website. "I get it lodged in my mind and I decide I'm going to do something with it. The names of pubs are incredible."

By the ninth book, *Five Bells & Bladebone* (1987), she appeared regularly on the *New York Times* list of bestsellers.

Though she has made departures for stand-alone novels and a new series featuring Emma Graham, a teenage heroine, and another about Andi Olivier and a theme of animal rights, she is quite comfortable writing about Jury and his friend Melrose Plant for as long as readers want her to. "If you write a mystery series it is almost impossible to have any other kind of book accepted by the critics," she said in an interview with Charles L. P. Silet. "They don't want you to write anything else. ... The advantage is I can keep on writing about the same people in book after book, and I really like them."

One of her departures, *The End of the Pier* (1993), is set in western Maryland (where Grimes, in her youth, had spent summers at her mother's hotel) and observes a serial killer's progress. At the same time the novel explores a stormy relationship between a woman and her son.

Grimes brought the Jury cast to the United States for *The Horse You Came in On* (1993) and *Rainbow's End* (1995), with settings in Baltimore and Santa Fe, respectively.

For a time the author published through Knopf, until the publisher's editor in chief decided he didn't want the Jury books any longer. She quickly landed a new publisher. And she made skewering light of the situation in the novel *Foul Matter,* issued by Signet in 2003. In the book, mystery writer Paul Giverney jumps at the opportunity to leave his old publisher and sign on with a new one—but only if the new publishing house drops a longtime literary star, Ned Isaly. Grimes takes readers inside the world of publishing, with a murderous angle, without fully admitting which characters are based on real people. But it's not hard to guess.

She wrote the book over a half-dozen years. "The book was a kind of safety valve," she said in a Bookreporter interview.

> Whenever I'd get fed up with Richard Jury or one of the other books I was writing, I'd just go back and write another chapter of *Foul Matter*. I loved writing this book. It was inspired. By an officious little note from the publisher's assistant returning my original manuscript.

The moral of the story is this: mess with a veteran mystery writer at your own risk.

Works by the Author

Send Bygraves (1989)

The End of the Pier (1993)

The Train Now Departing (1998), collection

Foul Matter (2003)

Andi Olivier Series

Biting the Moon (1999)

Dakota (2008)

Emma Graham Series

Hotel Paradise (1996)

Cold Flat Junction (2000)

Belle Ruin (2005)

Fadeaway Girl (2011)

Richard Jury Series

The Man with a Load of Mischief (1981)

The Old Fox Deceiv'd (1982)

The Anodyne Necklace (1983)

The Dirty Duck (1984)

The Jerusalem Inn (1984)

Deer Leap (1985)

Help the Poor Struggler (1985)

I Am the Only Running Footman (1986)

The Five Bells and Bladebone (1987)

The Old Silent (1989)

The Old Contemptibles (1991)

The Horse You Came In On (1993)

A Martha Grimes Omnibus: Three Great Richard Jury Mysteries (1993)

Rainbow's End (1995)

The Case Has Altered (1997)

The Stargazey (1998)

The Lamorna Wink (1999)

The Blue Last (2001)

The Grave Maurice (2002)

The Winds of Change (2004)

The Old Wine Shades (2006)

Dust (2007)

The Black Cat (2010)

For Further Information

Martha Grimes interview, Bookreporter, http://www.bookreporter.com/authors/au-grimes-martha.asp/ (viewed Dec. 17, 2009).

Martha Grimes website, http://www.marthagrimes.com/ (viewed Dec. 17, 2009).

Ryan, Ellen, "Martha Grimes: Woman of Mystery," *Washingtonian*, Aug. 1, 2008.

Silet, Charles L. P., "Martha Grimes Author Interview," Mystery Net, http://www.mysterynet.com/books/testimony/grimes/ (viewed Dec. 17, 2009).

Smith, Dinitia, "An Author Gets Back at Knopf," *New York Times*, Aug. 20, 2003.

Jane Haddam

Bethel, Connecticut
1951

Police Procedural, Private Detective
Benchmark Series: Gregor Demarkian

About the Author and the Author's Writing

Life changes have a way of affecting a writer's art. Orania Papazouglou, for example, began her career as a mystery novelist with five cozy books about Pay McKenna, a freelance writer in New York who wrote paperback romance novels (under an alias) to get by. Papazouglou launched a second series, featuring cop-turned-PI Gregor Demarkian. She wrote these books under the name Jane Haddam and has remained Jane Haddam since.

Papazouglou's husband, mystery novelist William DeAndrea, became gravely ill with cancer and died in 1996. She was left with two young sons and enormous medical bills—and a different outlook.

She found she couldn't write lighthearted prose any more.

She preferred darkness.

Her Demarkian books changed. They became longer and even more character- or issue-driven. She wrote on her blog, "Around the time that Bill died, something odd went on in my head, and you can literally chart the change in the books from there. Start with *True Believers,* which is the second book published by St. Martin's, and you can see it happen."

Haddam was no stranger to adversity, however. She once had a severe case of writer's block until fellow writer Warren Murphy urged her to just keep on writing. She did and was pleased with the final manuscript.

She didn't recognize the struggle when it recurred in 2009 until her editor delayed in sending a response to her latest manuscript. She reread it, found it didn't make sense, and rewrote the whole book. The new work, *Wanting Sheila Dead,* came out in 2010.

The author was born in Bethel, Connecticut, in 1951. She received a B.A. from Vassar College in 1973 and an M.A. from University of Connecticut in 1975; she also did doctoral study at Michigan State University from 1975 to 1980. In 1984 she married DeAndrea. She has taught writing and was executive editor with *Greek Accent* magazine from 1981 to 1983.

As a girl the author read Nancy Drew. She credits P. D. James with inspiring her to try writing a crime novel and recently has devoured Anthony Trollope's Barsetshire Chronicles.

She writes a good deal of nonfiction for periodicals and is thinking of starting a new series, but otherwise she has stuck close to her Demarkian novels.

"When I started the series," she said in a *Publishers Weekly* interview, it was supposed to be a contrast between Gregor, who was old-fashioned, and his love-interest, Bennis, who was more hip. He got more modern in his attitudes towards everything, except technology, but the series itself just got darker after I got darker.

A series has its pluses, however. "It provides you with a continuing frame—you don't have to reinvent the wheel every time you write a book. The biggest drawback is that there is no way for your continuing characters to have consistently exciting lives without the whole thing beginning to sound like a soap opera," she said in an interview with Jon Jordan for bookBytes.

But a series mustn't be taken for granted, she cautioned.

"Most series die because everybody, including the writer, gets sick of the detective," she said in a Literary Spotlight interview, suggesting that there is only so much to be said about one person, book after book. "That's why I like to have only a little about the detective and his circle in each book, with the major concentration being on the characters who make up the suspects."

Literary critic Susan Oleksiw ranks the writer's works high. In an essay in the *St. James Guide to Crime & Mystery Writers,* she said: "Although Papazouglou threads political arguments and social commentary through every novel, her greatest strength and perhaps least considered quality is her skill as a social observer."

Her grittier themes don't mean bloody murder scenes or inner-city violence; the author, one of several Connecticut mystery writers profiled in a *New York Times* article, said she believed readers were happier with suburban settings, in which she depicts "the evil under the nice."

And where better than in a crime novel?

Works by the Author

Writing as Jane Haddam, Gregor Demarkian Series

Not a Creature Was Stirring (1990)

Act of Darkness (1991)

Precious Blood (1991)

Quoth the Raven (1991)

A Feast of Murder (1992)

A Great Day for the Deadly (1992)

Murder Superior (1993)

A Stillness in Bethlehem (1993)

Dear Old Dead (1994)

Festival of Deaths (1994)

Bleeding Hearts (1995)

Fountain of Death (1995)

Baptism in Blood (1996)

And One to Die On (1997)

Deadly Beloved (1997)

Skeleton Key (2000)

True Believers (2001)

Somebody Else's Music (2002)

Conspiracy Theory (2003)

The Headmaster's Wife (2005)

Hardscrabble Road (2006)

Glass Houses (2007)

Cheating at Solitaire (2008)

Living Witness (2009)

Wanting Sheila Dead (2010)

Contributor

Canine Christmas, edited by Jeff Marks (1999), includes "Midnight Clear"

Once Upon a Crime: Fairy Tales for Mystery Lover, edited by Ed Gorman and Martin H. Greenberg (1999), includes "Rapunzel"

Creature Cozies, edited by Jill M. Morgan (2006), includes "Edelweiss"

Writing as Orania Papazouglou

Charisma (1986)

Sanctity (1992)

Patience McKenna Series

Sweet, Savage Death (1984)

Wicked, Loving Murder (1985)

Once & Always Murder (1986)

Rich, Radiant Slaughter (1988)

Death's Savage Passion (1990)

The author has also written romance novels as Nicola Andrews and Ann Paris.

For Further Information

Jane Haddam blog, http://blog.janehaddam.com/ Jan. 14, 2010 (viewed Jan. 20, 2010).

Jane Haddam website, http://www.janehaddam.com/ (viewed Dec. 17, 2009).

Jordan, Jon, "Interview with Jane Haddam," BookBytes, http://www.booksnbytes.com/auth_interviews/jane_haddam.html/ (viewed Dec. 17, 2009).

"Literary Spotlight; Orania Papazolou, Penname Jane Haddam," Writers News Weekly, May 14, 2009, http://www.writersnewsweekly.com/interview_haddam/ (viewed Dec. 17, 2009).

Oleksiw, Susan, Orania Papazouglou entry, *St. James Guide to Crime & Mystery Writers*, fourth edition, edited by Jay P. Pederson. Detroit: St. James Press, 1996.

Pace, Eric, "What Evil Lurks in Connecticut? The Novelists Know," *New York Times*, June 30, 1991.

Picker, Leonard, "It's Not Just about the Detective," *Publishers Weekly*, March 13, 2006.

James W. Hall

Hopkinsville, Kentucky
1947

Private Detective
Benchmark Series: Thorn Bates

Maggie Evans Silverstein

About the Author and the Author's Writing

Private detectives usually can't make ends meet, much less fall into a fortune. But *Key Largo*'s fishing bum Thorn is not only flush but, in his eleventh outing, *Silencer* (2010), has a nifty idea how to spend some of his riches. His business partner Rusty Stabler wants to bring environmental protection to 300 square miles that land schemers have their eyes on. Coquina Ranch belongs to Earl Hammond, who sponsors big-game hunting there but is willing to sell to keep it out of the hands of developers. Then Hammond is killed, Thorn is kidnapped, and things are off and running.

Thorn doesn't go looking for trouble. "Thorn is just this cranky, Henry David Thoreau I-want-to-look-at-my-pond-all-day kind of guy," author James W. Hall said of his series hero in a *St. Petersburg Times* interview. "He doesn't like anybody."

Hall was born in Hopkinsville, Kentucky, in 1947. He earned a B.A. from Florida Presbyterian College (now Eckerd College) in 1969, an M.F.A. from Johns Hopkins University in 1970, and a Ph.D. from the University of Utah in 1973. His wife, Evelyn, is a schoolteacher. Hall has held a variety of jobs ranging from lifeguard, tree planter, and yacht washer to meat slicer at a buffet restaurant. Since 1974, however, he has taught literature and creative writing at Florida International University in Miami. (One of his students was future crime novelist Dennis Lehane.)

His first efforts at writing were in what proved to be unsellable metafiction. So he wrote a mystery, *Under Cover of Daylight*, and it found a publisher in 1987. He didn't intend it to be the first of a series—until his publisher told him. He has since refined his hero and his rebellious take on life in Florida—Thorn being about halfway between John D. MacDonald's Travis McGee and some of Carl Hiaasen's heroes.

Hall enjoys reading, and learns from such authors as John Sanford, Sue Grafton, Ernest Hemingway, Charles Frazier, and Michael Chabon—also Robert B. Parker and Elmore Leonard. In other words, he reads a lot.

He also reads a lot in whatever theme he decides on for his next book, reading, going to locations, interviewing people. He usually gets up at 5 o'clock in the morning to begin his daily writing routine. He writes, and then rewrites, in part because he doesn't write full outlines. "I write for the same reason I read, to be surprised and to feel an excitement about the unfolding narrative and all the twists and turns and surprises," he said on his website. 'I want to discover real-life people, see into their depths and come to care about them."

He said he glances at "Wanted" mug shots at the post office, and incorporates what he imagines as their personalities into his bad guys. Thorn is an amalgam of an old neighbor and several other people, living and fictional.

Hall loves his home state—he lives in Miami, Florida—and uses the setting to great advantage. "I hate to see it hijacked by those who see it simply as a buck-making machine," he said in a *January Magazine* interview. "Of course, that's nothing new, but my approach to it is convey what I love about the place, not write sermonettes on what I don't love, or spend page after page lamenting the lost golden age of Florida."

A recent nonseries novel, *Forests of the Night* (2004), shifted the locale northward, to the North Carolina mountains where the Halls own a home. "I'd also had this story kicking around in my head for some time," he said in New Mystery Reader. "A father who discovers a son he doesn't know he had, a son who turns out to be a wanted criminal."

As a teen, Hall wrote poetry. At that time he had hoped that it would impress young women. But it proved to have another value: he relentlessly reworks his words, reshaping the language and the style. Whether or not readers notice, he needs to know he's done his best.

Works by the Author

Paper Products (1991), short stories

Bones of Coral (1992)

Hard Aground (1993)

Body Language (1998)

Rough Draft (2000)

Forests of the Night (2004)

Thorn Series

Under Cover of Daylight (1987)

Tropical Freeze (1990), also titled *Squall Line*

Mean High Tide (1994)

Gone Wild (1995)

Buzz Cut (1996)

Red Sky at Night (1997)

Blackwater Sound (2002)

Off the Chart (2003)

Magic City (2007)

Hell's Bay (2008)

Silencer (2010)

Contributor

Naked Came the Manatee, with Brian Antoni, Dave Barry, Edna Buchanan, Tananarive Due, Vicki Hendricks, Carl Hiaasen, Elmore Leonard, Paul Levine, Evelyn W. Mayerson, and Edna Standiford (1996)

The Putt at the End of the World, with Lee K. Abbott, Dave Barry, Richard Bausch, James Crumley, Tami Hoag, Tim O'Brien, Ridley Pearson, and Les Standiford (2000)

For Further Information

Bancroft, Colette, "Under Florida's Spell," *St. Petersburg Times*, March 18, 2007. http://www.sptimes.com/2007/03/18/Features/Under_Florida_s_spell.shtml (viewed Jan. 8, 2010).

James W. Hall interview, New Mystery Reader. http://www.newmysteryreader.com/james_w__hall.htm (viewed Jan. 8. 2010).

James W. Hall website. http://www.jameswhall.com/jameshallbiography.htm (viewed Jan. 8, 2010).

Smith, Kevin Burton, "Wingnut with a Keyboard: Crime Novelist James W. Hall," *January Magazine,* 2005. http://januarymagazine.com/profiles/jwhall.html (viewed Jan. 8, 2010).

Parnell Hall

Culver City, California
1944

Private Detective, Amateur Detective,
Legal Mystery
Benchmark Series: Stanley Hastings

Lynn Mandel

About the Author and the Author's Writing

Multitalented Parnell Hall sometimes acts (he appeared uncredited in Arnold Schwarzenegger's first film, *Hercules in New York*, in 1970), sometimes writes screenplays (well, one, anyway, *C.H.U.D.,* in 1984, the story of monsters hiding beneath city streets), often writes songs (such as the catchy "Signing at Waldenbooks"), quite often writes mystery novels (under two names), and, when he has to, crafts crossword puzzles (for his popular Cora Felton, the Puzzle Lady, series).

The author was born in 1944 in Culver City, California. He attended Marlboro College, receiving a B.A. in 1968. He married Lynn Mandel and they have two children. He worked as an actor with the Marlboro Theater Company; taught at Windsor Mountain School in Lenox, Massachusetts, from 1974 to 1975; then taught at Berkshire Community College in Pittsfield, Massachusetts (1975) and at Stockbridge (Massachusetts) School (1975 to 1976). He was a screenwriter from 1977 to 1984. From 1985 to 1987 he worked as an investigator with the Claims Investigation Bureau in Mount Vernon, New York. He became a full-time writer in 1987 with the publication of the first Stanley Hastings novel, *Detective.*

Stanley Hastings is the anti-Spade, the un-Spenser, the not-Milhone. As Marilyn Stasio wrote in the *New York Times Book Review* of *Client* (1990), the fourth book in the series, Hastings appears

> with no more confidence in himself than when he took up the tough profession for which he is so amusingly ill-suited. Still scared to death of guns and inept at stakeouts, Stanley would starve if he didn't moonlight for a Manhattan attorney as an ambulance chaser.

The reviewer, in fact, enjoyed the novel.

But that reputation for bungling has continued through some 17 novels now. Hastings in *Hitman,* said *Publishers Weekly* in 2007, is

> not to be confused with the macho type who carries a rod and gives or takes a beating in the course of his investigations, Stanley is more likely to have his ego beaten down

by his caustic wife, Alice; longsuffering Sergeant MacAuliff; or profit-hungry lawyer Richard Rosenberg, Stanley's only steady client.

In Hastings's defense, Hall said in a Mysterious Pen interview, "He's actually rather competent and he makes up for the fact that he does not have the tools of the TV or movie detective by figuring things out, getting around the fact that he doesn't have a gun."

Hall has a pretty good grasp of the details of what it takes to be a private detective, since he worked as one when he began to write crime fiction. He collected information from accident victims and took photographs of car fenders and sidewalk cracks. As he explained to Contemporary Authors, "While this was real detective work, it was not the type I was used to reading about in mystery novels, and it occurred to me how ill equipped I would be if I had to solve a murder. So that's how I began my novel."

Hall took on the alias J. P. Hailey to write five courtroom dramas featuring the character Steve Winslow (e.g., *The Underground Man* [1990], typically, finds Winslow defending a teenager against charges he killed his wealthy uncle), then used his own name again for the Cora Felton puzzlers.

Felton is a professional puzzler. Well, she is and she isn't. She has a nationally syndicated crossword puzzle column, but she can't construct crossword puzzles, so she hires her niece, Sherry, to do them. This gives her the time to investigate murders.

In *The Puzzle Lady vs. the Sudoku Lady* (2009), to describe one book, the Puzzle Lady has competition from Minami, a Japanese sudoku lady who is resentful that her books don't sell as well as Felton's. The two become rivals to solve the murder of Ida Felding. "That none of this is remotely plausible scarcely matters," said *Publishers Weekly*. "*New York Times* puzzle editor Will Shortz supplies four sudokus and two crosswords."

Hall constructed his own puzzles for the first books in the series, so that the clues would tie in with the plots. After a while he had an epiphany. Why not find professionals to make the puzzles? "When I started writing *And a Puzzle to Die On* [2004], birthday card crossword puzzles was the *only* idea I had for the book. I had nothing else. No other preconceived notions, no other plots. And a wonderful thing happened. Without the burden of having to weave a crossword puzzle into the story, I was suddenly free to do anything I wanted."

And the result spoke for itself.

Works by the Author

Cora Felton, the Puzzle Lady Series

A Clue for the Puzzle Lady (1999)

Last Puzzle and Testament (2000)

Puzzled to Death (2001)

A Puzzle in a Pear Tree (2002)

With This Puzzle I Thee Kill (2003)

And a Puzzle to Die On (2004)

Stalking the Puzzle Lady (2005)

You Have the Right to Remain Puzzled (2006)

The Sudoku Puzzle Murders (2008)

Dead Man's Puzzle (2009)

The Puzzle Lady vs. the Sudoku Lady (2009)

The KenKen Killings (2011)

Stanley Hastings Series

Detective (1987)

Favor (1988)

Murder (1988)

Strangler (1989)

Client (1990)

Juror (1990)

Shot (1991)

Actor (1993)

Blackmail (1994)

Movie (1995)

Trial (1996)

Scam (1997)

Suspense (1998)

Cozy (2000)

Manslaughter (2003)

Hitman (2007)

Caper (2010)

Contributor

Mystery's Most Wanted (1997), includes "Faking It"

The Shamus Game, edited by Robert J. Randisi (2000), includes "The Missing Heir"

Canine Christmas, edited by Maggie Bruce (2001), includes "Clicker Training"

Murder Most Feline, edited by Ed Gorman, Martin H. Greenberg, and Larry Segriff (2001), includes "The Witness Cat"

Murder Most Crafty (2005), includes "Oh, What a Tangled Lanyard We Weave"

Writing as J. P. Hailey, Steve Winslow Series

The Baxter Trust (1988)

The Anonymous Client (1989)

The Naked Typist (1990)

The Underground Man (1990)

The Wrong Gun (1992)

Parnell Hall also wrote the screenplay for *C.H.U.D.* (1984).

For Further Information

Hall, Parnell, "Crossword Puzzles Inspire Book," Mysterynet.com, http://www.mysterynet.com/hall/writing.shtml/ (viewed Dec. 17, 2009).

Hitman review, *Kirkus Reviews*, Sept. 15, 2007.

Hitman review, *Publishers Weekly,* Sept. 10, 2007.

Parnell Hall interview, Mysterious Pen, http://www.mysteriouspen.com/Hall.html/ (viewed Dec. 17, 2009).

Parnell Hall profile, Contemporary Authors. http://galenet.galegroup.com/servlet/BioRC/ (viewed Dec. 17 2009).

Parnell Hall website, http://www.parnellhall.com/ (viewed Dec. 17, 2009).

Puzzle Lady vs. the Sudoku Lady review, *Publishers Weekly*, Nov. 23, 2009.

Stasio, Marilyn, *Client* review, *New York Times Book Review*, July 15, 1990.

Zvirin Stephanie, *Stalking the Puzzle Lady* review, *Booklist*, Sept. 1, 2005.

Steve Hamilton

Detroit, Michigan
1961

Private Detective
Benchmark Series: Alex McKnight

Julia Hamilton

About the Author and the Author's Writing

Alex McKnight was a police officer in Detroit. His partner died in a shootout and McKnight himself was shot in the chest. This compounded his feelings of failure, stemming from his inability to make it as a minor-league baseball catcher and from his divorce. He moved to Paradise, an isolated town in Michigan's Upper Peninsula, to run the hunting camp his father had started years earlier. Except for a bar-owning pal, Jackie Connery, a sidekick of sorts, schleppy but reliable Leon Prudell, and a good Ojibwa friend, Vinnie Red Sky LeBlanc, he wants to be left alone.

But crimes with no easy solutions have a way of finding Alex.

That's the gist of Steve Hamilton's character-driven, brisk-paced mystery series that began in 1997 with *A Cold Day in Paradise*. The novel, after winning publication through the Private Eye writers of America/St. Martin's Press Best First Private Eye Novel Contest, also garnered Edgar and Shamus awards for best first novel.

The honors, first time out, put the pressure on his next novel, which was by then halfway done. "I wanted the second book to be better," he said in a *January Magazine* interview. "It didn't get any easier until I learned pretty much forget everybody else—especially editors and reviewers—and to just go back to the way I wrote the first one: Trust the story. Trust the voice."

Steve Hamilton was born in Detroit in 1961. He received a B.A. from the University of Michigan in 1983. He and his wife, Julia L. Antonietta, have two children. He lives in Cottekill, New York, and works as an information developer with IBM in Poughkeepsie.

He wrote his first novel—and his subsequent ones—after the rest of the family retired at night.

Hamilton had long wanted to write fiction. While at the university, he wrote a short literary novel that won the Hopwood Award. But he put off writing for publication while he became established as a technical writer and raised a family. A dozen years went by. He joined a small writing group, and that, along with the first-novel contest, gave him the spark to complete a manuscript.

From the start he knew he wanted to avoid the detective-with-an-office pattern. "I thought it would be a little different to set a hard-boiled crime novel in the most lonely,

221

out-of-the-way place I've ever known, which is Paradise, Michigan," he told William Kent Krueger for Mystery Readers International. "That was really the best place I could think of for Alex McKnight to end up, being such a solitary character."

Hamilton didn't have to do much research for his remote setting, since he grew up there and was familiar with its bitterly cold weather. He uses the setting, he told Andi Schechter of *Library Journal*,

> to set a mood: for many readers "noir" or "hardboiled" brings thoughts of Raymond Chandler's Los Angeles, with endless sun and palm trees. I think "cold" because there's something about a winter day with a foot of new snow and an icy wind . . . it's a battle just to get out the door.

Readers and reviewers appreciate the change of locale. "Hamilton expertly delivers sharply etched characters, a vivid setting and a thoroughly enjoyable hero, leaving us breathless, perched at the edge of our seats for this chilly ride," a *Publishers Weekly* critic wrote of *Ice Run* (2004).

With his first novel, he said in an interview with Martina Bexte,

> After trying to write what I thought would be a traditional private eye novel and totally failing at it, Alex was sort of just there waiting for me, if that makes any sense. I got this feeling about him and tried to follow it, with no idea in my head about what kind of book it would be, and certainly no idea it would turn into a series.

Hamilton starts a book with a premise but does not outline so as to avoid becoming formulaic. On the other hand, it can get him into a plotting pickle. As a result, he expects it will take four or five drafts before he has a serviceable manuscript.

While the author said he has plenty more ideas for Alex McKnight—including a further look at a potential romance with a Canadian police officer, Natalie Reynaud—he's taking a break for stand-alones such as *Night Work* (2007), about which David Pitt, in *Booklist,* said, "It's smartly paced with well-drawn characters and a constant claustrophobic sense of evil, as though something is about to lunge out of the darkness at us."

Repeatedly heard about Hamilton's books is praise for the well-conceived characters, and that's part of the advice he might offer beginning writers: "Listen to your characters, and then write it down," he said in a Writers Write conversation with Claire E. White. "If you try to put words in their mouths, it will never sound natural. And that will wreck your characters every time."

If the characters aren't convincing, setting and plot won't matter.

Works by the Author

Night Work (2007)

The Crimes of Michael K. (2009)

The Lock Artist (2010)

Alex McKnight Series

A Cold Day in Paradise (1998)

Winter of the Wolf Moon (2000)

The Hunting Wind (2001)

North of Nowhere (2002)

Blood Is the Sky (2003)

Ice Run (2004)

A Stolen Season (2006)

Misery Bay (2011)

For Further Information

Bexte, Martina, "Steve Hamilton Creates a Different Kind of Private Eye," Book-Loons.com, http://www.bookloons.com/cgi-bin/Columns.asp?name=Steve%20Hamilton&type=Interview/ (viewed Aug. 22, 2009).

Ice Run review, *Publishers Weekly*, May 24, 2004.

Krueger, William Kent, Steve Hamilton interview, Mystery Readers International, http://www.mysteryreaders.org/athome/athome_hamilton.html/ (viewed Aug. 22, 2009).

Pitt, David, *Night Work* review, *Booklist*, July 1, 2007.

Rainone, Anthony, "The Education of Steve Hamilton," *January Magazine,* http://januarymagazine.com/profiles/shamilton.html/ (viewed Aug. 22, 2009)

Schechter, Andi, "Q&A: Steve Hamilton," *Library Journal*, Sept. 1, 2006.

Steve Hamilton web page, http://www.authorstevehamilton.com/ (viewed Aug. 22, 2009).

White, Claire E., "A Conversation with Steve Hamilton," Writers Write, June 2003, http://www.writerswrite.com/journal/jun03/hamilton.htm/ (viewed Aug. 22, 2009).

Charlaine Harris

Tunica, Mississippi
1951

Amateur Detective; Paranormal
Benchmark Series: Sookie Stackhouse

Caroline Greyshock

About the Author and the Author's Writing

Bon Temps, Louisiana. Late at night. The body of Lafayette Reynold, short-order cook at Merlotte's Bar, turns up in the back seat of Andy Bellefleur's car. Bellefleur, a police detective, had hitched a ride home, too intoxicated to drive. Since this is Charlaine Harris's novel *Living Dead in Dallas* (2002), things quickly become strange. Telepathic (and slightly ditzy) cocktail waitress Sookie Stackhouse is afraid that her boyfriend, Bill Compton the vampire, knows some people who know something about the murder. (Vampires, by the way, have a newfound legitimacy, thanks to the availability of artificial blood. Still, they remain social pariahs.) Sookie starts tuning in on people's thoughts, looking for clues.

Harris's Sookie Stackhouse books are wildly popular urban fantasy. Actually, the author calls them rural fantasy, as they take place mostly in northern Louisiana. Unlike kick-butt Anita Blake, Vampire Hunter, in Laurell K. Hamilton's popular series, Stackhouse knows her limits and knows when to yell for help.

As she developed the first book in the series, Harris said in *Entertainment Weekly*,

> I knew only two things about this novel: The protagonist would be a woman who was dating a vampire, and the book would be both funny and bloody. In 1998, there were not that many strong women characters in the science-fiction field, and I was constructing my heroine from new material.

That the novel, the Anthony Award–winning *Dead Until Dark* (2001), contains many elements of traditional mysteries was no surprise, since the author already had two amateur detective series under her belt and would soon create another.

Charlaine Harris was born in 1951 in Tunica, Mississippi. She wrote stories and poems while in college, receiving a B.A. from Southwestern College at Memphis in 1973. From 1973 to 1978 she worked as a typesetter and darkroom technician. She and her second husband, Hal Schultz, live in Arizona. She has three children.

Her initial foray into novel writing produced two stand-alone novels. She decided to write a mystery featuring a librarian. The first lighthearted Aurora Teagarden book, *Real Murders*, came out in 1989.

In 1996, looking new directions, Harris created a darker series of mysteries featuring Lily Bard. Bard, a housekeeper, carries a good deal of emotional baggage as the result of having once been assaulted. She regularly works out and takes lessons in karate. New social relationships tend to unhinge her.

Harris's most recent series is about Harper Connelly. Connelly, like Stackhouse, has an unusual ability. Ever since she was struck by lightning, she has been able to sniff out corpses and discern their cause of death. "I wanted Harper's gift to be unique," the author said in an interview with Melissa Mia Hall for *Publishers Weekly*, "something that she's made work for her, instead of holding her back."

HBO has adapted the books for its television series *True Blood*, featuring actress Anna Paquin. "Excess and gall," said *New York Times* critic Ginia Bellafante. So what; seven of Harris's books were on the same newspaper's paperback mass-market-fiction best-seller list at the time. Interestingly, when she first proposed the series, Harris's agent had little interest. The agent came around, but nevertheless it took two years to land a contract.

"I was trying to figure out what kind of woman would date a vampire," Harris said of her inspiration in a Paraphernalia interview, "that's a pretty outrageous thing for an unsophisticated small-town waitress to do. And the answer, of course, is that she herself is not a run-of-the-mill individual."

The author amplified, in an interview with Crescent Blues, "Who would be more likely to hang out with a vampire? Well, someone who was an outcast herself. Why would she been an outcast? Because she couldn't tolerate the constant companionship of other humans." Telepathy, you see, is more of a curse than a blessing.

The whole vampire theme, according to the author, is a metaphor for gays. Still, "I am not a crusader," she said in a *New York Times* profile. "If you need a good adventure or a vacation from your problems, then I am your woman."

She has said she particularly enjoys creating characters. She sometimes researches real people by listening well and watching their reactions to various community or national events.

Harris has offered advice to aspiring writers: "Read everything you can cram into your head, for years," she said on her website.

She told interviewer Robert L. Hall, "I do most of my plotting in my head before I ever begin writing the book, at least establishing the main strokes. I think about plotting a lot while I'm in the shower, or while I'm driving."

That last may or may not be good advice.

Works by the Author

Sweet and Deadly (1980), also titled *Dead Dog*

A Secret Rage (1984)

Aurora Teagarden Series

Real Murders (1989)

A Bone to Pick (1992)

Three Bedrooms, One Corpse (1994)

The Julius House (1995)

Dead Over Heels (1996)

A Fool and His Honey (1999)

Last Scene Alive (2002)

Poppy Done to Death (2003)

Lily Bard, Shakespeare Series

Shakespeare's Landlord (1996)

Shakespeare's Champion (1997)

Shakespeare's Christmas (1998)

Shakespeare's Trollop (2000)

Shakespeare's Counselor (2001)

Sookie Stackhouse, Southern Vampire Mystery Series

Dead Until Dark (2001)

Living Dead in Dallas (2002)

Club Dead (2003)

Dead in Dixie (2003), includes *Dead Until Dark, Living Dead in Dallas*, and *Club Dead to the World* (2004)

Dead by Day (2005), includes *Dead to the World* and *Dead as a Doornail*

Dead as a Doornail (2005)

Definitely Dead (2006)

All Together Dead (2007)

From Dead to Worse (2008)

Dead and Gone (2009)

A Touch of Dead (2009), short stories

True Blood (2009), includes *Dead Until Dark, Living Dead in Dallas*, and *Club Dead*

Dead in the Family (2010)

Dead Reckoning (2011)

The Sookie Stackhouse Companion (2011), includes a new novella

Harper Connelly Series

Grave Sight (2005)

Grave Surprise (2006)

An Ice Cold Grave (2007)

Grave Secret (2009)

Contributor

Night's Edge, with Barbara Hambly and Maggie Shayne (2004)

Bite, with MaryJanice Davidson, Laurell K. Hamilton, Angela Knight, and Vickie Taylor (2005)

My Big Fat Supernatural Wedding, with L. A. Banks, Jim Butcher, Rachel Caine, P. N. Elrod, Esther Friesner, Lori Handeland, Sherrilyn Kenyon, and Susan Krinard (2006)

Blood Lite, with Kelley Armstrong, Jim Butcher, and Sherrilyn Kenyon (2008)

Must Love Hellhounds, with Ilona Andrews, Meljean Brook, and Nalini Singh (2009)

Editor

Many Bloody Returns: Tales of Birthdays with Bite, with Toni L. P. Kelner (2007)

Wolfsbane and Mistletoe, with Toni L. P. Kelner (2008)

Death's Excellent Vacation, with Toni L. P. Kelner (2010)

Adaptations in Other Media

True Blood (HBO, 2008–) based on Southern Vampire Mysteries

For Further Information

Bellafante, Ginia, "Necks Overflowing with Rivers of Metaphor," *New York Times*, Aug. 28, 2009.

"Charlaine Harris: Putting the Bit on Cozy Mysteries," Crescent Blues, http://www.crescentblues.com/4_4issue/int_charlaine_harris.shtml/ (viewed Aug. 5, 2009)

Charlaine Harris website. http://www.charlaineharris.com/ (viewed Aug. 6, 2009).

Hall, Melissa Mia, "The Gift of Lightning: Charlaine Harris Develops a New Sleuth," *Publishers Weekly*, Aug. 13, 2007.

Hall, Robert L., "Cozies with Teeth! An Interview with Charlaine Harris," Southern Scribe, http://www.southernscribe.com/zine/authors/Harris_Charlaine.htm/ (viewed Aug. 6, 2009).

Harris, Charlaine, "Sookie Stackhouse and Me," *Entertainment Weekly*, Aug. 7, 2009.

Motoko, Rich, "Vampire-loving Barmaid Hits Jackpot for Author," *New York Times*, May 20, 2009.

Sheridan, Barbara, "Love by the Light of the Moon!" Paranormal Romance/Paraphernalia, http://paranormalromance.org/CharlaineHarris.htm/ (viewed Aug. 6, 2009).

Carolyn Hart

Oklahoma City, Oklahoma
1936

Amateur Detective, Journalism Mystery,
Paranormal
Benchmark Series: Death on Demand

About the Author and the Author's Writing

Carolyn Hart's Death on Demand series takes place in Broward's Rock, a fictional island off the South Carolina coast. The main character, Annie Darling, manages a mystery bookstore, Death on Demand. In the 19th book in the series, *Dare to Die* (2009), she and her husband, Max, are planning a big party to celebrate their new home until water problems stymie their moving in. They hastily reschedule to a town pavilion and the event goes splendidly—until a body turns up.

Reviewer Joe Meyers praised the novel for its characters—comfortable without being too sweet. He said the book "is a quintessential Hart mystery, combining the writer's great faith in the essential goodness of most people with a deep understanding of the evil that can lie just under the surface of even the most idyllic place."

The author was born Carolyn Gimpel in Oklahoma City, Oklahoma, in 1936. At an early age she decided she wanted to be a newspaper reporter. She wrote in the *Washington Post*,

> I worked on school newspapers and majored in journalism at the University of Oklahoma, back in the days of hot type, pica poles and Speed Graphics. In j-school, I wore a trench coat, smoked Chesterfields (successfully discarded years ago) and was sure I would be the next Maggie Higgins [the prizewinning journalist who covered the Nuremburg trials].

She married Philip Hart, a young law student; worked for the *Norman Transcript*; issued press releases from a university public information office; then stayed at home to raise two children. From 1982 to 1985 she taught journalism at the University of Oklahoma, Norman, School of Journalism and Mass Communications. She still had the itch, so she entered a contest to write a novel for young adults. *The Secret of the Cellars* won the competition and was published by Dodd, Mead in 1964. She wrote a few more juveniles, then switched to adult novels.

When the market for her novels evaporated, she switched briefly to southern Gothics. Finally, grounded particularly in the depiction of relationships, she found the right approach to mysteries with the Death on Demand books. Her characters the Darlings are truly in love and have a solid marriage.

"In a mystery novel the point of the book is to figure out who committed a crime. When you do that, what you're really exploring . . . is what went wrong in the lives of these people," she said in Contemporary Authors. "How did these relationships become so tortured that violence resulted?"

Hart credits Agatha Christie with setting the model for her novels, but she also admires the work of Mary Roberts Rinehart, Phoebe Atwood Taylor, and Josephine Tey.

"I write mysteries because we live in an unjust world," the author told JoAnna Carl. "Mystery readers and writers long for a world where justice is served, goodness admired, and wrongs righted. We don't find that world in our everyday lives and that's why we revere mysteries, both reading and writing them."

Hart's next series features Henrietta O'Dwyer Collins, better known as Henri O, a former journalism professor, now widowed but still writing a newspaper article or two. She applies her skills in investigative reporting to solving crimes.

Hart prefers the cozy approach to crime fiction. "The truth of the matter is that murder in a mystery is simply an exaggeration of the kind of conflicts that people have in their everyday lives," she said in *Publishers Weekly*. "This is especially true in the traditional mystery."

The author knows the particulars when she sits down to write a novel—the protagonists, the victim, the setting, and probably the murderer—but otherwise she lets the characters take their own direction.

This unplanned approach to writing can have its drawbacks, bringing on moments of panic. "But one of the great joys of writing," she said to interviewer Kathy Moad of Oklahoma Writers Association, "is coming up against a blank wall and then little squiggles of thought begin and suddenly something happens, a character appears, a door opens, a message is left and hey, we're off and running again."

The approach continues to bring freshness to Hart's stories.

Works by the Author

Flee from the Past (1975)

A Settling of Accounts (1976)

Escape from Paris (1982)

Castle Rock (1983)

Death by Surprise (1983)

The Rich Die Young (1983)

Skulduggery (1984)

The Devereux Legacy (1986)

Brave Hearts (1987)

The Rich Die Young (2000)

Letter from Home (2003)

Bailey Ruth Raeburn Series

Ghost at Work (2008)

Merry, Merry Ghost (2009)

Ghost in Trouble (2010)

Henrie O Series

Dead Man's Island (1993)

Scandal in Fair Haven (1994)

Death in Lovers' Lane (1997)

Death in Paradise (1998)

Death on the River Walk (1999)

Resort to Murder (2001)

Set Sail for Murder (2007)

Death on Demand Series

Death on Demand (1987)

Design for Murder (1988)

Something Wicked (1988)

Honeymoon with Murder (1989)

A Little Class on Murder (1989)

Deadly Valentine (1990)

The Christie Caper (1991)

Southern Ghost (1992)

Mint Julep Murder (1995)

Yankee Doodle Dead (1998)

White Elephant Dead (1999)

Sugarplum Dead (2000)

April Fool Dead (2002)

Engaged to Die (2003)

Murder Walks the Plank (2004)

Death of the Party (2005)

Dead Days of Summer (2006)

Death Walked In (2008)

Dare to Die (2009)

Laughed 'Til He Died (2010)

Dead by Midnight (2011)

Editor

Crimes of the Heart (1995)

Love & Death (2001)

Contributor

Crime on Her Mind (1999)

Motherhood is Murder, with Mary Daheim, Jane Isenberg, and Shirley Rousseau Murphy (2003)

Secrets and Other Stories of Suspense (2003)

Adaptations in Other Media

Dead Man's Island (CBS TV movie, 1996)

The author has also written five mysteries for young adults.

For Further Information

Brundige, Kay, Carolyn Hart interview, *Publishers Weekly*, Mar. 7, 2005.

Carl, JoAnna, "Carolyn Hart at Home," Mystery Fanfare, April 2, 2009, http://mysteryreadersinc.blogspot.com/2009/04/carolyn-hart-at-homeinterviewed-by.html/ (viewed Sept. 17, 2009).

Carolyn Hart website, http://www.carolynhart.com/ (viewed Sept. 17, 2009).

Gorman, Ed, "Pro-File: Carolyn G. Hart," Gormania, March 1, 2006, http://edgorman rambles.blogspot.com/2006/03/pro-file-carolyn-g-hart.html/ (viewed Sept. 17, 2009).

Hart, Carolyn, "The Writing Life," *Washington Post*, Nov. 18, 2007.

Mead, Jean Henry, Carolyn Hart interview, Murderous Musings, Aug. 14, 2009, http://murderousmusings.blogspot.com/2009/08/carolyn-hart-interview.html/ (viewed Sept. 17, 2009).

Meyers, Joe, "The Comforting/Disturbing World of Carolyn Hart," ConnPost.com, http://forum.connpost.com/joe/archive/2009/05/the_comfortingd.html/ (viewed Sept. 17, 2009).

Moad, Kathy, "Carolyn on Writing," The Report, Oklahoma Writers' Federation, http://www.carolynhart.com/interview.html/ (viewed Sept. 17, 2009).

Pickard, Nancy, Carolyn Hart tribute, Malice Domestic XIX, http://www.carolynhart.com/malice.html/ (viewed Sept. 17, 2009).

John Harvey

London, England
1938

Police Procedural, Private Detective,
Westerns
Benchmark Series: Charlie Resnick

About the Author and the Author's Writing

"'My God!' Jackie Ferris exclaimed. 'What happened to you?'

"'Don't ask.' The skin around Resnick's swollen right eye was a dramatic purple tinged with yellow and green; the centre of his face, all around the nose, was blue shading into black. An artist's palette run amok."

John Harvey's British police hero Charlie Resnick is no superman. He takes his lumps in *Cold in Hand* (2008) and other books in the popular series.

The award-winning author introduced his longest-running detective character with *Lonely Hearts* (1989), and, according to the program notes for Bouchercon 2008, at which John Harvey was International Guest of Honor, "a buzz befell our community. The Times declared it one of the top 100 mysteries of the twentieth century. A gritty and realistic police procedural interspersed with humor. A protagonist who loves jazz, women and food enthralled us."

Charlie Resnick didn't come out of the blue. Harvey was a seasoned writer who took a different route to literary achievement. He was born in London in 1938 and earned a teaching certificate at Goldsmiths' College, University of London, and taught English and drama. While on staff at Stevenage, he pursued further studies himself and earned his M.A. in American Studies at the University of Nottingham. He has been twice married and has two children.

In 1975 Harvey became a full-time writer after an editor friend at New English Library persuaded him to write two Mick Norman biker paperbacks (which he did, under the name Thom Ryder). Another editor-friend, Angus Wells, sent other assignments (Hawk, Apache, Herne, Peacemaker) his way. And Harvey wrote, and wrote some more.

In a *This Is Nottingham* interview, he said,

> The first 60 or so [books] are what we'd call pulp fiction.. They were 120-page paper-backs, mostly westerns, written at the rate of one a month. It was me learning to write. It wasn't until I wrote the first Resnick book nearly 20 years ago that I slowed down and was able to do one a year instead of 12.

Harvey early on took a stab at the private detective genre with mysteries with character Scott Mitchell. It wasn't until he conferred with Dulan Barber, yet another editor friend, not long after he'd wound up an engagement on the television series *Hard Cases*, that he decided to try another crime novel. Protagonist Charlie Resnick, the Polish-descended detective from Nottingham, found an eager audience.

Harvey set about writing the first Resnick "with a clear sense of purpose; what I wanted to do was write a story which would simultaneously be English in its content and American in its influence," he told Contemporary Authors. He credited as influences Elmore Leonard and Ross Thomas, primarily, also Joseph Wambaugh and Ed McBain. While his books are driven by character and sharp on dialogue, he also found in these writers a keen sense of place, conveyed atmospherically rather than in travelogue style.

Critic Philip Northeast saw this: "The solution of the crime or mystery is there as a thread around which Harvey tells the real story of the lives of his police officers and the seamier side of Nottingham."

Harvey, in Otto Penzler's *The Lineup*, said that Resnick emerged from his own experiences: "What helped to make Resnick was a patchwork of things, memories that, as will happen, came back to me in the course of writing and that, where suitable, became in some altered state a part of his past."

Harvey has created two post-Resnick series, both which grew from short stories. Former detective Frank Elder (first seen in "Drive North") and his wife and teenage daughter are newly transplanted to Nottingham. The author felt he had more to say about their relationship, so he turned out *Flesh and Blood* (2004) and two sequels. Another policeman, Detective Inspector Will Grayson ("Snow, Snow Snow"), intrigued an anthology editor, Robert J. Randisi, who urged Harvey to expand on the character and his relationship with his partner Detective Sergeant Helen Walker. Thus came *Gone to Ground* (2007) and one sequel so far.

Aside from his fiction writing, Harvey has written and published poetry, written for television and radio, and from 1977 to 1999 overseen Slow Dancer Press.

Aspiring fiction writers "must have the wherewithal and self-discipline to write regularly," Harvey told interviewer Chris High. "Secondly, reading widely is essential. The more you read, the better you'll write. Thirdly, it is paramount to understand that, for the most part, in order to get published you must have a commercial proposition."

To publish is to mature and to move forward.

Works by the Author

One of Our Dinosaurs Is Missing (1976), film novelization

Herbie Rides Again (1977), film novelization

The Eagle's Wing (1978), as by Michael Syson, film novelization

Herbie Goes to Monte Carlo (1978), film novelization

Duty Free (1986), film novelization

More Duty Free (1986)

Hard Cases (1987), based on his own screenplay

In a True Light (2001)

Trouble in Mind (2007)

Nick's Blues (2008)

Minor Key (2009), short stories

Charlie Resnick Series

Lonely Hearts (1989)

Rough Treatment (1990)

Cutting Edge (1991)

Off Minor (1992)

Wasted Years (1993)

Cold Light (1994)

Living Proof (1995)

Easy Meat (1996)

Still Water (1997)

Last Rites (1998)

Now's the Time: The Complete Resnick Short Stories (1999), enlarged edition (2002)

Cold in Hand (2008)

Frank Elder Trilogy

Flesh and Blood (2004)

Ash and Bone (2005)

Darkness and Light (2006)

Will Grayson and Helen Walker Series

Gone to Ground (2007)

Far Cry (2009)

Scott Mitchell Series

Amphetamines and Pearls (1976)

The Geranium Kiss (1976)

Junkyard Angel (1977)

Neon Madman (1977)

Frame (1979)

Blind (1981)

Endgame (1982), as by James Mann

Dancer Draws a Wild Card (1985), as by Terry Lennox

As by J. B. Dancer, Lawmen Series

Evil Breed, Coronet (1977)

Judgement Day (1978)

The Hanged Man (1979)

As by J. D. Sandon, Gringos Series

Border Affair (1979)

Cannons in the Rain (1979)

Mazatlan (1980)

Wheels of Thunder (1981)

Durango (1982)

As by John B. Harvey Hart, the Regulator Series

Blood Trail (1980)

Cherokee Outlet (1980)

The Silver Lie (1980)

Tago (1980)

Blood on the Border (1981)

Ride the Wide Country (1981)

Arkansas Breakout (1982)

John Wesley Hardin (1982)

California Bloodlines (1983)

The Skinning Place (1983)

As by John J. McLaglen Herne, the Hunter Series

River of Blood (1976)

Death in Gold (1977)

Shadow of Vultures (1977)

Cross-Draw (1978)

Vigilante! (1979)

Billy the Kid (1980)

Sun Dance (1980)

Till Death . . . (1980)

Dying Ways (1982)

Hearts of Gold (1982)

Wild Blood (1983)

As by James Barton, Wasteworld Series

Angels (1984)

As by Jon Hart, Mercenaries Series

Black Blood (1977)

Guerilla Attack (1977)

High Slaughter (1977)

Triangle of Death (1977)

Death Raid (1978)

As by Jon Barton, Deathshop Series

Kill Hitler (1976)

Forest of Death (1977)

Lightning Strikes (1977)

As by L. J. Coburn, Caleb Thorn Series

The Raiders (1977)

Bloody Shiloh (1978)

As by Thom Ryder

Angel Alone (1975)

Avenging Angel (1975)

As by William M. James, Apache Series

Blood Rising (1979)

Blood Brother (1980)

Death Dragon (1981)

Death Ride (1983)

The Hanging (1983)

As by William S. Brady, Hawk Series

Blood Money (1979)

Blood Kin (1980)

Killing Time (1980)

Dead Man's Hand (1981)

Desperadoes (1981)

Death and Jack Shade (1982)

Sierra Gold (1982)

Border War (1983)

Killer! (1983)

Peacemaker Series

Whiplash (1981)

War-Party (1983)

Contributor

London Noir, edited by Maxim Jakubowski (1994), includes "Now's the Time," featuring Resnick

No Alibi, edited by Maxim Jakubowski (1995), includes "Dexterity," featuring Resnick

Now's the Time (1995), includes "Dexterity," featuring Resnick

Fresh Blood, edited by Mike Ripley and Maxim Jakubowski (1996), includes "She Rote," featuring Resnick

Orion Book of Murder, edited by Peter Haining (1996), includes "Confirmation," featuring Resnick

The Year's 25 Finest Crime & Mystery Stories (1996), includes "She Rote," featuring Resnick

City of Crime, edited by David Belbin (1997), includes "Cheryl," featuring Resnick

The Fatal Frontier, edited by Ed Gorman and Martin H. Greenberg (1997), includes "The Skinning Place"

The Cutting Edge (1998), includes "Bird of Paradise," featuring Resnick

Mean Time, edited by Jerry Sykes (1998), includes "My Little Suede Shoes," featuring Resnick

The Year's 25 Finest Crime & Mystery Stories, edited by Ed Gorman and Martin H. Greenberg (1998) includes "She Rote," featuring Resnick

Now's the Time (1999), includes "She Rote," Bird of Paradise," "Cheryl," "Work," "Stupendous," "My Little Suede Shoes," "Slow Burn," "Billie's Blues," and "Confirmation," featuring Resnick

Opening Shots, edited by Lawrence Block (2000), includes "Now's the Time," featuring Resnick

Birmingham Noir, edited by Joel lane and Steve Bishop (2002), includes "Smile," featuring Jack Kiley

Crime in the City, edited by Martin Edwards (2002), includes "Due North"

First Cases, edited by Robert J. Randisi (2002), includes "Now's the Time," featuring Resnick

The Best British Mysteries, edited by Maxim Jakubowski (2003), includes "Due North"

The Best British Mysteries 2006, edited by Maxim Jakubowski (2005), includes "Drummer Unknown"

Like a Charm, edited by Karin Slaughter (2004), includes "Favour," featuring Jack Kiley

Murder and All That Jazz, edited by Robert J. Randisi (2004), includes "Drummer Unknown"

The Best British Mysteries 2005, edited by Maxim Jakubowski (2005), includes "Chance," featuring Jack Kiley

Crime on the Move, edited by Martin Edwards (2005), includes "Asylum," featuring Jack Kiley

The Detective Collection, edited by Simon Brett (2005), includes "The Sun, the Moon and the Stars," featuring Resnick

Greatest Hits, edited by Robert J. Randisi (2005), includes "Snow, Snow, Snow"

Great TV & Film Detectives, edited by Maxim Jakubowski (2005), includes "Now's the Time," featuring Resnick

Murder Is My Racquet, edited by Otto Penzler (2005), includes "Promise," featuring Jack Kiley

Sunday Night & Monday Morning, edited by James Zurquhart (2005), includes "Home," featuring Resnick

The Best British Mysteries IV, edited by Maxim Jakubowski (2006), includes "Home," featuring Resnick

Damn Near Dead, edited by Duane Swiercznski (2006), includes "Just Friends"

Paris Noir, edited by Maxim Jakubowski (2007), includes "Minor Key"

The Penguin Book of Crime Stories, edited by Peter Robinson (2007), includes "Just Friends"

The Blue Religion, edited by Michael Connelly (2008), includes "Sack O'Woe"

Mammoth Book of Best British Mysteries, edited by Maxim Jakubowski (2008), includes "Just Friends"

Minor Key (2009), includes "Home," "Well, You Needn't," "The Sun, the Moon and the Stars," and "Billie's Blues," featuring Resnick, and "Minor Key"

Editor

Blue Lightning (1998), includes "Cool Blues," featuring Resnick

Men from Boys (2003), includes "Chance," featuring Jack Kiley

The author has also written young adult novels, including six books in the Tempest Twins series. And he has written screenplays for *Anna of the Five Towns* (1985), *Hard Cases* (1988), *Resnick* (1992–1993), and other series.

For Further Information

Cartwright, Bob, John Harvey interview, *SHOTS*, http://www.shotsmag.co.uk/interviews/2009/j_harvey/j_harvey.html/ (viewed Sept. 11, 2009)

High, Chris, "Author John Harvey Develops through Darkness and Light," http://www.twbooks.co.uk/crimescene/JohnHarveyDarknessandLightinterview.htm/ (viewed Sept. 11, 2009).

John Harvey interview, *This is Nottingham,* http://www.thisisnottingham.co.uk/entertainment/Books-John-Harvey-interview/article-1015666-detail/article.html/ (viewed Sept. 11, 2009).

John Harvey profile, Bouchercon 2008, Charmed to Death program, http://www.charmedtodeath.com/guests.html/ (viewed Sept. 11, 2009).

John Harvey profile, Contemporary Authors Online, http://galenet.galegroup,com/servlet/BioRC/ (viewed Sept. 11, 2009).

John Harvey Q&A, Masterpiece Mystery, http://www.pbs.org/wgbh/masterpiece/spotlight/jharvey.html?v=h/ (viewed Sept. 11, 2009).

John Harvey website. http://www.mellotone.co.uk/ (viewed Sept. 11, 2009).

Northeast, Philip, "John Harvey and Charlie Resnick: Successful British Detective Given New Life," Suite101.com, http://detective-fiction.suite101.com/article.cfm/john_harvey_and_charlie_resnick/ (viewed Sept. 11, 2009).

Penzler, Otto, ed. *The Lineup: The World's Greatest Crime Writers Tell the Inside Story of Their Greatest Detectives*. New York: Little, Brown, 2009.

Joan Hess

Fayetteville, Arkansas
1949

Police Procedural, Amateur Detective
Benchmark Series: Arly Hanks

About the Author and the Author's Writing

A town in Arkansas with a population of 755. Nothing amiss could happen here, could it? "Normally, Maggody is a hotbed of activity only from sunrise to sunset," we read in Joan Hess's *The Merry Wives of Maggody* (2010). "Most of the residents eat a supper at six o'clock, then settle in to watch television until they fall asleep on their sofas or in bulky faux leather recliners." The teens phone friends or chat via the Internet. Raccoons root through garbage cans.

But then there's Mrs. Jim Bob Buchanan's Maggody Charity Golf Tournament, a riotous affair when the men hastily take up the new sport so they'll have a chance at winning the $40,000 bass boat. Wouldn't you know, the braggadocios golf instructor Tommy Ridner, wins. Ridner's elation at slamming a hole-in-one is cut when someone bashes his head in with a golf club. Then Sheriff Arly Hanks tees up.

"What if golf columnist Dan Jenkins wrote a cozy ? Perhaps it would turn out something like this slaphappy cozy, raunchy but wise," opined a *Publishers Weekly* reviewer.

Joan Edmiston, born in Fayetteville, Arkansas, in 1949, received a B.A. in fine art from the University of Arkansas in 1971 and an M.A. in education from Long Island University in 1974. In 1973 she married Jeremy Hess. They had two children and later divorced. She sold real estate in Fayetteville from 1974 to 1980, then taught art for four years at a private preschool. In 1984 she became a freelance writer.

At the urging of a friend, she wrote a romance novel, then nine more. None found a publisher. She never read romances and admitted she couldn't figure them out. She did read mysteries, however. *Strangled Prose* (1986) was her first published novel, centering on a murdered romance writer. It featured her first series heroine, Claire Malloy, somewhat based on herself, just as its setting is somewhat like Fayetteville.

In *Mummy Dearest* (2008), atypically, Malloy leaves her bookstore in Farberville, Arkansas, behind to travel with her policeman husband Peter Rosen to Egypt. While he works on an assignment, she and her teenage daughter, Caron, and Caron's friend Inez encounter a kidnapping and two murders. Of course Malloy will investigate!

Having a main character's daughter as a running character is a departure in the mystery genre. "Even with a daughter, Claire can go hither and yon without having to arrange for a baby-sitter," Hess said in an *Armchair Detective* interview with Charles L. P. Silet. "If Claire were totally on her own, I would still have to manufacture someone for her to talk with. Caron provides an interesting foil, and on occasion she helps to complicate the plot."

"Humor, quirky characters, a rich mother-daughter relationship, and the fresh setting all add to this satisfying addition to Hess' long-running series," said Sue O'Brien in her review of the book for *Booklist*.

Hess still lives in Fayetteville, the Washington County seat, and adores its amenities on a scale somewhere between a city and a small town. She set out to recreate the feeling in her murder mysteries. Ariel "Arly" Hanks, whom we've already met, is a one-woman police force, often grabbing a bite at her mother's place, Ruby Bee's Bar & Grill. (Kate Jackson played Hanks and Polly Bergen was her mother in an unsold TV pilot several years ago.)

Hanks's personality also borrows from the author. "I'm certainly not as laid back as Arly," Hess told interviewer Michael Pettengell for *Mystery Scene*, "not as spontaneously clever as Claire who gets the chance to polish her words before they go into print. In general, when I'm getting to do a book, I have some ideas, not so much about the plot and the murder, but a situation which creates a closed community." As in *The Merry Wives of Maggody*, based on a charity golf tournament.

The author has served on the Mystery Writers of America board of directors and is former president of American Crime Writers League. She has frequently toured to book signings with other women mystery writers such as Dorothy Cannell and Diane Mott Davidson.

Hess keeps to a rigorous schedule when writing. "On a good day, I can turn out 15 pages of fairly polished prose," she told interviewer Dulcy Brainard.

Hess offers advice to new writers: keep busy. "Once you've finished a manuscript, tidied it up, and perhaps let a trusted friend read it, send it off, and start the next one," she said in a Suite101 interview. "Don't spend ten years trying to get your firstborn published. Take into consideration what you learned from writing the first/second/third/tenth one."

Works by the Author

Future Tense (1987)

To Kill a Husband: A Mystery Jigsaw Puzzle Thriller (1995)

Arly Hanks Series

Malice in Maggody (1987)

Mischief in Maggody (1988)

Much Ado in Maggody (1989)

Madness in Maggody (1991)

Mortal Remains in Maggody (1991)

Maggody in Manhattan (1992)

O Little Town of Maggody (1993)

Martians in Maggody (1994)

Miracles in Maggody (1995)

The Maggody Militia (1996)

Misery Loves Maggody (1998)

Murder@maggody.com (2000)

Maggody and the Moonbeams (2001)

Muletrain to Maggody (2004)

Malpractice in Maggody (2006)

The Merry Wives of Maggody (2010)

Claire Malloy Series

The Murder at the Mimosa Inn (1986)

Strangled Prose (1986)

Dear Miss Demeanor (1987)

A Really Cute Corpse (1988)

A Diet to Die For (1989)

Roll Over and Play Dead (1991)

Death by the Light of the Moon (1992)

Poisoned Pins (1993)

Tickled to Death (1994)

Busy Bodies (1995)

Closely Akin to Murder (1996)

A Holly Jolly Murder (1997)

A Conventional Corpse (2000)

Out on a Limb (2002)

The Goodbye Body (2005)

Damsels in Distress (2007)

Mummy Dearest (2008)

Tickled to Death (2010)

Collections

Death of a Romance Writer, and Other Stories (2002)

Big Foot Stole My Wife! and Other Stories (2003)

The Deadly Ackee and Other Stories (2003)

Contributor

Red Rover, Red Rover (1987), Crosswinds series

Sisters in Crime 2, edited by Marilyn Wallace (1990)

Sisters in Crime 4, edited by Marilyn Wallace (1990)

Under the Gun (1990)

Cat Crimes 1, edited by Martin H. Greenberg and Ed Gorman (1991)

Cat Crimes 2, edited by Martin H. Greenberg and Ed Gorman (1991)

Invitation to Murder, edited by Martin H. Greenberg and Ed Gorman (1991)

Malice Domestic 1, edited by Martin H. Greenberg and Elizabeth Peters (1991)

Deadly Allies 2, edited by Robert J. Randisi (1995)

Great Cat Mysteries, with Sharyn McCrumb and Larry Segriff (1996)

Malice Domestic 2, edited by Mary Higgins Clark (1996)

The Best of the Best (1997)

Malice Domestic 9 (2000)

Editor

Funny Bones 15: New Tales of Murder and Mayhem (1997)

The Year's 25 Finest Crime and Mystery Stories (1997)

Crime After Crime, with Martin H Greenberg (1998)

Writing as Joan Hadley, Theo Bloomer Series

The Night Blooming Cereus (1986)

The Deadly Ackee (1988)

For Further Information

Brainard, Dulcy, "Joan Hess: An Arkansas Native Mines Laughs in Her Regional Mysteries," *Publishers Weekly*, Dec. 20, 1993.

Ham, Lorie, "Interview with Well known Mystery Author, Joan Hess," Suite101.com, http://www.suite101.com/article.cfm/mystery_suspense_book_reviews/91198/ (viewed Dec. 9, 2009).

Hess, Joan, "The Life and Loves (and Twisted Fantasies) of a She-writer," *Mystery Scene* (1991).

Joan Hess website, http://www.maggody.com/ (viewed Dec. 9, 2009).

Pettengell, Michael, "The Maker of Maggody: An Interview with Joan Hess," *Mystery Scene* (1993).

Silet, Charles L. P., "Tickled to Death: An Interview with Joan Hess," *The Armchair Detective*, winter 1995.

Reginald Hill

West Hartlepool, England
1936

Police Procedural, Private Investigator
Benchmark Series: Andrew Dalziel and Peter Pascoe

About the Author and the Author's Writing

Opposites attract. In the case of Reginald Hill's long-running crime series duo, crude Detective Superintendent Andy Dalziel and compassionate Detective Chief Inspector Peter Pascoe are opposites who attract—a wide readership.

Hill first put the two together in *A Clubbable Woman* (1970). "From the opening paragraphs," critic Martin Edwards said,

> Dalziel has been a character destined to stay in the memory. Fat and coarse he may be, but to underestimate his shrewd insights into human nature is invariably to make a grave mistake. The contrast between gruff Fat Andy and the sensitive, liberal Pascoe is an enduring source of strength in the series.

While he has written other series, and under other names, Hill has continued to come back to the Yorkshire investigators, including *Midnight Fugue* (2009), in which Dalziel is back in harness after recovering from an injury from a terrorist's bomb. Gina Wolfe asks him to look into the disappearance of her policeman husband, Alex, who has been under internal affairs investigation. Authorities think Wolfe is dead. Wolfe wants him dead, or at least declared dead, so she can remarry. But she thinks she's seen him in a recently published magazine photo.

In the view of Euro Crime reviewer Mike Ripley,

> This is one of the fastest-paced—and funniest—books in the Dalziel . . ., with the action cutting almost cinematically between several view points as 'Fat Andy' does what he does best, which is to be both a catalyst and a focal point for the resolution of crimes past, present and possibly still to come.

Reginald Hill was born in 1936 in West Hartlepool, England. He showed no remarkable early bent for writing, if one measures by an anecdote he often relates of the head of English at his Stanwix primary school in Carlisle. As he remarked in an *Independent* interview with Jonathan Sale,

> He said I should get a job as a lorry-driver and write my first novel in transport caffs on the Great North Road. But I didn't have a driving license and I'd had the idea of going to Oxford because that's where people in schoolboy stories ended up.

He served with the British Army Border Regiment from 1955 to 1957 and received a B.A., with honors, from St. Catherine's College, Oxford, in 1960. That same year he married Patricia Ruell. They and their two Siamese cats live in Cambria, England. From 1962 to 1967 he taught secondary school, then was a lecturer in English literature at Doncaster College of Education until 1982. He became a full-time writer in 1980.

"It took me ten years to take that nervous step of giving up the day job," Hill said on his website, "but I have never regretted it. And now with forty books to my name I live amidst the loveliest scenery in the country (I think in the world)."

It's easy to categorize Hill's Dalziel and Pascoe books as police procedurals, but the author insists they are simply crime novels. Real policemen would scoff at the procedures his heroes employ.

Hill wrote a humorous essay for *SHOTS* magazine on how the Dalziel character emerged. He said he'd long told audiences

> that my initial intention was that Dalziel should be a caricature, a grotesque exaggeration of everything that made up the traditional old-fashioned, unsubtle, technologically Luddite, seat-of-the-pants cop; a foil in other words for the true hero of that first book, Peter Pascoe.

Ultimately, Hill said, that was wrong. Dalziel came from somewhere inside him. But, "I've no idea whatsoever where he came from."

Hill sometimes takes liberties with his Dalziel and Pascoe books. Some, such as *Midnight Fugue*, center on Dalziel, others such as *Death Comes for the Fat Man* (2007), focus more on Pascoe, as his partner is in and out of a coma for most of the book. Hill relates how the two teamed, not in a novel, but in a short story, "The Last National Serviceman," which appeared in *Asking for the Moon* (1996).

Hill has also written adventure thriller novels under the name Patrick Ruell, and the Joe Sixsmith series under his own name. Sixsmith is a schlumpy black private eye who, in *Singing the Sadness* (1999), saves a woman from a burning house, after which his injuries keep him from competing in the Llanffugiol Choral Festival in Wales. So instead, he looks into how the woman—naked at the time—happened to be in the enflamed building. *Publishers Weekly* found the characterizations sharp. "And Hill's swift pacing and keen dialogue make his modest, intelligent hero a winner in this intriguing tale of the seedy side of small-town life."

Hill has no great secret to his writing success. "It's just perseverance and hard work," he said in a *Guardian* interview with Sarah Kinson. "If you've got something to say or a good story to tell then the greatest problem is writing to the end of it. If you can do that, then even if it's not that good, you have got something to work at."

Works by the Author

Fell of Dark (1971)

A Fairly Dangerous Thing (1972)

A Very Good Hater (1974)

Another Death in Venice (1976)

The Spy's Wife (1980)

Who Guards a Prince? (1982)

Guardians of the Price (1983)

Traitor's Blood (1983)

No Man's Land (1985)

The Collaborators (1987)

There Are No Ghosts in the Soviet Union (1987), collection

Brother's Keeper (1992), collection

Singleton's Law (1997)

The Stranger House (2005)

The Woodcutter (2011)

Dalziel and Pascoe Series

A Clubbable Woman (1970)

An Advancement of Learning (1971)

Ruling Passion (1973)

An April Shroud (1975)

A Pinch of Snuff (1978)

Pascoe's Ghost, and Other Brief Chronicles of Crime (1979)

A Killing Kindness (1980)

Deadheads (1983)

Exit Lines (1984)

Child's Play (1986)

Under World (1988)

Bones and Silence (1990)

One Small Step (1990)

Recalled to Life (1992)

Pictures of Perfection (1994)

The Wood Beyond (1995)

Asking for the Moon (1996)

On Beulah Height (1998)

Arms and the Women (1999)

Dialogues of the Dead (2001)

Death's Jest Book (2002)

Good Morning, Midnight (2004)

For Love nor Money (2005), chapbook

Secrets of the Dead (2005), chapbook

Death Comes for the Fat Man (2007), also titled *The Death of Dalziel* (2007)

The Last National Serviceman (2007), chapbook, reprints 1994 short story "The Last National Serviceman"

A Cure for All Diseases (2008), also titled *The Price of Butcher's Meat* (2009)

Midnight Fugue (2009)

Joe Sixsmith Series

Blood Sympathy (1993)

Born Guilty (1995)

Killing the Lawyers (1997)

Singing the Sadness (1999)

The Roar of the Butterflies (2008)

Adaptations in Other Media

The Last Hit (1993), telefilm based on *The Long Kill* (as by Patrick Ruell)

Dalziel and Pascoe (1996–2007, BBC TV series)

The author has also written eight adventure novels as Patrick Ruell, two science fiction novels under the name Dick Morland, and two historical adventure novels as Charles Underhill.

For Further Information

Edwards, Martin, "Reginald Hill's Dalziel & Pascoe Series," TW Books, http://www.twbooks.co.uk/crimescene/rhillme.html/ (viewed Dec. 9, 2009).

Fletcher, Connie, *Death Comes for the Fat Man* review, *Booklist*, Dec. 1, 2006.

Hill, Reginald, "Deconstructing Dalziel," *SHOTS*, http://www.shotsmag.co.uk/Deconstructing%20Dalziel.htm/ (viewed Dec. 9, 2009).

Kinson, Sarah, Reginald Hill interview, *The Guardian*, April 9, 2008. http://www.guardian.co.uk/books/2008/apr/09/whyiwrite/ (viewed Dec. 9, 2009).

Midnight Fugue review, *Publishers Weekly*, Aug. 24, 2009.

Reginald Hill website, http://www.randomhouse.com/features/reghill/ (viewed Dec. 9, 2009).

Ripley, Mike, *Midnight Fugue* review, Euro Crime, http://www.eurocrime.co.uk/reviews/Midnight_Fugue.html/ (viewed Jan. 27, 2010).

Sale, Jonathan, "Passed/Failed: An Education in the Life of Reginald Hill, Author of the Dalziel and Pascoe Novels," *The Independent*, June 26, 2008, http://www.independent.co.uk/news/people/profiles/passedfailed-an-education-in-the-life-of-reginald-hill-author-of-the-dalziel-and-pascoe-novels-853993.html/ (viewed Dec. 9, 2009).

Singing the Sadness review, *Publishers Weekly*, Aug. 23, 1999.

Declan Hughes

Patrick Redmond

Dublin, Ireland
1963

Private Detective
Benchmark Series: Ed Loy

About the Author and the Author's Writing

When Declan Hughes turned to crime fiction in order to articulate some of his feelings about his native Ireland, he was keenly aware of both the British murder mystery tradition and of the rich possibilities a trio of California authors had pioneered.

"We have the rope of Agatha around our necks," he told Jordan Foster of *Publishers Weekly* in 2008. "She created an expectation that was great for when she was writing, but now we want to write about the society we live in and the Agatha Christie formula doesn't work anymore."

The author was born in Dublin, Ireland, in 1963. He partnered with Lynne Parker to establish the Rough Magic Theatre Company in 1984, and served as its artistic director until 1992 and writer in residence until 1999. His first play, *I Can't Get Started*, won the Stewart Parker Award and the BBC NI TV Drama Award in 1991. He wrote several other plays (some in association with the Abbey Theatre) and adaptations, and also directed plays. He also wrote screenplays, including *The Flying Scotsman* (2000), which was nominated for a Scottish BAFTA award for best screenplay.

When Hughes decided to take another direction, he figured his drama writing would serve him well. "It taught me how to tell a scene through dialogue, to make a story out of a series of scenes," he related to *New Mystery Reader*, "to have a sense of place, to have a very low boredom threshold, to 'cast' characters so a reader can 'see' them, to end a story at least three times."

Hughes spent some time in California. He absorbed the writing of Raymond Chandler for his romanticism, recognizing the misogyny that penetrates his Philip Marlowe novels, the author told *January Magazine*. He also absorbed the writing of Dashiell Hammett for his grittiness and realism. (Hughes' first play was about Hammett and Lillian Hellman and speculated on why Hammett stopped writing.) And he absorbed Ross Macdonald, for his reaching into hidden pasts, the forgotten or convoluted reasons for things happening today. He decided a private investigator would work just fine in Dublin.

His first Ed Loy novel, *The Wrong Kind of Blood*, came out in 2006. The hero had established himself as a private investigator in Los Angeles for two decades but came back to his homeland when his mother died. In no time, he's accepted a woman friend's plea to find her missing husband and enters a world of high-stakes real estate speculation and drug dealing.

Although reviews of Hughes's work were tepid at first, doubts vanished by the publication of *The Color of Blood* (2007), in which the hero has chosen to stay in Ireland and takes on a case of pursuing a missing young woman who has become tied in with a pornographer. Said Kevin Burton Smith in *January Magazine*,

If that first Loy outing was a warning shot fired across the bows of a genre that too often settles for a sort of anemic predictability, this second novel is no tentative warning— it's a direct hit, an audacious full-blooded scream in the night, a bruising, ferocious assault on the evil that families do. The third novel in Hughes's initial contract (since renewed) was *The Price of Blood* (2008), in which a parish priest's request takes Loy into a web of secrets and deceit, as well as abuse by clerics, while at the same time being alerted that one of the thuggish Harrigan family, fresh out of prison, is out to get him. "Beaten up, warned off and yet undaunted, Loy uncovers a horrific series of secrets, leading to a violent and labyrinthine conclusion at a famous Irish horse-racing festival," said *Publishers Weekly*. "This intelligent, often brutal thriller will have readers' hearts racing from start to finish."

Fourth time up, in *All the Dead Voices* (2009), Loy again juggles more than one case. Someone has killed a local soccer hero, and he tries to find the killer. And he has to figure out who killed Anne Fogarty's father 15 years before. "Hughes weaves all the history, background and conflict into clear, elegant prose," commented Margaret Cannon in *The Globe and Mail*. "This isn't a wordy novel with lots of filler, food and bad sex. Every paragraph matters, and the dialogue snaps, as Loy drifts from high Irish to Dublin drawl with wit and charm."

Claire Kilroy in *The Irish Times* summed up Hughes's impact on the genre:

Loy is a winning combination of caustic cynicism and romantic idealism, an adept at Beckettian failing better. The ladies fall for him, the criminals respect him. They even, in *All the Dead Voices*, try to hire him, but Loy has principles. His principles may not tally with accepted notions of right and wrong, but principles they are, nonetheless.

Works by the Author

Ed Loy Series

The Wrong Kind of Blood (2006)

The Color of Blood (2007)

The Dying Breed (2008), also titled *The Price of Blood* (2009)

All the Dead Voices (2009)

City of Lost Girls (2010)

The author has also written several plays, including *Digging for Fire* (1994) and *Shiver* (2003), and several screenplays, including *The Flying Scotsman* (2000).

For Further Information

Cannon, Margaret, *All the Dead Voices* review, *Globe and Mail*, Sept. 9, 2009.

Declan Hughes interview, New Mystery Reader, http://www.newmysteryreader.com/ declan_hughes.htm/ (viewed Sept. 18, 2009).

Declan Hughes profile, Irish Writers Online, http://www.irishwriters-online.com/ declanhughes.html/ (viewed Sept. 18, 2009).

Declan Hughes web page. http://www.declanhughesbooks.com/ (viewed Sept. 18, 2009).

Kilroy, Claire, "The Loy Is Back in Town," *Irish Times*, Apr. 4, 2009.

Pitt, David, *The Color of Blood* review, *Booklist*, May 1, 2007.

Price of Blood review, *Publishers Weekly*, Jan. 21, 2008.

Smith, Kevin Burton, "Bloodwork: Declan Hughes," *January Magazine,* http://januarymagazine.com/profiles/dhughes.html/ (viewed Sept. 18, 2009).

Wright, David, *The Wrong Kind of Blood* review, *Booklist*, Feb. 1, 2006.

J. A. Jance

Jerry Bauer

Watertown, South Dakota
1944

Police Procedural; Journalism Mystery
Benchmark Series: J. P. Beaumont

About the Author and the Author's Writing

J. A. Jance—born Judith Ann Busk in 1944 in Watertown, South Dakota—discovered L. Frank Baum's Wizard of Oz fantasy books while she was in second grade and immediately wanted to write her own stories. After growing up on Nancy Drew, Dana Girls, and Hardy Boys series adventures and later devouring John D. MacDonald and Lawrence Block, mysteries became a logical genre to pursue when she began to write.

The author received her B.A. in English and secondary education from the University of Arizona in 1966. An M.Ed. degree in library science followed four years later. She taught high school English in Tucson for two years; then worked as K-12 librarian for the Indian Oasis School District near Tucson for five years. In 1980 she received a Chartered Life Underwriters (C.L.U.) degree from American College. Two years later, resettled from Arizona to Seattle, divorced and raising two children, she sold life insurance full time. Then Jance decided to write a true crime book, but it failed to find a publisher. Her agent urged her to try fiction, and the result was *Until Proven Guilty* (1985), the first case involving her Seattle detective.

She said on her website that

> The eighteen years I spent while married to an alcoholic have helped shape the experience and character of Detective J. P. Beaumont. My experiences as a single parent have gone into the background for Joanna Brady—including her first tentative steps toward a new life after the devastation of losing her husband in *Desert Heat*.

Jance also modeled Beaumont on a Pima County homicide cop she met when he was investigating a series of Arizona serial killings. She has said that her characters are like old friends to her, and as they age, things change in their lives. When she's occasionally been away from Beaumont to write a Brady or other book, coming back is like visiting again with an old friend. For her Brady books, she changed the setting to arid Arizona. (Today she has homes in both Arizona and Washington, which she shares with her second husband, William Alan Schilb, a retired electronics engineer.) Jance gave Brady a demanding family to deal with at the same time she solved crimes—a daughter, helpful in-laws, a pushy mother, a new husband, and their respective complications.

At the urging of readers, Beaumont and Brady have twice shared cases—in *Partner in Crime* (2002) and *Fire and Ice* (2009).

Jance's other fiction includes *Hour of the Hunter* (1992)—drastically rewritten from her first, unpublished attempt at fiction—and two sequels, all featuring Sheriff Brandon Walker. And there's a fourth series, about newscaster Ali Reynolds who, deemed too old for television, finds new vitality as a blogger—and, of course, as a crime solver.

Since doing research is easier than writing a book, Jance said in a Bestsellers World interview, she tries to limit the time she spends digging up background material. She said she mostly writes on deadline.

Jance told iVillager that she does not outline her books: "First, I usually come up with a name; then I figure out who's dead. I spend the rest of the book trying to find out who did it, and why."

The first 20 percent of the book is the most critical, she said in *The Writer*. It's when the characters are introduced, the setting established, the tone set. "Like the foundation of a house," she wrote, "those first few chapters have to be strong enough to support the rest of the book. They also have to be interesting and engaging."

The spark for *Dead to Rights*, she explained, was a friend's loss of his wife to a drunk driver. Jance opens her novel with a man handing out Mothers Against Drunk Driving leaflets outside the office of a veterinarian. The man's wife was killed by the vet in a DWI accident. When the vet soon turns up dead, the man is the first—but of course wrong—suspect. The dead dentist in *Improbable Cause* (1988)? "I finally managed to wreak personal revenge on a sadistic dentist who had haunted a whole generation of kids in my home town by practicing Novocain-free dentistry," she wrote in *Mystery Scene*.

Brady doesn't long anticipate her characters. She introduced Butch Dixon in *Shoot, Don't Shoot* (1995), for example, and didn't expect to see him again. "If I had known he was a character who I was just not going to be able to ditch—that he was going to marry Joanna Brady—I would have given him a better name," she said in a Crime Factory interview.

When she gets stuck with one of her characters, she told *January Magazine* interviewer Linda Richards,

> What I've learned to do is go back and tweak the motivation instead of throwing everything away. And because in the mysteries the murder hardly ever happens onscreen, all I have to do is the hardest thing authors ever do, which is change my mind and decide somebody else is the killer.

Jance said in a Barnes and Noble interview that the storyteller's mission "is to beguile the time. And that's how I see my book—as storytelling."

Works by the Author

Ali Reynolds Series

Edge of Evil (2006)

Hand of Evil (2007)

Web of Evil (2007)

Cruel Intent (2008)

Trial by Fire (2008)

Fatal Error (2011)

Brandon Walker Series

Hour of the Hunter (1992)

Kiss of the Bees (2000)

Day of the Dead (2004)

Queen of the Night (2010)

Joanna Brady Mysteries

Desert Heat (1993)

Tombstone Courage (1994)

Shoot, Don't Shoot (1995)

Dead to Rights (1996)

Skeleton Canyon (1997)

Rattlesnake Crossing (1998)

Outlaw Mountain (1999)

Devil's Claw (2000)

Paradise Lost (2001)

Exit Wounds (2003)

Dead Wrong (2006)

Damage Control (2008)

Joanna Brady and J. P. Beaumont Mystery

Partner in Crime (2002)

Fire and Ice (2009)

J. P. Beaumont Mysteries

Until Proven Guilty (1985)

Injustice for All (1986)

Trial by Fury (1986)

Taking the Fifth (1987)

Improbable Cause (1988)

More Perfect Union (1988)

Dismissed with Prejudice (1989)

Minor in Possession (1990)

Payment in Kind (1991)

Without Due Process (1992)

Failure to Appear (1993)

Lying in Wait (1994)

Name Withheld (1995)

Breach of Duty (1999)

Birds of Prey (2001)

Sentenced to Die (2005), omnibus including *Until Proven Guilty, Injustice for All,* and *Trial by Fury*

Long Time Gone (2006)

Justice Denied (2008)

Contributor

Cat Crimes, edited by Martin H. Greenberg and Ed Gorman (1991)

The Mysterious West (1994)

Partners in Crime (1994)

No Alibi (1995)

Vengeance Is Hers (1997)

Midnight Louie's Pet Detective (1998)

More Murder, They Wrote (1999)

Fathers & Daughters, edited by Jill Morgan (2000)

First Cases IV (2002)

For Further Information

Exit Wounds review, *Publishers Weekly*, June 9, 2003.

Goldberg, Rylla, "J. A. Jance," *Mystery Scene*, Jan./Feb. 1996.

J. A. Jance biography, Meet the Writers, Barnes & Noble, http://www.barnesand noble.com/writers/writer.asp?cid=881721/ (viewed May 6, 2003).

J. A. Jance books, Mystery Women Authors, http://members.fortunecity.com/le10/ authors/authorsH-P/jajance.htm/ (viewed May 6, 2003).

J. A. Jance interview, BestsellersWorld (June 2, 2002), http://www.bestsellersworl. dcom/interview-jajance.com/ (viewed April 11, 2003).

J. A. Jance interview, iVillagers, http://www.ivilage.com/books/intervu/myst/articles /0,11872,240795_91812,00.html/ (viewed April 11, 2003).

J. A. Jance profile, *January Magazine,* http://www.januarymagazine.com/profiles/ jajance.html/ (viewed April 11, 2003).

J. A. Jance website, http//jajance.com/ (viewed Aug. 20, 2009).

Jance, J. A., "Dead to Rights," *Mystery Scene*, July/Aug. 1996.

Jance, J. A., "The Long Slide Home: The Author of 30 Mysteries Shares Her Secrets for Getting from Start to Finish," *The Writer,* Jan. 2004.

McDonald, Craig, J. A. Vance interview, Crime Factory, http://www.crimefactory. net/cfOLM-001h.html/ (viewed Aug. 20, 2009).

Richards, Linda, J. A. Jance interview, *January Magazine,* February 2001, http:// januarymagazine.com/profiles/jajance.html/ (viewed Aug. 20, 2009).

Sturgeon, Julie, "Stranger than Fiction: With J. A. Jance, the Line between the Two Blurs Beautifully," *Pages*, Sept./Oct. 2003.

Michael Jecks

Courtesy of the author

Surrey, England
1960

Historical Mystery
Benchmark Series: Knights Templar

About the Author and the Author's Writing

Michael Jecks set his detective series in 14th-century Britain to take advantage of its violent, mysterious, and dynamic events. In October 1307, in the latter days of the Crusades when the Holy Land was lost, members of the Knights Templar, the famed Christian military order, loyal Christians all, were arrested, and the disgraced order soon disbanded.

"At the time this was a cataclysmic event," the author said on his website.

All the most highly respected warriors in a society based upon courage, chivalry and religion were accused of sodomy, murder, cannibalism, and many other trumped-up charges from the over-imaginative agents of the Pope and the French King. They wanted the Templars' wealth.

In that century, with Christianity in turmoil, relentless crop failures, spreading disease, and the seventh Plantagenet king, King Edward II, maintaining ill control of his country (until he was deposed in 1327), British society was ripe for crime.

And it was ripe for Jecks's heroes, the former Knight Templar Sir Baldwin Furnshill, now keeper of the king's peace, and his friend, Simon Puttock, bailiff of Lyford Castle.

Chapel of Bones (2004), typically, finds the pair at Exeter Cathedral Close, where a mason installing stonework is killed by a falling rock. A saddler turns up dead in the Charnel Chapel. Sir Baldwin and Simon have a puzzle on their hands.

"Together they uncover a complicated tale of religious dissension and misplaced revenge," noted reviewer Barbara Hoffert in *Library Journal*, delighted with the plot, adding, "What's just as good is the characterization."

Michael Jecks was born in Redhill, Surrey, England, in 1960. He attended Caterham School, Surrey, and City University, London. He and his wife, Jane Susan Bond, have two children. He trained as an actuary but worked in computer software and hardware sales for 13 years. During an idle time of employment, he leapt at an opportunity to fulfill a dream.

When he and his wife were on their honeymoon in Devon, they visited Fursdon House. Jecks came away with an idea for a crime tale set in medieval times. That idea grew into *The Last Templar,* which sold to Headline in 1994. Simon & Schuster picked up the series for hardcover publication in the United States with *The Oath* (2010).

Jecks thrives on the Devon setting. "For me the landscape is crucial to my stories," he said in an interview on the HarperCollins website. "I believe men are formed by the land even as they change it through mining or farming. The moors are very special: they are atmospheric, hauntingly beautiful, and unspoiled."

Too, he said, the moors are little changed from centuries ago, the period in which his mysteries take place. As well as the setting, the author has made use of local lore. For instance, the legend of the monks of Tavistock inspired *The Devil's Acolyte* (2002). In that book, set in 1322, a body is discovered on the moors, coincidental with the realization someone has stolen wine from the private cellar of the abbot.

When he's not writing, Jecks is often found striding Dartmoor with his dogs or camping or playing the fiddle or melodeon. He may also be Morris dancing, working at his wood lathe, or snapping photographs.

When he is writing, he's also doing a lot of research.

"My books are ruthlessly, historically accurate," Jecks told Sibylle Barrasso for an article for International Thriller Writers, "with the events depicted taken from actual cases. But this is not ancient, dead history: my stories are modern, gritty thrillers that happen to be set in the past."

His research takes him deep into archives for period materials. He has examined court dockets, death certificates, church ledgers, and more.

At the same time, he takes keen interest, the author has said, in personalities and their interactions, in humanity and brutality, love and betrayal.

Jecks has chaired the Crime Writers' Association, where he instigated its Debut Dagger award and judged the Ian Fleming Steel Dagger prize. He has participated in Medieval Murderers with a handful of fellow writers, all of whom have contributed interconnected novelettes to another series of books set in the Dark Ages.

As much as he knows about its history, settings, and characters, the author said he doesn't always know where the story will take him. "I think it's fair to say, though, that of the [then] twenty-four books in the series, more have started with a scene or a theme, and I have tended to take that initial concept and built on it as I write," he said. "The story develops and grows as I write."

Jecks, you might say, makes a living rewriting history.

Works by the Author

Knights Templar Series

The Last Templar (1995)

The Merchant's Partner (1995)

A Moorland Hanging (1996)

The Crediton Killings (1997)

The Abbot's Gibbet (1998)

The Leper's Return (1998)

Squire Throwleigh's Heir (1998)

Belladonna At Belstone (1999)

The Boy-Bishop's Glovemaker (2000)

The Traitor of St. Giles (2000)

The Sticklepath Strangler (2001)

The Tournament of Blood (2001)

The Devil's Acolyte (2002)

The Mad Monk of Gidleigh (2002)

The Outlaws of Ennor (2003)

The Templar's Penance (2003)

The Chapel of Bones (2004)

The Tolls of Death (2004)

The Butcher of St. Peter's (2005)

A Friar's Blood Feud (2005)

The Death Ship of Dartmouth (2006)

Dispensation of Death (2007)

The Malice of Unnatural Death (2007)

The Templar, the Queen and Her Lover (2007)

The King of Thieves (2008)

The Prophecy of Death (2008)

The Bishop Must Die (2009)

No Law in the Land (2009)

The Oath (2010)

King's Gold (2011)

Historical Mysteries issued as by The Medieval Murderers (Philip Gooden, Susanna Gregory, Michael Jecks, Bernard Knight, Karen Maitland, Philip Gooden, Simon Beaufort, Ian Morson, Maxim Jakubowski, and C. J. Sansom in various combinations).

The Tainted Relic (2005)

Sword of Shame (2006)

House of Shadows (2007)

The Lost Prophecies (2008)

King Arthur's Bones (2009)

The Sacred Stone (2010)

Contributor

Chronicles of Crime, edited by Maxim Jakubowski (1999), includes "The Coroner's Tale"

Murder Most Foul, edited by Martin H. Greenberg and John Helfers (2000), includes "For the Love of Old Bones"

Mammoth Book of Historical Whodunits, edited by Mike Ashley (2001), includes "The Amorous Armourer"

Murder Most Catholic, edited by Ralph McInerny (2002), includes "A Clerical Error"

The Mammoth Book of Roman Whodunits, edited by Mike Ashley (2003), includes "The Hostage to Fortune"

The Best British Mysteries 2005, edited by Maxim Jakubowski (2004), includes "No One Can Hear You Scream"

Crimes of Identity, edited by Martin Edwards (2006), includes "A Case of Identity"

Mammoth Book of Jacobean Whodunits, edited by Mike Ashley (2006), includes "The Tower's Man"

For Further Information

Barrasso, Sylvia, "King of Thieves by Michael Jecks," International Thriller Writers, http://www.thrillerwriters.org/2009/01/king-of-thieves-by-michael-jecks.html/ (viewed July 29, 2009).

Hoffert, Barbara, *Chapel of Bones* review, *Library Journal*, Mar. 15, 2005.

"Interview with Michael Jecks," HarperCollins, http://www.harpercollins.com/author/authorExtra.aspx?authorID=28798&isbn13=9780060763442&displayType=bookinterview/ (viewed July 29, 2009).

King of Thieves review, *Publishers Weekly*, May 18, 2009.

"Michael Jecks, '. . . A Case of Sudden Need,'" *Quarterdeck*, May 2007, http://www.mcbooks.com/pdf/Quarterdeck-05–07.pdf/ (viewed July 29, 2009).

Michael Jecks website, http://www.michaeljecks.co.uk/ (viewed July 29, 2009).

H.R.F. Keating

St. Leonards-on-Sea, East Sussex,
England
1926

Police Procedural
Benchmark Series: Inspector Ghote

About the Author and the Author's Writing

H.R.F. Keating despaired of breaking into the American crime fiction market—he was told his books were too British—until he came up with his mild-mannered but adept Inspector Ganesh Ghote of the Mumbai Criminal Investigation Division in India.

"Out of nowhere, into my head there came this man, or some part of him," Keating said in the introduction to *Inspector Ghote, His Life and Crime* (1989). "A certain naiveté, which should enable him to ask the questions about the everyday life around him, to which my potential readers might want answers."

Asking Questions (1996), typically, tosses the Bombay inspector a locked-room dilemma: who poisoned snake handler Chandra Chagoo? "Deferential and persistent, Ghote uncovers many little mysteries before he finally asks the right questions and presents an elegant solution," remarked the *Publishers Weekly* reviewer.

Henry Reymond Fitzwalter Keating, known to his friends as Harry, was born in St. Leonards-on-Sea, Sussex, England, in 1926. He married Sheila Mary Mitchell in 1953; they have four children. Keating worked as a journalist and editor for the *Evening Advertiser*, 1952 to 1955, the *Daily Telegraph*, 1955 to 1957, and the *Times*, 1957 to 1960, where he was crime fiction critic. He began to write fiction, and at the urging of his actress wife, took a stab at a genre he enjoyed reading: mysteries.

"The tone and manner of Keating's crime stories are wholly original in modern crime fiction," in the view of fellow crime writer Julian Symons. "They spring from a mind attracted by philosophical and metaphysical speculation, with a liking for fantasy held in check by the crime story's requirements of plot."

Keating threads humor and Indian customs throughout his stories, with great success. He portrayed his characters and settings, mind you, for a decade (and nine novels) before he actually visited India, "proof that you don't always need to write from direct experience. He actually felt that the books were harder to write after his visit," according to journalist Christopher Fowler.

"Keating's most remarkable skill (along with solid plots and excellent dialogue) lies in his ability to induce in the most provincial reader an interest in, and a sympathy for, characters facing mystery in unusual environments," said fellow mystery writer William L. DeAndrea.

Keating brought his Ghote series to a close with *Breaking and Entering* (2000), but before decade's end, found he had more to reveal about his character. In *Inspector Ghote's First Case* (2009), he related how Ghote was sent into the hills of Mahabaleshwar to determine whether a young woman married to a British friend had died a suicide or was murdered. "From dialogue to setting, Keating's story is lush with the detail and heat of Bombay," said *Booklist*'s Jessica Moyer, "making for an intensely atmospheric tale."

Keating then developed another police character, this one a woman: Detective Superintendent Harriet Martens of the Great Birchester Police. She is nicknamed "the Hard Detective" for her determined personality. In *A Detective at Death's Door* (2005), she has to figure out who slipped poison into her drink at a party. She is not at full faculty at first, and uncomfortably watches her colleagues try to sort out the clues.

Keating has also written highly praised nonfiction, including *Sherlock Holmes: The Man and His World* (1979), and *Crime and Mystery Fiction: The One Hundred Best Books* (1987). He also edited *Agatha Christie: First Lady of Crime* (1977). His awards include a Gold Dagger from the Crime Writers Association, an Edgar from the Mystery Writers of America for *The Perfect Murder* (1964), and Lifetime Achievement awards from that organization in 1996 and from Malice Domestic in 2005.

Keating has always found the mystery form sufficiently flexible for his interests. "The crime story can, to a small extent or to quite a large extent, do what the pure novel does," he said in Martin Edwards' profile in *Mystery Scene*. "It can make a temporary map for its readers out of the chaos of their surroundings—only it should never let them know."

Works by the Author

Death and the Visiting Firemen (1959)

Zen There Was Murder (1960)

A Rush On the Ultimate (1961)

The Dog It Was That Died (1962)

Death of a Fat God (1963)

Is Skin-Deep, Is Fatal (1965)

The Strong Man (1971)

The Underside (1974)

A Remarkable Case of Burglary (1975)

Murder by Death (1976), novelization of screenplay by Neil Simon

A Long Walk to Wimbledon (1978)

The Murder of the Maharajah (1980)

Mrs. Craggs: Crimes Cleaned Up (1985), short stories

The Body in the Billiard Room (1987)

The Rich Detective (1993)

The Good Detective (1995)

In Kensington Gardens Once . . . (1997), short stories

The Soft Detective (1997)

The Bad Detective (1999)

Jack the Lady Killer (1999), novel in verse

Harriet Martens Series

The Hard Detective (2000)

A Detective in Love (2001)

A Detective Under Fire (2002)

The Dreaming Detective (2003)

A Detective at Death's Door (2005)

One Man and His Bomb (2006)

Rules, Regs and Rotten Eggs (2007)

Inspector Ghote Series

The Perfect Murder (1964)

Inspector Ghote's Good Crusade (1966)

Inspector Ghote Caught in Meshes (1967)

Inspector Ghote Hunts the Peacock (1968)

Inspector Ghote Plays a Joker (1969)

Inspector Ghote Breaks an Egg (1970)

Inspector Ghote Goes by Train (1971)

Inspector Ghote Trusts the Heart (1972)

Bats Fly Up for Inspector Ghote (1974)

Filmi, Filmi, Inspector Ghote (1976)

Inspector Ghote Draws a Line (1979)

Go West Inspector Ghote (1981)

The Sheriff of Bombay (1984)

Under a Monsoon Cloud (1986)

Dead on Time (1988)

Inspector Ghote, His Life and Crimes (1989), short stories

The Iciest Sin (1990)

Cheating Death (1992)

Doing Wrong (1993)

Asking Questions (1996)

The Inspector Ghote Mysteries: An Omnibus (1996), reprints first three novels in the series

Bribery, Corruption Also (1999)

Breaking and Entering (2000)

Inspector Ghote's First Case (2009)

A Small Case for Inspector Ghote? (2009)

Editor

Crime Writers (1978)

Crime Waves 1 (1991)

The Man Who . . . (1992)

Written as by Evelyn Hervey

The Governess (1983)

The Man of Gold (1985)

Into the Valley of Death (1986)

Adaptations in Other Media

"Hunt the Peacock" episode, *Detective* (1969), based on the novel

"Inspector Ghote Moves In" episode, *Storyboard* (1983), teleplay

The Perfect Murder (1988), screenplay based on the novel

Sherlock Holmes and the Leading Lady (1991), teleplay

Keating has also written and edited nonfiction books and scripted several radio plays.

For Further Information

Asking Questions review, *Publishers Weekly*, Jan. 20, 1997.

DeAndrea, William L. *Encyclopedia Mysteriosa*. New York: Prentice Hall General Reference, 1994.

Edwards, Martin, H.R.F. Keating: Putting the Reader First," *Mystery Scene* 89 (spring 2006), http://www.mysteryscenemag.com/articles/89hrfkeating.pdf/ (viewed Oct. 24, 2009).

Fletcher, Connie, *A Detective at Death's Door* review, *Booklist*, May 1, 2005.

Fowler, Christopher, "Forgotten Authors No. 33: HRF Keating," *The Independent,* May 17, 2009, http://www.independent.co.uk/arts-entertainment/books/features/ forgotten-authors-no33-hrf-keating-1684411.html/ (viewed Oct. 24, 2009).

H.R.F. Keating website. http://hrfkeating.com/ (viewed Oct. 24, 2009).

Keating, H.R.F. *Writing Crime Fiction*, second edition. London: A&C Black Publishers, 1986.

Moyer, Jessica, *Inspector Ghote's First Case* review, *Booklist*, July 1, 2009.

Symons, Julian, H.R.F. Keating entry, *The Oxford Companion to Crime and Mystery Writing*, edited by Rosemary Herbert. New York: Oxford University Press, 1999.

Laurie R. King

Oakland, California
1952

Private Detective, Police Procedural,
Historical Mystery
Benchmark Series: Mary Russell

About the Author and the Author's Writing

Laurie R. King had no intention, when she set about to write her first mystery novel, to do the expected. This applied to her craft—she produced 300 pages of her first draft within a month's time—and to her character—Mary Russell was a feisty, freethinking, determined young woman. King wrote a second manuscript featuring Russell and her new friend, Sherlock Holmes, then a third novel with a contemporary San Francisco homicide detective, Kate Martinelli. The third book was the first to appear in print, though the other two were not far behind.

All this, from a woman who began writing at age 35 when, with her younger child starting preschool, she had a few morning hours to herself each week.

The author always intended the books would launch series, she said in the *St. James Guide to Crime & Mystery Writers*. "I do not write classic 'whodunits'; I write stories about people within the format of the mystery genre." And she had a lot to explore in Kate Martinelli and Mary Russell.

Born Laurie Richardson in Oakland, California, in 1952, the author graduated from the University of California, Santa Cruz, in 1977 with a B.A. In 1984, she earned an M.A. from Graduate Theological Union. She married Noel Q. King, a college professor, in 1977; they have two children. Before she began writing full time in 1993, she managed a coffee shop and worked as a counselor for La Leche League International.

While her depiction of Arthur Conan Doyle's classic private investigator invited the ire of purists, King, in an interview with Gayle Surrette, said that "Sherlockians appreciate it when a writer plays 'the game,' treating Holmes as an historical character, and makes the kinds of in-jokes in the books that only they notice."

King insists her works are not Holmes pastiches but justifiable crime novels that just happen to include mysterydom's best-known hero. She uses the novels to explore a variety of topics. "One of the joys of mysteries is that you can weave all kinds of interests and abilities into them—house building, child rearing, life in Papua New Guinea, Greek verbs, holy fools, trench warfare, the hills of north India," she said on her Web site.

When we first encounter Mary Russell, she is a teenage girl who wants to find out who kidnapped the daughter of a U.S. senator. She asks a retiree who now keeps bees at a small farm on the Sussex Downs for some useful tips on being a detective.

"I can allow the character of Holmes to develop in ways that someone who is writing a Holmes pastiche could not," King told *Publishers Weekly's* Robert C. Hahn. "After all, the Mary Russell novels take place after Conan Doyle was through with Holmes and I'm not bound by the Holmesian canon."

As the series progresses, King ages her characters, and before long, Russell is Mrs. Holmes. In *The Language of Bees* (2009), the author revisits the canon sufficiently to create a heretofore unknown son of Holmes, Damien Adler, who is addicted to narcotics and has been the suspect in a number of crimes and murders. King gives it her trademark skew. While Holmes gallops off in pursuit of Damien's missing wife and child, Russell adopts a disguise and pursues her own ideas in Damien's Bohemian London sphere. "While the detective's shrewdly observant brother, Mycroft, and other Doyle regulars appear, fans of the original Holmes stories should be prepared for a strong feminist slant," said *Publishers Weekly*.

King peppers her novels with details. "For the Russell books, I tend to use an unstructured approach to research," she told interviewer Mia Stampe, "wandering into areas in the library with no particular goal in mind, and picking up books in bookstores and catalogues that have some interest and are in my period—memoirs are particularly valuable."

As mentioned, King did not abandon Martinelli; the SFPD veteran has continued to appear in such cases as *Night Work*, in which victims are tasered, strangled, and decorated with candy. Of the series, Emily Melton in *Booklist* said, "it's a solid choice for those who like tough female cops. The feminist slant of this story will also draw readers interested in women's issues."

But King doesn't anticipate running out of ideas for Russell and Holmes anytime soon. Jokingly dropping into reverie, she told Bookreporter, "I could put Russell into a life-threatening coma and let Holmes take over for one book; that would certainly keep things from going stale."

The casebook remains open.

Works by the Author

A Darker Place (1998), also titled *The Birth of a New Moon*

Folly (2001)

Keeping Watch (2003)

Kate Martinelli Series

A Grave Talent (1993)

To Play the Fool (1995)

With Child (1996)

Night Work (2000)

The Art of Detection (2006)

Mary Russell Series

The Beekeeper's Apprentice: or, On the Segregation of the Queen (1994)

A Monstrous Regiment of Women (1995)

A Letter of Mary (1996)

The Moor (1998)

O Jerusalem (1999)

Justice Hall (2002)

The Game (2004)

Locked Rooms (2005)

The Language of Bees (2009)

The God of the Hive (2010)

Writing as Leigh Richards

Califia's Daughters (2004)

Touchstone (2007)

Contributor

Naked Came the Phoenix, with Nevada Barr, Mary Jane Clark, Diana Gabaldon, J. A. Jance, Faye Kellerman, Val McDermid, Pam and Mary O'Shaughnessy, Anne Perry, Nancy Pickard, J. D. Robb, Lisa Scottoline, and Marcia Talley (2001)

For Further Information

Hahn, Robert C., "PW Talks with Laurie R. King," *Publishers Weekly*, Feb. 18, 2002.

Language of Bees review, *Publishers Weekly*, Mar. 9, 2009.

Laurie R. King profile, Bookreporter, 2005, http://www.bookreporter.com/authors/au-king-laurie.asp/ (viewed Nov. 11, 2009).

Laurie R. King website, http://www.laurierking.com/ (viewed Nov. 11, 2009).

Melton, Emily, Night Work review, *Booklist*, Dec. 1, 1999.

Oleksiw, Susan, Laurie R. King profile, *St. James Guide to Crime & Mystery Writers*, fourth edition, edited by Jay P. Pederson. Detroit: St. James Press, 1996.

Russell, Mary J., Laurie R. King interview, Laurie R. King website, http://www.laurierking.com/?page_id=907/ (viewed Nov. 11, 2009).

Stampe, Mia, "Interview with Laurie R. King," Sherlockiana, 1999, http://www.sherlockiana.dk/shklub/artikler/interview.shtml/ (viewed Nov. 11, 2009).

Surette, Gayle, "Interview; Laurie R. King," Gumshoe: A literary investigation, April 13, 2009, http://www.gumshoereview.com/php/Review-id.php?id=1729/ (viewed Nov. 11, 2009).

William Kent Krueger

Torrington, Wyoming
1950

Police Procedural, Private Detective
Benchmark Series: Cork O'Connor

Tony Nelson

About the Author and the Author's Writing

Cork O'Connor entered the barn, fearful of what he might find, desperate to spot a clue to where his missing wife Jo might be.

> A chair sat in the middle of the room. It was empty, but an uncoiled length of rope lay like a long, dead snake on the ground around it . . . . His finger nestled the rifle trigger, and he eased himself farther into the barn.

> What he saw stopped him cold.

It wasn't his wife. But it was a gruesome scene, in *Heaven's Keep* (2009), a tense novel in William Kent Krueger's award-winning crime series.

Although he has gathered a large following in the United States and abroad, particularly in Japan, the author thinks of himself as a regionalist. He lovingly depicts, as an example, the Quetico-Superior Wilderness in Minnesota on the Canadian border, more than 2 million acres of forest and rivers with white-water rapids, in *Boundary Waters* (1999). "I begin with place," he told Lynn Kaczmarek for *Mystery News*, "and I populate it with the kind of characters who would live in that place and everything kind of comes from there. . . . I'm unabashedly a regional author."

In Krueger's initial novel, *Iron Lake* (1998), his hero O'Connor, of Irish and Anishinaabe ancestry, was originally a Chicago cop. He lost his job as Aurora sheriff in a bitter election, became involved in a dispute with local Indians over fishing rights, got caught up in a murder and a missing boy, and faced a malevolent windigo. So he moved with his lawyer wife and their two daughters to northern Minnesota, where he had grown up, hoping for a change, hoping to preserve his marriage. The book won the Anthony Award for best first novel.

Krueger was born in 1950 in Torrington, Wyoming. His father taught high school English. His mother was a musician. He knew, after a story he wrote in third grade garnered huge praise from his teacher, that he wanted to become a writer. He attended Stanford for a year. He has worked as a journalist, logger, construction worker, and child development researcher. Krueger's wife, Diane, is an attorney; they have two children.

It took the author three years to complete the manuscript for his first novel, working an hour each morning, before he went to his day job. "The first hurdle authors need to get over is that you can complete the first novel," he told interviewer Kristin Johnson. While he gained practice writing short stories, "I like to paint on a larger canvas that a novel offers and particularly a series."

Urged by his writing group to submit his novel to an agent, he failed to find a New York agent willing to represent him. An agent in Chicago, however, took an interest and recommended he shorten his draft. That took another year. When *Iron Lake* was finished, it ended up commanding a brief bidding exchange between two interested publishers. Pocket Books brought it out in 1998.

"Krueger makes Cork a real person beneath his genre garments," said *Publishers Weekly*, "mostly by showing him dealing with the needs of his two very different teenage daughters. And the author's deft eye for the details of everyday life brings the town and its peculiar problems to vivid life."

In addition to his belief that character rises from place, the author told interviewer Jonathan Maberry, "I also think setting contributes significantly to plot and to motive. Things that happen in a story happen because of the kind of place the story is set."

For example, as the author said on his website,

> The idea at the heart of *Heaven's Keep* was given to me many years ago during a discussion with a guy from "up North." He was telling me about the vast stretches of peat bog in northern Minnesota and how treacherous they can be. "A person could disappear there and never be found, not a trace."

And that's just what happened in that novel, the ninth in the O'Connor series.

Krueger frequently introduces Indian characters and lore. He researches extensively in books, "And then, of course, I began to meet and get to know the Ojibwe," he told Bookreporter. "It's an ongoing journey, understanding this remarkable culture and these amazing people."

Krueger offers advice to budding authors on his website: "always tie up loose ends at books' end, and never kill off a family pet." He does a lot of thinking ahead of time about his plot before he begins writing, usually in longhand in a notebook. "It frees me from having to worry about plot as I'm going along and I can concentrate on the actual prose, the words and sentences and paragraphs, which is the most compelling part of the writing for me," he told Ali Karim.

With characters, setting, theme, all that's left is craft. "Every story, to be compelling, demands tension," he told interviewer Craig Johnson of Backyard Writer. "And despite the fact that we work in a genre that generally gets a lot of mileage out of putting people in jeopardy, I think it's really the emotional dynamics that drive readers' interest."

Works by the Author

The Devil's Bed (2003)

Cork O'Connor Series

Iron Lake (1998)

Boundary Waters (1999)

Purgatory Ridge (2001)

Blood Hollow (2004)

Mercy Falls (2005)

Copper River (2006)

Thunder Bay (2007)

Red Knife (2008)

Heaven's Keep (2009)

Vermillion Drift (2010)

Northwest Angle (2011)

Contributor

Resort to Murder: Thirteen Tales of Mystery by Minnesota's Premier Writers, edited by Lance Eaton (2009)

For Further Information

Iron Lake review, *Publishers Weekly*, May 25, 1998.

Johnson, Craig, William Kent Krueger interview, Mystery Fanfare, Aug. 10, 2009, http://mysteryreadersinc.blogspot.com/2009/08/william-kent-krueger-inter viewed-by.html/ (viewed Oct. 21, 2009).

Johnson, Kristin, "An Interview with William Kent Krueger," Backyard Writer, http://www.whistlingshade.com/0503/krueger.html/ (viewed Oct. 21, 2009).

Kaczmarek, Lynn, "William Kent Krueger: Magic in the Northwoods," *Mystery News*, February/March 2001, http://www.blackravenpress.com/Author%20 pages/kreuger.htm/ (viewed Oct. 21, 2009).

Karim, Ali, "William Kent Krueger Speaks to Ali Karim for Shots Ezine," *SHOTS*, http://www.shotsmag.co.uk/shots23/intvus_23/wkkrueger.html/ (viewed Oct. 21, 2009).

Maberry, Jonatahan, Regional Mysteries and Thrillers, http://jonathanmaberry.com/ regional-mysteries-and-thrillers/ (viewed Sept. 17, 2010).

William Kent Krueger interview, *Bookreporter,* July 27, 2007. http://www.bookre porter.com/authors/au-krueger-william-kent.asp/ (viewed Oct. 21, 2009).

William Kent Krueger website, http://www.williamkentkrueger.com/about.html/ (viewed Oct. 21, 2009).

Joe R. Lansdale

Gladewater, Texas
1951

Police Procedural, Amateur Detective,
Horror Western
Benchmark Series: Hap Collins and
Leonard Pines

Alex McVey

About the Author and the Author's Writing

"Mojo" writing, Joe R. Landsdale explains, is a muscular, over-the-top storytelling style that he came by thanks to having been born (1951) in east Texas (Gladewater). "Texas is so wrapped up in myth and legend, it's hard to know what the state and its people are really about," Landsdale said on his website. "Real Texans raised on these myths and legends sometimes become legends themselves."

A varied life experience—he has worked as a custodian, carpenter, bodyguard, bouncer, goat farmer, rose-field laborer, and plumber's helper—hadn't hurt as Lansdale embarked on his writing career.

"I sold my first piece, a nonfiction piece—when I was 21. Right before I turned 22. I wrote it with my mother. It was an article on planting shrubs as a way of therapy," he said in an interview with Nick Gevers for the Infinity Plus website. He next sold a short story to *Mike Shayne Mystery Magazine*, then more tales of private detective Ray Slater. Then a crime novel, *Act of Love* (1980), followed by a Western novel, *The Texas Nightriders* (1983).

Lansdale has reached into nearly all genres, though he seems most drawn to horror and crime fiction. As he said in a *Locus* interview, he often uses his fiction as "a kind of hot, burning lens you can look through that makes things bigger than life, that distorts everything into something bigger than it really is."

Lansdale attended Tyler Junior College, the University of Texas at Austin, and Stephen F. Austin State University. He and his wife since 1973, Karen Ann Morton, live in Nacogdoches, Texas.

Among his literary influences, he includes Homer, Rudyard Kipling, Edgar Rice Burroughs, Mark Twain, and Flannery O'Connor as well as fantasy writers including Robert Bloch, Ray Bradbury, William F. Nolan, and Charles Beaumont.

The literary world has certainly taken appreciative notice of Lansdale. He has earned six Bram Stoker Awards from Horror Writers of America and an Edgar for best novel from Mystery Writers of America for *The Bottoms* (2000), a novel about the search for a killer of black prostitutes that evidences his disgust for racism. Honors have also come to Lansdale from abroad; he has received the Italian Grinzane Cavour Literature Prize for lifetime achievement.

The author's best-known mystery series began in 1990 and features the duo of Hap Collins and Leonard Pines, the former at various times a factory security guard or construction worker, the latter his gay, black, Vietnam War–era veteran friend. If the two are not quite private detectives, they do manage to uncover crimes and solve puzzles and get in a lot of fights. Incorrigible friends, their sense of right is often bigger than circumstances should allow. Hap and Leonard are relentlessly straight with each other, as in this exchange from *Vanilla Ride* (2009):

"'My motto,' I said, 'is if you've got it, flaunt it.'"

"'What you're flauntin' is enough to make a man turn a gun on himself,' Leonard said."

Lansdale acknowledges that the books are violent. "People are drawn to it, and even though we might not ourselves be involved in these kinds of adventures, it seems to be the engine for stories that people want to read and have been reading for a long time," the author told Jeff Salamon for *American-Statesman*.

One expects unusual plots from Lansdale. *Lost Echoes* (2006), for instance, has a hero who has the ability to hear the sounds of violence that took place in the past. Where do this and other ideas come from? "I have to wait on them," he said in a UnitShifter conversation. "*Bubba Ho-Tep* [2003] was actually several years in the making. I had the title. I had tried to write an Elvis story before . . . and, of course, I loved mummy movies. It all came together when I was asked to write an Elvis story."

Lansdale holds belts in Aikido and Combat Hapkido. He suggested, in a *Publishers Weekly* discussion, with Melissa Mia Hall, that martial arts have guided his writing. "One of the five key elements is deception—if you make the reader believe one thing and surprise them with something else, there's deception, correct?"

That's part of Lansdale's mojo.

Works by the Author

Act of Love (1980)

Dead in the West (1983)

The Nightrunners (1983)

Texas Night Riders (1983), originally issued as by Ray Slater

The Magic Wagon (1986)

The Steel Valentine (1986), chapbook

Cold in July (1989)

Drive-By, with Gary Gianni (1993)

Jonah Hex: Two Gun Mojo (1994), graphic novel

Tarzan: The Lost Adventure, with Edgar Rice Burroughs (1996), graphic novel

The Boar (1998)

Freezer Burn (1999)

Something Lumber This Way Comes (1999)

Waltz of Shadows (1999)

The Big Blow (2000)

Blood Dance (2000)

The Bottoms (2000)

Zeppelins West (2001)

A Fine Dark Line (2002)

Bubba Ho-Tep (2003)

Sunset and Sawdust (2004)

Flaming London (2005)

Lost Echoes (2006)

Conan and the Songs of the Dead (2007), graphic novel

The God of the Razor (2007)

The Shadows Kith and Kin (2007)

Leather Maiden (2008)

Flaming Zeppelins: The Adventures of Ned the Seal (2010)

All the Earth, Thrown to the Sky (2011)

Crucified Dreams (2011)

Drive-In Series

The Drive-In (1988)

The Drive-In 2: Not Just One of Them Sequels (1989)

The Complete Drive-In (2010)

Hap Collins and Leonard Pine Series

Savage Season (1990)

Mucho Mojo (1994)

The Two-Bear Mambo (1995)

Bad Chili (1997)

Rumble Tumble (1998)

Captains Outrageous (2001)

Vanilla Ride (2009)

Red Devil (2011)

Collections

Stories by Mama Lansdale's Youngest Boy (1975)

The Long Ones (1985)

Bestsellers Guaranteed (1986)

By Bizarre Hands (1987)

On the Far Side of the Cadillac Desert with the Dead Folks (1988)

Tight Little Stitches on a Dead Man's Back (1988), also titled *Tight Little Stitches*

Electric Gumbo (1994)

Writer of the Purple Rage (1994)

A Fist Full of Stories (and Articles) (1996)

Atomic Chili (1997)

The Good, the Bad and the Indifferent (1997)

High Cotton: Selected Stories (1997)

Private Eye Action as You Like It, with Lewis Shiner (1998)

Selected Stories (2001)

For a Few Stories More (2002)

Bumper Crop (2004)

Mad Dog Summer: And Other Stories (2004)

The King and Other Stories (2005)

Sanctified and Chicken-Fried: The Portable Lansdale (2009)

The Best of Joe R. Lansdale (2010)

Dead in the West (2010)

Contributor

Fears (1984)

Book of the Dead (1989)

More Tales Of Zorro, with Kage Baker, Matthew Baugh, Johnny D Boggs, Keith R. A. DeCandido, Carole Nelson Douglas, Win Scott Eckert, Jennifer Fallon, Alan Dean Foster, Craig Shaw Gardner, Joe Gore, and Timothy Zahn (2009)

Editor

Best of the West (1986)

The New Frontier: The Best of Today's Western Fiction (1989)

Razored Saddles, with Pat Lo Brutto (1989)

Dark at Heart: All New Tales of Dark Suspense, with Karen Lansdale (1992)

The West That Was, with Thomas W. Knowles (1994)

Wild West Show, with Thomas W. Knowles (1994)

Weird Business, with Richard Klaw (1995)

The author has also written several screenplays including *Bubba Nosferatu and the Curse of the She-Vampires* (2008)

For Further Information

Gevers, Nick, "With Mojo Aforethought: An Interview with Joe R. Lansdale," Infinity Plus, http://www.infinityplus.co.uk/nonfiction/intjl.htm (viewed Aug. 5, 2009).

Hall, M. M., "PW Talks with Joe R. Lansdale," *Publishers Weekly*, Aug. 27, 2001.

Hall, Melissa Mia, "Blue Collar-Writer," *Publishers Weekly*, Dec. 11, 2006.

Joe R. Lansdale interview, Locus online, http://www.locusmag.com/2007/Issue05_Lansdale.html/ (viewed Aug. 5, 2009).

Joe R. Lansdale interview, Unitshifter, http://www.unitshifter.com/lansdale.html/ (viewed Aug. 6, 2009).

Joe R. Lansdale website, http://www.joerlansdale.com/ (viewed Aug. 5, 2009).

Salamon, Jeff, "The Further Adventures of Hap and Leonard," *American-Statesman*, July 4, 2008, http://www.statesman.com/life/content/life/stories/books/2009/07/04/0704lansdale.html/ (viewed Aug. 6, 2009).

Donna Leon

New Jersey
1942

Police Procedural
Benchmark Series: Guido Brunetti

About the Author and the Author's Writing

Venezia (Venice) is in the Veneto region of northern Italy. Population 300,000. Tourist mecca boasting the Doge's Palace, the Basilica di San Marco, and the Piazza San Marco. Hundreds of churches. Dramatic architecture. Dazzling history. Sparkling night life.

And, of course, crime.

The Grand Canal and other water courses in Venice are plagued by pollution. In *About Face* (2009), author Donna Leon's 18th crime novel featuring Commissario Guido Brunetti, "Brunetti becomes an ecological expert when an investigator with the carabiniere wants him to look into illegal hauling that has resulted in a truck driver's murder," said a *Publishers Weekly* reviewer, who called the series "wickedly entertaining."

Donna Leon, of Irish/Spanish descent, was born in New Jersey in 1942. She studied 18th-century novelists for her doctorate through a university in Indiana. She has taught in Switzerland, Saudi Arabia, Iran, and China; was a professor of English literature in Italy; and also taught at American military bases there. She first ventured to Italy in 1965 and settled there permanently in 1981. She founded Il Complesso Barocco, an opera company in Venice. She wrote the libretto for a comic opera, *Donna Galliana*. And in 1992, she wrote her first Brunetti mystery, at the suggestion of a conductor friend. After all, she knew the genre inside and out, having been a crime reviewer for the *Sunday Times* of London for many years. (She has said that her favorite authors include Ruth Rendell, Reginald Hill, Frances Fyfield, and P. D. James.)

Leon wrote *Death at la Fenice* (1992) just to show that she could. She set the manuscript aside, then submitted it for the prestigious Suntory Prize for Social Sciences and Humanities in Japan. She won the prize for best suspense novel in 1991, and with it a two-book contract with HarperCollins.

Her books deal more with the circumstance of a crime than the particulars. "'Who' is just a noun," the author told reporter Tim Heald, "'why' is a verb. Who someone leaves his wife for is dull, but why he leaves his wife is interesting."

Leon allows her character a home life, and readers have come to know his dazzling wife, Paola, a university professor, and their teenage children.

"Brunetti is no ordinary lone police officer," Rachel Pollack explained in *The St. Petersburg Times*. His "secret to finding out information in Venice—perhaps all of Italy—according to Brunetti, is knowing someone who knows someone and is familiar with gossip about that person."

Although dedicated to his vocation, Brunetti sometimes dances cautiously through some moral dilemmas. "The reality of daily life makes Guido Brunetti cynical," said John Stankevicz of Hubpages, "but his soul won't allow him to quit. Donna Leon writes the life of a man that you would like to know and spend time with. He is a perfect series character."

Leon disdains the technical jabber of forensics in favor of the psychology of the characters. She places violence mostly offstage. "I don't think it's good for us to read that stuff, more so to write that stuff," she said in a conversation with Elaine Petrocelli. "I've never had a television and I don't go to the movies so I am perhaps more attuned to the vision of violence. I just can't do it."

In his second appearance, *Death in a Strange Country* (1993), Brunetti's search for the killer of an American soldier conflicts with his supervisor Patta's fears of what word of the case might do to the city's tourism.

"Venice looms large as a well-painted backdrop," said *Publishers Weekly* in reviewing the book, "crumbling beauty and tourist-mobbed sites are as vivid in Leon's depiction as the rich tang of espresso boiling over or the chill of a morgue tucked away on the cemetery island of San Michele."

Venice is so important to the novels, and Leon's descriptions are so dead-on that Toni Sepeda has written a companion book, *Burnetti's Venice: Walks Through the Novels* (2009), which shadows the fictional hero through the canal city's highlights.

Although the author speaks Italian, she writes in English. Her books have come out in 20 other languages. So far she has not allowed translation into Italian, however, as she tries to avoid celebrity in her adopted country. She sends her new books to Diogenes, a German-language press in Zurich, Switzerland. She went through a brief lapse in American publishers in the late 1990s, but is now firmly in Atlantic Monthly's catalog.

Leon has seen her cultured detective hero evolve through the course of the series. "Guido's vision of the world grows increasingly black and pessimistic with each book," she told journalist Stephen Anable for *Publishers Weekly*. "It's difficult to view politics today, everywhere in the world, without being pessimistic and cynical. But, like Brunetti, I have a personal life that is happy, that allows optimism to coexist with a historical sense that is very different."

Leon has become quite comfortable with her literary achievement—and a character who has now also generated a cookbook and a book of walking tours. Brunetti has truly come alive.

Works by the Author

Guido Brunetti Series

Death at la Fenice (1992)

Death in a Strange Country (1993)

The Anonymous Venetian (1994), also titled *Dressed for Death*

A Venetian Reckoning (1995), also titled *Death And Judgment*

Acqua Alta (1996), also titled *Death in High Water*

The Death of Faith (1997), also titled *Quietly in Their Sleep*

A Noble Radiance (1997)

Fatal Remedies (1999)

Friends in High Places (2000)

The First Donna Leon Collection (2001)

A Sea of Troubles (2001)

The Second Donna Leon Collection (2002)

Willful Behaviour (2002)

Uniform Justice (2003)

Doctored Evidence (2004)

Blood from a Stone (2005)

Through a Glass Darkly (2006)

Suffer the Little Children (2007)

The Girl of His Dreams (2008)

About Face (2009)

A Question of Belief (2010)

Drawing Conclusions (2011)

Nonfiction

Brunetti's Venice: Walks with the City's Best-Loved Detective, by Toni Sepeda (2009), with introduction by Donna Leon

Brunetti's Cookbook, by Roberta Pianaro (2010), with essays and excerpts from novels by Donna Leon

For Further Information

About Face review, *Publishers Weekly*, Feb. 23, 2009.

Anable, Stephen, "Deaths in Venice: PW Talks with Donna Leon," *Publishers Weekly*, Aug. 4, 2003.

Death in a Strange Country review, *Publishers Weekly*, June 28, 1993.

Donna Leon website, http://www.donnaleon.co.uk/ (viewed Oct. 16, 2009).

Donna Leon website, http://www.groveatlantic.com/leon/author.htm/ (viewed Oct. 16, 2009).

"Exclusive interview with Donna Leon," Italian Mysteries, May 5, 2003, http://italian-mysteries.com/leon-interview.html/ (viewed Oct. 16, 2009).

Heald, Tim, "Donna Leon Talks about Corruption and Death in Venice: Interview," *London Telegraph*, May 7, 2009, http://www.telegraph.co.uk/culture/books/

bookreviews/5291489/Donna-Leon-talks-about-corruption-and-death-in-Ven ice-interview.html/ (viewed Oct. 16, 2009).

Leon, Donna, with Roberta Pianaro, *At Table with the Brunettis*. London: William Heinemann, 2010.

Petrocelli, Elaine, "At Lunch with Donna Leon," Book Passage, http://www. groveatlantic.com/grove/leon/lunch.htm/ (viewed Oct. 16, 2009).

Pollack, Rachel, "Under the Surface in Venice," *St. Petersburg Times*, Sept. 22, 2009.

Sepeda, Toni, *Burnetti's Venice: Walks Through the Novels*. London: William Heinemann, 2009.

Stankevicz, John, "Discover Donna Leon, the Mystery Writer Who Takes Us to Venice." Hubpages, http://hubpages.com/hub/Discover_Donna_Leon/ (viewed Oct. 16, 2009).

Jeff Lindsay (Jeffrey P. Freundlich)

Miami, Florida
1952

Rogue Detective
Benchmark Series: Dexter

About the Author and the Author's Writing

As much as they love private detectives and police investigators, many readers have an equal fascination with the other side—the criminals. And we're talking not just career criminals such as Lawrence Block's sneak thief Bernie Rhodenbarr or Richard Stark's holdup specialist Parker but assassins such as Barry Eisler's John Rain or vile psychotics such as Thomas Harris's Dr. Hannibal Lector.

Dexter Morgan kills those he believes deserve to be killed. He's a forensic blood spatter analyst for Miami PD by day, a usually convenient, sometime uncomfortable place to hide his avocation. Dexter is morally reprehensible except for one trait: His adoptive father disciplined him to kill only those who are deserving of being killed. This usually means other serial killers. Dexter lives by a strict moral code—of a sort. Besides the nature of his targets, his stepfather also trained him how to blend into society and avoid detection.

Author Jeff Lindsay pulls off his freakish series "by keeping a very light touch on what it is that Dexter actually does, and with a great deal of humor," suggests reviewer Matthew Lewin in *The Guardian*. "There are genuinely funny situations, very clever plots and many excellent one-liners. Dexter has a way of—ouch—getting under your skin and making you like him."

The first book in Lindsay's series, *Darkly Dreaming Dexter* (2004), was nearly nominated for a Mystery Writers of America Edgar Award for best first novel, only it wasn't his first novel.

The author was born Jeffrey P. Freundlich in 1952 and grew up in Miami, Florida. He graduated from Middlebury College in Vermont in 1975 with a B.A. in literature and writing. Three years later he graduated from Carnegie-Mellon University with a double M.F.A. in theater direction and playwriting. He attended Celebration Mime Clown School. He taught literature and writing courses at Florida Gulf Coast University. Freundlich worked in standup comedy and theater. He wrote some 22 plays and several screenplays.

Freundlich married Hilary Hemingway, the daughter of Ernest Hemingway's brother Leicester, and they co-authored *Hunting with Hemingway: Based on the Stories of Leicester Hemingway* (2000). He and Hilary Hemingway also collaborated on two novels in the late 1990s, for which he used the byline Jeffrey P. Lindsay. An earlier novel, *Tropical Depression* (1994), came out under his actual name, Jeffrey P. Freundlich. It is about Billy

Knight, a transplanted former LAPD officer, now trying to make a go of it in Key West, Florida, and unable to resist a friend's plea for help solve his son's murder.

Lindsay's career picked up pace when he had an inspiration "while attending a civics group luncheon in his home state of Florida," according to Carol Memmott in *USA Today*. "'An idea just popped into my head that a serial killer isn't always a bad thing.' By the time lunch was over, he had outlined most of the story on a napkin."

His manuscript found a publisher and a television producer who took the affable killer to Showtime for a series that began its fifth season in 2010.

In that first book, Dexter's comfort level is challenged when another, even more gruesome serial killer, nicknamed Dr. Danco, stalks victims in Miami.

"This new killer seems to be doing more than copying Dexter—he seems to be saying, 'Come out and play.' Dexter's secret life makes for a lonely existence, even a lovable monster can be intrigued by the prospect of finding a friend," observed a Powell's Books reviewer.

While the popular television series' first season (featuring Michael C. Hall) was based on Lindsay's first novel, later seasons took their own direction, killing some characters and adding new ones (including a family). Lindsay in his slower pace with books, meanwhile, proceeded as if the television Dexter didn't exist.

"Dexter is an amusing narrator," reviewer Eleanor Bukowsky of Mostly Fiction said of the second book, *Dearly Devoted Dexter* (2005), "with an extremely sick mind, and he is very funny. Not all readers will appreciate the many dismemberment puns. . . . However, the strong of stomach will get a kick out of Lindsay's satirical send-off of the many formulaic serial killer novels that flood the literary market every year."

The author admitted in an *Entertainment Weekly* Q&A that he made a slight misstep with *Dexter in the Dark* (2007), in which he suggested that the antihero might be possessed by demons.

"I had to rethink things," he told *EW*. "How much do I follow my instincts? What do I owe my readers? I made a deliberate choice to write something people would enjoy. . . . I feel like I'm back in the groove" with the next book, *Dexter by Design* (2009).

Has Dexter on TV become more famous than Dexter on page? The author, on his Random House website, admitted as much.

> That takes some getting used to, even though there are perks. It has given me some wonderful moments—like riding into Times Square in a taxi and seeing Dexter 60 feet tall on the side of the building. "Have you seen that program?" the driver asked me.

And what was the author's killer answer?

Works by the Author

Tropical Depression: A Novel of Suspense (1994), as by Jeffrey P. Freundlich

Dreamland: A Novel of the UFO Cover-up, (1995), as by Jeffrey P. Lindsay with Hilary Hemingway

Dreamchild (1998), as by Jeffrey P. Lindsay with Hilary Hemingway

Hunting with Hemingway: Based on the Stories of Leicester Hemingway (2000), as by Jeffrey P. Lindsay with Hilary Hemingway

Dexter Series, as by Jeff Lindsay

Darkly Dreaming Dexter (2004)

Dearly Devoted Dexter (2005)

Dexter in the Dark (2007)

Dexter: An Omnibus (2008), includes first three novels

Dexter by Design (2009)

Dexter is Delicious (2010)

Double Dexter (2011)

Adaptations in Other Media

Dexter (Showtime, 2006–)

For Further Information

Budak, Bertan, "Interview: Jeff Lindsay," Askmen.com, http://uk.askmen.com/celebs/interview_250/273_jeff_lindsay_interview.html/ (viewed Sept. 12, 2009).

Bukowsky, Eleanor, *Darkly Dreaming Dexter* review, MostlyFiction Book Reviews, http://www.mostlyfiction.com/sleuths/lindsay.htm/ (viewed Sept. 12, 2009).

Bukowsky, Eleanor, *Dearly Devoted Dexter* review, MostlyFiction Book Reviews, http://www.mostlyfiction.com/sleuths/lindsay.htm/ (viewed Sept. 12, 2009).

Darkly Dreaming Dexter review, Powells.com, http://www.powells.com/biblio/8–1400095913–0/ (viewed Sept. 16, 2009).

Dexter Crew, Showtime website, http://dexterwiki.sho.com/page/Dexter+Crew/ (viewed Sept. 15, 2009).

Dexter web page, Random House, http://www.randomhouse.com/doubleday/dexter/ (viewed Sept. 12, 2009).

Jeff Lindsay interview, Curled Up With a Good Book, http://www.curledup.com/intlinds.htm/ (viewed Sept. 12, 2009).

Lewin, Matthew, "Death's Head Boy," *The Guardian*, Feb. 28, 2009.

"Middlebury College Acquires Archival Materials of Ernest Hemingway and the Hemingway Family," *Middlebury*, Aug. 21, 2007, http://www.middlebury.edu/about/pubaff/news_releases/2007/pubaff_633232903059489308.htm/ (viewed Sept. 12, 2009).

Mudge, Alden, Jeff Lindsay interview, BookPage, http://www.bookpage.com/0508bp/jeff_lindsay.html/ (viewed Sept. 12, 2009).

Peter Lovesey

Kate Shemilt

Middlesex, England
1936

Historical Mystery, Police Procedural
Benchmark Series: Sergeant Cribb

About the Author and the Author's Writing

Peter Lovesey wobbled into the mystery field in 1970. Four decades later, he is solidly established as a master of the genre.

The author won 1,000 pounds for *Wobble to Death* (1970), his entry in a *Sunday Times* first-crime-novel contest. Its main characters, Sergeant Cribb and Constable Thackery, appeared in another eight books and were featured in a television series.

Lovesey had three goals in mind when he crafted that crime story—goals he'd adopted after writing a history of long-distance foot racing, *The Kings of Distance* (1968): Write interestingly, plan, and keep everything. From the nonfiction sports book, he had a mound of research material that he put to good use in *Wobble to Death*, the story of a killer among runners in 1879 London.

He thought the book was a one-shot. But it soon became clear "that a second novel was expected," he told interviewer Annie Chernow of *Crimespree Magazine*. "So I turned to another sport—bareknuckle boxing—played safe and stayed in the Victorian period for *The Detective Wore Silk Drawers* [1971]." In this sequel he explored further themes of seaside resorts, Irish nationalists, and music halls.

Lovesey has said he enjoys shaping his plots. His Peter Diamond novel, *Bloodhounds* (1996), is a throwback to classic detective novels, such as those written by Arthur Conan Doyle and John Dickson Carr. "The challenge was to construct a puzzle that worked, and was plausible in a modern setting. I enjoyed trying out the possibilities. The art, I suspect, is like a conjuring trick in which the presentation matters as much as the mechanics," he told interviewer Martin Edwards of Crimescene.

The author was born in Whitton, Middlesex, England in 1936. World War II became a tumultuous time in the Lovesey household after a flying V1 bomb wrecked the family home in 1944, while his father was working at the bank, his mother was shopping, and he was at school. His brothers survived the blast. He wrote of some of this experience in *Rough Cider* (1986).

Lovesey earned a B.A. from University of Reading, with honors, in 1958. He served in the Royal Air Force from 1958 to 1961 as an education officer and a flying officer. Thereafter, until 1969, he was a lecturer at Thurrock Technical College. He then headed the general education department at Hammersmith College for Further Education in London until 1975.

Lovesey delights in the short as well as the long form and has contributed to a number of periodicals and anthologies. His first short story was "The Bathroom" for *Ellery Queen's Mystery Magazine* in 1973. Eventually he became a full-time writer of novels, though he shaped several manuscripts for the television series based on his Cribb stories and was story consultant for another series, *Rosemary & Thyme*, from 2003 to 2006.

Lovesey was firmly entrenched as a writer of Victorian mysteries for many years. "I've heard it suggested that readers like to escape into the past when so much about the present is depressing," he said on his website. "I find I'm more intrigued by things that haven't changed. It's amusing to discover that human nature hasn't altered in thousands of years."

The author's Peter Diamond books are police procedurals set in modern Bath, England. The main character is a former rugby player who disdains modern forensics methods.

Bertie is the nickname of another ongoing character, Albert Edward, Prince of Wales, son of Queen Victoria, who, at Lovesey's hand, has an affinity for solving crimes. These books are written in the first person and are keyed to actual historical events. *Bertie and the Tin Man* (1987), for instance, has the main character investigating the apparent suicide of jockey Fred Archer, who frequently rode his horses.

Chief Inspector Henrietta Mallin has shown up in two books so far. "She's had to compensate for being short and female in a job dominated by men," he told Leonard Picker of *Publishers Weekly*. "She picked the toughest job because she wanted to win respect from her family."

Ideas for his novels and stories come from many sources, he said in a *Strand* magazine interview.

> It might be something I've heard in a teashop. It might be something I've read. It might be two things that coalesce. . . . For about six weeks before I write a word, I'll be working out plotlines and writing things down on bits of paper and throwing them away and trying to devise a plot that I think will work.

And they've all worked.

Works by the Author

The False Inspector Dew (1982)

Keystone (1984)

Rough Cider (1986)

On the Edge (1989)

The Reaper (2000)

In Suspense (2001)

Dead Gorgeous (2002)

Albert Edward, Prince of Wales Series

Bertie and the Tin Man (1987)

Bertie and the Seven Bodies (1990)

Bertie and the Crime of Passion (1993)

Inspector Henrietta Mallin Series

The Circle (2005)

Circle/Do Not Exceed the Stated Dose (2008), omnibus

The Headhunters (2008)

Inspector Peter Diamond Series

The Last Detective (1991)

Diamond Solitaire (1992)

The Summons (1995)

Bloodhounds (1996)

Upon A Dark Night (1997)

Do Not Exceed The Stated Dose (1998) stories

The Vault (1999)

Diamond Dust (2002)

The House Sitter (2003)

Bloodhounds/Diamond Dust (2004) omnibus

The Last Detective/Diamond Solitaire (2005) omnibus

House Sitter /Upon a Dark Night (2007) omnibus

The Secret Hangman (2007)

The Headhunters (2008)

Skeleton Hill (2009)

Sergeant Cribb Series

Wobble to Death (1970)

The Detective Wore Silk Drawers (1971)

Abracadaver (1972)

Mad Hatter's Holiday (1973)

The Tick of Death (1974), also issued as *Invitation to A Dynamite Party* (1974)

A Case of Spirits (1975)

Swing, Swing Together (1976)

Waxwork (1978)

Collections

Butchers: And Other Stories of Crime (1987)

The Staring Man and Other Stories (1989)

The Crime of Miss Oyster Brown and Other Stories (1994)

A Dead Giveaway, with Clare Curzon, Gillian Linscott, Dorothy Simpson, and Margaret Yorke (1995)

The Sedgemoor Strangler: And Other Stories of Crime (2002)

Murder on the Short List (2008)

Editor

The Black Cabinet: Stories Based on Real Crimes (1989)

Third Culprit, with Liza Cody and Michael Z. Lewin (1996)

The Verdict of Us All (2006)

Contributor

Winter's Crimes 5 (1973), includes "The Bathroom"

Winter's Crimes 10 (1978), includes "The Locked Room"

The Bell House Book (1979), includes "A Slight Case of Scotch"

Mystery Guild Anthology (1980), includes "How Mr. Smith Traced His Ancestors"

Winter's Crimes 14 (1982), includes "Butchers"

John Creasey's Mystery Crime Collection (1983), includes "The Virgin and the Bull"

Winter's Crimes 15 (1983), includes "Belly Dance"

Butchers and Other Stories of Crime (1985), includes "The Corder Figure," "Woman and Home," "Trace of Spies," "The Staring Man," and "Private Gorman's Luck"

Winter's Crimes 17 (1985), includes "The Secret Lover"

Woman's Own (1985), includes "Murder in Store"

New Adventures of Sherlock Holmes (1987), includes "The Curious Computer"

Winter's Crimes 19 (1987), includes "The Pomeranian Poisoning"

Winter's Crimes 20 (1988), includes "Where Is Thy Sting?"

Mistletoe Mysteries (1989), includes "The Haunted Crescent"

New Crimes (1989), includes "Youdunnit"

The Rigby File (1989), includes "The Munich Posture"

Winter's Crimes 21 (1989), includes "A Case of Butterflies"

A Classic English Crime (1990), includes "The Lady in the Trunk"

Winter's Crimes 22 (1990), includes "Shock Visit"

Winter's Crimes 23 (1990), includes "Being of Sound Mind"

Cat Crimes (1991), includes "Ginger's Waterloo"

Midwinter Mysteries (1991), includes "The Crime of Miss Oyster Brown"

Midwinter Mysteries 2 (1992), includes "You May See a Strangler"

The Man Who . . . (1992), includes "The Man Who Ate People"

Midwinter Mysteries 3 (1993), includes "Pass the Parcel"

Murder for Halloween (1994), includes "The Odstock Curse"

Royal Crimes (1994), includes "Bertie and the Fire Brigade"

The Dead Giveaway (1995), includes "Wayzgoose"

Midwinter Mysteries 5 (1995), includes "The Mighty Hunter"

No Alibi (1995), includes "Quiet, Please—We're Rolling"

A Proper English Crime (1995), includes "The Proof of the Pudding"

Crime Through Time (1996), includes "Bertie and the Boat Race"

Malice Domestic 5 (1996), includes "A Parrot Is Forever"

Perfectly Criminal (1996), includes "Disposing of Mrs. Cronk"

Malice Domestic 6 (1997), includes "The Corbett Correspondence"

Whydunit: Perfectly Criminal 2 (1997), includes "Because It Was There"

Past Poisons (1998), includes "Showmen"

More Holmes for the Holidays (1999), includes "The Four Wise Men"

Crime Through Time 3 (2000), includes "Dr. Death"

Mammoth Book of Locked Room Mysteries & Impossible Crimes (2000), includes "The Amorous Corpse"

Murder Through the Ages (2000), includes "Problem of Stateroom 10"

Scenes of the Crime (2000), includes "Interior, With Corpse"

Death by Horoscope (2001), includes "Star Struck"

Malice Domestic 10 (2001), includes "Away with the Fairies"

Mysterious Press Anniversary Anthology (2001), includes "The Usual Table"

The Sedgemoor Strangler and Other Stories of Crime (2001), includes "The Stalker"

Green for Danger (2003), includes "The Field"

Mysterious Pleasures (2003), includes "The Man Who Jumped for England"

The Mammoth Book of Roaring Twenties Whodunits (2004), includes "Bullets"

Murder Is My Racquet (2005), includes "Needle Match"

ID: Crimes of Identity (2006), includes "A Blow on the Head"

The Verdict of Us All (2006), includes "Popping Round to the Post"

Red Herrings (2008), includes "Agony Column"

Issued as by Peter Lear

Goldengirl (1977)

Spider Girl (1980)

The Secret Of Spandau (1986)

Teleplays with Jacqueline Ruth Lovesey

"The Horizontal Witness," "Something Old, Something New," "Murder, Old Boy?," "The Choir That Wouldn't Sing," "The Hand That Rocks the Cradle," and "The Last Trumpet," episodes of *Cribb* television series (Granada/PBS, 1980–1981)

Adaptations in Other Media

Goldengirl (1979) motion picture

Dead Gorgeous (telefilm, 2002) based on *On the Edge*

Cribb (Grenada/PBS television series, 1980–1981)

For Further Information

Chernow, Annie, Peter Lovesey interview, *Crimespree Magazine*, July/Aug. 2007.

Edwards, Martin, Peter Lovesey interview, Crimescene. http://www.twbooks.co.uk/crimescene/ploveseyme.html (viewed Feb. 18, 2011).

Moules, Joan M., "He Started with a Wobble," *Writer's Forum*," May 2005.

Muller, Adrian, Peter Lovesey interview, in *Speaking of Murder*, edited by Ed Gorman. New York: Berkeley Prime Crime, 1998.

Peter Lovesey interview, *Strand Magazine,* http://www.strandmag.com/lovesey1.htm/ (viewed July 22, 2009).

Peter Lovesey web page, http://www.peterlovesey.com/ (viewed July 22, 2009).

Picker, Leonard, "An up-to-date Victorian," *Publishers Weekly*, Mar. 28, 2005, http://www.twbooks.co.uk/crimescene/ploveseyme.html/ (viewed July 22, 2009).

Margaret Maron

Courtesy of the author

Greensboro, North Carolina
Date not disclosed

Police Procedural, Amateur Detective,
Legal Mystery
Benchmark Series: Judge Deborah Knott

About the Author and the Author's Writing

"Oyez, oyez, oyez!" intoned the bailiff in my courtroom next morning. "This honorable court for the County of Colleton is now open and sitting for the dispatch of its business. God save the state and this honorable court, the Honorable Judge Deborah Knott pleasant and presiding. Be seated."

The sheepish bailiff quickly corrected himself; he meant "present and presiding," of course. But the amusing gaffe, in Margaret Maron's *Death's Half Acre* (2008), only reinforces this folksy, cozy, yet serious series from a veteran North Carolina author.

Margaret Maron was born in the Tar Heel State's Greensboro and grew up on a tobacco farm. The author attended college for two years, took a summer job at the Pentagon, married, traveled to Italy. But after a few years' residence in Brooklyn, she's again living on part of the ancestral farm, luxuriating in all that her home state has to offer.

"The mystery is the peg upon which I hang my love and concerns for North Carolina as the state transitions from agriculture to high tech, from a largely rural countryside to one increasingly under assault by housing developments and chain stores," she said on her website.

Maron was well grounded in the mystery genre when she began writing short stories and novels. She lists among her favorite authors Mary Roberts Rinehart, Josephine Tey, Agatha Christie, Grace Lathem, Rex Stout, and Erle Stanley Gardner.

Above all, she believes in fair play, "which means that I have to show the reader everything Deborah sees," she said in an Art & Literature interview. "Playing fair with the reader is harder than keeping things up my sleeve, but I can always misdirect readers by showing them more than is actually relevant."

Earlier in her career Maron wrote a series about a New York police detective, Sigrid Harald, whose father was also a cop. A cop killed in the line of duty.

"I made her a loner so she would have a prickly personality," the author told Mary Carroll of *Booklist*. "I saw humor in all these people trying to intrude on her solitude and bring her out when she didn't necessarily want to be brought out. And I do like to see the amusing sides of people's personalities."

She quickly found that setting was as important a part of a good book as solid characters, puzzling crime, and interesting characters. *Past Imperfect* (1991), typically, follows Harald's investigation of the fatal shooting of an off-duty detective. According to *Publishers Weekly*, "Providing continuity and atmosphere with details of the snowy cityscape, Maron writes a terse, technically expert police procedural, its hard-boiled plot undiluted by sentimentality."

With the Judge Deborah Knott series, the author set herself up for a richer array of personalities and a canvas of rural—and often national—issues, from immigration to the pressures of real estate development to church burnings. Knott has her own anxieties— her father was an infamous North Carolina bootlegger, after all—but she is a more settled character than Harald.

For a time, Maron alternated between the series. "I've noticed as I've gotten older and 'mouthier' I've given these more self-confident character traits to Deborah. Sigrid is painfully shy. I feel more protective of Sigrid because Deborah is like the younger, prettier sister," she said in an interview with Pat Koch of *Publishers Weekly*.

Maron is undaunted in taking the point of view of a male or African American character. In *Home Fires* (1998), for instance, an examination of southern race relations, she features a young black assistant DA, Cyl DeGraffenried. "I keep going back to Walt Whitman, who said, 'I am large. I contain multitudes.' Imagining yourself into a different consciousness is the very essence of being a writer," she said in a MysteryNet.com interview. "I try to present different viewpoints and let the characters speak for themselves."

Maron writes a compact novel, according to the *New York Times Book Review's* Marily Stasio, who said of *High Country Fall* (2006):

> Nothing is extraneous in Margaret Maron's seamlessly constructed mysteries featuring Deborah Knott . . . Deborah's narrative voice, with its engaging tone of amusement at the human foibles she witnesses in her travels, is just the ticket for this dramatic view of the spectacular Blue Ridge Mountains.

This tightness comes from the author's skill; she outlines only minimally. "I am constantly surprised by where the story and the characters take me," she said in a My Tote Bag website conversation. "Although the first victim remains constant, if there's a second victim, it's usually unplanned. I have written several books in which the killer keeps changing."

But then, Maron has been adept in figuring out conundrums since childhood. "I used to love it when my shoelaces got knotted," she told interviewer Scott Nicholson. "I would drop a ball of string and then spend a few days sorting out the tangles. I like to create chaos and then resolve the chaos."

A puzzler at heart has found her niche.

Works by the Author

Bloody Kin (1985)

Shoveling Smoke (1997), Culleton County short stories

Last Lessons of Summer (2003)

Suitable for Hanging (2004), short stories

Deborah Knott Series:

Bootlegger's Daughter (1992)

Southern Discomfort (1993)

Shooting at Loons (1994)

Up Jumps the Devil (1996)

Killer Market (1997)

Home Fires (1998)

Storm Track (2000)

Uncommon Clay (2001)

Slow Dollar (2002)

High Country Fall (2004)

Rituals of the Season (2005)

Winter's Child (2006)

Hard Row (2007)

Death's Half-Acre (2008)

Sand Sharks (2009)

Christmas Mourning (2010)

Sigrid Harald Series

One Coffee With (1981)

Death of a Butterfly (1984)

Death in Blue Folders (1985)

The Right Jack (1987)

Baby Doll Games (1988)

Corpus Christmas (1989)

Past Imperfect (1991)

Fugitive Colors (1995)

Contributor

Return to the Twilight Zone (1994)

Malice Domestic 8 (1999)

Very Merry Christmas, with M. C. Beaton and Charlotte MacLeod (1999)

For Further Information

Carroll, Mary, Margaret Maron interview, *Booklist*, May 1, 2001.

Death's Half Acre review, *Publishers Weekly*, June 9, 2008.

"Interview with Margaret Maron," Art & Literature, http://artandliterature.wordpress. com/2008/11/30/an-interview-with-margaret-maron/ (viewed Sept. 17, 2009).

Koch, Pat, "PW Talks with Margaret Maron," *Publishers Weekly*, April 9, 2001.

Margaret Maron interview, My Tote Bag, http://www.authorsoundrelations.com/ MTB/beyondbook/beyondbook-margaretmaron.htm/ (viewed Sept. 17, 2009).

"Margaret Maron Talks about 'Sand Sharks,'" Art & Literature, http://artandlit erature.wordpress.com/2009/09/08/margaret-maron-talks-about-sand-sharks/ (viewed Sept. 17, 2009).

Margaret Maron web page. http://www.margaretmaron.com/ (viewed Sept. 17, 2009).

Nicholson, Scott, "Margaret Maron: Bootlegger Belle," Haunted Computer, http:// www.hauntedcomputer.com/ghostwr28.htm/ (viewed Sept. 17, 2009).

Past Imperfect review, *Publishers Weekly*, Jan. 4, 1991.

Stasio, Marilyn, *High Country Fall* review, *New York Times Book Review*, Aug. 22, 2004.

Taylor, Art, "Margaret Maron Author Interview," MysteryNet.com, http://www.mys terynet.com/books/testimony/homefires.shtml/ (viewed Sept. 17, 2009).

Wilkinson, Joanne, *Winter's Child* review, *Booklist*, May 1, 2006.

Steve Martini

San Francisco, California
1946

Amateur Detective, Legal Mystery
Benchmark Series: Paul Madriani

About the Author and the Author's Writing

Steve Martini learned courtroom drama by watching. "I was a reporter starting in 1969," he said in a Bookreporter interview, "living in Southern California. I went to work for the LA *Daily Journal*, a legal newspaper. . . . I covered all of the Manson case. It was a major circus." But it reinforced his desire to attend law school.

Born in San Francisco in 1946, Martini grew up in the Bay Area. He graduated with a B.A. from the University of California at Santa Cruz in 1968 and worked for the *Daily Journal* from 1970 to 1975. He was a military reservist while in college, frequently assigned to the jail ward at Los Angeles County General Hospital. After attending night classes at the University of the Pacific, McGeorge School of Law, he received his J.D. in 1974. From 1975 to 1980, he was in private practice. He became a state attorney and, later, deputy director of consumer affairs and deputy director of the California Office of Administrative Hearings. He also worked as special counsel to the California Victims of Violent Crimes Program. He was a legislative representative for the State Bar of California. He was an administrative law judge and supervising hearing officer. He and his wife, Leah, have one child.

Degree in hand, Martini soon missed his old newspaper days and the satisfaction of composing words at a keyboard. He wrote *The Simeon Chamber*, the story of a San Francisco attorney who finds that holding long-lost diaries of the explorer Sir Francis Drake is a dangerous proposition. Shortly after the book came out (1988), he quit the law to become a full-time writer. It was 1991.

"For me the mix of law and fiction was natural," he said in *Contemporary Authors*. "For me, a good courtroom story must cut very close to the bone of reality to have true value."

He mentions John D. MacDonald as a mystery author he has enjoyed; otherwise he reads a great deal of history and biography. A favorite subject is Abraham Lincoln.

Martini's 1992 novel *Compelling Evidence* had as the main character Paul Madriani, a lawyer kicked out of his large firm because he had an affair with his boss's wife. When the boss turns up dead and the wife is accused of his murder, Madriani becomes her unlikely defense lawyer. The bestselling novel kicked off a series featuring Madriani, the author using his courtroom dramas to explore a range of themes from corrupt judges to the witness protection program to the world of publishing. Ideas come from daily headlines, he has said.

But it is his veracity that holds his readers. He calls them legal procedurals.

"*Shadow of Power*, Steve Martini's ninth legal thriller featuring San Diego criminal defense attorney Paul Madriani, is so meticulously researched and well written that it is virtually impossible to discern where fiction ends and fact begins," said a *Mysterious Reviews* critic in 2008. A long missing Thomas Jefferson letter may hold the key to his client's freedom, Madriani finds.

Two of Martini's novels have been adapted as television miniseries.

Martini in a Powell's Q&A described what makes a good writer: "A good novelist will either have innate talent or will have developed a keen perception regarding human motivation—what stimulates a person to commit what may be an extreme act of violence, and how to make it believable."

His advice to aspiring writers? In a *Bestsellers World* interview, he said:

> Write. You have to be persistent in your self-criticism, develop an ear for dialogue and narrative and be willing to toss material that doesn't work and start again. The real answer is to rewrite until you have honed your work to a fine edge. .

Works by the Author

The Simeon Chamber (1988)

The List (1997)

Critical Mass (1998)

Paul Madriani Series

Compelling Evidence (1992)

Prime Witness (1993)

Undue Influence (1994)

The Judge (1995)

The Attorney (2000)

The Jury (2001)

The Arraignment (2002)

Double Tap (2005)

Shadow of Power (2008)

Guardian of Lies (2009)

The Rule of Nine (2010)

Trader of Secrets (2011)

Adaptations in Other Media

Undue Influence (CBS, 1996), television miniseries

The Judge (NBC, 2001), television miniseries

For Further Information

Shadow of Power review, Mysterious Reviews, http://www.mysteriousreviews.com/mystery-book-reviews/martini-shadow-power.html/ (viewed Aug. 19, 2009).

Steve Martini entry, *Contemporary Authors*, 2009. Reproduced in Biography Resource Center, http://galenet.galegroup.com/servlet/BioRC/ (viewed July 10, 2009).

Steve Martini interview, *Bestsellers World*, Jan. 9, 2003, http://www.bestsellersworld.com/interviews-martini.htm/ (viewed July 10, 2009).

Steve Martini interview, *Bookreporter*, Feb. 21, 1997, http://www.bookreporter.com/authors/au-martini-steve.asp (viewed July 10, 2009)

Steve Martini interview, Powell's Q&A. http://www.powells.com/ink/stevemartini.html/ (viewed July 10, 2009).

Steve Martini website, http://www.stevemartini.com/ (viewed July 23, 2009).

Archer Mayor

Thetford, Vermont
1959

Police Procedural
Benchmark Series: Joe Gunther

About the Author and the Author's Writing

Rampant crime in the idyllic Green Mountain State? Yes, Vermont has its share of arsonists, drug dealers, murderers, corporate manipulators, and rapists, as depicted in Archer Mayor's series of Joe Gunther mysteries. There's not so much crime (for real) that there's a Vermont Bureau of Investigation, however. That's an agency the author made up, to give his characters more resources and freedom to roam.

Gunther first appeared on the scene in *Open Season* (1988), in which an unknown person nudges the Brattleboro police department into reopening an old case. Each year since then the homicide detective has reappeared and, as the *New York Times Book Review* critic Marilyn Stasio noted in a review of *The Surrogate Thief* (2004),

> Mayor has devised a vivid overview of the kinds of criminal behavior—from domestic violence to interstate drug trafficking—that relentlessly wear down the social fabric in the postindustrial mill and factory towns of northern new England, giving people the uneasy feeling that they are losing control over their lives.

Archer Mayor was born in Mount Kisco, New York, in 1950. He has been twice married and has two children. After receiving a bachelor of arts degree from Yale in 1973, he led a peripatetic life until he settled into writing the Gunther mysteries. He traveled to more than 30 countries. He was a researcher and writer for Time-Life Books, editor for a university press, political aide, consultant to the Lyndon Baines Johnson Library, photographer, lab technician, illustrator, and rescue squad member and EMT. Since 2002, he has been an assistant medical examiner for the state of Vermont.

Why did he become a fiction writer? Beyond having enjoyed the writing of Dashiell Hammett, Raymond Chandler, and Ross Macdonald, he has a natural curiosity, he said in a Bookbrowse conversation. "My writing, while in the context of (I hope) an entertaining and compelling series of police procedurals, allows me to meet people I normally wouldn't get to meet and to visit places I normally wouldn't get to explore."

Mayor was immediately comfortable with the conventions of mystery novels. "Mysteries were no longer about good or bad guys and car chases, they were about human beings who happen to be good or bad guys, and what they do. I don't like pure puzzle mysteries. I like mysteries about three-dimensional human beings who interact," he told Louise Jones of *Publishers Weekly*.

He thrives on series fiction. "The trick is, don't overanalyze and overplot," he said in *The Writer*. "Do pay attention to reality, and let the story unfold like life—the more mechanisms you introduce into your writing process, the more mechanistic it becomes. I like to let readers fill in the blanks." Thus, he's never given a physical description of Joe Gunther, for example.

Mayor has given enhanced roles to some of Joe Gunther's co-workers, among them the one-armed, wily, and sharp-tongued investigator Willy Kunkle and his softer-spoken but no less capable girlfriend Sammie Martens. Gunther, long divorced, cultivated a relationship with Gail Zigman for several books and supported her after a traumatic rape. Both have since moved on, and Gunther now has a new romantic interest, Lyn Silva, who lives on the Maine coast.

Gunther's part-time position as a medical examiner serves as a solid foundation for his depiction of procedures and brutal deaths. "I use the feelings I encounter on my other jobs, some of the techniques, occasionally a phrase or one-liner," Mayor said on his website. "I would never want to cross the line between the integrity and/or privacy of an actual case and any of my novels."

Mayor's books have consistently received good reviews. Yet, his first publisher didn't have a good handle on the series (and how to take it beyond regional popularity), Mayor said, so he switched to St. Martin's Press. At the same time, his first dozen novels had gone out of print. So he established AMPress to bring them back into publication. Thus, while still thriving on the frontlist, he had control of the backlist. "The whole thing about getting mad and getting even, I'm doing something in between. I'm trying to be part of the solution," he told Judith Rosen of *Publishers Weekly*.

Works by the Author

Joe Gunther Series

Open Season (1988)

Borderlines (1990)

Scent of Evil (1992)

The Skeleton's Knee (1993)

Fruits of the Poisonous Tree (1994)

The Dark Root (1995)

The Ragman's Memory (1996)

Bellows Falls (1997)

The Disposable Man (1998)

Occam's Razor (1999)

The Marble Mask (2000)

Tucker Peak (2001)

The Sniper's Wife (2002)

Gatekeeper (2003)

The Surrogate Thief (2004)

St. Alban's Fire (2005)

The Second Mouse (2006)

Chat (2007)

The Catch (2008)

The Price of Malice (2009)

Red Herring (2010)

For Further Information

Archer Mayor interview, BookBrowse, http://www.bookbrowse.com/biographies/ index.cfm?author_number=1229/ (viewed July 17, 2009)

Archer Mayor website. http://www.archermayor.com/ (viewed Aug. 7, 2009).

Haley, Carolyn, "Archer Mayor Interview," *The Writer*, Aug. 2008.

Jones, Louise, "PW Talks with Archer Mayor," *Publishers Weekly*, Oct. 15, 2001.

Rosen, Judith, "Commercial Frontlist, His Own Backlist: Crime Writer Solves His Own Problem," *Publishers Weekly*, Oct. 8, 2007.

Stasio, Marilyn, "Not Just a Nut with a Gun," *New York Times Book Review*, Nov. 7, 2004.

Toth, Susan Allen, *Open Season* review, *New York Times Book Review*, Oct. 9, 1988.

Alexander McCall Smith

Bulawayo, Southern Rhodesia
(Zimbabwe)
1948

Amateur Detective, Private Detective
Benchmark Series: The No. 1 Ladies'
Detective Agency

Graham Clark

About the Author and the Author's Writing

Alexander McCall Smith has a light, deft touch when it comes to shaping fictional characters. Mma Precious Ramotswe, the savvy Botswanan private detective, for example, is irresistible.

Although he was an experienced author, McCall Smith wrote *The No. 1 Ladies' Detective Agency*, Mma Ramotswe's first book, in 1998, not really thinking of it as a mystery novel and certainly not expecting to turn the genre on its ear.

"There is not a great deal of actual crime," the author confessed to Charles L. P. Silet for *Mystery Scene*, "and it's fairly incidental to the other problems that Mma Ramotswe deals with. Mystery readers read the books as mysteries; novel readers read them as novels."

There was a good chance no one would read them, as *No. 1* came out initially in a small edition from Polygon, the fiction imprint of Edinburgh University Press. After three books, Columbia University Press acquired rights in the United States. Independent bookstores in particular discovered the books' charms, and a glowing review in *The New York Times Book Review* gave it deserving attention by 2002. Anchor Books assumed U.S. rights and launched a major marketing campaign.

McCall Smith appreciated the sudden fame, having labored for years writing legal texts (such as *Butterworths Medico-Legal Encyclopedia* in 1987) and children's books (including *The Popcorn Pirates* in 1999).

How did an academic, a Scotsman at that, come to write novels about an African tribal woman? Alexander McCall Smith was born in 1948 in Southern Rhodesia, now Zimbabwe. He also lived in Switzerland and studied law in Scotland. He has been a professor of medical law at Edinburgh University and has also taught law at the University of Botswana. He helped create a criminal code for Botswana, though "it was never enacted," he told *Publishers Weekly* in 2002. He is married with two daughters.

The character of Mma Ramotswe came, McCall Smith told that same publication, from his admiration for women of the African villages. "They really keep the show on the road."

McCall Smith has often related the genesis of his heroine to a woman he saw one day in a village called Mochudi. It was Botswana National Day. A village woman wanted to make a gift of a chicken to McCall Smith's friends. In a Readers Read interview, the author said,

> I watched as this woman—traditionally built, like Mma Ramotswe—chased the chicken round the yard and eventually caught it. She made a clucking noise as she ran. The chicken looked miserable. She looked very cheerful. At that moment I thought that I might write a book about a cheerful woman of traditional build.

He thought she must have had a fascinating backstory, the author elaborated in an interview with Dave Welch. "She had probably brought up a number of children with very little money. Her yard was nicely swept—it was a respectable house in which she was living. She was probably, with very little in a material sense, making a good life for herself."

In McCall Smith's books, Mma Ramotswe is in her thirties, divorced, and the proprietor of a small agency that she started with a modest inheritance. She is assisted by Mma Makutsi, her office secretary, and J.L.B. Matekoni, a mechanic. Most of her cases are of the domestic dispute or employee relations type. But once in a while, there's a crime to solve.

"Every novel presents a slice of life," McCall Smith told journalist Toby Clements. "A noir policier for example presents one slice, one that perhaps addresses social dysfunction or some sort of pathology, while mine present a slice that is more upbeat and affirmative. I think it is a perfectly defensible view."

With one successful mystery series under his belt, McCall Smith wasted no time in establishing another. And another. And another. His bumbly Dr. Moritz-Maria von Igelfield books, starting with *Portuguese Irregular Verbs* in 2003, are set in Scotland, as are the novels with Pat, Bertie, Domenica, Angus, and the dog Cyril (all live in the same Georgian townhouse). These last, starting with *44 Scotland Street* in 2005, originated as serials and are very lighthearted. More serious but still cozy are the Isabel Dalhousie books, beginning with *The Sunday Philosophy Club* (2004). These are centered on a 40-something divorcee in Edinburgh who edits an ethics journal and leads an ethical life.

McCall Smith often addresses serious matters in a nonserious way. Fiction doesn't have to be dreary, he reasons. "If you look at music, do we expect all composers to write dirges? The answer surely is no. There are many other emotions and moods which music can deal with or engage with," he said in a conversation with journalist Gilbert Cruz of *Time*.

At that, Alexander McCall Smith is an adept one-man band.

Works by the Author

La's Orchestra Saves the World (2008)

Corduroy Mansions (2009)

The No. 1 Ladies' Detective Agency Series

The No.1 Ladies' Detective Agency (1998)

Tears of the Giraffe (2000)

Morality for Beautiful Girls (2001)

The Kalahari Typing School for Men (2002)

The Full Cupboard of Life (2003)

In the Company of Cheerful Ladies (2004), also titled *The Night-Time Dancer*

Blue Shoes and Happiness (2006)

The Good Husband of Zebra Drive (2007)

The Miracle at Speedy Motors (2008)

Tea Time for the Traditionally Built (2009)

The Double Comfort Safari Club (2010)

Precious and the Puggies: Precious Ramotswe's Very First Case (2010), for younger readers, translated from the Scots by James Robertson for U.S. edition (2011)

The Saturday Big Tent Wedding (2011)

Isabel Dalhousie Series

The Sunday Philosophy Club (2004)

Friends, Lovers, Chocolate (2005)

The Right Attitude to Rain (2006)

The Careful Use of Compliments (2007)

The Comfort of Saturdays (2008), also titled *The Comforts of a Muddy Saturday*

The Lost Art of Gratitude (2009)

The Charming Quirks of Others (2010)

Scotland Street Series

Espresso Tales (2005)

44 Scotland Street (2005)

Love over Scotland (2006)

The World According to Bertie (2007)

The Unbearable Lightness of Scones (2008)

2½ Pillars of Wisdom Series

At the Villa of Reduced Circumstances (2003)

The Finer Points of Sausage Dogs (2003)

Portuguese Irregular Verbs (2003)

Collections

Children of Wax: African Folk Tales (1991)

Heavenly Date: And Other Flirtations (1995)

The Girl Who Married a Lion: And Other Tales from Africa (2004)

Adaptations in Other Media

No. 1 Ladies' Detective Agency (BBC television series, 2008)

The author has also written children's books, including the Harriet Bean series, and nonfiction.

For Further Information

Abbott, Charlotte, "From Africa, with Love," *Publishers Weekly*, July 22, 2002.

Alexander McCall Smith interview, Readers Read, Feb. 2003, http://www.reader sread.com/features/alexandersmith.htm (viewed Sept. 30, 2009).

Alexander McCall Smith website, http://www.alexandermccallsmith.co.uk/ (viewed Sept. 30, 2009).

Clements, Toby, "Alexander McCall Smith: Interview," *Telegraph*, Sept. 18, 2009.

Cruz, Gilbert, "Q&A: Alexander McCall Smith," *Time*, Apr. 30, 2009.

Penzler, Otto, ed. *The Lineup: The World's Greatest Crime Writers Tell the Inside Story of Their Greatest Detectives*. New York: Little, Brown, 2009.

Quinn, Mary Ellen, "Andrew McCall Smith's Isabel Dalhousie Novels and 44 Scotland Street Series," *Booklist*, Dec. 1, 2008.

Silet, Charles L. P., "The Possibilities of Happiness: An Interview with Alexander McCall Smith, Author of *The Full Cupboard of Life* & *The No. 1 Ladies' Detective Agency*," *Mystery Scene* 80 (summer 2003).

Welch, Dave, "Red Bush Tea with Alexander McCall Smith," Powells Books, http://www.powells.com/authors/smith.html/ (viewed Sept. 30, 2009).

Val McDermid

Kirkcaldy, Scotland
1955

Police Procedural, Private Detective,
Amateur Detective
Benchmark Series: Carol Jordan/
Tony Hill

Mimsy Moller

About the Author and the Author's Writing

Val McDermid is a master of the "tartan noir" novel—Ian Rankin is another—a subgenre of crime fiction that draws inspiration from Robert Louis Stevenson's *Strange Case of Dr. Jekyll and Mr. Hyde* (1886). She writes intense psychological novels that look at the why more than the who or how of a murder. They stretch the expectation of British crime fiction.

"We have the rope of Agatha around our necks," the author said in a *Publishers Weekly* interview with Jordan Foster. "She created an expectation [about British mystery writers] that was great for when she was writing, but now we want to write about the society we live in and the Agatha Christie formula doesn't work anymore."

McDermid read Christie's *The Murder at the Vicarage* over and over as a youth, but it was Sara Paretsky's initial V. I. Warshawski private eye novel in 1982, *Indemnity Only,* that gave her the impetus to write a crime novel. Her all-time favorite book? "Robert Louis Stevenson's *Treasure Island* is pure pleasure," she told the *Telegraph*, "fantastic storytelling, great characters, beautifully written. It's got everything you want in a novel."

McDermid was born in Kirkcaldy, Scotland, in 1955. Both of her grandfathers were coal miners in eastern Scotland. She was the first state school student to be admitted to Oxford, and, once she had trained herself to speak English (and drop her native Fife accent), she graduated from St. Hilda's College with a B.A. in 1975. For the next 16 years, she worked as a reporter with newspapers in Devon and Manchester, England as well as in Glasgow, Scotland. While she has been a correspondent for BBC Radio 4 and BBC Radio Scotland, since 1991 she has made her living as a writer of nonfiction and fiction. She, her partner, and her son live in South Manchester, England.

McDermid developed a keen interest in becoming a writer from childhood, when her family lived across the road from the Kirkcaldy public library.

"I had always wanted to write, ever since I realized that real people actually produced all those books in the library," she said on her web page. She was told she should find a proper job for security. "I knew I wasn't the sort of person who would be suited to a proper, nine to five job with a neat hierarchical career structure, so I became a journalist."

Journalism carried another advantage. "What it gave me," she related to Hallie Ephron for *The Writer*, "was a window into people's worlds that I might otherwise never have had. It gave me a great chance to observe human nature. Showed me how people behaved in crisis. It taught me, more than anything, not to be precious about the act of writing."

Reporters collect information in their notebooks. For her first mystery novel, McDermid assembled color-coded index cards as she shaped her books. She found her pace with her third book, she has said. Eventually, she found that she could write the books as she went, in her head, without index cards, freeing the actions of her characters and producing stronger first drafts.

McDermid has three mystery series. Lindsay Gordon, featured in her first book, *Report for Murder* (1987), is a lesbian journalist with a half dozen cases so far. Kate Brannigan, who first appeared in *Dead Beat* (1992), is a private investigator who specializes in computer fraud. And Bradfield Detective Chief Inspector Carol Jordan, who works closely with profiler Dr. Tony Hill, has been featured in another series that started with *The Mermaids Singing* in 1995. The author didn't anticipate the strong reaction that came from male readers of that book, who were shocked by the depiction of a killer who preyed on male victims.

The second book in the series, *The Wire in the Blood* (1997), became an ITC television series. *A Place of Execution* (2000), the earlier multi–award-winning nonseries novel, was the basis for a three-part television series.

Only with the recent *A Darker Domain* (2008) did McDermid model a character—Detective Inspector Karen Pirie—on herself, both physically (solidly built) and emotionally (a dynamo with a sharp tongue) in a story that caroms off a major mining disaster—such as the one in 1967 in Kirckaldy.

"I don't set out to address particular issues, but as I work out a story, important issues arise from the experiences of characters," the author told Ralph Menconi of *Publishers Weekly*. "I first focus on the story's structure. Then I examine characters and how they become the people they are."

She is very comfortable with the mystery novel's constraints. "Readers actually want to read things that have a beginning, a middle and an end," she said in *The Writer* in 2003. "I think most of us have given up the fight for respectability [from literary reviewers] some time ago. I think we are content to be read."

With strong characters and solid stories, McDermid is assured a substantial audience.

Works by the Author

The Writing on the Wall: And Other Stories (1997)

A Place of Execution (1999)

Killing The Shadows (2000)

The Distant Echo (2003)

Stranded (2005), stories

Cleanskin (2006), novella

The Grave Tattoo (2006)

A Darker Domain (2008)

Trick of the Dark (2011)

Carol Jordan/Tony Hill Series

The Mermaids Singing (1995)

The Wire in the Blood (1997)

The Last Temptation (2002)

The Torment of Others (2004)

Beneath the Bleeding (2007)

Fever of the Bone (2009)

Kate Brannigan Series

Dead Beat (1992)

Kick Back (1993)

Crack Down (1994)

Clean Break (1995)

Blue Genes (1996)

Star Struck (1998)

Lindsay Gordon Series

Report for Murder (1987)

Common Murder (1989)

Final Edition (1991), also titled *Open and Shut*

Union Jack (1993), also titled *Conferences Are Murder*

Booked for Murder (1996)

Hostage to Murder (2003)

Contributor

Naked Came the Phoenix, with Nevada Barr, Mary Jane Clark, Diana Gabaldon, J. A. Jance, Faye Kellerman, Laurie R. King, Pam and Mary O'Shaughnessy, Anne Perry, Nancy Pickard, J. D. Robb, Lisa Scottoline, and Marcia Talley (2001)

The Best New British Mysteries, edited by Maxim Jakubowski (2005)

*Magnetic North: New Work from North East Writer*s, with Neil Astley, Andrew Crumey, Julia Darling, Sean O'Brien, and Jacob Polley (2005)

Nonfiction

A Suitable Job for a Woman: The World of Female Private Investigators (1994)

Adaptations in Other Media

A Place of Execution (ITV, 2000)

Wire in the Blood (ITV, 2002–2009), based on the Carol Jordan/Tony Hill series

For Further Information

"According to Scottish Crime Novelist Val McDermid," *The Writer*, Apr. 2003.

Ephron, Hallie, "Murder in Tartan Plaid," *The Writer*, Aug. 2009.

Foster, Jordan, "The Cozy Gets the Hard-boil: Edgy British Mysteries Come to the U.S.," *Publishers Weekly*, Apr. 21, 2008.

Jones, Louise, "PW Talks with Val McDermid," *Publishers Weekly*, Aug. 12, 2002.

Menconi, Ralph, "PW Talks with Val McDermid: A Charmingly Plausible Mystery," *Publishers Weekly*, Dec. 18, 2006.

"Val McDermid: Just a Minute," *The Telegraph*, Sept. 4, 2009, http://www.telegraph.co.uk/culture/books/books-life/6138387/Val-McDermid-just-a-minute.html/ (viewed Sept. 18, 2009).

Val McDermid website, http://www.valmcdermid.com/ (viewed Sept. 18, 2009).

Penny Mickelbury

Atlanta, Georgia
1948

Police Procedural, Journalism Mystery,
Private Detective
Benchmark Series: Gianne Maglione/
Mimi Patterson

Peggy Blow

About the Author and the Author's Writing

Nuyorican. That's a word you don't see often. It's Spanish for "New Yorker of Puerto Rican descent" and describes Phil Rodriguez, a private investigator who has appeared in two books so far in Penny Mickelbury's crime series.

"The character was born out of my experiences living in New York and my fondness for frequenting the Village, both East and West," the author said on her web page. It was there that she encountered the fascinating culture of Louisaida—the Lower East Side.

In his first published case, *Two Graves Dug* (2005), Rodriguez and his partner, Yolanda Maria Aquirre, accept two commissions: one from parents and community members who want the detectives to track down a serial rapist in Louisaida and another from an underworld figure who wants them to find the man who is pressuring an African American therapist.

"Fast pacing, multiple plotlines, and interesting secondary characters distinguish the first-person narration, which offers a likable, honorable main character who has his own code of ethics and is willing to circumvent the law to achieve justice," reviewer Sue O'Brien said in *Booklist*.

Mickelbury has no trouble finding convincing plots in city neighborhoods. She spent nearly 20 years as a newspaper, radio, and television reporter in Washington, D.C. She writes what she knows. And where she knows. The author's two other crime series are set in D.C.

The author was born in 1948 in Atlanta, Georgia. She attended the University of Georgia from 1966 to 1971. She worked for Atlanta's *Voice* and *Banner-Herald* newspapers in Georgia and the *Washington Post* in D.C. From 1972 to 1975 she was public relations director for the National Center on Black Aged in Washington. She was a news reporter for WHUR-FM from 1975 to 1978, then reporter and later assistant news director for WJLA-TV, both in Washington, from 1978 to 1984. She taught at City Kids Repertory Company in New York City until 1987. In 1990 she cofounded Alchemy: Theater of Change in New York and was its managing director until 1993. She taught writing in Washington, D.C., and Baltimore, Maryland, beginning in 1994. She now lives in California, where she guest lectures at colleges and universities and at public libraries.

Mickelbury has written mysteries steadily since 1994—that's when her first novel featuring Gianna Magione and Mimi Patterson came out—but she has also written short stories and dramas. California's African-American Museum selected one of her works for its Radio Theater program, as did the TriBeCa Film Studio for its Staged Reading Series. Mickelbury's play *Waiting for Gabriel* came in second in the Theodore Ward Competition in 2006. Fountain Theater included her *Hush* in its 2006 New Works series.

The Magione/Patterson book previously mentioned is *Keeping Secrets*. Its main characters, an Italian police officer who heads D.C.'s Hate Crimes Unit and a black newspaper reporter pursue a serial killer who targets gays. And they pursue each other, as they, too, are gay.

"Professionally, Gianna and Mimi circle each other warily, yet they must come to terms with a mutual attraction so powerful that when one is targeted by the killer, the other is also drawn into danger," the *Publishers Weekly's* reviewer said. "Gianna and Mimi imbue the tale with a certain winning zest.

Mickelbury's third series concerns an African American detective (and former lawyer), Carole Ann Gibson, who, in the first book, *One Must Wait* (1998), lost her husband to a murderer. Her life a shambles, she abandons her career in law and, with partner and ex-cop Jake Graham, starts a high-tech security agency in D.C. Gibson and Graham "work well together," said *Publishers Weekly* in a review of *Paradise Interrupted* (2001), "although they spend a lot of time arguing good-naturedly over their different approaches to criminal justice."

Keenly aware of current events, and of minority frustrations, Mickelbury in her recent Rodriguez outing, *A Murder Too Close* (2008), looks at the fallout of the September 11 attacks on New York City. "The story line looks closely at people who lost loved ones on 9/11 and how they have reacted since, while also providing a deep glimpse into the lives of Muslims, Hindu and Sikh residents trying to make it in an atmosphere of hate," Harriet Klausner wrote in *The Mystery Gazette*.

"Every word I write originates in the reality of having been born female, black, and southern," the author told Contemporary Authors, "of having been dipped in the waters that proclaim the sanctity of clan and land, and in the belief in the eventual and ultimate triumph of good over evil."

Good crime stories know no boundaries.

Works by the Author

Carole Ann Gibson Series

One Must Wait (1998)

Where to Choose (1999)

The Step Between (2000)

Paradise Interrupted (2001)

Gianna Magione/Mimi Patterson Series

Keeping Secrets (1994)

Night Songs (1995)

Love Notes (2002)

Darkness Descending (2005)

Phil Rodriguez Series

Two Graves Dug (2005)

A Murder Too Close (2008)

Contributor

The Mysterious Naiad: Love Stories, edited by Katherine V. Forrest and Barbara Grier (1994)

Spooks, Spies, and Private Eyes: Black Mystery and Suspense Fiction, edited by Paula Woods (1995)

Shades of Black: original Mystery Fiction by African-American Writers, edited by Eleanor Taylor Bland (2004)

The author has also written plays.

For Further Information

Keeping Secrets review, *Publishers Weekly*, Jan. 31, 1994.

Klausner, Harriet, *A Murder Too Close* review, The Mystery Gazette, Oct. 20, 2008, http://themysterygazette.blogspot.com/2008/10/murder-too-close-penny-mickelbury.html/ (viewed Aug. 5, 2009).

Leber, Michele, *A Murder Too Close* review, *Booklist*, Oct. 1, 2008.

Murder Too Close review, Mystery Gazette, http://themysterygazette.blogspot.com/2008/10/murder-too-close-penny-mickelbury.html/ (viewed Aug. 5, 2009)

O'Brien, Sue, *Two Graves Dug* review, *Booklist*, July 2005.

Paradise Interrupted review, *Publishers Weekly*, Dec. 18, 2000.

Penny Mickelbury profile, *Contemporary Authors Online*, Biographical Resource Center, http://galenet.galegroup.com/servlet/BioRC/ (viewed July 31, 2009).

Penny Mickelbury website, http://www.pennymickelbury.com/ (viewed July 31, 2009).

Marcia Muller

Craig Prographica

Detroit, Michigan
1944

Private Detective
Benchmark Series: Sharon McCone

About the Author and the Author's Writing

Capable female private eyes are so much a part of the mystery fiction genre these days that few appreciate that the way they had to muscle their way onto the scene. Marcia Muller's Sharon McCone was a pioneer with her first case, *Edwin of the Iron Shoes* (1997). Within five years, it was followed by the debut novels of Sarah Paretsky's V. I. Warshawski and Sue Grafton's Kinsey Millhone.

McCone's appearance came only after Muller had written and submitted two earlier crime novels. An editor at the David McKay Co. urged her to try one more time. The manuscript was accepted. But then McKay abruptly ended its line of mystery fiction. In 1982 Muller found a new home at St. Martin's Press and has continued the series through nearly a book a year since, through life-threatening encounters, miserable dates, family crises, wrenching murder scenes, and more.

"My greatest fear is that Sharon McCone will show up on my doorstep with her .357 and get even for all the dreadful experiences I've put her through!" the author joked in a BookBrowse interview.

Marcia Muller was born in 1944 in Detroit, Michigan. She received a B.A. from the University of Michigan in 1966 and an M.A. from the same school in 1971. She worked in the administration of *Sunset* magazine from 1967 to 1969 and was a field interviewer for the University of Michigan Institute for Social Research from 1971 to 1973. Even though one of her university instructors attempted to discourage her efforts at creative writing, she decided to try fiction as a career. So since 1973 she has been a freelance writer and novelist full time. In a second marriage, she wed crime novelist Bill Pronzini in 1992.

Although she works very much within the private eye genre and is fond of the writings of Ross Macdonald, Dashiell Hammett, and Raymond Chandler, Muller does not consider herself a noir writer. Rather, she strives to depict a strong character with a close group of friends who interact much as the rest of us do.

"I am attempting to explore various problems of contemporary American society through the eyes of women who become involved in situations which compel them to seek the solutions to various crimes," she said in *St. James Guide to Crime & Mystery Writers*.

Muller has no shortage of ideas, starting with her own life experiences, which have inspired some of her plots. A friend's mother was stabbed to death by her husband, for example, and another friend's father died when an airplane blew up. These later became plot threads for the author.

Muller purposely made her character McCone much different than herself. "I was vehemently opposed to Sharon's background being similar to mine, lest I fall into the trap of undisciplined autobiographical writing," she said in *Mystery Scene*.

Muller writes each book with a general idea in mind but no detailed outline. She said the McCone novels are very linear—the stories have a day-to-day beginning and end—and are easier to pull together than her recent stand-alone novels, which contain a lot of flashbacks and changing points of view. However, she admitted to interviewer Michael Pettengell, of *Mystery Scene,*

> Sometimes I will be writing along and I'll look at what I've written and say, now wait a minute. I didn't plan that. What causes it is that my subconscious has been working in that direction all along and just chose that moment to let [the character] act it out.

Muller has on occasion collaborated with her husband, and even when they're not working together, they frequently bounce ideas off each other. "We exchange pages on a biweekly basis whenever we feel that we have enough to show," Muller said in *Booklist*. "If a problem comes up, we are free to pop into the office and say 'Help.'"

Muller has written other series. The Elena Oliverez books are about a museum curator; the Joanna Stark cases are about a security specialist in the art museum field. The author ran dry on ideas for the Oliverez books. The Starks were a planned trilogy. But what began as a single novel set in a made-up Soledad County, California, *Point Deception* (2001), has now had two follow-ups.

"Each project is more ambitious—which keeps me from getting bored with writing series—so there's always another challenge to meet, always a facet of the craft that needs refining. It *never* gets easier," Muller told interviewer Jan Grape of *Mystery Scene*.

One theme that Muller comes back to frequently in her novels is mistakes made years ago and things are long buried that suddenly come back to haunt her characters. "A guilty secret or a past crime that an individual feels he or she has put to rest is in danger of being exposed," she said on her website, "thus threatening the character's very existence. How one deals with that threat and the choices one makes is central to my fiction."

The readers of crime novels seek resolution, in the author's view.

"I'm more interested in the 'why' than the 'what,'" she told *Publishers Weekly's* Tim Peters. "And readers like the fact that at the end, even though someone is dead or damaged, you have the answers, that things are wrapped up."

Case closed.

Works by the Author

The Lighthouse, with Bill Pronzini (1986)

Waiting Heart (1993)

Crucifixion River: Western Stories, with Bill Pronzini (2007)

Elena Oliverez Series

The Tree of Death (1983)

The Legend of the Slain Soldiers (1985)

Beyond the Grave, with Bill Pronzini (1986), also features Pronzini's Quincannon

Joanna Stark Series

The Cavalier in White (1986)

There Hangs the Knife (1988)

Dark Star (1989)

Sharon McCone Series

Edwin of the Iron Shoes (1977)

Ask the Cards A Question (1982)

The Cheshire Cat's Eye (1983)

Double, with Bill Pronzini (1984), also features Pronzini's Nameless

Games to Keep the Dark Away (1984)

Leave A Message for Willie (1984)

There's Nothing to Be Afraid of (1985)

Eye of the Storm (1988)

The Shape of Dread (1989)

There's Something in A Sunday (1989)

Trophies and Dead Things (1990)

Where Echoes Live (1991)

Pennies on A Dead Woman's Eyes (1992)

Wolf in the Shadows (1993)

The McCone Files (1994) stories

Till the Butcher's Cut Him Down (1994)

A Wild and Lonely Place (1995)

The Broken Promise Land (1996)

Both Ends of the Night (1997)

While Other People Sleep (1998)

McCone and Friends (1999), stories

A Walk Through the Fire (1999)

Listen to the Silence (2000)

Dead Midnight (2002)

The Dangerous Hour (2004)

Vanishing Point (2006)

The Ever-Running Man (2007)

Burn Out (2008)

Locked in (2009)

Coming Back (2010)

Soledad County Series

Point Deception (2001)

Cyanide Wells (2003)

Cape Perdido (2005)

Editor

The Web She Weaves: An Anthology of Mystery & Suspense Stories by Women, with Bill Pronzini (1983)

Child's Ploy: An Anthology of Mystery and Suspense Stories, with Bill Pronzini (1984)

Witches Brew: Horror and Supernatural Stories by Women, with Bill Pronzini (1984) includes 'Kindling Point"

Chapter and Hearse: Suspense Stories About the World of Books, with Bill Pronzini (1985)

Dark Lessons: Crime & Detection on Campus, with Bill Pronzini (1985)

The Deadly Arts: A Collection of Artful Suspense, with Bill Pronzini (1985)

Kill or Cure: Suspense Stories About the World of Medicine, with Bill Pronzini (1985)

She Won the West An Anthology of Western and Frontier Stories by Women, with Bill Pronzini (1985)

The Wickedest Show on Earth: A Carnival of Circus Suspense, with Bill Pronzini (1985)

1001 Midnights: The Aficionado's Guide to Mystery and Detective Fiction, with Bill Pronzini (1986), nonfiction

Lady on the Case: 21 Stories and 1 Complete Novel Starring the World's Great Female Sleuths, with Bill Pronzini and Martin H. Greenberg (1988)

Kill or Cure: Suspense Stories About the World of Medicine, with Bill Pronzini (1989)

A Century of Mystery: 1980–1989, with Bill Pronzini (1997)

Detective Duos: The Best Adventures of Twenty-Five Crime-Solving Twosomes, with Bill Pronzini (1997)

Crucifixion River: Western Stories, with Bill Pronzini (2007)

Collections

Deceptions (1991)

Criminal Intent: 1, with Ed Gorman and Bill Pronzini (1993)

Time of the Wolves: Western Stories (2003)

Somewhere in the City: Selected Stories (2007)

Contributor

Great Tales of Mystery and Suspense (1981) includes "Merrill-Go-Round"

The Shamus Winners: America's Best Private Eye Stories, Vol. 1, 1982–1995 (2010) edited by Robert J. Randisi

For Further Information

Bibel, Barbara, Marcia Muller interview, *Booklist*, May 1, 2000.

Grape, Jan, "Interview: Pronzini and Muller," *Mystery Scene*, Feb. 1992.

Howe, Alexander N., and Christine A. Jackson. *Marcia Muller and the Female Private Eye: Essays on the Novels That Defined a Subgenre*. Jefferson, N.C.: McFarland, 2008.

Marcia Muller interview, Books 'n Bytes, http://www.booksnbytes.com/auth_inter views/marcia_muller.html/ (viewed Sept. 12, 2009).

Marcia Muller interview, Mystery One, http://www.mysteryone.com/MarciaMuller Interview.htm/ (viewed Sept. 12, 2009).

Marcia Muller profile, Bookbrowse, http://www.bookbrowse.com/biographies/index. cfm?author_number=669/ (viewed Sept. 12, 2009).

Marcia Muller website, http://marciamuller.com/ (viewed Sept. 12, 2009).

Muller, Adrian, Marcia Muller entry, *St. James Guide to Crime & Mystery Writers*, fourth edition, edited by Jay P. Pederson. Detroit: St. James Press, 1996.

Muller, Marcia, "Developing a Series Character," *Mystery Scene,* No. 69, 2000.

Peters, Tim, "Muller and McCone: Parboiled Touch," *Publishers Weekly*, Aug. 31, 2009.

Pettengell, Michael, "The First Lady of Female Detection: An Interview with Marcia Muller," *Mystery Scene* 35 (1992).

Carol O'Connell

New York, New York
1947

Police Procedural
Benchmark Series: Kathleen Mallory

About the Author and the Author's Writing

Beauty is in the eye of the beholder. But sociopathy lurks beneath the surface and may elude quick detection. Carol O'Connell's series character Kathleen Mallory is lanky, her physical good looks belying a barely controlled anger. Growing up on the streets, she got by by stealing. A New York City police inspector took her in and, with his wife, raised her. She trained as a computer expert, and she joined the police force, quickly working her way into a posting as a detective. Her mentor is murdered, setting her on a grief-filled track to solve the crime, and perhaps take revenge.

Critics praised O'Connell's debut novel, *Mallory's Oracle*, for elbowing the genre's traditions.

Mallory wasn't O'Connell's first choice for lead character. Her unpublished manuscript was about a different gruff cop, Louis Markowitz. Mallory was a peripheral character. But she won the author's heart. For her to succeed, however, Markowitz had to die. Her first case, *Mallory's Oracle*, involved finding his killer.

Nine novels later, in *Find Me* (2006), Mallory has lost none of her grit. She drew praise from *Library Journal*'s Devon Thomas: "Arrogant, cold, and sometimes brutal, New York detective Kathy Mallory has always been as scary as the murderers she pursues."

O'Connell appreciates her character's foibles. "She's a sociopath," she told John Orr for Triviana. "I get letters asking if I would write a kinder, gentler Mallory, but I tell them if I did that, I've got no career."

The author's childhood was nowhere near as dramatic as those of her characters, but she did struggle for several years in Greenwich Village, failing in efforts to become a painter and scratching up rent money with small jobs in the editorial field. She put together a manuscript for a crime novel and had no success finding a publisher. Inspired to try an offshore publisher, she sent her unagented manuscript to Hutchinson in England. An editor found it in the slush pile, and while he didn't accept it, he wrote an encouraging letter. She wrote a second manuscript, which the editor bought and which came out in 1993. U.S. rights sold to Putnam for $800,000. Rights were also sold for Dutch, French, German, and Norwegian editions. O'Connell became an overnight success.

Born in 1947 in New York City, O'Connell earned a B.F.A. from Arizona State University and also attended the California Institute or Arts/Chouinard.

Claiming she has no time for hobbies or other interests, O'Connell is a compulsive writer. Writing, she told reporter John Orr for the *Oakland Tribune*, is "always the largest chunk of my day when I am on a roll. It can go on for a very long time, 16 hours. If it goes too long I have to tell myself to stop because you don't want to burn out." It generally takes her a year to finish a manuscript; she does a great deal of rewriting.

Mallory may represent some wishful thinking on the author's part. O'Connell stands 5 foot 4 inches; her heroine is 6 foot 1 inch. O'Connell is a peaceable sort. Mallory is prone to solving problems with violence.

The author has ventured twice into freestanding novels. For *Judas Child*, she visited Cooperstown, New York, to research her fictional Maker's Village. The rural setting for the novel was quite a leap from her generally urban setting. But she was anxious to change her venue—not the tension. Critic Mick McAllister has observed the trademark dark tone of O'Connell in *Judas Child*, in which a child is placed in jeopardy to draw out a kidnapper: "The ferocity of the priest, the madness of the psychiatrist, the toothy mean-ness of the killer, and the terrible relationship between Ali Cray and her ex-lover all play against the sentimental touches."

"I perceive the whole universe as a rather violent place," the author said in a *Booklist* interview with Emily Melton. "I don't think there are any truly safe places anymore. And I think once you get the idea out of your head that there's such a thing as a safe place, life is much easier."

The safest place, surely, is nestled in an armchair with the latest O'Connell novel.

Works by the Author

The Judas Child (1998)

Bone by Bone (2008)

Kathleen Mallory Series

Mallory's Oracle (1994)

The Man Who Lied to Women (1995); U.S. title, *The Man Who Cast Two Shadows*

Killing Critics (1996)

Flight of the Stone Angel (1997); U.S. title, *Stone Angel*

Shell Game (1999)

Crime School (2002)

The Jury Must Die (2003); U.S. title, *Dead Famous*

Winter House (2004)

Find Me (2006) also titled *Shark Music* (2007)

Shell Game (2010)

For Further Information

Carol O'Connell web page, Berkley Prime Crime, http://berkleysignetmysteries.com/ author215/ (viewed Oct. 7, 2009).

McAllister, Mick, "Watching Mallory Grow a Soul," Dancing Badger, http://www. dancingbadger.com/carol_oconnell.htm/ (viewed Oct. 14, 2009).

Melton, Emily, Carol O'Connell interview, *Booklist*, Apr. 15, 1998.

Menkes, Vivenne, "First Novel Sold to Putnam for $800K," *Publishers Weekly*, Jan. 10, 1994.

Orr, John, "Carol O'Connell Rises to the Task," Triviana, http://triviana.com/books/ oconn/carol03.htm/ (viewed Oct. 7, 2009).

Orr, John, "Mystery Author Carol O'Connell Drops by San Mateo," *Oakland Tribune*, Jan. 3, 2009.

Penzler, Otto, ed. *The Lineup: The World's Greatest Crime Writers Tell the Inside Story of Their Greatest Detectives*. New York: Little, Brown, 2009.

Thomas, Devon, *Find Me* review, *Library Journal*, Nov. 15, 2006.

Katherine Hall Page

New Jersey
1947

Amateur Detective, Culinary Mystery
Benchmark Series: Faith Fairchild

Jean Fogelberg

About the Author and the Author's Writing

The writer of cozy murder mysteries faces a challenge. The work has to include a death, to make the stakes sufficiently high. But for the comfort of readers, the passing can't be too gruesome, the investigation too clinical. Katherine Hall Page, to lend her mysteries some civility, began including recipes (with *The Body in the Cast*, the fifth book in her Faith Fairchild series, in 1893).

Page already knew her readers would want intriguing puzzles (corpses, or rather, bodies, found in belfry, veranda, and attic) and agreeable characters when she wrote her first crime novel, *The Body in the Belfry*, featuring the upscale caterer with a taste for crime solving, published in 1989.

"I had just finished a doctorate, my son was almost two, and my husband, who is a professor, took [the family on] a sabbatical in France. It was the first time that I really had free time—and the gift of time that all writers dream about," the author related to Lynn Kaczmarek for *Mystery News*.

It won the 1991 Agatha Award for best first mystery novel.

Page was born in New Jersey in 1947. She earned a B.A. in English from Wellesley in 1969 and taught high school English and history. She earned an Ed.M. in secondary education from Tufts University in 1974. From 1969 to 1980 she was a director of programs for youths with emotional disabilities. She spent five years developing and nurturing an in-school program for adolescents and dealt with truancy, substance abuse, and relationship matters. After receiving a Ph.D. in administration from Harvard University in 1985, she became an educational consultant. Her husband, Alan Hein, is on the faculty at the Massachusetts Institute of Technology. They have a grown son.

When she began to think about writing mysteries, Page relied for inspiration on favorite writers Virginia Rich (who also nurtured a culinary theme), Rex Stout, and Dorothy L. Sayers, among others.

The author gave her heroine an unsettling environment: newly married, Faith Fairchild moves with her minister husband to suburban Aleford, Massachusetts, west of Boston (the author herself lives in Lincoln, Massachusetts), so he can teach at Harvard Divinity School.

"As Faith explores the byways of Boston and Cambridge in search of dangerous past secrets," said *Publishers Weekly* reviewer of *The Body in the Attic* (2004), "both cities come to vivid life."

Page nails the personalities of her various characters, in the world served by Fairchild's Have Faith food-provision business. As reviewer Marilyn Stasio pointed out in *The New York Times Book Review*, in discussing *The Body in the Snowdrift* (2005), the author capably handles "the complicated social dynamics within large families."

But having a theme, a setting, and characters only gets you started; you need mastery of the mechanics of a mystery. *Booklist* reviewer Connie Fletcher noted how Page approached this matter and overcame it in *The Body in the Gallery* (2008), which takes place in an art gallery: "Page has to work a bit to get Faith on scene for the investigation, since the local cops want nothing to do with her, but a temporary posting to the gallery café gives the intrepid sleuth all the opportunity she needs."

And you need a knack for good stories. Page "remains an unabashed eavesdropper," she said on her website, "and will even watch your slides or home movies to hear your narration. Her books are the product of all the strands of her life and she plans to keep weaving."

Works by the Author

Faith Fairchild Series

The Body in the Belfry (1989)

The Body in the Kelp (1990)

The Body in the Bouillon (1991)

The Body in the Vestibule (1992)

The Body in the Cast (1993)

The Body in the Basement (1994)

The Body in the Bog (1996) also titled *The Body in the Marsh* (1996)

The Body in the Fjord (1997)

The Body in the Bookcase (1998)

The Body in the Big Apple (1999)

The Body in the Moonlight (2001)

The Body in the Bonfire (2002)

The Body in the Lighthouse (2003)

The Body in the Attic (2004)

The Body in the Snowdrift (2005)

The Body in the Ivy (2006)

The Body in the Gallery (2008)

The Body in the Sleigh (2009)

Have Faith in Your Kitchen (2010), recipes from the Fairchild mysteries

The Body in the Gazebo (2011)

Contributor

Mistletoe and Mayhem, with Judi McCoy, Joanne Pence, and Christie Ridgway (2004)

Young Adult Fiction

Club Meds (2006)

Christie and Company Series

Christie and Company (1996)

Down East (1997)

In the Year of the Dragon (1997)

Bon Voyage (1998)

For Further Information

Body in the Attic review, *Publishers Weekly*, Apr. 26, 2004.

Fletcher, Connie, *The Body in the Gallery* review, *Booklist*, Apr. 1, 2008.

Kaczmarek, Lynn, "Katherine Hall Page: The Body in The. . . ," *Mystery News,* Apr./May 2000. Katherine Hall Page website, http://www.katherine-hall-page.org/ (viewed July 24, 2009).

Stasio, Marilyn, "A Funny Thing Happened," *New York Times Book Review*, Apr. 24, 2005.

George Pelecanos

Washington, D.C.
1957

Private Detective, Historical Mystery
Benchmark Series: Derek Strange/Terry Quinn

About the Author and the Author's Writing

Many think of Washington, D.C., as largely populated by members of Congress, Pentagon workers, Supreme Court jurists, and Smithsonian Institution staff. George Pelecanos, in his novels set in those 61.4 square miles, has preferred to hold a lens to the black and Greek neighborhoods—and particularly the lowlifes who peddle sex, drugs, or violence.

The author was born in Washington, D.C., in 1957, the son of a Greek restaurant owner and his administrator wife. A film major, Pelecanos received a B.A. from the University of Maryland in College Park in 1980. He and his wife, Emily Hawk, have three children.

Pelecanos was everything from a short-order cook to an appliance store clerk to a shoe salesman until, in 1990, he joined Circle Films, producers and distributors of theatrical films including John Woo's *The Killer* and early films made by the Coen brothers. Pelecanos eventually produced the third, 2004 season of HBO's hit series *The Wire*, set in Baltimore, and scripted the series.

With his favorite writers being Ross Macdonald, Raymond Chandler, and Dashiell Hammett, Pelecanos had by then begun to write crime fiction. He developed a Greek American detective, Nick Stefanos, for his first novel, *A Firing Offense*, published in 1992. Since then he has produced a novel a year. The writer upped the ante for *The Big Blowdown* (1996), a denser, more ambitious novel set in the 1940s and '50s. His *King Suckerman* (1997) introduced an African American veteran of the Vietnam War era, Marcus Clay, who owns a record store in D.C., and Dimitri Karras, his Greek American friend. Those books and two others form a linked series that explores the immigrant experience.

Clay, Pelecanos said, is his attempt to depict a more regular black character than is usually found in literature. "You've either got the Superspade guy or you've got the other side, the very pious family man. I just wanted to write a man, a guy who has a business. But he certainly has his faults, he's just a guy," the author said in a conversation with Bob Cornwell of twbooks.

As Ben Greeman wrote in *The New Yorker*,

Pelecanos wasn't as hilariously deadpan as Elmore Leonard or as dourly intense as Dennis Lehane, but his characters, even the villains, were motivated by a mixture of self-interest and existential despair which made the battle between good and evil unusually compelling.

Pelecanos's ninth novel featured another pair of heroes, a black ex-cop named Derek Strange and a white ex-cop named Terry Quinn, who are thrust deep into D.C.'s criminal underbelly. Sometimes they take matters into their own hands.

"There has always been a strong element of vigilantism in American culture," the author told interviewer Ali Karim for *SHOTS* magazine, "and a distrust of authority and the law, which is why our citizens are so violently opposed to any laws that might restrict their rights to own guns."

Not all of Pelecanos's books wrap up neatly. The murder solution rate in mystery novels is close to 100 percent. In real life, it's maybe 50 percent or less. Strange and Quinn don't nail the killer in *Soul Circus*, for example. "They are constantly one step behind the police throughout the book, as they would be. You know, private detectives don't solve murders. Police do. It's trying to show the futility of what they're doing," Pelecanos related to Robert Birnbaum for Identitytheory.com.

Pelecanos amplified for the *New York Times*,

> When somebody's dead, they're dead forever, and it ripples out into the community and into people's lives. The world is forever off balance. And I don't want to make people feel comfortable with it. I want them to be entertained but also uncomfortable by the time they finish a book.

Uncomfortable, but not so uncomfortable they won't watch for the next Pelecanos novel.

Works by the Author

The Night Gardener (2006)

The Turnaround (2008)

The Way Home (2009)

The Cut (2011)

D.C. Quartet

The Big Blowdown (1996)

King Suckerman (1997)

The Sweet Forever (1998)

Shame the Devil (2000)

Derek Strange/Terry Quinn Series

Right as Rain (2001)

Hell to Pay (2002)

Soul Circus (2003)

Hard Revolution (2004)

Drama City (2005)

Nick Stefanos Series

A Firing Offense (1992)

Nick's Trip (1993)

Shoedog (1994)

Down by the River Where the Dead Men Go (1995)

Contributor

Best American Mystery Stories 1997, edited by Robert B. Parker and Otto Penzler (1997), includes "When You're Hungry"

Measure of Poison, edited by Dennis McMillan (2002)

Editor

D.C. Noir (2006)

George Pelecanos has also been a film producer and was a producer and writer for the HBO series *The Wire*, which aired from 2002 to 2008, and a writer for *The Pacific* miniseries in 2009.

For Further Information

Birnbaum, Robert, George Pelecanos interview, Identitytheory.com, 2003. http://www.identitytheory.com/interviews/birnbaum100.html/ (viewed July 15, 2009).

Cornwell, Bob, "Hard-Boiled Heaven," twbooks, http://www.twbooks.co.uk/crime scene/pelecanosinterviewbc.htm/ (viewed Sept. 18 2010).

George Pelecanos interview, Bookreporter, 2004, http://www.bookreporter.com/authors/au-pelecanos-george.asp (viewed July 15, 2009).

Greenman, Ben, "The Capital Crime Novels of George P. Pelecanos," *New Yorker*, Apr. 8, 2002.

Maslin, Janet, "The Crimes They Are A-changin'," *New York Times*, May 13, 2002.

Rich, Motoko, "George Pelecanos Dreams of Literary and Commercial Success," *New York Times*, July 26, 2006.

Louise Penny

Gary Matthews

Toronto, Ontario
1958

Police Procedural
Benchmark Series: Three Pines
Mysteries

About the Author and the Author's Writing

Louise Penny agrees there's a certain Canadian-ness to her half-dozen crime novels featuring Chief Inspector Armand Gamache of the Sûreté du Québec. She told *Mystery Fanfare* interviewer David Cole,

> As Canadians we really are the product of a belief system that includes social justice, a social safety net. Medicine and education for everyone. A belief that a meritocracy isn't good enough. Wee need to help each other. It's our obligation, as citizens.

But that's only the icing. The cake is still murder, and Gamache and his force must grapple with reluctant witnesses, puzzling clues, and distrust in the upper ranks.

Although Penny writes police procedurals, she credits mystery author Agatha Christie for inspiring her "cozy" direction. "She's my template. When I started writing I intentionally set out to create a modern sense of a classic Christie," the author said in Soho Noir. "I hope, though, mine have a little more character development."

Born in Toronto, Ontario, in 1958, the author took up a career as a journalist and radio host for the Canadian Broadcasting Corporation, first in Toronto, then in Thunder Bay. In Winnipeg, she produced documentaries and hosted an afternoon show. She advanced to a morning program in Québec City, where she met her husband, Michael Penny, a physician. They live in a rural community south of Montreal, Québec.

With her background, she thought it would be a snap to write a book. She left the CBC and immediately suffered writer's block. She couldn't complete a manuscript. In frustration, she read novels by Christie, Ngaio Marsh, Michael Innes, and Dorothy L. Sayers. And she came to realize that she shouldn't be attempting a literary crime novel, she should simply write the kind of book she liked to read.

"A classic traditional mystery. Set in a village, not unlike the ones in my area of Québec," she said in *New Mystery Reader*. "And since I knew it might take years to write and sell, I figured I'd better populate it with people I'd want to spend years with. And shops I'd love to wander, with food I'd eat. In the loveliest of settings. So I created Three Pines."

She offered a further reason for fabricating a setting rather than taking a real one. With an imagined place, she didn't have to remember precise streets or building locations—she could make them up. Three Pines is both familiar and unusual enough for readers in the United States to set it apart.

"She deftly uses the bilingual, bicultural aspect of Quebecois life as well as arcane aspects of archery and art to deepen her narrative," *Publishers Weekly* said of *Still Life* (2005), Penny's initial novel and winner of a Crime Writers of America New Blood Award.

She took particular care in shaping her main character, Gamache. "He's a man with a moral center," she told interviewer Jeri Westerson. "A man who, while flawed, will always try to do the right thing, not the easy thing. . . . He was created because I never wanted to tire of my main character. He, uniquely, was created with the long view in mind."

Penny builds her plots in layers, with deeper levels for those who are perceptive.

"Arthur Ellis Award-winner Penny paints a vivid picture of the French Canadian village," said *Publishers Weekly* of *The Cruellest Month* (2007), "its inhabitants and a determined detective who will strike many Agatha Christie fans as a 21st-century version of Hercule Poirot."

As there must always be tension in mystery novels, Penny makes sure Gamache and his superiors in the Sureté bang heads.

Besides its charming rural setting, *A Fatal Grace* (2007) has one of the more unusual murder weapons seen in some time: the victim is electrocuted while sitting in a chair on a frozen lake watching a curling match. Her husband gave her the idea, Penny said. The idea, but not how it was accomplished. That she had to devise on her own.

The author works out her stories, she told Soho Noir, starting with the why of it all, then shaping a backdrop, adopting a theme (jealousy, redemption). She builds village characters. Everything is in place except how her police heroes will get from cold body to murderer. That comes during the writing.

Penny boldly overcame her writer's block, and became a risk-taker. She said she once heard that writer P.D. James wrote crime novels with a particular killer in mind, then at the last minute switched to a different killer. The concept intrigued Penny, and that's how she wrote *A Fatal Grace*, her second novel.

Penny's first books are each set each in a different season of the year at Three Pines. The fourth, *The Brutal Telling* (2009), was nominated for both Agatha and Dilys awards. *Bury Your Dead* (2010) shifts some of its setting to Québec City, in part to find some new types of crimes and killers, in part to explore a new venue.

"Penny is a careful writer," *Booklist* reviewer David Pitt said, "taking time to establish character and scene, playing around with a large cast, distracting us so we won't see the final twists coming until they're upon us."

Works by the Author

Three Pines Mysteries

Still Life (2005)

A Fatal Grace (2007) *Dead Cold* (Canada and United Kingdom, 2006)

The Cruelest Month (2008), *The Cruellest Month* (United Kingdom, 2007)

A Rule Against Murder (2009), *The Murder Stone* (United Kingdom, 2008)

The Brutal Telling (2009)

Bury Your Dead (2010)

For Further Information

Cole, David, "Louise Penny: Cool Canadian Crime," Mystery Fanfare, http://my steryreadersinc.blogspot.com/2009/06/louise-penny-cool-canadian-crime.html/ (viewed July 8, 2009).

Coon, Judy, *Rule Against Murder* review, *Booklist*, Jan. 1, 2009.

Cruelest Month review, *Publishers Weekly*, Jan. 7, 2008.

Interview with Louise Penny, New Mystery Reader Magazine, http://www.newmy steryreader.com/louise_penny.htm/ (viewed July 8, 2009).

Louise Penny interview, Soho Noir, http://www.sohonoir.co.uk/louisepenny.html/ (viewed July 8, 2009).

Louise Penny website, http://www.louisepenny.com/ (viewed July 15, 2009).

Pitt, David, *A Fatal Grace* review, *Booklist*, Mar. 15, 2007.

Still Life review, *Publishers Weekly*, May 1, 2006.

Westerson, Jeri, Interview with author Louise Penny, getting medieval, http://www.getting-medieval.com/my_weblog/2009/05/interview-with-author-louise-penny.html/ (viewed July 16, 2009).

Anne Perry

London, England
1938

Amateur Detective, Historical Mystery
Landmark Series: William Monk

About the Author and the Author's Writing

Anne Perry started writing fiction set in the Victorian era after her stepfather one day revealed to her his candidate for the real Jack the Ripper. "I found that I was totally absorbed by what happens to people under the pressure of investigation, how old relationships and trusts are eroded, and new ones formed," she said on her website. She wrote *The Cater Street Hangman* (1979), and a long-running series was born.

The author was born Juliet Marion Hulme in Blackheath, London, and spent her early years there. Her father was an astronomer, mathematician, and nuclear physicist. Frequent family relocations in wartime and her poor health interrupted her education in private schools. An avid reader, her early favorite authors included Lewis Carroll and Charles Kingsley.

She held clerical and retail jobs. She was an airline stewardess. She was an assistant buyer in Newcastle Upon Tyne. Residing in California from 1967 to 1972, she was a limousine dispatcher and insurance underwriter for Muldoon and Adams. She lived in the Bahamas and Toronto briefly. Today she resides in Portmahomack, Scotland.

Perry has not married. She converted to Mormonism. She generally writes six days a week, in longhand, starting with a detailed draft.

"I figure that to make a good mystery," she said to reporter Wilder Penfield III.

> The motive must be understandable and powerful—passionate, and intense, and real, at least to the person concerned. . . . Fear makes people behave very, very differently from the way they normally do. How people behave under pressure is what the story's always about, I think.

"I write about the Victorian era because there is demand for it," Perry said in an AbeBooks conversation.

The Cater Street Hangman introduced Inspector Thomas Pitt and his upper-class wife, Charlotte. Perry said she was drawn to the time period by the dramatic class differences, wealth living so close to squalor, high manners coexisting with crude rowdyism. "Having forsaken her comfortable upper-middle-class lifestyle . . . [to marry Pitt], the intelligent and socially conscious Charlotte aids her educated and sensitive husband in all his cases," explained Jean Swanson and Dean James in *By a Woman's Hand*.

"I write Victorian plots but they are transferable to any other era because it would be pointless to write about issues that no longer exist," she elaborated in an e-mail.

Perry writes darker books about another policeman, William Monk, and Crimean war nurse Hester Latterley. This series is set in the 1850s and 1860s. Monk is an amnesiac; he has no recollection of his past life.

Hester has something of a sharp tongue. "It's much more fun to have a character who's tart," the author told Bethanne Kelly Patrick. "Laughing is good for you and just because I'm writing mysteries doesn't mean there can't be humor." Hester and Monk married later in the series, and for a time Monk became a private investigator.

A third mystery series, beginning with *No Graves as Yet: 1914* (2003), is set in World War I. That time period interests her, as her grandfather was a military chaplain during the conflict.

"I just wanted to try something different," she told *Publishers Weekly* in 2003. "I love the Victorian era, but I want to stretch and tell another story. World War I gives me the opportunity to examine different sorts of ethical problems. I like to write stories in which there is a real moral conflict."

"I listen to what people say at my book signings," she told Crescent Blues. "They tell me they like historical backgrounds. They have certain expectations. They know which writers will never give them graphic violence, or hurt animals. You must keep the promises you've implicitly made."

Works by the Author

The One Thing More (2000)

A Dish Taken Cold (2001)

The Sheen on the Silk (2010)

Charlotte and Thomas Pitt Series

The Cater Street Hangman (1979)

Callander Square (1980)

Paragon Walk (1981)

Resurrection Row (1982)

Rutland Place (1983)

Bluegate Fields (1984)

Death in the Devil's Acre (1985)

Cardington Crescent (1987)

Silence in Hanover Close (1988)

Bethlehem Road (1990)

Highgate Rise (1991)

Belgrave Square (1992)

Farriers' Lane (1993)

The Hyde Park Headsman (1994)

Traitors Gate (1995)

Pentecost Alley (1996)

Ashworth Hall (1997)

Brunswick Gardens (1998)

Bedford Square (2000)

Half Moon Street (2000)

The Whitechapel Conspiracy (2001)

Southampton Row (2002)

Seven Dials (2003)

Long Spoon Lane (2005)

Buckingham Palace Gardens (2008)

Treason at Lisson Grove (2011)

Christmas Series

A Christmas Journey (2003), also titled *Journey Towards Christmas*

A Christmas Visitor (2004)

A Christmas Guest (2005)

An Anne Perry Christmas: The First Two Christmas Novels (2006)

A Christmas Secret (2006)

A Christmas Beginning (2007)

Anne Perry's Christmas Mysteries (2008), includes second two Christmas novels

A Christmas Grace (2008)

Anne Perry's Silent Nights: Two Victorian Christmas Mysteries (2009)

A Christmas Promise (2009)

A Christmas Odyssey (2010)

William Monk Series

The Face of a Stranger (1990)

A Dangerous Mourning (1991)

Defend and Betray (1992)

A Sudden, Fearful Death (1993)

The Sins of the Wolf (1994)

Cain His Brother (1995)

Weighed in the Balance (1996)

The Silent Cry (1997)

A Breach of Promise (1998), also titled *The Whited Sepulchres*

The Twisted Root (1999)

Slaves and Obsession (2000)

A Funeral in Blue (2001)

Death of a Stranger (2002)

The Shifting Tide (2004)

The William Monk Mysteries: The First Three Novels (2005)

Dark Assassin (2006)

Execution Dock (2009)

World War I Series

No Graves as Yet: 1914 (2003)

Shoulder the Sky: 1915 (2004)

Angels in the Gloom: 1916 (2005)

At Some Disputed Barricade: 1917 (2006)

We Shall Not Sleep: 1918 (2007)

Editor

Death by Horoscope, with Martin H. Greenberg (2001)

Much Ado About Murder (2002)

Death by Dickens (2004)

Contributor

Holmes for the Holidays (1996)

Murder for Love (1996)

Crime Through Time (1997)

Crime Through Time II (1997)

Holmes for the Holidays II (1997)

Malice Domestic 6, edited by Martin H. Greenberg (1997)

Canine Crimes, edited by Jeffrey Marks (1998)

Murder They Wrote II, edited by Elizabeth Foxwell (1998), includes "Brodie and the Regrettable Incident of the French Ambassador"

Women of Mystery (1998)

First Lady Murders, edited by Nancy Pickard (1999)

A Century of British Mystery & Suspense (2000)

Malice Domestic 10, edited by Nevada Barr (2000)

Midnight Louie's Pet Detectives, edited by Carole Nelson Douglas (2000)

Murder for Obsession, edited by Otto Penzler (2000)

Unholy Orders (2000)

World's Finest Mystery and Crime Stories, edited by Edward Gorman (2000)

I'll Kill for That, with Rita Mae Brown, Jennifer Crusie, Linda Fairstein, Lisa Gardner, Heather Graham, Kay Hooper, Katherine Neville, Kathy Reichs, Julie Smith, and Tina Wainscott (2001)

Naked Came the Phoenix, with Nevada Barr, Mary Jane Clark, Diana Gabaldon, J. A. Jance, Faye Kellerman, Laurie R. King, Val McDermid, Pam and Mary O'Shaughnessy, Nancy Pickard, J. D. Robb, Lisa Scottoline, and Marcia Talley (2001)

World's Finest Mystery and Crime Stories: Fourth Annual Collection, edited by Ed Gorman and Martin H. Greenberg (2003)

The Mighty Johns and Other Stories, edited by Otto Penzler (2004)

Adaptations in Other Media

The Cater Street Hangman (television movie, 1998)

The author has also written the fantasy novels *Tathea* and *Come Armageddon* as well as historical novels.

For Further Information

Anne Perry interview, AbeBooks, http://www.abebooks.com/docs/authors-corner/anne-perry.shtml/ (viewed Nov. 18, 2009).

Anne Perry interview, Crescent Blues, http://www.crescentblues.com/2_2issue/perry.shtml/ (viewed Nov. 18, 2009).

Anne Perry website. http://www.anneperry.net/ (viewed Nov. 13, 2009).

Borck, Helga, Anne Perry entry, *St. James Guide to Crime & Mystery Writers*, fourth edition, edited by Jay P. Pederson. Detroit; St. James Press, 1996.

Patrick, Bethanna Kelly, "In the Trenches," *Pages* (Jan./Feb. 2003).

Peacock, Scot, ed., Anne Perry entry, *Contemporary Authors New Revision Series*, vol. 84. Detroit: Gale Research, 2000.

Penfield, Wilder III, "Heavenly Creature-Turned-Hit Novelist Anne Perry Survives Exposure," *Toronto Sun* (Feb. 5, 1995).

Penzler, Otto, ed. *The Lineup: The World's Greatest Crime Writers Tell the Inside Story of Their Greatest Detectives*. New York: Little, Brown, 2009.

Perry, Anne, "Breach of Promise," *Mystery Scene* No. 62 (1999).

Swanson, Jean, and Dean James. *By a Woman's Hand: A Guide to Mystery Fiction by Women*. New York: Berkley, 1996.

Nancy Pickard

Walt Whitaker Photography

Kansas City, Missouri
1945

Amateur Detective
Benchmark Series: Marie Lightfoot

About the Author and the Author's Writing

"Writing is a path as full of darkness as it is of light," Nancy Pickard said in *Seven Steps on the Writer's Path* (2003), her nonfiction guide to writing, "and so the way ahead is hard to see. There are so many ominous shadows, unpredictable gusts of wind, unexpected, blinding shafts of sunlight. It's easy to get lost." But Pickard and her coauthor, psychologist Lynn Lott, skillfully guide their readers through a comfortable course to writing success.

Four-time Agatha Award–winning Pickard came by her appreciation of the seven steps over time; when she started out, at age 35, she was a mystery fan without knowing quite what it was that made one work. Her first manuscript, an editor told her, couldn't make up its mind if it wanted to be romantic suspense or mystery. Pickard listened, and started fresh. Her next manuscript found a home.

Generous Death (1984) introduced her series character Jenny Cain, director of a charitable foundation in Port Frederick, Massachusetts. The books, according to critic Ed Blachman, "have been worthy accomplishments indeed. Pickard's mysteries are appropriately mysterious, her characters gripping; and Cain's position has allowed Pickard to tell important tales of social realities in modern-day America."

Publishers Weekly, in discussing *Bum Steer* (1990), said, "Pickard writes fluidly on family ties, both good and bad, while her appealing detective displays warmth, intelligence and a social conscience as she perseveres in her search for the truth."

Pickard told interviewer Dean James she based her heroine in part on herself, in part on Louisa May Alcott's Jo March, and in part on a popular juvenile series character. "I love hearing Jenny referred to a 'Nancy Drew all grown up,' though she's definitely a 'Nancy' who's been through the sixties, don't you think?"

The author was born in Kansas City, Missouri, in 1945. She received a bachelor's degree in journalism from the Missouri School of Journalism in 1967. From 1967 to 1969, she worked as a reporter and editor with *The Squire* in Overland Park, Kansas, then as a writer and supervisor with Western Auto in Kansas City until 1972. In 1973 she became a freelance writer. She married rancher Guy Pickard in 1976 and had one son. She is now divorced. A founding member of Sisters in Crime, she served as president in 1988–1989.

Among her several awards was a Shamus in 1991 for the short story "Dust Devils." The author has not written many short stories, finding the form more difficult than novels—that is, until the day she overheard another writer say a short story must have an epiphany. "Well, I had one right there," she said on her web page. "Light bulb going off in my head, the whole ah ha moment in a flash. I realized my stories lacked that crucial turning point where somebody changes, or the plot changes in some entertaining way."

While she has become more accomplished at her craft, Pickard said in an interview with Elizabeth Zelvin that she still disdains tight outlines. "I write a proposal in order to go to contract, and then I mostly ignore my own proposal and let the book develop as it will. I revise constantly."

At the request of an editor, she agreed to finish Virginia Rich's manuscript for a novel in her series, then went on to write two more Eugenia Potter culinary mysteries. The books proved more of a challenge than Pickard expected. "It was incredibly tough, until it dawned on me that I should focus on capturing the character of Mrs. Potter and then everything else would take care of itself," she told Susan McBride for Between the Pages Past.

Pickard took a new direction when she wrote a trilogy of puzzlers featuring true-crime writer Marie Lightfoot. And these days she has shifted to writing stand-alone crime novels. *The Virgin of Small Plains* took the author back to the state where she grew up, Kansas, for a story a review for *Publishers Weekly* said had "some cleverly planted surprises and the convincing portrait of small-town life [that] make this a memorable read."

Pickard now gives greater thought to her characters, she said in a conversation with fellow mystery author Julia Spencer-Fleming.

> When something happens in a story, I don't just wait for them to do what they do—I think about how they'd be reacting to it, and what their options might be, and what effect that might have on the people around them. And I'm finding that this is deepening my feeling for them.

That's how she finds her way through the shadows.

Works by the Author

Storm Warnings (1999), short stories

The Virgin of Small Plains (2006)

The Scent of Rain and Lightning (2010)

Eugenia Potter Series

The 27-Ingredient Chili Con Carne Murders, with Virginia Rich (1992)

The Blue Corn Murders (1998)

The Secret Ingredient Murders (2001)

Jenny Cain Series

Generous Death (1984)

Say No to Murder (1985)

No Body (1986)

Marriage Is Murder (1987)

Dead Crazy (1988)

Bum Steer (1989)

I.O.U. (1991)

But I Wouldn't Want to Die There (1993)

Confession (1994)

Twilight (1995)

Marie Lightfoot Series

The Whole Truth (2000)

Ring of Truth (2001)

The Truth Hurts (2002)

Contributor

Cat Crimes for the Holidays (1997)

Mary Higgins Clark Presents The Plot Thickens (1997)

Murder, They Wrote, with Mary Daheim, Jane Dentinger, Marjorie Eccles, Sally Gunning, Jean Hager, Ellen Hart, Kate Kingsbury, Janet Laurence, and Marlys Millhiser (1997)

The Year's Best Fantasy and Horror Eleventh Annual Collection (1998)

Naked Came the Phoenix, with Nevada Barr, Mary Jane Clark, Diana Gabaldon, J. A. Jance, Faye Kellerman, Laurie R King, Val McDermid, Pam and Mary O'Shaughnessy, Anne Perry, J D Robb, Lisa Scottoline, and Marcia Talley (2001)

The Shamus Winners: America's Best Private Eye Stories, Vol. 1 1982–1995 (2010), edited by Robert J. Randisi

Editor

Nancy Pickard Presents Malice Domestic (1994)

The First Lady Murders (1999)

Mom, Apple Pie & Murder (1999)

For Further Information

Blachman, Ed, *Bum Steer* review, *The Drood Review of Mystery*, Feb. 1990.

James, Dean, "Interview with Nancy Pickard," *Mystery Scene,* No. 41, 1993.

Marks, Jeffrey, "An Interview with Nancy Pickard," *The Armchair Detective*, spring 1993.

McBride, Susan, "Nothing but the Truth: An Interview with Nancy Pickard," Between the Pages Past, July 2001, http://www.myshelf.com/betweenthepages/01/pickard.html/ (viewed Dec. 2, 2009).

Nancy Pickard website, http://www.nancypickard.com/ (viewed Dec. 2, 2009).

Pickard, Nancy, and Lynn Lott. *Seven Steps on the Writer's Path: The Journey from Frustration to Fulfillment*. New York: Ballantine, 2003.

Secret Ingredient Murders review, *Publishers Weekly*, Nov. 6, 2000.

Spencer-Fleming, Julia, "A Conversation with Nancy Pickard," The Narthex, http://www.juliaspencerfleming.com/Nancy-Pickard.html/ (viewed Dec. 2, 2009).

Steinberg, Sybil, *Bum Steer* review, *Publishers Weekly*, Jan. 12, 1990.

Virgin of Small Plains review, *Publishers Weekly*, Mar. 20, 2006.

Zelvin, Elizabeth, "Interview with Nancy Pickard," Poe's Deadly Daughters, July 19, 2007, http://poesdeadlydaughters.blogspot.com/2007/07/interview-with-nancy-pickard.html/ (viewed Dec. 2, 2009).

Bill Pronzini

Petaluma, California
1943

Private Detective, Westerns, Historical
Mystery
Benchmark Series: Nameless

Marcia Muller

About the Author and the Author's Writing

Bill Pronzini's Nameless Detective really does have a name. You're just not likely to see it in one of the books—which number more than three dozen, issued by eight publishing houses. "Nameless is nameless because, in the beginning, I could never think of a name that suited him," the author said, in 1980, in a letter to the compiler of this reference book.

> And as the series began to grow, and the character grew in my mind, I realized that I was endowing him with more and more of my own likes, dislikes, weaknesses, world views, etc. So he really does have a name: Bill Pronzini. He's me . . . in an alternate universe where I happened to have become a private detective instead of a professional writer.

Pronzini was born in Petaluma, California, in 1943. He devoured his grandfather's science fiction digests, sought out used copies of *Manhunt*, and assembled a large collection of vintage pulp fiction magazines. After attending junior college, he lived in West Germany and Majorca. He worked as a news clerk, plumbing supply vendor, newspaper sports reporter, typist, parking lot attendant, and civilian guard for the U.S. Marshal's Service. He sold his first short story, "You Don't Know What it's Like," to *Shell Scott Mystery Magazine* for its November 1966 issue. He wrote stories for digest magazines under the house names Brett Halliday, Romer Zane Grey, and Robert Hart Davis. His first novel was *The Stalker* (1971).

Pronzini, who received the Private Eye Writers of America Lifetime Achievement Award in 1987, said he modeled his crime-solving heroes not on those of Raymond Chandler or Dashiell Hammett or their wise-cracking, supercapable derivatives but on Thomas B. Dewey's Mac novels. Mac, Pronzini said, was more compassionate, more human.

"Many fictional detectives are vigilantes—they're running around, committing felonies. Nameless is a private eye who is an honest citizen and a decent man," he told Connie Fletcher of *Booklist*.

Nameless has aged at about the same pace as his chronicler. He has weathered marital problems, a cancer scare, the loss of his partner to suicide, the acceptance of new partners Jake Runyon and Tamara; and Pronzini admits it's become a challenge to keep his hero realistic in an age of DNA tests and other technologies that have transformed criminal investigation.

Pronzini wrote a handful of novels under his own name and as Jack Foxx and Alex Saxon before his first Nameless case made its way into print: *The Snatch* in 1971. He has collaborated with other writers, including Barry N. Malzberg, John Lutz, Collin Wilcox, Jeffrey Wallman, and Jack Anderson—and also with Marcia Muller, who became his third wife in 1992. The two were named Mystery Writers of America Grand Masters—he in 2008, she in 2005. Pronzini has been a prolific anthologist of both mystery and western stories. He has become a student of the crime novel, with Muller compiling *1001 Midnights* (1986), a collection of short reviews, and *Gun and Cheek* (1982) and *Six Gun in Cheek* (1987), tongue-in-cheek overviews of less literary efforts at crime and western fiction.

The Pronzini–Muller household is a professional one. "Writing is more than just a business for us. It's who and what we are," Pronzini told *Library Journal*. "We work on regular schedules, five and sometimes six days a week, but even when we're not actually writing, we're thinking or talking about it."

The writing has gotten harder, Pronzini said in an interview with *Mystery Scene*'s Jan Grape, as "I've become more of a perfectionist, less easily satisfied with scenes, descriptions, passages of dialogue, etc., and therefore do a lot more rewriting than I used to. This makes the finished product better, but it's damned hard work along the way."

Pronzini said he does not model his characters on particular individuals, though at times he has fallen to temptation. He told Jon Jordan for Books 'n' Bytes,

> Bits and pieces of certain individuals have been fused into characters. Murder victims, mainly. There's nothing more gratifying than creating a composite of people who have done you dirt or who for one reason or another you simply don't like and then bumping him or her off.

Works by the Author

The Stalker (1971)

Panic! (1972)

Snowbound (1974)

Games (1976)

The Running of Beasts, with Barry N. Malzberg (1976)

Acts of Mercy, with Barry N. Malzberg (1977)

Night Screams, with Barry N. Malzberg (1979)

Prose Bowl, with Barry N. Malzberg (1980)

The Cambodia File, with Jack Anderson (1981)

Masques (1981)

The Eye, with John Lutz (1984)

Graveyard Plots (1985), collection

San Francisco (1985)

The Lighthouse, with Marcia Muller (1986)

Small Felonies (1988) collection

Firewind (1989)

The Hangings (1989)

The Jade Figurine (1991)

Stacked Deck (1991) collection

Carmody's Run (1993)

With an Extreme Burning (1994), also titled *The Tormentor* (2000)

Blue Lonesome (1995)

A Wasteland of Strangers (1997)

Nothing But the Night (1999)

Sleuths (1999), collection

Oddments (2000), collection

All the Long Years (2001), collection

In an Evil Time (2001)

More Oddments (2001), collection

Step to the Graveyard Easy (2002)

A Wasteland of Strangers (2002)

Problems Solved, with Barry N. Malzberg (2003), collection

The Alias Man (2004)

The Crimes of Jordan Wise (2006)

Snowbound/Games (2007), omnibus

Dago Red (2008), collection

The Other Side of Silence (2008)

Crucifixion River, with Marcia Muller (2009)

The Hidden (2010)

Nameless Detective Series

The Snatch (1971)

Undercurrent (1973)

The Vanished (1973)

Blowback (1977)

Twospot, with Colin Wilcox (1978)

A Killing in Xanadu (1980), chapbook

Labyrinth (1980)

Hoodwink (1981)

Dragonfire (1982)

Scattershot (1982)

Bindlestiff (1983)

Casefile (1983), collection

Double, with Marcia Muller (1984)

Nightshades (1984)

Quicksilver (1984)

Bones (1985)

Deadfall (1986)

Shackles (1988)

Dragonfire/Casefile (1990), omnibus

HoodwinkScattershot (1990), omnibus

Jackpot (1990)

Labyrinth/Bones (1990), omnibus

Breakdown (1991)

Quarry (1991)

Epitaphs (1992)

Demons (1993)

Spadework: A Collection of Nameless Detective Stories (1994)

Hardcase (1995)

Sentinels (1996)

Illusions (1997)

Boobytrap (1998)

Crazybone (2000)

Bleeders (2001)

Spook (2002)

Scenarios (2003), collection

Nightcrawlers (2005)

Mourners (2006)

Savages (2007)

Fever (2008)

Schemers (2009)

Betrayers (2010)

Camouflage (2011)

Quincannon Series

Quincannon (1985)

Beyond the Grave, with Marcia Muller (1986)

Carpenter and Quincannon: Professional Detective Services (1998)

Quincannon's Game (2005)

Contributor

The Mammoth Book of Short Crime Novels (1986)

The Mammoth Book of Short Spy Novels (1986)

The Mammoth Book of Private Eye Stories (1988)

Criminal Intent: 1, with Ed Gorman and Marcia Muller (1993)

Problems Solved, with Barry N. Malzberg (2003)

The Shamus Winners: America's Best Private Eye Stories, Vol. 1, 1982–1995 (2010)
    edited by Robert J. Randisi

Editor

Tricks and Treats, with Joe Gores (1976)

Midnight Specials (1977)

Mystery Writers' Choice, with Joe Gores (1977)

The Edgar Winners (1980)

Great Tales of Mystery and Suspense, with Martin H. Greenberg and Barry N. Malzberg (1981)

The Arbor House Treasury of Mystery and Suspense, with Martin H. Greenberg and Barry N. Malzberg (1982)

Arbor House Treasury of Detective and Mystery Stories from the Great Pulps (1983)

The Web She Weaves, with Marcia Muller (1983)

Child's Ploy, with Marcia Muller (1984)

The Mystery Hall of Fame: An Anthology of Classic Mystery and Suspense Stories Selected by Mystery Writers of America, with Martin H. Greenberg and Charles G Waugh (1984)

Chapter and Hearse, with Marcia Muller (1985)

Dark Lessons: Crime And Detection On Campus, with Marcia Muller (1985)

Deadly Arts, with Marcia Muller (1985)

The Ethnic Detectives: Masterpieces of Mystery Fiction, with Martin H. Greenberg (1985)

Murder in the First Reel, with Martin H. Greenberg and Charles G. Waugh (1985)

The Wickedest Show on Earth, with Marcia Muller (1985)

Women Sleuths, with Martin H. Greenberg (1985)

Great Modern Police Stories (1986)

Locked Room Puzzles 3, with Martin H. Greenberg (1986)

Mystery in the Mainstream: An Anthology of Literary Crimes, with Martin H. Greenberg (1986)

101 Mystery Stories (1986)

Tales of Mystery (1986)

Tales of the Dead (1986)

Manhattan Mysteries, with Martin H. Greenberg and Carol-Lynn Waugh (1987)

Prime Suspects, with Martin H. Greenberg (1987)

Suspicious Characters, with Martin H. Greenberg (1987)

Uncollected Crimes, with Martin H. Greenberg (1987)

Cloak and Dagger: A Treasury of 35 Great Espionage Stories, with Martin H. Greenberg (1988)

Criminal Elements, with Martin H. Greenberg (1988)

Homicidal Acts, with Martin H. Greenberg (1988)

Deadly Doings (1989)

Felonious Assaults, with Martin H. Greenberg (1989)

Kill or Cure: Suspense Stories About the World of Medicine, with Marcia Muller (1989)

Crime and Crime Again: Unexpected Mystery Stories by the World's Great Writers, with Martin H. Greenberg and Barry N. Malzberg (1990)

Night Freight (1992)

Hard-boiled, with Jack Adrian (1995)

American Pulp, with Ed Gorman (1997)

A Century of Mystery: 1980–1989, with Marcia Muller (1997)

Detective Duos, with Marcia Muller (1997)

Giant Book of Short Crime Stories, with Martin H. Greenberg (1997)

Giant Book of Private Eye Stories, with Martin H. Greenberg (1997)

Duo, with Marcia Muller (1998)

Pure Pulp, with Ed Gorman and Martin H. Greenberg (1999)

Marksman and Other Stories by William Campbell Gault (2002)

The Danger Zone: Stories by Erle Stanlely Gardner (2004)

The Casebook of Sidney Zoom: Stories by Erle Stanley Gardner (2006)

The Exploits of the Patent Leather Kid: Stories by Erle Stanley Gardner (2010)

Ten Thousand Blunt Instruments: Stories by Philip Wylie (2010)

Writing as Alex Saxon

A Run in Diamonds (1973)

The Dying Time (1999)

Writing as Jack Foxx

The Jade Figure (1972)

Dead Run (1975)

Freebooty (1976)

Wildfire (1978)

Writing as William Jeffrey

Duel at Gold Buttes, with Jeffrey Wallman (1981)

Border Fever, with Jeffrey Wallman (1983)

Day of the Moon (1983)

Writing as Robert Hart Davis, Charlie Chan Series

Charlie Chan in the Pawns of Death (2002)

Charlie Chan in The Temple of the Golden Horde (2002)

The author has also written science fiction and western novels; edited science fiction, horror, and western anthologies; and written nonfiction books in the mystery genre.

For Further Information

Bill Pronzini interview, *Mystery Scene* No. 68, 2000.

Bill Pronzini profile, Thrilling Detectives, http://www.thrillingdetective.com/trivia/pronzini.html/ (viewed Oct. 24, 2009).

Carlson, Joseph L., *Mourners* review, *Library Journal*, May 1, 2006.

Carpenter and Quincannon review, *Publishers Weekly*, Oct. 26, 1998.

Fletcher, Connie, "Story behind the Story: Bill Pronzini's Fever," *Booklist*, May 1, 2008.

Grape, Jan, "Interview: Pronzini and Muller," *Mystery Scene* 33 (1991).

Jordan, Jon, Bill Pronzini interview, Books 'n Bytes, August 2002, http://www.booksnbytes.com/auth_interviews/bill_pronzini.html/ (viewed Oct. 24, 2009).

Shechter, Andi, Marcia Muller and Bill Pronzini interview, *Library Journal*, July 15, 2006.

Ian Rankin

Cardenden, Fife, Scotland
1960

Police Procedural
Benchmark Series: Inspector Rebus

Rankin

About the Author and the Author's Writing

Ian Rankin wouldn't so hastily have named his Edinburgh policeman hero had he known that *Knots and Crosses* (1987) would be the start of such a successful series. He offhandedly thought that Oxford had an Inspector Morse (in books written by Colin Dexter), a code, so he would have an Inspector Rebus, a puzzle.

The first novel was an attempt to recast Robert Louis Stevenson's *Dr. Jekyll and Mr. Hyde*. Rankin then wrote a thriller, and only when his publisher asked for another Rebus did he revisit Rebus, and secondary characters such as Siobhan Clarke, with new interest.

"The reasons I keep writing about them, especially Rebus, is that there are still things I don't know about them. Rebus continues to surprise me and there are bits of his history I don't know about, bits of his psychology," the author told interviewer George Lewis.

When readers first met John Rebus, the policeman was 40. He was 60 by the time of *Exit Music* (2007), described as the inspector's final case (though the author has left room for more stories of the crime solver in retirement).

While Rankin has been true to time with his prickly character and delved more deeply into his psyche with each book, he has been more cavalier with the conventions of crime fiction. In *The Writer*, he said the hero often seems like "something of a cipher, dragging the plot forward." Miraculously, by the last chapter, there was resolution. "Real life isn't like that. I want the novels to be realistic to the extent that [they aren't] always neatly wrapped up at the end."

Ian Rankin was born in Cardenden, Fife, Scotland, in 1960. He earned an M.A. (with honors) in American literature from the University of Edinburgh in 1982. He and his wife, Miranda Harvey, have two sons. Rankin's life experience was diverse, to say the least. He tended pigs, collected taxes, sang in a punk rock band, and researched alcohol use among teens. He began work toward a Ph.D. in Scottish literature, then decided to write fiction instead. His first novel, *The Flood*, came out in 1986. Four years later he became a full-time writer.

Rankin knew little about true police procedures, so he shadowed real detectives working out of a station in Leith. He later said that when he described his plot idea to them, it was so close to an actual case they were working on that they gave him a grilling first hand.

He was content to turn out his series novels, one a year, until his publisher began to yawn. With *Black and Blue* (1997), he changed course. He based the story on a real-life crime. His inspiration came in part from reading the dark crime novels of James Ellroy. *Black and Blue* won the Crime Writers' Association Gold Dagger and was nominated for a Mystery Writers of America Edgar.

The character of Rebus changed in that book. "He was much more erudite than he should be [in the first books]," Rankin told *Contemporary Authors*, "basically he's got too much of Ian Rankin peering out of his eyes."

The author still disdained violence. "I don't think you need to be graphic," he told Bookreporter. "In fact, I feel graphic violence is both lazy and salacious. You can allude to horror without sticking people's noses in it."

The author's audience appreciated the new direction. "What makes Rankin's Rebus tales so appealing is their distinctly unappealing main protagonist," summarized J. Kingston Pierce in *January Magazine*. "Rebus is cynical, antisocial and full of barely repressed anger, a cop who harbors animosities and makes terrible blunders out of impatience. Yet he is also an attentive observer and a relentless investigator."

Rebus exhibited a fondness for alcohol—something that did not go unnoticed by Orkney distillers Highland Park, which honored the fictional drinker with his own single malt, Rebus20.

Rankin is at the top of his form. As reviewer Mark Sanderson wrote of *Exit Music* in *The Evening Standard*, "Every page crackles with energy. Ian Rankin's skill and pawky wit make even the most routine interview a pleasure to read."

Reviewer N. J. Cooper, in the *Globe and Mail*, echoed the praise in discussing *The Complaints* (2009): "if the point of crime fiction is to make you think while entertaining you—and I believe it is—then Ian Rankin definitely does it better than most."

Rankin has written a handful of standalone novels, and four books issued originally under the penname Jack Harvey. Even though he has retired Rebus, he has no intention to quit writing.

Professional as he is, Rankin still encounters interesting challenges, such as when he wrote what he anticipated would be the first of a trilogy about the Scottish parliament. "But a guy who was going to be in all three books, well, I bumped him off on page 50," he said in a Mystery One interview. "Didn't want to; the story made me do it. No idea who killed him or why."

Such are the challenges for the hard-working mystery novelist.

Works by the Author

The Flood (1986)

Watchman (1988)

Westwind (1990)

Death Is Not the End (1998)

Doors Open (2008)

The Complaints (2009)

A Cool Head (2009), entry in Quick Reads Series

Dark Entries, with Werther Dell'Edera (2009), graphic novel

Inspector Rebus Series

Knots and Crosses (1987)

Hide and Seek (1990)

A Good Hanging: And Other Stories (1992)

Strip Jack (1992)

Tooth and Nail (1992), also issued as *Wolfman*

The Black Book (1993)

Mortal Causes (1994)

Let It Bleed (1995)

Black and Blue (1997)

The Hanging Garden (1998)

Dead Souls (1999)

Rebus: The Early Years (1999), omnibus

Set in Darkness (2000)

The Falls (2001)

Rebus: The St Leonard's Years (2001), omnibus

Three Great Novels: Strip Jack/The Black Book/Mortal Causes (2001)

Resurrection Men (2002)

A Question of Blood (2003)

Rebus: The Lost Years (2003), omnibus

Capital Crimes (2004), omnibus

Fleshmarket Close (2004), also issued as *Fleshmarket Alley*

The Naming of the Dead (2006)

Exit Music (2007)

Collections

A Good Hanging and Other Stories (1992)

Herbert in Motion: And Other Stories (1997)

Beggars Banquet (2002)

Complete Short Stories: The Hanging Garden, Beggars Banquet, and *Atonement* (2005)

Editor

Ian Rankin Presents Criminal Minded: A Collection of Short Fiction from Canongate Crime (2000)

Contributor

One City, with Alexander McCall Smith and Irvine Welsh (2006)

Crimespotting (2009)

Ox-Tales: Earth (2009)

Written as by Jack Harvey, reprinted as by Ian Rankin

Witch Hunt (1993)

Bleeding Hearts (1994)

Blood Hunt (1995)

The Jack Harvey Novels (2000), omnibus

Adaptations in Other Media

Four Rebus mysteries were adapted for ITV telefilms. The author hosted *Ian Rankin's Evil Thoughts* on the BBC (2002) and was a contributor to BBC2's *Newsnight Review*.

Selected Nonfiction

Rebus' Scotland: A Personal Journey (2004)

For Further Information

Cooper, N. J., *The Complaints* review, *Globe and Mail*, Sept. 11, 2009.

Ephron, Hallie, "Inspector Rebus Takes the Crime Novel to a New Level," *The Writer*, Dec. 2007.

Ian Rankin entry, Contemporary Authors Online, http://galenet.galegroup.com/servlet/BioRC/ (viewed Aug. 7, 2009).

Ian Rankin interview, Bookreporter, Aug. 7, 2009, http://www.bookreporter.com/authors/au-rankin-ian.asp#top/ (viewed Aug. 26, 2009).

Ian Rankin interview, Murder One Bookstore, http://www.mysteryone.com/IanRankin.htm/ (viewed Aug. 26, 2009).

Ian Rankin website, http://www.ianrankin.net/ (viewed Aug. 26, 2009).

Keller, Julia, "Inspector Rebus Solves His Final Case," *Chicago Tribune*, Oct. 11, 2008.

Lewis, George, "Making it Up," Powells.com, http://www.powells.com/authors/rankin.html/ (viewed Aug. 26, 2009).

Maslin, Janet, "Scottish Detective Goes off into the Heater. Is He over the Hill?" *New York Times*, Sept. 24, 2008.

Pierce, J. Kingston, "Ian Rankin: The Accidental Crime Writer," *January Magazine,* http://januarymagazine.com/profiles/ianrankin.html/ (viewed Aug. 26, 2009).

Penzler, Otto, ed. *The Lineup: The World's Greatest Crime Writers Tell the Inside Story of Their Greatest Detectives*. New York: Little, Brown, 2009.

Sanderson, Mark, *Exit Music* review, *Evening Standard*, Sept. 3, 2007.

Simpson, Alan, "Rebus Malt? I'll Drink to That, Says Detective," *Daily Mail*, Nov. 23, 2006.

Peter Robinson

Castleford, Yorkshire, England
1950

Police Procedural
Benchmark Series: Inspector Alan Banks

Jerry Bauer

About the Author and the Author's Writing

Peter Robinson splits his time between continents. His time in Toronto, Ontario, serves him well, he has said, as it gives him wonderful perspective from which to shape his fictional British characters and settings. The Eastvale of his books is based on Ripon and Richmond (where he now lives part of the year) in North Yorkshire, England. "I had to make it much larger than those towns, of course, otherwise who would believe there could be that many murders? I've probably killed the population of the Yorkshire Dales three times over as it is!" he said on his web page.

Robinson's richly textured, deeply plotted, and entertaining crime novels feature Chief Inspector Alan Banks. In the course of the series Banks loses a wife, Sandra, and one girlfriend, Detective Inspector Annie Cabbot; but cultivates another, Detective Inspector Michelle Hart. Over time, his hero has become increasingly a loner, Robinson told interviewer Michael Connelly. While Robinson hasn't planned Banks's personal travails very far ahead,

> He does seem to be becoming increasingly isolated and introspective, but whether this will change significantly in future books, I don't know yet. I can see him working more urban cases, which might even mean a transfer to West Yorkshire, to my hometown of Leeds.

The key word here is *change*; Robinson is not at all reluctant to allow his hero to mature and change.

Robinson was born in Castleford, Yorkshire, England, in 1950, the son of a photographer and a homemaker. Growing up in England, his first attempts at writing were retellings of "Robin Hood" and other stories, complete with his own illustrations, in a notebook. After he earned a B.A., with honors, from the University of Leeds in 1974, he went to Canada to study creative writing at the University of Windsor in Ontario. "I think the main thing I learned from Joyce Carol Oates [his instructor there] was to take myself seriously as a writer, to believe in myself," he said in a HarperCollins interview.

In 1983, he completed requirements for a Ph.D. at York University in Ontario. He is married to Sheila Halladay, a lawyer.

Reading his father's copies of books by Raymond Chandler and Georges Simenon inspired Robinson to try his hand at a mystery novel.

"Crime fiction was immediately attractive because of its formal and structured nature," he said in an interview on the HarperCollins web page, "though I have tried to move away from some of the stricter requirements since then—that's probably what keeps me there, the feeling that you can push at the boundaries, go further with each book."

Opera-loving Banks is freshly arrived in the Dales in the first book, *Gallows View* (1987), but he finds the countryside far from tranquil, as he has to immediately deal with a peeping tom, a burglar, and a murderer. While he may have similarities to Simenon's Inspector Jules Maigret or Rendell's Chief Inspector Reginald Wexford, Robinson said he has made him more modern, more musical, more political, more proletarian, and more rebellious.

Solving the puzzle is only part of his task, Robinson believes.

"I'm far more interested in what combination of circumstances caused a person to commit a crime," he told Tim Peters of *Publishers Weekly*. "My novels are often less about Banks as detective than they are about Banks and what happens to the people around him, in his work and his life."

A full-time writer since 1987, Robinson has also taught community college writing and literature classes for 20 years. Hobbies include music, reading, travel, walking, and visiting pubs.

Among Robinson's awards are the Mystery Writers of Canada Arthur Ellis Awards in 1990 and 1991 for *The Hanging Valley* (1989) and *Past Reason Hated* (1991), respectively, and a French Grand Prix de Littérateur Policiére in 2000 for *In a Dry Season* (1999). He has also received the British Crime Writers Association Dagger in the Library award.

"Robinson quietly pushes the boundaries of crime fiction while shrugging off the genre wars," observed Brian Bethune in *Maclean's*.

He does not try to replicate true-life conversation. "I just look at dialogue as an extension of narrative," he said in *The Writer*. "I try to keep in mind that when two people are talking, each wants something from the other or is trying to get something across. I think if you keep that in mind, it helps you to focus the dialogue."

The author does not outline his books. He starts with a plot nugget and watches it develop. He commented further in a Mystery One conversation,

> I let the characters and events take me places, and sometimes those places turn out to be dead ends. It's not a method I'd recommend. I always tell my students to know how their story ends before they begin writing it, but [I] don't practice that technique myself.

What a crime.

Works by the Author

Fiction

The First Cut (1990), published in Great Britain as *Caedmon's Song*

No Cure for Love (1995)

Inspector Banks Series

Gallows View (1987)

A Dedicated Man (1988)

The Hanging Valley (1989)

A Necessary End (1989)

Past Reason Hated (1991)

Wednesday's Child (1992)

Final Account (1994), published in Great Britain as *Dry Bones That Dream*

No Cure for Love (1995)

Innocent Graves (1996)

Blood at the Root (1997), published in Great Britain as *Dead Right*

Cold is the Grave (2000)

Aftermath (2001)

Close to Home (2002), published in Great Britain as *The Summer That Never Was*

Playing With Fire (2004)

Strange Affair (2005)

Piece of My Heart (2006)

Friend of the Devil (2007)

All the Colors of Darkness (2008)

The Price of Love, and Other Stories (2009)

Bad Boy (2010)

Collections

Not Safe After Dark (1998)

In a Dry Season (1999)

Contributor

Cold Blood II, edited by Peter Sellers (1989), includes "Fan Mail"

Cold Blood III, edited by Peter Sellers (1990), includes "Innocence"

Canadian Mystery Stories, edited by Albergo Manguel (1991), includes "Fan Mail"

Cold Blood IV, edited by Peter Sellers (1992), includes "Anna Said . . . " (Banks short story)

Criminal Shorts, edited by Howard Engel and Eric Wright (1992), includes "Not Safe After Dark"

Year's Best Mystery and Suspense Stories, 1992, edited by Edward D. Hoch (1992), includes "Innocence"

Cold Blood V, edited by Peter Sellers (1994), includes "Lawn Sale"

No Alibi, edited by Maxim Jakubowski (1995), includes "Carrion"

Best American Mystery Stories 1997, edited by Robert B. Parker (1997)

First Cases 2, edited by Robert J Randisi (1997), includes "Anna Said . . ."

Malice Domestic 6, edited by Anne Perry (1997), includes "The Two Ladies of Rose Cottage"

Blue Lightning, edited by John Harvey (1998), includes "Blue Lightning"

Best American Mystery Stories 1999, edited by Ed McBain (1999)

Television Programs Based on the Author's Work

Aftermath (2010, ITV), based on the novel

For Further Information

Bethune, Brian, "Working-class Boys Made Good," *Maclean's*, Feb. 23, 2004.

Colley, Kimberly, *Closer to Home* review, *RT Bookclub* (Feb. 2003).

Peter Robinson interview, HarperCollins, http://www.harpercollins.com/hc/features/mystery/0380978083fea.asp/ (viewed Apr. 21, 2003).

Peter Robinson interview, Mystery One bookstore, http://www.mysteryone.com/PeterRobinsonInterview.htm/ (viewed Apr. 20, 2003).

Peter Robinson website, http://www.inspectorbanks.com/ (viewed Aug. 6, 2009)

Peters, Tim, "Inspector Banks Goes Home (PW Talks with Peter Robinson)," *Publishers Weekly* (Dec. 9, 2002).

Robinson, Peter, "How I write," *The Writer* (Sept. 2003).

David Rosenfelt

Brandy Allen

Paterson, New Jersey
1949

Amateur Detective, Legal Mystery
Benchmark Series: Andy Carpenter

About the Author and the Author's Writing

When we first meet him in David Rosenfelt's *Open and Shut* (2002), Andy Carpenter is a New Jersey lawyer with low aspirations. His dying father, a former district attorney, makes an unusual request: Represent Willis Miller in an appeal of his conviction for the murder of Denise McGregor in the alley behind a bar in Teaneck, New Jersey. Nelson Carpenter has new details about the case, but he dies before he can pass them on. And he leaves his son $22 million. So Andy feels obliged to help Miller get off death row.

Oh, and there's a subplot. Dogs. "There is nothing like a golden retriever," Andy Carpenter says at one point. "I know, I know, it's a big planet with a lot of wonderful things, but golden retrievers are the absolute best. Mine is named Tara."

Mystery fiction is a third career for Rosenfelt, who was born in 1949 in Paterson, New Jersey. He graduated from New York University and went to work for his uncle's business—United Artists. Rosenfelt became president of marketing for Tri-Star Pictures.

"I left the movie marketing business, to the sustained applause of hundreds of disgruntled producers and directors," he said on his web page. "I decided to try my hand at writing. I wrote and sold a bunch of feature films, none of which ever came close to being actually filmed, and then a bunch of TV movies." He wrote 12 film screenplays and 10 teleplays, one of which was the 2000 TNT picture *Deadlocked*, featuring Charles Dutton and David Caruso, and the 2005 Lifetime feature *Deadly Isolation* with Sherilyn Fenn.

Then he had an idea for a book. That book grew into a series.

"I don't consider myself a real writer because I came to it so late in life," he said. "I never learned the process. I just sat down and did it."

The result was a cleverly plotted courtroom drama with a wisecracking hero who deftly maneuvers his client to freedom. Suddenly a man of wealth, the first thing Andy Carpenter does is create a foundation to help homeless dogs.

And that's just what the author himself, together with his wife, did in establishing the Tara Foundation in 2002, named for a favored pet (a golden retriever, naturally) that died of cancer. At any given time, the Rosenfelt household in southern California has two dozen or more guests, usually elderly dogs waiting to find a retirement home.

"We rescued almost 4,000 dogs, many of them Goldens, and found them loving homes," he told interviewer Rochelle Lesser.

Our own home quickly became a sanctuary for those dogs that we rescued that were too old or sickly to be wanted by others. They surround me as I write this. It's total lunacy, but it works, and they are a happy, safe group.

Rosenfelt is a friendly, affable man, much like his hero.

"As satisfying as the nuts and bolts of the case are," said *Publishers Weekly* in a review of the second book, *First Degree* (2003), it's the sheer likability of Andy and the odd assortment of his friends and a staff that lifts the story from merely enjoyable to genuinely delightful."

Carpenter temporarily loses his love interest when police detective Laurie Collins pulls up stakes to take a position as police chief in Wisconsin. When she phones for help with a case, he is again by her side.

Rosenfelt has created another hero, Tim Wallace in *Don't Tell a Soul* (2008), co-owner of a small construction company who has to figure out who's trying to sabotage his business. Thomas Gaughan in *Booklist* called it "high-voltage entertainment from an author who plots and writes with the verve and wit of Elmore Leonard."

Rosenfelt acknowledges as his favorite writers Robert B. Parker, Lee Child, Michael Connelly, and Harlan Coben.

While Rosenfelt has written a second stand-alone thriller, he is not likely to stray far from Carpenter.

"I've just always found the courtroom to be an amazing source of human drama," he told Melissa Mia Hall of *Publishers Weekly*. "[I] don't think there's any moment with more tension than when a verdict is being read. Besides that, lawyer is the only job I can think of where one can be argumentative and badgering and be praised for it."

Works by the Author

Don't Tell a Soul (2008)

Down to the Wire (2010)

On Borrowed Time (2011)

Andy Carpenter Series

Open and Shut (2002)

First Degree (2003)

Bury the Lead (2004)

Sudden Death (2005)

Dead Center (2006)

Play Dead (2007)

New Tricks (2009)

Dog Tags (2010)

For Further Information

David Rosenfelt website. http://www.davidrosenfelt.com/ (viewed Sept. 2, 2009).

First Degree review, *Publishers Weekly*, March 10, 2003.

Gauthan, Thomas, *Don't Tell a Soul* review, *Booklist,* May 1, 2008.

Geiger, Mia, "Success Is Golden for This Dog Lover," *Denver Post*, Aug. 10, 2008.

Hall, Melissa Mia, "Andy in the Endzone: PW Talks with David Rosenfelt," *Publishers Weekly*, Mar. 7, 2005.

Lesser, Rochelle, "Golden Retriever Rescuer & Author, David Rosenfelt," Land of PureGold Foundation, Sept. 5, 2007, http://landofpuregold.wordpress.com/2007/09/05/golden-retriever-rescuer-author-david-rosenfelt/ (viewed Sept. 16, 2009).

New Tricks review, *USA Today*, Aug. 6, 2009.

Pitt, David, *Dead Center* review, *Booklist*, Mar. 15, 2006.

C. J. Sansom

Location not identified
1952

Amateur Detective, Historical Mystery, Legal Mystery
Benchmark Series: Matthew Shardlake

About the Author and the Author's Writing

C. J. Sansom is a lawyer who writes about a lawyer/crime solver. But there the comparison with John Grisham ends. Matthew Shardlake, Sansom's series character, wears robe and cape rather than a Brooks Brothers suit. His practice, after all, is in 16th century England during the reign of Henry VIII.

Sansom was born in England in 1952. He obtained a law degree from Birmingham University and was in practice for several years before he wrote his first medieval mystery, *Dissolution* (2003). He long aspired to be a writer, but only after becoming secure in his law career was he able to take the time to try it. John Le Carre, P. D. James, Ruth Rendell, and John Steinbeck are among his favorite authors. An avid amateur historian, he was keen on the period when monasteries were in turmoil.

"To interpret the time to modern readers," he said in an interview on the Penguin website, "I needed a protagonist who was 'apart' from his time—through intellectual rigor and honesty, but also in more subtle ways." Shardlake is a hunchback; "perhaps it symbolizes the weight he carries as a person of integrity in that grim time."

Sansom needed a wise hero to sort out the intricate plots he devises. The author admitted that his legal background provides him both with the compulsion to explore difficult themes and crimes and to construct them. He typically writes a first chapter and then outlines in good detail where things will go. This tightness, however, still allows some flexibility for plot twists and character development as he works his way through the manuscript.

In *Dissolution*, Shardlake confronts a series of killings on the grounds of a monastery. It is the time of the English Reformation and Lord Thomas Cromwell, King Henry VIII's vicar, is on a tirade against Catholics. When Cromwell's first investigator is killed, Shardlake is handed the assignment to solve the murders. He and his companion, Mark Poer, are soon embroiled in intrigue.

"Shardlake is a memorable protagonist, a compassionate man committed to Cromwell's reforms, but increasingly doubtful of the motives of his fellow reformers," said a *Publishers Weekly* reviewer. "With this cunningly plotted and darkly atmospheric effort, Sansom proves himself to be a promising newcomer."

The author isn't just interested in the past for history's sake; he's also interested in how it can relate to the modern day. "Though he avoids any allegorizing of characters or scenes, Sansom wrestles with issues that still press upon us," said Ralph C. Wood in *The Christian Century*, "the loss of faith, the rise of the tyrannous nation-states, the seizure of wealth by political machination, the pandemic of fear lying just beneath the surface of things, the cruel violence underlying everything."

In *Revelation* (2009), Shardlake has to figure out a youth who has been imprisoned in Bedlam for his religious rantings. The case soon involves murder. "Like its predecessors, this installment in the series is sophisticated entertainment, with an intricately but not confusingly wrought plot," Brad Hooper said in a review for *Booklist*.

Sansom's standing as a historical novelist gained him entry to The Medieval Murders consortium within the Crime Writers' Association. He, Philip Gooden, Susanna Gregory, Michael Jecks, Bernard Knight, Philip Gooden, Simon Beaufort, and Ian Morson in various combinations have written a half dozen Historical Mystery books of murder, magic and mayhem so far. Each follows a single object or artifact through time.

Sansom moved forward in history for the novel *Winter in Madrid* (2007), a crime story set against the backdrop of the Spanish Civil War. This book required new research and the author is a stickler for accuracy. "Everything about what was going on politically at the period is accurate," he said in a BookBrowse conversation, "and I have made the setting as authentic as I can. On one or two occasions where I have made small alterations to historical fact, I have said so in the Historical Note."

The story is about Harry Brett, a British Intelligence agent, and the unexpected trouble he gets into in pursuit of Madrid businessman and Franco associate Sandy Forsyth. "Sansom deftly plots his politically charged tale for maximal suspense," said *Publishers Weekly*, "all the way up to its stunning conclusion."

The book was a challenge, Sansom said on his Pan Macmillan web page. "You don't have a framework of characters and settings in a standalone, and in *Winter in Madrid* there were three third-person narrators, not one first-person narrator. That gives you a great deal more freedom, but it is hard work."

Sansom is not averse to a challenge, however, as his fan base shows.

Works by the Author

Winter in Madrid (2007)

Matthew Shardlake Series

Dissolution (2003)

Dark Fire (2005)

Sovereign (2006)

Revelation (2008)

Heartstone (2011)

Contributor to Historical Mysteries issued as by The Medieval Murderers

The Tainted Relic (2005)

Sword of Shame (2006)

House of Shadows (2007)

The Lost Prophecies (2008)

King Arthur's Bones (2009)

The Sacred Stone (2010)

For Further Information

C. J. Sansom interview, Historical Novels, http://www.historicalnovels.info/CJ-Sansom.html/ (viewed Jan. 9, 2010).

C. J. Sansom interview, Pan Macmillan, http://www.panmacmillan.com/Interviews/ (viewed Jan. 9, 2010).

C. J. Sansom interview, Penguin, http://us.penguingroup.com/static/rguides/us/dissolution.html/ (viewed Jan. 9, 2010).

"Conversation with C. J. Sansom, Author of *Winter in Madrid*," BookBrowse, http://www.bookbrowse.com/author_interviews/full/index.cfm?author_number=1517/ (viewed Jan. 9, 2010).

Dissolution review, *Publishers Weekly*, Mar. 17, 2003.

Hooper, Brad, *Revelation* review, *Booklist*, Feb. 15, 2009.

Medieval Murderers, Michael Jecks website, http://www.michaeljecks.co.uk/medievalmurder/index.html/ (viewed Jan. 9, 2010).

Winter in Madrid review, *Publishers Weekly*, Sept. 24, 2007.

Wood, Ralph C., "Mysteries and Morals: The Historical Fiction of C. J. Sansom" *The Christian Century,* May 1, 2007.

Martin Cruz Smith

Reading, Pennsylvania
1942

Police Procedural, Historical Mystery
Benchmark Series: Arkady Renko

About the Author and the Author's Writing

During the heart of the Cold War, the rest of the world held a rather grim picture of what life was like inside the Soviet Union. Paperback novelist Martin Cruz Smith had an idea for an ambitious hardcover novel about forensic reconstruction of a victim's face. He wanted to have an American policeman visit the USSR.

Once he went to the country, collected information, made sketches, interviewed a few people—without authorities being concerned—he changed his mind. He wanted a Russian as his main character. Thus emerged Arkady Renko, a dour investigator in Moscow who appeared in Smith's first novel, *Gorky Park*, in 1981—and he has lived on in six more novels, in which he has seen the fall of the Berlin Wall, the fracture of the Soviet Union, and the continued horror of Siberia. Amid the gloom, he does find a romantic interest, Irina. For a brief time, Renko carries on.

"Deep down Renko is a patriot," Timothy L. O'Brien wrote in the *New York Times*. "He loves the promise of Russia—its poetry, music and people—even though he is routinely battered and emotionally scarred. That's also why he's so often disgusted with the operatic corruption and indignities that swarm around him." Renko should leave, but he can't.

Martin William Smith was born in 1942 in Reading, Pennsylvania. His father was a jazz musician, his mother a jazz singer and Native American activist. In 1964 he received a B.A. from the University of Pennsylvania. He married Emily Arnold in 1968; they have three children. After spending several years as a journalist, he worked as a writer and editor from 1966 to 1969 at *For Men Only* magazine. He wrote novels under the pseudonym Simon Quinn and two early Slocum paperback westerns for Playboy Press in 1976 and 1977. Smith continued to write the series for successor publisher Berkley from 1990 on. He also wrote novels under his own name, including *Nightwing* (1977). With an unanticipated windfall from *Nightwing*'s production as a film, Smith was able to complete his long-in-the-works manuscript about a crime in Moscow. His original publisher balked, so Smith paid back his advance and held out for a $1 million advance from another publisher.

With the appearance of *Gorky Park*, the author substituted his mother's middle name for his, to become Martin Cruz Smith. The public's reaction was enthusiastic. The book sold some 6 million copies.

"Martin Cruz Smith has managed to combine the gritty atmosphere of a Moscow police squad room with a story of detection as neatly done as any English manor-house puzzlement," said reviewer Peter Andrews in the *New York Times Book Review*. "I have no idea as to the accuracy of Mr. Smith's descriptions of Russian police operations. But they ring as true as crystal."

The author's intense research—he had visited Moscow in 1973—paid off. The only ones disappointed were the Soviet bureaucrats, who banned the novel and barred Smith from the country.

Smith returned to Russia several times, but only in print. *Wolves Eat Dogs* (2005) drops Renko into the investigation of a businessman's suicide. A second death and various clues lead the investigator to Chernobyl, site of a nuclear reactor meltdown in 1986.

Why Chernobyl? "People speak so glibly about nuclear power," Smith told *USA Today*, "but Chernobyl is a reference point that people don't know about. So this is as much a story about what will happen someplace else." Again, the author immersed himself in the story, speaking with members of the Russian mob and actually getting as close to Chernobyl as safety would allow.

Smith went on to place novels in Cuba and Japan, partly from a longtime interest in sociology. As he said in *Geographical*,

> The interesting aspect of writing a detective novel from a sociological point of view is that you're allowed to examine society—you're allowed to ask questions of your betters and you're forced to ask questions of those worse of than you. It's a great vehicle for examining much more than just a murder mystery.

As concerned as he is with the accuracy of his characters and setting, Smith deals loosely with his plot outlines. In *Tokyo Station*, also titled *December 6* (2001), "I had no idea where this story was going," he told *Publishers Weekly*'s Dorman T. Shindler. He placed several characters in a room, among them the war hero Ishigami. "I let Ishigami take over. And Ishigami, as those who read the book will learn, is a character given to drastic and immediate solutions."

It's less the plot than the movement toward resolution that interests Smith. "What appeals to me about this genre is the excuse it gives a character to ask really hard questions that would otherwise land him in jail," he told Anna Mundrow for *The Boston Globe*. Investigators—at least the ones I know—are slightly dubious characters socially. But they can open the book on society and read it."

Works by the Author

The Indians Won (1970)

The Analog Bullet (1972)

Nightwing (1977)

Stallion Gate (1986)

Rose (1996)

Tokyo Station (2001) also titled *December 6*

Roman Grey Series

Gypsy in Amber (1971)

Canto for a Gypsy (1972)

Arkady Renko Series

> *Gorky Park* (1981)
>
> *Polar Star* (1989)
>
> *Polar Star/Gorky Park* (1991)
>
> *Red Square* (1992)
>
> *Havana Bay* (1999)
>
> *Polar Star/Rose* (2002)
>
> *Gorky Park/Nightwing* (2003)
>
> *Wolves Eat Dogs* (2004)
>
> *Stalin's Ghost* (2006)
>
> *The Golden Mile* (2009)
>
> *Three Stations* (2010)

Editor

> *Death by Espionage: Intriguing Stories of Betrayal and Deception* (1970)

Written as Simon Quinn

> *Human Factor* (1975)

Inquisitor Series

> *The Devil in Kansas* (1974)
>
> *His Eminence, Death* (1974)
>
> *The Last Time I Saw Hell* (1974)
>
> *Nuplex Red* (1974)
>
> *Last Rites for the Vulture* (1975)
>
> *The Midas Coffin* (1975)

Films based on the author's work

> *The Art of Crime* (1975), screenwriter, based on *Gypsy in Amber*
>
> *Nightwing* (1979), screenwriter, based on the novel
>
> *Gorky Park* (1983), based on the novel

> The author has also written Slocum western novels under the house name Jake Logan.

For Further Information

Amodeo, Christian, "Q&A: Martin Cruz Smith," *Geographical*, Dec. 2002.

Andrews, Peter, "Murder in Moscow, Arkady Renko on the Case," *New York Times Book Review*, Apr. 5, 1981.

Majewski, Sophie, "Working in a Coal Mine," Salon.com, http://www.salon.com/weekly/interview960520.html/ (viewed Oct. 1, 2009).

Martin Cruz Smith website, http://literati.net/MCSmith/ (viewed Oct. 1, 2009).

Mundow, Anna, "Inside Renko, and a Darker Russia," *Boston Globe*, June 17, 2007.

Nawotka, Edward, "Gorky Park Author Answers Call of Russia with Wolves," *USA Today*, Jan. 6, 2005.

O'Brien, Timothy, "Martin Cruz Smith's Arkady Renko Series: A Trail of Clues to the Russian Soul," *New York Times*, Aug. 6, 2007.

Ott, Bill, *Stalin's Ghost* review, *Booklist*, May 1, 2007.

Shindler, Dorman T., "PW Talks with Martin Cruz Smith," *Publishers Weekly*, Aug. 5, 2002.

Julia Spencer-Fleming

Plattsburgh, New York
Date not revealed

Amateur Detective, Police Procedural,
Ecclesiastical Mystery
Benchmark Series: Clare Fergusson/Russ
Van Alstyne

Lisa Bowe

About the Author and the Author's Writing

Miller's Kill, New York, exists only in Julia Spencer-Fleming's murder mysteries. But it's close enough to communities around Plattsburgh, where the author was born, to be emblematic both of the Adirondack region and of small towns across America.

The setting and, of course, the characters who flow in and out, provide the author with a lively backdrop to explore a variety of themes ranging from abandoned babies to migrant workers to soldiers returning from the Iraq war.

Julia Spencer-Fleming, a self-described military brat, grew up in New York, Alabama, Italy, and Germany. Her father died when she was six months old when the B-47 he was flying out of an Air Force Base in Plattsburgh crashed on a training mission. Her mother remarried, and the author took a hyphenated last name, combining the names of her birth father Spencer and her stepfather Fleming.

She graduated from Ithaca College and George Washington University and received her J.D. from the University of Maine. After practicing law for a few years, she took a break from law to stay at home with her young children and decided to write a mystery novel. (She and her husband, Ross Hugo-Vidal, have three children.) She admits that the earliest mystery she read was Walter Brooks's Freddy the Detective. But she quickly caught up on current writers and credits Margaret Maron and Archer Mayor with making strong use of setting in their South Carolina and Vermont crime novels, respectively.

Even though she now lives in Maine, she still had a keen recollection of the rich topography and the tired communities of upper New York State. So she chose that setting.

"The books take an unsentimental look at the hardscrabble existence in an economically depressed Adirondack town, explore the life-altering effect of violence on people's lives, and include what I hope is heart-pounding, adrenalin-inducing action," the author said on her website.

For a detective, she wanted someone who could logically be at the center of things and ask the necessary questions. She decided on an Episcopal priest. But Clare Fergusson wasn't just any minister. "I wanted to have extremely dynamic stories and I thought by giving her a military background [as a helicopter pilot], it would be feasible that she could confront danger, that she would have the skills necessary to disarm someone who is coming after her with a gun," she said in a *Publishers Weekly* interview with Kay Brundige.

To contrast with Fergusson, the author shaped a younger, married, recovering alcoholic, agnostic male, Police Chief Russ van Alstyne.

"The characters of Russ and Clare really sort of intrigued me," the author said in a *Maine Bar Journal* interview, "the idea of two different people with two different points of view, but similar backgrounds, interacting."

And interact they did. The chemistry of the two characters was a magnet for readers. And readers were appreciative that the relationship has stayed Platonic.

"I think people like the bittersweet romance because unattainable love is so emotion-filled: lust, longing, hopelessness, happiness," she said in an interview with Jeri Westerson of the Getting Medieval website.

Keenly aware of how skillfully Lee Child plots his novels, how Steve Hamilton uses lean prose, and how Elizabeth George depicts society, Spencer-Fleming added her own occasional twist, structurally, to her novels. One takes place in a 24-hour period. Another seesaws back and forth in time. Another presents multiple points of view.

Her books titles all come from Episcopal hymns.

The author wanted to confront social issues. As she said in an All About Romance conversation,

> One thing I try to do is present different facets of the issue, as it's experienced by different individuals. I don't want you to read a treatise on homophobias. I want you to feel what it's like to be a small-town, semi-closeted guy, and a gung-ho liberal pastor, and a middle-aged cop who's uncomfortable around openly gay men.

With the seventh Fergusson/Van Alstyne book, the author plans to abandon the pair and write a stand-alone novel set at a prison in Maine. When she returns to Miller's Kill, it likely will be to take up the story of side characters she has introduced, notably one of the officers in the town's police department who is a single mother.

"As a writer," the author said in an Internet conversation with J. A. Konrath, "I love the intimacy that comes from having all my characters' lives intertwined."

Works by the Author

Clare Fergusson/Russ Van Alstyne Series

In the Bleak Midwinter (2002)

A Fountain Filled with Blood (2003)

Out of the Deep I Cry (2004)

To Darkness and to Death (2005)

All Mortal Flesh (2006)

I Shall Not Want (2008)

One Was a Soldier (2011)

For Further Information

Brundige, Kay, "From Helicopters to Holy Orders: PW Talks with Julia Spencer-Fleming," *Publishers Weekly*, Mar. 8, 2004.

Conversation with Julia Spencer-Fleming and J. A. Konrath, http://www.jakonrath.com/JAinterview.pdf/ (viewed Sept. 4, 2009).

Julia Spencer-Fleming interview, Bookreporter, June 13, 2008, http://www.bookreporter.com/authors/au-spencer-fleming-julia.asp/ (viewed Sept. 2, 2009).

Julia Spencer-Fleming interview, *Maine Bar Journal*, fall 2002, http://www.likesbooks.com/juliaspencerfleming.html/ (viewed Sept. 2, 2009).

Julia Spencer-Fleming website, http://www.juliaspencerfleming.com/ (viewed 2009).

Potter, Rachel, "Julia Spencer-Fleming Combining Romance and Mystery in Wonderful Ways," All About Romance, http://www.likesbooks.com/juliaspencerfleming.html/ (viewed Sept. 2, 2009).

Westerson, Jeri, Julia Spencer-Fleming interview, Getting Medieval, http://www.getting-medieval.com/my_weblog/2008/09/interviewing-julia-spencer-fleming.html/ (viewed Sept. 2, 2009).

Dana Stabenow

Anchorage, Alaska
1952

Police Procedural
Benchmark Series: Kate Shugak

About the Author and the Author's Writing

Dana Stabenow's three series characters are outsiders. Star Svensdotter is a colonist in Terra-Luna-Sol in a science fiction trilogy. Kate Shugak is an Aleut living in Alaska with her dog Mutt in a mystery series. And, in a second crime series, Liam Campbell is a recovering alcoholic state trooper punished with a remote Alaskan posting.

The experience of being an outsider is not unknown to the author, having grown up on a fishing boat, where her mother home-schooled her.

Born in Anchorage, Alaska, in 1952, Stabenow enjoyed a childhood of outdoors adventure. Her mother worked on a fishing tender in the Gulf of Alaska for five years. "During the winters we tied up to the old fuel dock in Seldovia," the author told interviewer Adrian Muller, "but one year I went trapping on Knight and Montague Islands in Prince William Sound, so my mother home-schooled instead."

After graduating from Seldovia High School in 1969, she worked as an egg grader, bookkeeper, and general problem solver for Whitney-Fidalgo Seafoods in Anchorage to pay her way through college. In 1973 Stabenow graduated from the University of Alaska with a B.A. in journalism. She traveled to Europe. She worked on the Alyeska Pipeline at Galbraith Lake and became an innkeeper for British Petroleum in Prudhoe Bay. In 1982 she left the oil pipeline to pursue an M.F.A., which she received from University of Alaska in 1985.

"My goal was to sell a book before I went broke and I just barely made it. *Second Star* was bought by Ace Science Fiction in 1990. It fell with an almighty thud on the marketplace and was never heard from again," the author said on her web page. Actually, *Second Star* had two sequels before Stabenow decided to write a mystery. Favorite writers when she was growing up included Georgette Heyer, Nevil Shute, Anya Seton, and Thomas B. Costain.

Being an outsider, living in the 49th state, made it a challenge to sell her first novel. "If you're trying to get an agent from Alaska, the difficulty compounds geometrically," she said in a MysteryNet.com essay. "like interest owed to a loan shark. My manuscripts returned regularly like little homing pigeons accompanied by letters which read, 'Alaska? Where is that?'"

Heroine Kate Shugak, the former star investigator for the Anchorage district attorney's office now turned freelance, made her debut in Stabenow's Edgar-nominated *A Cold Day for Murder* in 1992 and proved to be a durable character.

"She was very, very angry in the beginning," the author said in a Writers Write interview, "and very isolated by that anger. She was mad at everybody, mad at the child abusers in Anchorage that she went after for five years, mad at Jack [Morgan, her former colleague], mad at her grandmother, mad at the world."

Shugak worked past the anger, though she remains a loner in the books. By *Whisper to the Blood* (2009), she has a permanent boyfriend, Alaska state trooper Jim Chopin, and a foster son, Johnny Morgan, as well as a suitable puzzle to solve: a series of robberies by snowmobile-riding thieves. "No one writes more vividly about the hardships and rewards of living in the unforgiving Alaskan wilderness and the hardy but frequently flawed characters who choose to call it home," said the *Publishers Weekly* reviewer.

Stabenow's editor moved from Berkley/Putnam to Roc/Dutton and asked her to write a new mystery series based on the ongoing Shugak character Chopper Jim. She couldn't do that contractually but instead wrote what have been four books so far featuring Liam Campbell. Campbell is a state trooper and a recovering alcoholic. His love interest, Wyanet Choinard, gives the books a slightly spicier tone than those featuring the Shugaks. In *Better to Rest* (2002), the storyline involves Alaskan history as Campbell puzzles out murder victims found in a World War II–era airplane wreck hidden for years in a glacier. "Passionate about his work and perhaps more clear-headed about his professional life than his personal life, Campbell makes an engaging hero," *Publishers Weekly* said.

Stabenow is committed to the crime genre. "It's the eternal struggle of good versus evil, and the attractive thing about writing (and reading) crime fiction is that, unlike in real life, good usually wins," she said in an interview with Jan Burke for Mystery Readers International. "Crime fiction offers a relief from real life, where the crooks get off on technicalities or through deals made with the cops and courts or just plain don't get caught."

Outsiders, insiders, crime doesn't pay.

Works by the Author

Blindfold Game (2006)

Prepared for Rage (2008)

Kate Shugak Series

A Cold Day for Murder (1992)

A Fatal Thaw (1992)

Dead in the Water (1993)

A Cold-blooded Business (1994)

Play With Fire (1995)

Blood Will Tell (1996)

Breakup (1997)

Killing Grounds (1998)

Hunter's Moon (1999)

Midnight Come Again (2000)

The Singing of the Dead (2001)

A Fine and Bitter Snow (2002)

A Grave Denied (2003)

A Taint in the Blood (2004)

A Deeper Sleep (2007)

Whisper to the Blood (2009)

A Night Too Dark (2010)

Though Not Dead (2011)

Liam Campbell Series

Fire and Ice (1998)

So Sure of Death (1999)

Nothing Gold Can Stay (2000)

Better to Rest (2002)

Editor

The Mysterious North (2002)

Alaska Women Writers (2003)

Powers of Detection (2004)

Wild Crimes (2004)

At the Scene of the Crime: Forensic Mysteries from Today's Best Writers (2008)

Unusual Suspects: Stories of Mystery & Fantasy (2008)

Contributor

The Mysterious West (1994)

Star Colonies (2000)

And the Dying is Easy (2001)

Our Alaska (2001)

The author has also written three humorous science fiction novels featuring Star Svensdotter.

For Further Information

Better to Rest review, *Publishers Weekly*, Aug. 19, 2002.

Burke, Jan, Dana Stabenow interview, Mystery Readers International, http://www. mysteryreaders.org/athomedana.html/ (viewed Oct. 7, 2009).

Dana Stabenow website, http://www.stabenow.com/ (viewed Oct. 7, 2009).

Muller, Adrian, Dana Stabenow profile, *Mystery Scene*, No. 64, 1999.

Rowen, John, *A Taint in the Blood* review, *Booklist*, Sept. 1, 2004.

Stabenow, Dana, "Writing North of the Fifty-three," Mysterynet.com, http://www.my sterynet.com/books/testimony/writing-alaska-mysteries.shtml/ (viewed Oct. 7, 2009).

Whisper in the Blood review, *Publishers Weekly*, Dec. 1, 2008.

White, Claire E., "A Conversation with Dana Stabenow," Writers Write, http://www. writerswrite.com/journal/feb00/stabenow.htm/ (viewed Oct. 7, 2009).

James Swain

Location not given
1957

Private Detective
Benchmark Series: Tony Valentine

About the Author and the Author's Writing

Ever since his mother died, James Swain has been haunted by something that happened to her years ago. She had been the victim of a parental abduction when she was a child. He researched the subject—her situation was far from unique—and, when he wrote his latest mystery novel featuring his series character Jack Carpenter, he unexpectedly anticipated the shocking case, revealed in September 2009, of California's Jaycee Dugard, who disappeared from her home when she was 11 and fled her captor only 18 years later.

Swain wasn't surprised to learn that the accused captor was also suspected of having kidnapped a girl before he victimized Dugard. He was probably a serial rapist.

The Night Monster (2009) was the author's third novel to feature Carpenter, a one-time investigator for the Broward County Sheriff's Department specializing in missing persons. Booted from the force for hammering on a suspect, Carpenter began to work directly with parents.

"Carpenter can do things the police can't," Swain said to *St. Petersburg Times* reporter Colette Bancroft. "A law enforcement officer pointed out to me that Jack was an avenging angel. He's more interested in justice than the law."

In *The Night Monster*, Carpenter immediately recalls a troubling cold case in which the main suspect was a 6-foot, 10-inch heavyweight when his college student daughter phones to say a man is stalking one of her basketball teammates at Florida State. "In his incredibly fast-paced third case, private investigator Jack Carpenter refuses to allow a second abduction to haunt him like the first one still does," according to Harriet Klausner in *Mystery Gazette*.

Born in 1957, Swain graduated from New York University and worked for many years in advertising. He came to own his own agency. He also performed magic professionally. With his knowledge of card manipulation and of how gambling casinos function, he created Tony Valentine, his first series hero, a retired cop who now works for casinos, helping them spot and discourage cheaters, particularly cross-roaders who specialize in ripping off casinos.

With the current enormous interest in poker and regular televising of major tournaments such as the World Series of Poker, he had a sure audience for *Grift Sense* when it was released in 2001.

The *New York Times Book Review's* Marilyn Stasio was taken with the second Valentine book, *Funny Money* (2002), saying of Swain that "his direct style works just fine as a navigational aid to the cons, grifts and hustles that Valentine identifies for his clueless clients—often, with the insouciance of a professional magician, over the phone!"

Swain has spotted his novels with a variety of secondary characters. Stasio, in reviewing *Sucker Bet* (2003), was appreciative. "Both con artists and victims are a colorful lot, and none are more endearing than Mr. Beauregard, a chimpanzee who can look into your eyes and play your favorite song on his ukelele. Even Valentine can't explain that one."

Some have mistaken Swain for his hero Valentine. Not so, according to Swain, who points out that Valentine doesn't gamble. Swain does. Valentine doesn't drink. Swain does, on occasion. And Valentine despises hustlers. Swain numbers hustlers among his friends.

Swain certainly isn't opposed to card games. "Poker is socialization," he told journalist Susan L. Rife. "You have to sit down at a table with a group of people and you have to be friendly. You have to play by the rules. For three or four hours, it's like the good old days, and I think that's great."

However, Swain says the scams described in his books are real.

"My knowledge of scams has certainly helped me understand human nature and the criminal mind," he said on the Tony Valentine website, Grift Sense. "It has also helped me tremendously when it comes to plotting my books. Good scams are entertaining to the people that are being ripped off. The same is true of a good book."

Works by the Author

The Man Who Walked Through Walls (1989)

Jack Carpenter Series

Midnight Rambler (2007)

The Night Stalker (2008)

The Night Monster (2009)

"The Program" (2010), Kindle story

Tony Valentine Series

Grift Sense (2001)

Funny Money (2002)

Sucker Bet (2003)

Loaded Dice (2004)

Mr. Lucky (2005)

Deadman's Bluff (2006)

Deadman's Poker (2006)

"Jackpot" (2010) Kindle story

Wild Card (2010)

The author has also written three books about handling playing cards.

For Further Information

Bancroft, Colette, "Jaycee Dugard Comes to Mind in Reading 'The Night Monster' by James Swain," *St. Petersburg Times*, Sept. 13, 2009.

James Swain interview, Tony Valentine website, http://www.jimswain.com/old22/interview.htm/ (viewed Oct. 9, 2009).

James Swain website, http://www.jimswain.com/about.html/ (viewed Oct. 9, 2009).

Klausner, Harriet, The Night Monster review, Mystery Gazette, http://themystery gazette.blogspot.com/2009/08/night-monster-james-swain.html/ (viewed Oct. 9, 2009).

On Writing Mr. Lucky, Tony Valentine website, http://www.jimswain.com/old22/writing.htm/ (viewed Oct. 9, 2009).

Rife, Susan L., "Cheating Holds a Fascination for Mystery Author Swain," Sarasota *Herald-Tribune*, June 11, 2006.

Stasio, Marilyn, *Dead Man's Poker* review, *New York Times Book Review*, May 7, 2006.

Stasio, Marilyn, *Funny Money* review, *New York Times Book Review*, June 23, 2002.

Stasio, Marilyn, *Sucker Bet* review, *New York Times Book Review*, April 20, 2003.

Andrew Taylor

© Caroline Silverwood Taylor

Stevenage, Hertfordshire, England
1951

Police Procedural, Private Detective,
Historical Mystery
Benchmark Series: Lydmouth

About the Author and the Author's Writing

Andrew Taylor is interested in the near as well as distant past.

His Lydmouth novels take place in a community on the Anglo–Welsh border in the turbulent 1950s. They feature journalist Jill Francis, who is originally from London, and Detective Inspector Richard Thornhill, who hails from East Anglia. They're both outsiders, thrown together, in *An Air That Kills* (1994), when she seeks news and he seeks a killer of a newborn baby found in an abandoned privy.

His stand-alone *The American Boy* (2003) takes place a century and a half earlier, in London, when a youthful Edgar Allan Poe arrives in the city only to become involved in a criminal investigation after a bank building collapses and a mutilated body is found in the rubble.

One can expect the unexpected from the author, who has written thriller, espionage, and young adult novels; but mostly he writes crime puzzlers. "The flexibility of the genre is immensely attractive," he said in *St. James Guide to Crime & Mystery Writers*. "I began by writing what are more or less straight crime novels—the Dougal series."

William Dougal is an opportunist of sometimes dubious moral fiber. He later becomes a private investigator, but Dougal is still a postgrad knowledgeable in medieval manuscripts in *Caroline Minuscule* (1982). He makes a fascinating discovery about an ancient crime, revealed on a brittle page. Then his tutor is murdered. Dougal doesn't advise the police. Instead, with girlfriend Amanda in tow, he races to find a newly revealed prize—diamonds.

Taylor said in a Mystery One interview that he felt Patricia Highsmith's influence when he wrote that first novel. "I wanted to write about a nice character who was capable of doing nasty things (as most of us are). Goodies and baddies have always bored me in fiction; it's far more interesting to write about the shifting shades of grey."

Taylor also crafted the Roth Trilogy, which starts with the kidnapping of a girl and in each book follows the characters backwards, to see the crime taking shape.

Writing as Andrew Saville, he penned six books about Jim Bergerac, a detective sergeant, divorced, and a recovering alcoholic on the island of Jersey. Taylor's books were based on the popular BBC television series created by Robert Banks Stevens, which aired from 1981 to 1991.

"Although he has written more than one novel series, he has never become formulaic," said a reviewer on the Powys Web site, "often taking a new direction in stand-alone books."

Taylor was born in 1951 in Stevenage, England. He grew up in the Fen country of East Anglia. His father was a teacher and clergyman, his mother a physiotherapist. He graduated with honors from Emmanuel College, Cambridge with a B.A. in 1973. In 1979 he received an M.A. from University of London. He married librarian Caroline Silverwood in 1979. He worked as a boat builder, wages clerk, teacher, and librarian (from 1976 to 1981) before becoming a freelance writer. From 2004 to 2006 he edited the Society of Authors' quarterly journal *The Author*.

Taylor wrote the first draft of his first novel by hand and later typed it. In recent years, because he suffers repetitive strain injury, he uses a recorder. "I dictate my novels, which often involves me prancing up and down my workroom and talking to myself in silly voices," he said on his website. "In fine weather I sit under one of the apple trees and talk to myself in the fresh air instead. [His children] Sarah and Will believe I have an unhealthy relationship with the Oxford English Dictionary."

Taylor is so far the only mystery novelist to twice receive the Crime Writers Association's Ellis Peters Historical Dagger—for *The Office of the Dead* in 2000 and for *The American Boy* in 2003.

He doesn't shun the present, but Taylor enjoys his excursions into the past. His research for *The American Boy* was often intense. "I read memoirs, diaries and letters. I read and re-read novels of the period," he said in a *SHOTS* magazine interview. "In a sense I was spending more time in 1819–20 than in 2001–02. (I was even dreaming in semi-colons.) I suspect there's a connection between how people speak and how they think."

Whatever time period he's writing about, Taylor adds a sociologist's touch to his crime novels.

Works by the Author

The Raven on the Water (1991)

The Barred Window (1993)

The American Boy (2003), also titled *An Unpardonable Crime* (2004)

A Stain on the Silence (2006)

Bleeding Heart Square (2008)

The Anatomy of Ghosts (2011)

Blaines Trilogy

Blacklist (1988)

The Second Midnight (1988)

Toyshop (1990)

William Dougal Series

Caroline Minuscule (1982)

Waiting for the End of the World (1984)

Our Fathers' Lies (1985)

An Old School Tie (1986)

Freelance Death (1987)

Blood Relation (1990)

The Sleeping Policeman (1992)

Odd Man Out (1993)

Lydmouth Series

An Air that Kills (1994)

The Mortal Sickness (1995)

The Lover of the Grave (1997)

The Suffocating Night (1998)

Where Roses Fade (2000)

Death's Own Door (2001)

Calling the Dying (2004)

Naked to the Hangman (2006)

Roth Trilogy

The Four Last Things (1997)

The Judgment of Strangers (1998)

The Office of the Dead (2000)

Requiem for an Angel (2002), omnibus

Writing as Andrew Saville, Jim Bergerac Series

Bergerac (1985)

Bergerac Is Back! (1985)

Bergerac and the Fatal Weakness (1988)

Bergerac and the Jersey Rose (1988)

Bergerac and the Moving Fever (1988)

Bergerac and the Traitor's Child (1989)

The author has also written books for young adults and children, some under the name John Robert Taylor.

For Further Information

Andrew Taylor interview, Mystery One Bookstore, http://www.mysteryone.com/oldsite/AndrewTaylorInterview.htm/ (viewed Dec. 10, 2009).

Andrew Taylor interview, *SHOTS*, http://www.shotsmag.co.uk/SHOTS%2019/Taylorinterview.htm/ (viewed Dec. 10, 2009).

Andrew Taylor web page, Powys, http://www.powys.gov.uk/index.php?id=5135&L=0/ (viewed Dec. 10, 2009).

Andrew Taylor website, http://www.lydmouth.co.uk/ (viewed Dec. 10, 2009).

Plowden, Philip, Andrew Taylor entry, *St. James Guide to Crime & Mystery Writers*, fourth edition, edited by Jay P. Pederson. Detroit: St. James Press, 1996.

Aimée and David Thurlo

Cuba and New Mexico
Dates not revealed

Police Procedural, Amateur Detective,
Journalism Mystery, Paranormal
Benchmark Series: Emma Clah

About the Authors and the Authors' Writing

Aimée and David Thurlo work off each other's strengths as fiction writers. David has a knack for plotting and laying out action scenes. Aimée skills are conceiving dialogue and shaping character. With their Lee Nez police procedural series with a paranormal bent, David drafts a plot summary, Aimée revises it, David writes a first draft and rewrites it before he gives it to Aimée to do the next two drafts. They pass it back and forth until the manuscript is ready to send to the publisher.

"We are free to change, edit, add, delete, as we go, and we get together any time there is a question about a scene, character, or detail," the authors told interviewer Linda Suzanne. "We leave notes for each other in the text as we write, but, because our work habits are so different, we have separate offices."

For the Emma Clah and Sister Agatha books, their roles reverse and Aimée does the outline and first draft, while David still takes a strong hand in plotting and writing the action scenes.

The Thurlos have different writing habits and quite different backgrounds. Aimée was born in Havana, Cuba, and grew up and still lives in New Mexico. David was born in Shiprock, New Mexico, on the Navajo Indian Reservation. He attended the University of New Mexico and taught math and science for several years. The couple married in 1970. Their first writing together was for periodicals such as *Grit* and *Popular Mechanics*.

They began to cowrite romance and romantic suspense novels, most published under Aimée Thurlo's name (including the *Four Winds* trilogy for Harlequin in 1997), Aimée Martel, or Aimée Duvall.

Their first mystery fiction was *Blackening Song* (1995) for Forge. It appeared with a joint byline. The main character, Emma Clah, is an FBI agent and a Navajo. She is called back to the Shiprock Reservation from Los Angeles after her father, a Christian minister, is murdered. Her brother, Clifford, a traditional medicine man, is the main suspect. Reviewers praised the book for merging the latest in crime-fighting techniques of the FBI and the ritualistic world of the Navajo.

In subsequent books, Clah quits the FBI and goes to work for the Navajo Tribal Police as a special investigator. In *Earthway* (2009), typically, Clah pursues a group of antinuclear activists who are planting pipe bombs. "The authors smoothly blend personal and professional concerns, as the Navajo police sort through a tangle of lies and loyalties while respecting the values of traditionalists and adapting to modern intrusions," said a *Publishers Weekly* reviewer.

A second series character, Lee Nez, is also a tribal policeman—with a big difference. He is a daywalker, a vampire who, with the help of a savvy medicine man, is able to tolerate some sunshine and gets by drinking animal blood. Navajo skinwalkers (shapeshifters) dart in and out of the story as Nez follows approved investigative routines to solve murders. In the second book, *Blood Retribution* (2004), Nez and FBI Agent Diane Lopez look into the deaths of two undercover officers who have been on the track of jewelry smugglers. The smugglers are skinwalkers.

A third series is about motorcycle-riding Sister Agatha, an investigative reporter-turned- nun in a southwestern convent. In *The Prodigal Nun* (2008), Sister Agatha seeks the killer of one of the parishioners of Our Lady of Hope Monastery but runs afoul of the local police when clues suggests one of his officers may be involved.

That the Thurlos are able to juggle three mystery series and produce occasional stand-alone novels attests to their years of experience, during which they've recognized many important elements to good fiction writing. "Keep the stories fresh and true to character," they said in an interview for Poe's Deadly Daughters. "Also, know your readers and what they expect from your characters—though it's important to keep them guessing a bit."

Works by the Authors

Second Shadow (1990)

The Spirit Line (2004)

Ella Clah Series

Blackening Song (1995)

DeathWalker (1996)

Bad Medicine (1997)

Enemy Way (1999)

Shooting Chant (2000)

Red Mesa (2001)

Changing Woman (2002)

Plant Them Deep (2003)

Tracking Bear (2003)

Wind Spirit (2004)

White Thunder (2005)

Mourning Dove (2006)

Turquoise Girl (2007)

Coyote's Wife (2008)

Earthway (2009)

Never-ending Snake (2010)

Lee Nez Series

Second Sunrise (2002)

Blood Retribution (2004)

Pale Death (2005)

Surrogate Evil (2006)

Sister Agatha Series

Bad Faith (2002)

Thief in Retreat (2004)

Prey for a Miracle (2006)

False Witness (2007)

The Prodigal Nun (2008)

Bad Samaritan (2009)

The Thurlos have also written romance novels, including entries in the Harlequin Intrigue series, many published under Aimée Thurlo's byline or as by Aimée Martel or Aimée Duvall.

For Further Information

Aimée and David Thurlo interview, Poe's Deadly Daughters, Oct. 25, 2008, http://poesdeadlydaughters.blogspot.com/2008/10/guest-interview-aime-and-david-thurlo.html/ (viewed Oct. 15, 2009).

Aimée and David Thurlo website, http://www.aimeeanddavidthurlo.com/ (viewed Oct. 14, 2009).

Aimée Thurlo profile, Answers.com, http://www.answers.com/topic/-280/ (viewed Oct. 15, 2009).

David Thurlo profile, Answers.com, http://www.answers.com/topic/-281/ (viewed Oct. 15, 2009).

Earthway review, *Publishers Weekly*, Sept. 7, 2009.

Fletcher, Connie, *Coyote's Wife* review, *Booklist*, Sept. 1, 2008.

Fletcher, Connie, *Turquoise Girl* review, *Booklist*, Ap. 1, 2007.

Pale Death review, *Publishers Weekly*, Aug. 8, 2005.

Prodigal Nun review, *Publishers Weekly*, May 19, 2008.

Suzane, Linda, David and Aimée Thurlo interview, Suite101.com, http://www. suite101.com/article.cfm/vampire_ebook_authors/116342/ (viewed Oct. 15, 2009).

Peter Tremayne

Coventry, Warwickshire, England
1943

Amateur Detective, Legal Mystery, Historical Mystery, Ecclesiastical Mystery
Benchmark Series: Sister Fidelma

About the Author and the Author's Writing

Before we talk about Peter Tramayne we need to talk about Peter Berresfort Ellis, since they are one and the same.

Ellis has been a member of the Celtic League, the Scrif-Celt, the London Association for Celtic Education, the Royal Historical Society, the Royal Society of Antiquaries of Ireland, the Irish Brigades Association of the United States of America, the Irish Literary Society and . . . well, you get the drift. He knows his Celtic history. And so naturally, when he wanted to write a crime novel, he chose a particular setting (Munster in Ireland), a particular time (the seventh century), and a particular character (a woman lawyer) that one doesn't often, if ever, encounter in the genre.

There's a story that goes with this. In the 1980s Ellis lectured at Toronto University on the role of women at the time of the ancient Celts. Afterward, a student, aware that Ellis had written a historical novel, suggested that a woman lawyer from that time period would make an interesting character in a mystery novel. A decade later, called on to offer a short story to a collection that anthologist Peter Haining was putting together, he recalled the idea and wrote a story about Sister Fidelma. The collection came out in 1993, as did three other collections that same year with three other Sister Fidelma stories. The publisher Headline liked the stories and asked for a novel, offering a three-book contract. A detective series was launched.

The novels appear under the name Peter Tremayne. And there's a story to go with this, too. Asked one time to write a review of the first Brother Cadfael novel, Ellis felt it would confuse readers to see someone named Peter Ellis review a book by Ellis Peters. So he kept the Peter and added Tremayne, the name of a place in Cornwall that he had enjoyed. When he needed a name for his own crime series, Peter Tremayne was handy.

The author was born in Coventry, Warwickshire, England in 1943. His father was a journalist who also turned out pulp fiction. In fact, Ellis came from a family of writers and scribes going back several centuries. In 1943 he married Eva Daisy Randell. He studied at Brighton College of Art and University of East London and earned a B.A. and an M.A. in Celtic history. Ellis then became a journalist/editor and historian (after a few side trips as a rifle range attendant and dishwasher) until he turned to writing full time in 1975.

Although he writes a considerable amount of nonfiction, Ellis has dabbled in several fiction genres besides his historical mysteries. He has written a pastiche of E. C. Hornung's Raffles (as Tremayne), two historical novels (under his own name), and eight thrillers (under the pen name Peter MacAlan). Writing crime novels was an obvious choice, given that he was a longtime fan of Arthur Conan Doyle, Raymond Chandler, Colin Dexter, Georges Simenon, Dorothy L. Sayers, Margery Allingham, and Patricia Highsmith, to name a few.

Ellis's abilities in shaping people, places, and puzzles, however, largely come to him naturally. He does not outline ahead of time; he simply sits down and writes where his characters take him.

The author insists on veracity in his settings. If he writes about a place, whether in Ireland or Rome or elsewhere, he's been there, he's studied it, and he knows it sufficiently to describe it accurately.

He also insists on historical accuracy. "Nothing is quoted in the Fidelma books that cannot be found in written form in the laws," he told interviewer Tylwa Racz of the Historical Mystery Appreciation Society Journal. "We not only know the names of female lawyers and judges but we know women wrote some of the law texts. . . . The books are reflective of life in seventh century Ireland in all its forms."

Why a woman series character? There's a last story to tell.

"I chose a female protagonist because this was the most intriguing aspect of the seventh-century Irish system which placed women in a co-equal role to men," he told Sarah Cuthbertson of the Historical Novel Society website. "A fact that seemed forgotten. And it was inevitable that she had to be a religious, for, as Fidelma has explained in the stories, in pre-Christian days all the professionals and intellectuals were part of the Druid caste."

History becomes herstory, with a criminal twist.

Works by the Author

Writing as Peter Tremayne

The Return of Raffles (1991)

An Ensuing Evil: Fourteen Historical Mystery Stories (2006)

Sister Fidelma Series

Absolution By Murder (1994)

Shroud for the Archbishop (1995)

Suffer Little Children (1995)

The Subtle Serpent (1996)

The Spider's Web (1997)

Valley of the Shadow (1998)

Act of Mercy (1999)

The Monk Who Vanished (1999)

Hemlock at Vespers (2000)

Our Lady of Darkness (2000)

Smoke in the Wind (2001)

The Haunted Abbot (2002)

Badger's Moon (2003)

The Leper's Bell (2004)

Whispers of the Dead (2004)

Master of Souls (2005)

A Prayer for the Damned (2007)

The Council of the Cursed (2008)

Dancing With Demons (2008)

The Dove of Death (2009)

The Chalice of Blood (2010)

Contributor

Constable New Crime No. 2, edited by Maxim Jakubowski (1993), includes "Murder by Miracle"

Great Irish Detective Stories, edited by Peter Haining (1993), includes "Murder in Repose"

Mammoth Book of Historical Whodunnits, edited by Mike Ashley (1993), includes "The High King's Sword"

Midwinter Mysteries 3, edited by Hilary Hale (1993), includes "Hemlock at Vespers"

Midwinter Mysteries 4, edited by Hilary Hale (1994), includes "A Canticle for Wulfstan"

Year's Best Mystery & Suspense Stories 1994, edited by Edward D. Hoch (1994), includes "Murder by Miracle"

Mammoth Book of Historical Detectives, edited by Mike Ashley (1995), includes "Abbey Sinister"

Minister Mysteries 5, edited by Hilary Hale (1995), includes "Tarnished Halo"

Murder at the Races, edited by Peter Haining (1995), includes "The Horse That Died for Shame"

Classical Whodunnits, edited by Mike Ashley (1996), includes "The Poison Chalice"

Past Poisons: An Ellis Peters Memorial Anthology of Historical Crime, edited by Maxim Jakubowski (1998), includes "Invitation to a Poisoning"

Chronicles of Crime—The Second Ellis Peters Memorial Anthology of Historical Crime, edited by Maxim Jakubowski (1999), includes "Those Who Trespass"

Great Irish Stories of Murder and Mystery, edited by Peter Haining (1999) includes "Holy Blood"

Dark Detectives: Adventures of the Supernatural Sleuths, edited by Steve Jones (2000), includes "Our Lady of Death"

The Mammoth Book of Locked-Room Mysteries and Impossible Crimes (2000)

Murder Most Devine, edited by Ralph McInerny and Martin H. Greenberg (2000), includes "Those Who Trespass"

Murder Most Medieval, edited by Martin H. Greenberg and John Heifers (2000), includes "Like a Dog Returning"

Murder Through the Ages, edited by Maxim Jakubowski (2000), includes "Scattered Thorns"

World's Finest Crime and Mystery Stories, edited by Ed Gorman (2000), includes "Those Who Trespass"

And the Dying Is Easy, edited by Joseph Pittman and Annette Riffle (2001), includes "Corpse on a Holy Day"

Death by Horoscope, edited by Anne Perry (2001), includes "The Astrologer Who Predicted His Own Murder"

The Mammoth Book of Historical Whodunnits (Brand New Collection), edited by Mike Ashley (2001), includes "Death of an Icon"

Murder Most Catholic, edited by Ralph McInerny (2001), includes "Whispers of the Dead"

The Mammoth Book of Roman Whodunnits, edited by Mike Ashley (2003), includes "The Lost Eagle"

Whispers of the Dead (2004), includes "Cry Wolf!" "The Forsterer," and "The Heir Apparent"

The Mammoth Book of Historical Whodunnits, Third Collection, edited by Mike Ashley (2005) includes "The Spiteful Shadow"

Thou Shalt Not Kill: Biblical Mystery Stories, edited by Anne Perry (2005), includes "Does God Obey His Own Laws?"

Writing as Peter MacAlan

The Judas Battalion (1983)

Airship (1984)

The Confession (1985)

Kitchener's Gold (1986)

The Valkyrie Directive (1987)

The Doomsday Decree (1988)

Fireball (1991)

The Windsor Protocol (1993)

The author has also written numerous horror and fantasy novels as Peter Tremayne; he has written Celtic and other histories under his real name, Peter Berresford Ellis.

For Further Information

Cuthbertson, Sarah, "The Fascination for Sister Fidelma," Historical Novel Society, http://www.historicalnovelsociety.org/solander/fidelma.htm/ (viewed Dec. 2, 2009).

Peter Tremayne website, http://www.sisterfidelma.com/tremayne.html/ (viewed Dec. 2, 2009).

Racz, Twyla, "Peter Berresford Ellis interview about Sister Fidelma," Murder: Past Tense, Historical Mystery Appreciation Society Journal, http://www.sisterfidelma.com/interview.html/ (viewed Dec. 2, 2009).

Elaine Viets

Don Crinklaw

St. Louis, Missouri
1950

Amateur Detective, Journalism Mystery
Benchmark series: Dead-End Job

About the Author and the Author's Writing

One wouldn't wish on anyone all the drudgy, low-paying jobs Helen Hawthorne has had. But author Elaine Viets said that she herself has done them all and more. And they became a good resource for her popular Dead-End Job series of mystery novels.

The books, she has said, came in the post–September 11 era, when many middle-class people had to take on second or third jobs. "Instead of talking about buying a new house, going to Europe, or retiring early, they were suddenly wondering where their next nickel was coming from," she told interviewer Pamela James for Mystery File. "My series is a funny look at a serious subject, the minimum wage world. My main character, Helen Hawthorne, works these jobs—and so do I."

Hawthorne, Viets's protagonist, once took home six figures at her glamorous job in St. Louis. Then she caught her out-of-work husband in an indelicate position with a female neighbor. She took matters (and a crowbar) into her own hands, and smashed his SUV. Told by a judge to pay alimony, she ended up on the run—in South Florida, working a series of thankless jobs. Clerk in a dress shop. Dog groomer. Hair stylist. Telemarketer. Viets did them all. All except topless bartending (Hawthorne's employment in *Dying to Call You* in 2004).

Viets was born in St. Louis in 1950. She attended the University of Missouri at both St. Louis and Columbia, earning her bachelor's degree from the latter in 1972. A devout fan of the newspaper comic strip "Brenda Starr" as a teen, she became a fashion writer for the *St. Louis Post-Dispatch* beginning in 1972. She moved up to become youth page editor and then columnist in 1979. She has hosted "Travel Holiday Magazine," a syndicated radio program. She and her husband, journalist and actor Don Crinklaw, live in Hollywood, Florida.

Viets has written nonfiction, including *How to Commit Monogamy: A Lighthearted Look at Long-Term Love* (1997). Personal experiences that fed the collection of essays also served her lighthearted crime novels. She has taken inspiration from mystery writers including Sue Grafton, Lawrence Block, and Dorothy L. Sayers. Mainstream influences include Mark Twain, John Steinbeck, and Daphne Du Maurier.

Viets has two other mystery series, one featuring Josie Marcus, a one-woman consumer protection agency, the other Francesca Vierling, a newspaper reporter.

"My books are known for their accurate depiction of modern newspapers," she told Contemporary Authors. "My ideas for my [Vierling] mysteries are based on events that I covered as a reporter, from a transvestite beauty pageant to the Leather and Lace Bikers Society Ball."

Viets has a nontraditional writing schedule. She usually gets up at 3 A.M., writes for three hours, then goes back to bed. After breakfast, she writes some more.

Her main characters are pretty much takeoffs on herself and people in her circle, with a slant. Francesca Vierling, for example, is Viets at age 30. Emma, the daughter in the Josie Marcus books, is based on a good friend's daughter.

The Vierling books take place in St. Louis. "Readers expect the Midwest to have standards, morals, and taste," Viets said on her web page. "South Florida [where Helen Hawthorne lives] has none of these handicaps. That's why my Dead-End Job series hit the national bestseller lists—no standards, no morals, and especially no taste."

Josie Marcus is a single mother who lives with her shopaholic mother. She's a mystery shopper, a profession that by its nature is secretive and invisible. The books take place in Maplewood, near St. Louis—the place that Viets still knows the best and finds very comfortable to write about.

The hardest part of her craft, the author told Mystery File, is developing convincing plots and leaving no loose plot threads. She outlines her books for her editors, sometimes taking as many as 28,000 words to describe what her characters will do.

But she then lets the characters do their thing. As she told Writerspace,

> Margery Flax, the Marlboro-smoking landlady in the [Hawthorne] series, is a very strong character. She can really take over a story. I'm partial to her, because she's such a vital older woman. She's what I want to be when I grow up.

Though some of her plots may get a little, well, goofy, they can also be quite serious. *Doc in the Box* (2000), a Vierling series entry, for example, discusses needless deaths caused by neglectful health-care professionals.

"Every year, as many as 98,000 Americans die of preventable medical errors, according to the Institute of Medicine," she said in a Crescent Blues conversation. "This is scary."

Scary—but a font of ideas for the mystery novelist.

Works by the Author

Dead-End Job Series

Murder Between the Covers (2003)

Shop Till You Drop (2003)

Dying to Call You (2004)

Just Murdered (2005)

"Killer Blonde," in *Drop-Dead Blonde* (2005), with Victoria Laurie, Nancy Martin, and Denise Swanson

Murder Unleashed (2006)

Murder with Reservations (2007)

Clubbed to Death (2008)

Killer Cuts (2009)

Half-Price Homicide (2010)

Pumped for Murder (2011)

Francesca Vierling Series

Backstab (1997)

Rubout (1998)

The Pink Flamingo Murders (1999)

Doc in the Box (2000)

Josie Marcus, Mystery Shopper Series

Dying in Style (2005)

High Heels Are Murder (2006)

An Accessory to Murder (2007)

Murder with All the Trimmings (2008)

The Fashion Hound Murders (2009)

An Uplifting Murder (2010)

Collections

Urban Affairs: Tales from the Heart of the City (1988)

Contributor

Blood on Their Hands, edited by Lawrence Block (2003), includes "Red Meat"

High Stakes, edited by Robert Randisi (2003), includes "Sex and Bingo"

Chesapeake Crimes, edited by Stuart M. Kaminsky (2004) includes "Wedding Knife"

Show Business Is Murder, edited by Stuart M. Kaminsky (2004), includes "Blonde Moment"

World's Finest Mystery and Crime Stories: Fifth Annual Collection, edited by Ed Gorman and Martin H. Greenberg (2004)

Drop-Dead Blonde, with Nancy Martin, Denise Swanson, and Victoria Lurie (2005), includes "Killer Blonde"

Many Bloody Returns, edited by Charlaine Harris and Toni L. P. Kelner (2007), includes "Vampire Hours"

For Further Information

"Elaine Viets: Tall Order," Crescent Blues, http://www.crescentblues.com/3_3issue/viets.shtml/ (viewed July 9, 2009).

Elaine Viets profile, Contemporary Authors Online, http://galenet.galegroup.com/servlet/BioRC/ (viewed July 23, 2009).

Elaine Viets web page, http://www.elaineviets.com/ (viewed July 9, 2009).

Felt, Elizabeth Caulfield, "How to Commit Monogamy: A Lighthearted Look at Long-term Love," *Library Journal*, June 15, 1977.

James, Pamela, "An Interview with Elaine Viets," Mystery File, http://www.mysteryfile.com/viets/html/ (viewed July 9, 2009).

"Writerspace Interview with Elaine Viets," http://www.writerspace.com/interviews/eviets0205.html/ (viewed July 9, 2009).

Joseph Wambaugh

East Pittsburgh, Pennsylvania
1937

Police Procedural
Benchmark Series: LAPD

About the Author and the Author's Writing

As a kid growing up in East Pittsburgh, Joseph Wambaugh often had his nose in books, many of them borrowed from the Carnegie Library in Braddock. "That was the entertainment," he told reporter Dennis Marsili of the *Pittsburgh Law Enforcement Examiner*.

> I was always a reader so when I started college I naturally gravitated toward literature; that was what I loved. So I got a degree in English literature. When I was a cop I got a master's degree in literature. I thought that I would be an English teacher when I retired.

Wambaugh did retire from one career, but he's yet to quit his second one, which is his great love—writing.

It was inevitable that Wambaugh would become a policeman. His father was on the force. Born in East Pittsburgh in 1937, the younger Wambaugh attended Chaffey College, then California State College in Los Angeles (now California State University). He served in the U.S. Marine Corps from 1954 to 1957. He was a patrolman, then a detective sergeant with the Los Angeles Police Department from 1960 to 1974. His "clientele" was nothing if not interesting; one time he and his partner questioned two suspicious individuals in a parking lot. One was child actor and future *Baretta* star Robert Blake. (There was no arrest.)

He wrote his first two novels in spare moments while still with the department. The success of his work created an uncomfortable situation with his superiors, who felt that the books left a negative impression of cops. Fellow officers, on the other hand, knew he spoke the truth, Wambaugh has said. Wambaugh took a leave from the department, long enough to write a nonfiction book, the gripping *Onion Field* (1973), the story of an attempted arrest gone awry. He went back on assignment, then left permanently to pursue writing as a career. Besides novels, he has written more nonfiction, scripted motion pictures, and developed and written two television series: *Police Story* and *The Blue Knight*.

While Wambaugh has plenty of knowledge of police procedure, he nevertheless is a relentless interviewer, whether for his nonfiction or his fiction. The more he knows, the better he can shape his characters and their stories.

"I do more than fifty police interviews before starting any novel," he said in an interview with Scott Butki for Newsvine. "The anecdotes and characters are born from those chats over dinner and drinks."

"My characters are pretty much composites of people I've met," he said in a Bookreporter dialogue in 2008. "Sometimes they're pretty close to the living people. My work is character driven, and by that I mean that once I create the characters I start narrating their story without a clear idea of where they are going."

The author enjoys, among contemporary crime novelists, Michael Connelly, James Ellroy, and Robert Crais. "As for inspiration, for me it comes from the cops themselves," he told Patrick Millikin of *Publishers Weekly*. "I cannot write a novel, a script, or anything else without interviewing dozens of cops."

Wambaugh has become known for his colorful heroes. "But each scene—whether outlandish or poignant—has a sense of authenticity," said *Sun Sentinel* reviewer Oline H. Cogdill. "The officers are a mixed bag united in respect for their job."

After a decade-long hiatus to work in films and television, Wambaugh returned to the printed page with a series featuring Flotsam and Jetsam, the surfer cops; Nate "Hollywood" Weiss and his partner Dana Vaughn; and other officers as they grapple with new politically correct directives in dealing with some of the wackiest felons imaginable.

"Fat fast-food junkie officers have been replaced by 'granola-crunching coppers probably worried about *E. coli* in their Evian,'" observed *Guardian* reviewer Mark Lawson. "A woman officer, recently returned from maternity leave, stops her black-and-white during a patrol to express breast-milk in a restroom."

Times certainly have changed.

"What other author could present cops, street people, and career criminals with such deadeye credibility?" asked reviewer Connie Fletcher in discussing *Hollywood Moon* (2009) for *Booklist*. "Or transpose slang up and out from the drug world into cop speak with absolute perfect pitch?"

Some aspects of police work can be researched—but some can only be experienced.

Works by the Author

The New Centurions (1971)

The Blue Knight (1972)

The Choirboys (1975)

The Black Marble (1978)

The Glitter Dome (1981)

The Delta Star (1983)

The Secrets of Harry Bright (1985)

The Golden Orange (1990)

Fugitive Nights (1992)

Finnegan's Week (1993)

Floaters (1996)

LAPD Series

Hollywood Station (2006)

Hollywood Crows (2008)

Hollywood Moon (2009)

Hollywood Hills (2010)

Wambaugh has also written award-winning nonfiction and screenplays for *The Onion Field* and *The Black Marble*, the CBS-TV miniseries *Echoes in the Darkness,* and the NBC-TV series *Fugitive Nights*. He created the NBC-TV series *Police Story* and *The Blue Knight*.

For Further Information

Butki, Scott, Joseph Wambaugh interview, Newsvine, http://sbutki.newsvine.com/_news/2008/03/25/1388871-my-newsvine-interview-with-joseph-wambaugh-about-his-new-novel-hollywood-crows/ (Nov. 24, 2009).

Cogdill, Oline H., "Colorful Cops Are Still Stars in Trilogy Finale," *Sun Sentinel* (Fort Lauderdale, Fla.), Nov. 26, 2009.

Fletcher, Connie, *Hollywood Moon* review, *Booklist*, Oct. 1, 2009.

Joseph Wambaugh interview, Bookreporter, Mar. 28, 2008, http://www.bookreporter.com/authors/au-wambaugh-joseph.asp/ (viewed Nov. 24, 2009).

Joseph Wambaugh interview, *Pittsburgh Law Enforcement Examiner*, Nov. 3, 2009, http://www.examiner.com/x-16576-Pittsburgh-Law-Enforcement-Examiner~y2009m11d3-Exclusive-interview-with-author-Joseph-Wambaugh-Part-1-of-2?cid=examiner-email/ (viewed Nov. 24, 2009).

Joseph Wambaugh website. http://josephwambaugh.net/ (viewed Nov. 24, 2009).

Lawson, Mike, *Hollywood Station* review, *The Guardian*, Jan. 6, 2007.

Millikin, Patrick, "Political Correctness and the LAPD: PW Talks with Joseph Wambaugh," *Publishers Weekly*, Oct. 9, 2006.

Jacqueline Winspear

Kent, England
1955

Private Detective, Historical Mystery
Benchmark Series: Maisie Dobbs

About the Author and the Author's Writing

A California resident since 1990, Jacqueline Winspear found that distance from her native England was to her advantage in writing her bestselling Maisie Dobbs mystery novels.

"Fate brought me to live on this side of the Atlantic!" she said in a Bookreporter interview. "I can look back at England in the time I have created and not be distracted by the truth of the country today." The small town where she grew up in Kent (where she was born in 1955), she added, is little changed from Edwardian times. Still vivid in her mind, she easily reconstructs its setting in her books.

The author was born in 1955 and grew up in Kent County, England. She graduated from the University of London Institute of Education; worked in publishing, marketing and communications; and taught in London. When she came to the United States in 1990, she was a personal and professional coach while launching her writing career. Her list of favorite authors ranges from F. Scott Fitzgerald and Ernest Hemingway to Zadie Smith and John Paul Herren. Among crime fiction writers, she admires Jonathan Kellerman and Patricia Cornwell.

It was rather a dramatic vision—she calls it a "moment of artistic grace"—one day when she had stopped at a traffic light and daydreamed her character Maisie Dobbs coming out of a train station, speaking with a news vendor, and walking away. The time period was between the world wars.

"She is very much a woman of her time in Britain," Winspear said of her private detective heroine in an interview with Julia Spencer-Fleming of The Narthex. "I'm very interested in the lives of women in Europe at that time—their experience differs somewhat from that of American women, in that they were the first generation to go into war work in large numbers."

Maisie Dobbs is nothing if not striking. This is how we meet her in the first book:

> Even if she hadn't been the last person to walk through the turnstile at Warren Street tube station, Jack Barker would have noticed the tall, slender woman in the navy blue, thigh-length jacket with a matching pleated skirt short enough to reveal a well-turned ankle. She had what his old mother would have called "bearing."

Maisie was a nurse on the front lines during World War I. She was once wounded, and she lost her boyfriend. Afterwards, she put her skills of psychology and detection to professional use.

"I wanted to look at what happened to these 'surplus women'—women who sacrificed their sweethearts and potential husbands to the war," the author said in *USA Today*.

To look at one of the books, *An Incomplete Revenge* (2008): Maisie Dobbs accepts a commission to look into a series of unusual fires each harvest season in a village in Kent. She speaks with villagers but comes to believe that they aren't telling her everything. "Winspear paints a historical cozy featuring intriguing characters and surprising twists. Maisie is absolutely compelling not only as an investigator but also as a psychologist while she probes the hearts and minds of those she meets," Susan O. Moritz wrote in *Library Journal*.

Winspear enjoys researching the time period. Some things she learned from her own family. Her grandfather, for example, was wounded by shrapnel at the Battle of the Somme in 1916. Pieces of metal still worked their way through his skin up until his death in 1966. Information she collects otherwise she uses judiciously, not wanting to overwhelm the story with details of setting.

Maisie Dobbs, however, is not Jacqueline Winspear. "There is actually very little of me in Maisie Dobbs," the author told interviewer Ayo Onatade of *SHOTS* magazine, "I think she is much cleverer than me. She's also extremely intuitive to a very high degree; I am not going to say that I am that intuitive, but it is a muscle I like to use."

She has a cursory outline in mind, a map of sorts, when she begins a novel. "The wonderful thing about a map is that it allows you to be more of an adventurer, because if you lose your way, you have something to come back to," she said on her website. "Though I have key markers in the plot mapped out, I am also able to go off down another road if I am led there by curiosity, a dream or just my fingers on the keyboard."

Works by the Author

Maisie Dobbs Series

Maisie Dobbs (2003)

Birds of a Feather (2004)

Pardonable Lies (2005)

Messenger of Truth (2006)

An Incomplete Revenge (2008)

Among the Mad (2009)

The Mapping of Love and Death (2010)

A Lesson in Secrets (2011)

For Further Information

Donahue, Deirdre, "WWI's Fascinations Prove an Inspiration," *USA Today*, Sept. 29, 2005.

Jacqueline Winspear profile, Bookreporter, http://www.bookreporter.com/authors/au-winspear-jacqueline.asp/ (viewed Oct. 15, 2009).

Jacqueline Winspear website, http://www.jacquelinewinspear.com/ (viewed Oct. 15, 2009).

Knight, Virginia R., "Jacqueline Winspear: Definint azRtist grace," *Mystery News*, June/July 2006.

Moritz, Susan O., *An Incomplete Revenge* review, *Library Journal*, Jan. 1, 2008.

Onatade, Ayo, "Jacqueline Winspear Speaks to Ayo Onatade for Shots Ezine," *SHOTS*, http://www.shotsmag.co.uk/shots23/intvus_23/jwinspear.html/ (viewed Oct. 15, 2009).

Spencer-Fleming, Julia, "A Conversation with Jacqueline Winspear," The Narthex, http://www.juliaspencerfleming.com/Jacqueline-Winspear.html/ (viewed Oct. 15, 2009).

Mark Richard Zubro

Chicago Area
Date not disclosed

Amateur Detective, Police Procedural
Benchmark Series: Tom Mason and Scott Carpenter

About the Author and the Author's Writing

Mark Richard Zubro arrived on the mystery scene in the 1990s, when the gay detective novel came into its own. He admits that the acceptance of his first manuscript was a fluke; the first editor he submitted it to, at St. Martin's Press, liked it.

Little biographical information is available about the author. He lives in Mokena, Illinois, a suburb of Chicago. Among writers who have inspired him are Robert B. Parker, Jonathan Kellerman, and J.R.R. Tolkien. If he modeled his detectives on anyone, it was Sherlock Holmes—and Freddy the Pig, the protagonist in Walter R. Brooks's juvenile novels. Zubro taught eighth-grade English at Summit Hill Junior High until he retired in 2006. He wrote his first novels late at night, after work. His two crime series are set in Cook County and Chicago.

His first series is about Tom Mason, a teacher and the union representative at Grover Cleveland High School in Chicago. Mason is an ex-marine and Vietnam War vet who has a knack for solving crimes. His first puzzle is the killing of a math teacher, who turns out to have been a blackmailer and child abuser. When one of his students becomes a suspect, Mason steps in and, with an assist from his boyfriend Scott Carpenter, a professional baseball player, discovers the murderer and shuts down a homosexual child prostitution ring. The first Tom and Scott book, *A Simple Suburban Murder*, won the Lambda Award for Gay Men's Mystery in 1989, and four subsequent novels were nominated for the same honor.

The books offer a positive portrayal of a gay relationship.

Zubro told *Chicago Sun-Times* reporter Avis Weatherbee that he purposely made the Tom and Scott relationship a strong, happy, ideal one in large part because they are so rare in literature. He admitted, however, that "they were so much in love that it was just a bit much," and he soon went for a more realistic balance.

Not wanting to pass up opportunity, Zubro told the journalist it's no accident that most of the murder victims in his books are homophobes.

Mason himself is suspect in *Schooled in Murder* (2008), when two of his colleagues are killed (teaching is a more dangerous profession than you might imagine). Zubro ratchets up the tension, *Booklist* reviewer Carol Haggas noted: "The deeper Tom probes into the faculty's transgressions, the greater their hostility against him, and their increased opposition quickly shifts Tom from probable suspect to potential victim."

The second series features widower Paul Turner, a Chicago police detective who is raising his two teenaged sons. He is gay. He is often partnered with rough-and-tumble (but poetry-loving) Buck Fenwick.

To learn more about police procedures, Zubro did a lot of homework. "I talk to real police officers as often as I can. [It's] my most current example of research," he said in a Q&A with Stonewall Inn Mysteries. For a book he was working on at the time, he said, "I have had to read a voluminous amount on the rock/pop music scene."

Zubro, in personal retirement, also temporarily retired his series characters so he could work with writers Barbara D'Amato and Jeanne M. Dams on a thriller, *Foolproof* (2009). A software security firm, born in the aftermath of the Twin Towers bombing in New York City in 2001, takes a side interest in terrorist activity, and its agents stumble on a plot to hijack the election of a U.S. president.

The novel suggests that Zubro will explore new directions.

Works by the Author

Paul Turner Series

Sorry Now? (1991)

Political Poison (1993)

Another Dead Teenager (1995)

The Truth Can Get You Killed (1997)

Drop Dead (1999)

Sex and Murder.Com (2001)

Dead Egotistical Morons (2003)

Nerds Who Kill (2005)

Hook, Line, and Homicide (2007)

Tom Mason and Scott Carpenter Series

A Simple Suburban Murder (1989)

Why Isn't Becky Twitchell Dead? (1990)

The Only Good Priest (1991)

The Principal Cause of Death (1992)

An Echo of Death (1994)

Rust on the Razor (1996)

Are You Nuts? (1998)

One Dead Drag Queen (2000)

Here Comes the Corpse (2002)

File Under Dead (2004)

Everybody's Dead but Us (2006)

Schooled in Murder (2008)

Contributor

Foolproof, with Barbara D'Amato and Jeanne M. Dams (2009)

Editor

Next Year, Kankakee: Cat Crimes III (1992)

One Shot—He's Dead: Homicide Host Presents (1996)

For Further Information

Haggas, Carol, *Schooled in Murder* review, *Booklist*, June 1, 2008.

Mark Richard Zubro interview, Stonewall Inn Mysteries, http://www.echonyc.com/~stone/Features/SexDotInter.html/ (viewed Oct. 16, 2009).

Mark Richard Zubro profile, Uncommon Detectives, http://www.neiu.edu/~mystery/zubro.html/ (viewed Oct. 16, 2009).

Mark Richard Zubro website, http://www.markzubro.com/ (viewed Oct. 16, 2009).

Pebworth, Ted-Larry, "Mystery Fiction: Gay Male," glbtq: An Encyclopedia of Gay, Lesbian, Bisexual, Transgender, & Queer Culture, http://www.glbtq.com/literature/myst_fic_gay.html/ (viewed Oct. 16, 2009).

Scott, Whitney, *Everyone's Dead but Us* review, *Booklist*, May 15, 2006.

Sex and Murder.com review, *Publishers Weekly*, July 30, 2001.

Weathersbee, Avis, "Author Brings Gay Detectives Back for Overseas Caper," *Chicago Sun-Times*, July 16, 2006.

Mystery & Detection

Amateur Detective

Susan Wittig Albert

Donna Andrews

Nancy Atherton

Donald Bain

Linda Barnes

M. C. Beaton

Gail Bowen

Rhys Bowen

Rita Mae Brown

James Lee Burke

Jan Burke

Laura Childs

Ann Cleeves

Max Allan Collins

Susan Conant

Bill Crider

Nancy Daheim

Diane Mott Davidson

Carole Nelson Douglas

Aaron Elkins

Janet Evanovich

Joanne Fluke

Earlene Fowler

Margaret Frazer

Frances Fyfield

Robert Goddard

Sarah Graves

Kerry Greenwood

Robert O. Greer

Martha Grimes

Parnell Hall

Carolyn Hart

Joan Hess

Joe R. Landale

Margaret Maron

Steve Martini

Alexander McCall Smith

Val McDermid

Katherine Hall Page

Anne Perry

Nancy Pickard

David Rosenfelt

C. J. Sansom

Julia Spencer-Fleming

Aimée and David Thurlo

Peter Tremayne

Elaine Viets

Mark Richard Zubro

Academic Mystery

Gail Bowen

Bill Crider

Culinary Mystery

Susan Wittig Albert

Nancy Atherton

Susan Conant

Diane Mott Davidson

Kerry Greenwood

Katherine Hall Page

Ecclesiastical Mystery

Julia Spencer-Fleming

Peter Tremayne

Journalism Mystery

Jan Burke

G. M. Ford

Carolyn Hart

J. A. Jance

Penny Mickelbury

Aimée and David Thurlo

Elaine Viets

Legal Mystery

Lawrence Block

James Lee Burke

Frances Fyfield

Martha Grimes

Parnell Hall

Margaret Maron

Steve Martini

David Rosenfelt

C. J. Sansom

Peter Tremayne

Police Procedural

Donald Bain

M. C. Beaton

Giles Blunt

Rhys Bowen

C. J. Box

Ken Bruen

James Lee Burke

Ann Cleeves

Max Allan Collins

Patricia Cornwell

Bill Crider

Deborah Crombie

Barbara D'Amato

James D. Doss

Aaron Elkins

Margaret Frazer

Elizabeth George

Jane Haddam

John Harvey

Joan Hess

Reginald Hill

J. A. Jance

H.R.F. Keating

Laurie R. King

William Kent Krueger

Joe R. Lansdale

Peter Lovesey

Margaret Maron

Archer Mayor

Val McDermid

Penny Mickelbury

Carol O'Connell

Ian Rankin

Peter Robinson

Martin Cruz Smith

Julia Spencer-Fleming

Dana Stabenow

Andrew Taylor

Aimée and David Thurlo

Joseph Wambaugh

Mark Richard Zubro

Detection Specialists

Max Allan Collins

Patricia Cornwell

Aaron Elkins

Jeff Lindsay

Private Detective

Linda Barnes

Cara Black

Lawrence Block

Ken Bruen

Jim Butcher

Max Allan Collins

John Connolly

Bill Crider

Barbara D'Amato

Paul C. Doherty

James Ellroy

Earl W. Emerson

Loren D. Estleman

G. M. Ford

Ed Gorman

Sue Grafton

Robert O. Greer

Martha Grimes

Jane Haddam

James W. Hall

Parnell Hall

Steve Hamilton

John Harvey

Reginald Hill

Declan Hughes

Laurie R. King

William Kent Krueger

Alexander McCall Smith

Val McDermid

Penny Mickelbury

Marcia Muller

George Pelecanos

Bill Pronzini

James Swain

Andrew Taylor

Jacqueline Winspear

Rogue Detectives

Lawrence Block

Tim Dorsey

Loren D. Estleman

Jeff Lindsay

Historical Mystery

Susan Wittig Albert

M. C. Beaton

Rhys Bowen

Max Allan Collins

Paul C. Doherty

Carole Nelson Douglas

Loren D. Estleman

Margaret Frazer

Kerry Greenwood

Michael Jecks

Laurie R. King

Peter Lovesey

George Pelecanos

Anne Perry

Bill Pronzini

C. J. Sansom

Martin Cruz Smith

Andrew Taylor

Peter Tremayne

Jacqueline Winspear

Western Mystery

Bill Crider

Loren D. Estleman

Ed Gorman

John Harvey

Bill Pronzini

Paranormal Mystery

Nancy Atherton

Jan Burke

Jim Butcher

Carole Nelson Douglas

Charlaine Harris

Carolyn Hart

Aimée and David Thurlo

Index

Featured authors are in **bold** print.

About the Author

BERNARD A. DREW is a freelance writer/editor and author of numerous articles and books, including 100 Most Popular African American Authors (Libraries Unlimited, 2006) and 100 Most Popular Thriller and Suspense Authors (Libraries Unlimited, 2009). He lives in Great Barrington, Massachusetts. He has also written books about Hopalong Cassidy creator Clarence E. Malford and civil rights activist W. E. B. DuBois. He is now completing research on a book about Western Massachusetts during the French and Indian War and Revolutionary War era.